ultimate impression left by the poetry is of gradual loss of a vitality and confidence too easily won and precariously held; of diminishing faith in the power of man; of a growing gap between the material and the spiritual and a deepening doubt; of affirmation hardening into an incantatory rhetoric sharply at odds with the perceptions and experiences it conveys. The history of Romantic poetry becomes in part the history of a syntax that proved inadequate to the demands placed upon it."

As a starting point for his examination of the work of the major Romantic poets, the author chooses in each case important unfinished poems—Wordsworth's *The Recluse,* Coleridge's *Kubla Khan* and *Christabel,* Keats' *Hyperion* and *The Fall of Hyperion,* Shelley's *The Triumph of Life,* Byron's *Don Juan.* These illustrate dramatically the impasse to which each of the poets was led as the gap between his private vision and his experience of reality grew steadily wider. As a result Wordsworth and Coleridge retreated back to orthodoxy, while Shelley and Keats withdrew into a dream world of the self. Only Byron, through the comic exploitation of disillusionment, found a way of expanding outward in his poetry.

Edward E. Bostetter, professor of English at the University of Washington, is the author of numerous articles and reviews on the Romantic movement and editor of one of the volumes in the forthcoming edition of the collected works of Coleridge.

THE ROMANTIC VENTRILOQUISTS

Wordsworth, Coleridge, Keats, Shelley, Byron

Edward E. Bostetter

The Romantic Ventriloquists

WORDSWORTH, COLERIDGE, KEATS, SHELLEY, BYRON

University of Washington Press

Seattle, 1963

This book is published with the assistance
of a grant from the Ford Foundation.

For Betty

Now as Heaven is my lot, they're the Pest of the Nation!
Wherever they can come,
With clankum and blankum
'Tis all Botheration, & Hell & Damnation. . . .
Those muttering
Spluttering
Ventriloquogusty
Poets. . . .

COLERIDGE

A Soliloquy of the Full Moon,
She Being in a Mad Passion

ACKNOWLEDGMENTS

THIS book was planned and writing on it began during a sabbatical leave spent at the Henry E. Huntington Library in the winter and spring of 1954. I wish to express my gratitude to the staff of the library for their courtesy and invaluable aid. I wish also to express deep gratitude to the Agnes H. Anderson Research Fund Committee of the University of Washington for a travel grant in 1954, and for a generous grant in support of the publication of the book.

Portions of the book have appeared in altered form in the following articles: "Wordsworth's Dim and Perilous Way," *PMLA*, LXXI (June, 1956), 433–50; *"Christabel:* the Vision of Fear," *Philological Quarterly*, XXXVI (April, 1957), 183–94; "The Eagle and the Truth: Keats and the Problem of Belief," *The Journal of Aesthetics and Art Criticism*, XVI (March, 1958), 362–72; "Shelley and the Mutinous Flesh," *University of Texas Studies in Literature and Language*, I (Summer, 1959), 203–13; "Byron and the Politics of Paradise," *PMLA*, LXXV (December, 1960), 571–76; "The Nightmare World of *The Ancient Mariner*," *Studies in Romanticism*, I (Summer, 1962), 241–54. I wish to thank the editors of the above-mentioned periodicals for their courtesy in granting permission to reprint material from these articles.

E. E. B.

September, 1962
Seattle, Washington

[ix]

CONTENTS

ILLUSTRATIONS

THE ROMANTIC VENTRILOQUISTS

Wordsworth, Coleridge, Keats, Shelley, Byron

1: INTRODUCTION

Ever since Professor Lovejoy so dramatically documented in *The Great Chain of Being* the profound change that took place during the eighteenth century in the ways of thinking about the universe and man's role in it, students of Romanticism have been busily exploring the effect of this change upon English poetry.[1] Recently, in *The Subtler Language,* Earl Wasserman has vividly summed up the acute artistic problems that the breakdown of traditional religious and social patterns created for the poet. Until the end of the eighteenth century there were certain "cosmic syntaxes" in the public domain, such as the Christian interpretation of history and the concept of the great chain of being, which the poet could expect his audience to recognize and accept. He

> . . . could transform language by means of them, and could survey reality and experience in the presence of the world these syntaxes implied. . . . By the nineteenth century these world pictures had passed from consciousness for the purpose of public poetry, and no longer did men share in any significant degree a sense of cosmic design.[2]

Therefore, says Wasserman, the Romantic poets—and poets ever since—have been forced to formulate their own cosmic syntax and "shape the autonomous poetic reality that the cosmic syntax permits."

Actually, the formulation of a new cosmic syntax had begun early in the eighteenth century and by the end of the century had been pretty well completed. As a result, the Romantics, instead of being forced to formulate their own syntax, as perhaps would have been better for

[3]

them, exhausted much of their creative energy in an effort to adapt to their own particular needs the one that lay to hand. This syntax, building upon the scientific and philosophical speculations that stemmed from Newton and Locke, was designed both to absorb and to take the place of traditional Christian syntax.[3] Though it varied widely in detail from poet to poet, at its core were to be found certain simple organizing principles: that the universe revealed to science was a moral universe; that a creative and benign power expressed itself in and through nature and was manifest to the imagination of man; that as an "inmate" of this moral universe man was naturally good and perfectible, though at present corrupted by his society and education.

Perhaps the most important of these principles, because it underlay the others, was the conviction that the imagination rather than the "discursive" reason was the source of knowledge. The imagination assumed a religious function like the "inner light" of the Puritans; it became, in Ernest Tuveson's words, "a means of grace . . . a means of reconciling man, with his spiritual needs and his desire to belong to a living universe of purpose and values, with a cosmos that begins to appear alien, impersonal, remote and menacing."[4] The artist in particular cultivated the imagination as the half-passive, half-creative medium through which ultimate truth revealed itself. "I regard truth as a divine ventriloquist," said Coleridge, and he took for granted that it spoke through the lips of the poet.[5]

Among the Romantic poets one of the favorite analogies for the poetic imagination was the ventriloquistic image of the aeolian harp. As Coleridge's use of the image vividly demonstrates, it was difficult for the poet to distinguish the imagination as the passive instrument upon which the "intellectual breeze" played from the imagination as creative source of its own music.[6] Thus was engendered an immense egoism in which the poet assumed that the center of reality was within himself: the universe existed as he imagined it. Where in the traditional syntax an objective universe focused upon man as the center of creation, in the new syntax the universe expanded outward from the human imagination.[7] The poet became in reality the divine ventriloquist projecting his own voice as the voice of ultimate truth.

The result was a syntax of almost unqualified optimism and affirmation. The traditional view of the Romantics is that they not only utilized it successfully in their art but triumphantly justified it as a philosophy of life. The extent to which this view is still prevalent

[4]

Introduction

among Romantic scholars is indicated by the essays in *The Major English Romantic Poets: A Symposium in Reappraisal,* published in 1957 "as a cross section of opinion and appraisal" by leading scholars and critics. In the introduction the editors state that the terms in which most modern critics have sought to describe the uniqueness of the Romantic movement are "expressive of vitality, confidence, largeness of view" and then go on to say:

Readers of this book will be interested to see how many of our contributors have in one way or another commented on the positive qualities of the Romantics, on their confidence in the power of man to meet his problems, to bridge the gap between the seen and the unseen, the material and the spiritual, to do something to remedy the ills of the world.[8]

But even a cursory examination of the writings of the major Romantic poets reveals that the traditional view is seriously oversimplified and misleading. The Romantic movement did indeed produce a body of magnificent poetry that was "expressive of vitality, confidence, largeness of view." But all too often these qualities were purchased at the expense of ignoring or rationalizing crucial areas of experience and knowledge. What seems at first glance triumphant affirmation is revealed on closer observation as a desperate struggle for affirmation against increasingly powerful obstacles. The ultimate impression left by the poetry is of gradual loss of a vitality and confidence too easily won and precariously held; of diminishing faith in the power of man; of a growing gap between the material and the spiritual and a deepening doubt; of affirmation hardening into an incantatory rhetoric sharply at odds with the perceptions and experiences it conveys. The history of Romantic poetry becomes in part the history of a syntax that proved inadequate to the demands placed upon it.

Given the organizing principles of the syntax, its ultimate failure was almost inevitable; for these principles represented simply one half of a doubtful dialectic, and they were always haunted by the specters of their contraries. They dared not be exposed too long to the harsh scrutiny of reason or experience. They could not finally resolve the problems of social and natural evil; they could only ignore or explain them away. Dependent as they were upon subjective evidence, they were at the mercy of shifting moods and circumstances, and the shadow of doubt was ever threatening. What if there was nothing behind the ventriloquistic voice of truth but the poet's own wishful thinking? Ultimately the disparity between Romantic principles and the

[5]

world in which men lived became so great that the principles could be affirmed only in psychological if not physical isolation.

As a result the movement of most Romantic poetry was a retreat back to a traditional and orthodox syntax, as with Wordsworth and Coleridge, in order to protect fundamental illusions, or a withdrawal into a dream world of the self, as with Shelley and Keats. Only Byron, who is generally looked upon as the most negative of the great Romantics, ironically became an exception to this movement; starting from the narrow ground of self he alone found a way of expanding outward in his poetry. In the comic exploitation of a disintegrating syntax, he paradoxically discovered a source of artistic power.

This book is an attempt to test the foregoing generalizations through a re-examination of the characteristic themes and attitudes of the five most influential Romantic poets.[9] As a vantage point from which first to survey comprehensively the work of each poet and thus to find a way in to the more detailed examination of his major poetry, I have used those unfinished poems in which each poet made his most determined effort to solve the esthetic and philosophical problems that confronted him: Wordsworth's *The Recluse;* Coleridge's *Kubla Khan* and *Christabel;* Keats' *Hyperion* and *The Fall of Hyperion;* Shelley's *The Triumph of Life;* and Byron's *Don Juan.*

For a number of reasons these unfinished poems are peculiarly fitted to be points of departure. In each the problems are left unresolved in the process of being either challenged or tested. In several of the poems an impasse has obviously been reached. The ultimate end that the poet desires is evident; but in the poem he has come up against formidable obstacles that rise like escarpments barring his way. Thereupon we as readers are suddenly confronted with the necessity of assessing the strength and weakness of the poet's position. And we become aware that an assessment of this poem involves an assessment of the rest of his poetry, or at least of his characteristic thought and manner.

Furthermore, each poem breaks off at a memorably dramatic point—as if a motion picture were abruptly frozen at the moment of critical action. Thus we are able to contemplate the action so frozen until detail after detail is impressed upon our minds. We become abnormally aware also of the action leading to the point of suspension, and find ourselves probing and analyzing the attitudes embodied by the action, as we do not in other poems where these attitudes pass unchallenged and uninterrupted. The sudden distortion forced upon us by the abrupt breaking off of the poem has a tremendous shock value; we see what we have not seen before; familiar things become unfamiliar, and the insignificant stock situation or image or idea to which we ordinarily no longer respond looms as the clue to the interpretation of the poet's attitude which we have so long sought. A brief preliminary glimpse of the questions raised by each poem will bring these observations into focus.

The climactic episode of Wordsworth's *The Excursion,* the only completed portion of *The Recluse,* is a picnic, a symbol of harmony which suggests that all questions have been answered, all problems resolved. But the final action shows the despondent and unreconstructed Solitary turning off to his own cottage followed by Wordsworth's half-hearted and unfulfilled promise: "How far those erring notions were reformed . . . my future labours may not leave untold." Wordsworth had intended *The Recluse* to be the great philosophical epic that would once and for all settle the questions of the day and provide a convincing faith based upon an elaborate examination of the interrelationship of "man, nature and society." That faith was originally meant to be the faith in nature asserted in the first two books of *The Prelude* and the first book of *The Recluse* (1800). In the Solitary, Wordsworth presents a man who once held such a faith. But he has been betrayed and disillusioned, and, as a result, he raises questions aimed at the very foundations of Romantic optimism: How can we account for the suffering of those who live by "genial faith" in "genial good," giving themselves unreservedly into nature's power? If this faith is not justified and there is no power beyond nature, is not human life stripped of meaning and purpose? "What avails imagination high / Or question deep" if nowhere a better sanctuary from doubt and sorrow can be attained "than the senseless grave?" Do not all human efforts become futile? What can the thinking man do other than withdraw within himself to wait in a state of stoical repose for the stillness of death? The arguments of the Wanderer and the stories of the Pastor become the desperate effort to answer the Solitary's questions by appeal to what is in essence the faith of the previous century. But his lonely retreating figure at the end of the poem becomes an ironic comment on the effort. And it provides us with the perspective from which we can look back to the jubilant figure of the young Wordsworth singing on the road from Bristol in the opening lines of *The Prelude.*

Kubla Khan ends with a vision of the divinely maddened and omnipotent poet Coleridge longed to be. But the vision is one of frustration as well as hope, for its fulfillment hangs upon a condition: only if the poet can recall the symphony and song of the Abyssinian Maid can he build with his music the dome and the caves of Kubla Khan's paradise. What prevents him from recalling the symphony and song? What, quite literally, has prevented Coleridge from realizing his creative power except in a handful of poems? In seeking the answer, we are confronted by the clash between his desire to affirm a benevolent universe and his awareness of evils that inflict themselves upon him and threaten to suspend his "shaping spirit of imagination." The clash is dramatized in *Christabel,* which so far as it goes is a nightmare vision of evil triumphant. Not only has the virtuous Christabel been invaded and violated without cause or warning, but in the end she is taking on the loathsome characteristics of the invader. The final action of the poem leaves her helpless and abandoned as Sir Leoline turns away with Geraldine, with no answers for the questions of how evil is to be defeated and virtue to prevail, or of how Coleridge is to break through the barriers that are thwarting his poetic power.

Keats' *Hyperion* breaks off abruptly with the shriek of the young Apollo dying into life, becoming a god while Mnemosyne upholds her arms "as one who prophesied." The action comes as a climax to a description of Apollo as the poet who will be transformed into a god through knowledge spontaneously revealed. In the silent face of Mnemosyne he reads "a wondrous lesson" and cries, "Knowledge enormous makes a God of me." We are left with the question: What is the truth or knowledge to be revealed? It is the question for which Keats sought an answer in all his major poetry. He wanted to believe, and he constantly hoped to prove through his poetry, that the poet's imagination spontaneously discovers ultimate truths: "What the imagination seizes as Beauty must be truth." The knowledge revealed to Apollo would have demonstrated the supremacy of the poetic experience. But the abandonment of the poem at the point of revelation was a sign of doubt and imaginative failure. From then on the question became: *Can* the truth be revealed through the visionary experience? So important was it to Keats' artistic health that he answer the question that he began to recast the whole of *Hyperion* in the form of a vision in which he as the poet took on the role of Apollo. It was as if, by putting himself in the god's place, he hoped to see what had been revealed to Apollo but denied to himself in the first *Hyperion*. When at last he stands before Moneta (the new name for Mnemosyne), asking why he was brought where other laborers for human good need not come, she castigates him scornfully:

> What benefit canst thou do, or all thy tribe,
> To the great world? Thou art a dreaming thing,
> A fever of thyself. . . .
>
> [*Fall of Hyperion*, I.167–69]

The intent of the vision that Moneta begins to unfold is obviously to provide him with the knowledge that will transform him from worthless dreamer into true poet. So far as it goes the vision is of a dying golden age, revealed by one whose face is

> . . . bright blanch'd
> By an immortal sickness which kills not.
> . . . deathwards progressing
> To no death was that visage.
>
> [*Fall of Hyperion*, I.257–58, 260–61]

Again the vision breaks off abruptly, and the question remains unanswered.

The Triumph of Life is interrupted by Shelley's death just at the point where the crippled Rousseau is about to answer the poet's question: "Then what is life?" The question comes as the climax to a series of symbolic actions that are completely the reverse of corresponding actions in other poems of Shelley. Rousseau's vision of the ideal and his touching of the cup of nepenthe have been followed by the intrusion of the triumphal procession of life, and as Rousseau is whirled along he becomes aware that from every face the masks of beauty and youth are falling. The question asked by the poet, therefore, demands reconsideration of the whole complex interrelationship of the ideal and the reality as it evolves through the poetry of Shelley—a backward survey to determine how the question had been resolved in the past. The question involves particularly an examination of the increasing tension that had been developing between the millennial view of *Prometheus Unbound*, looking toward the perfectibility of man on earth, and the Platonic view of *Adonais,* in which life is a sick dream, a nightmare, and the ideal is attainable only through death, a view paradoxically reasserted by Ahasuerus in the strangely muted and qualified revolutionary poem, *Hellas:*

[9]

The Romantic Ventriloquists

. . . this Whole
Of suns, and worlds, and men, and beasts, and flowers . . .
Is but a vision;—all that it inherits
Are motes of a sick eye, bubbles and dreams;
Thought is its cradle and its grave. . . .
[*Hellas*, lines 775–76, 780–82]

But if thought is the only reality, and earthly life is a dream, is not every human effort to realize the ideal doomed to failure or corruption? It is the question Shelley faces in *The Triumph*, but as the poem proceeds the problem seems to be inverting itself in accordance with the reversal of the imagistic pattern, becoming: What if the ideal is the illusion, and the vision of life the reality? Upon the question at the end of the poem, Shelley's poetic career seems to pause deliberately suspended.

Byron's *Don Juan* is cut off running in full career. At the point at which Byron abandons it, Juan and the Duchess Fitz-Fulke have appeared at breakfast looking wan and worn following Juan's discovery of the night before that the phantom monk was really "her frolic Grace." This is the first step in the development of an intrigue of monstrous complexity for which Byron has been painstakingly setting the stage in the last four cantos. Just as the narrative grows more elaborate and complex, so the role of the narrator grows more subtle and ambiguous. The dominating attitude is one of amused skepticism:

For me, I know nought; nothing I deny,
Admit, reject, contemn; and what know *you*
Except perhaps that you were born to die?
And both may after all turn out untrue.
[*DJ*, XIV.3 (stanza)]

But this skepticism does not lead to paralysis or despair. On the contrary, it leads to increased intellectual and artistic vigor. *Don Juan* is in full growth when it breaks off: there is no sign of impasse or deterioration. Perched upon his "humbler promontory / Amidst life's infinite variety," Byron has discovered in his contemplation of the clash between illusion and reality an almost inexhaustible source of inspiration. The last cantos of *Don Juan* offer us in turn the perfect promontory on which to perch and look back upon the career of Byron and try to answer the question: How did the hero who started out as "the wandering outlaw of his own dark mind," seeing himself with gloomy exuberance predestined to a life of sin and misery, stirred to titanic defiance of society and the universe—how did he find his way here? On these poems the book has been built. They have been used to give coherence and form to the chapters on the individual poets and finally to the book as a whole. Each chapter begins with the unresolved questions and problems raised by one of the unfinished poems, moves into a reconstruction of the poet's development in the course of which the questions are used as touchstones for testing and evaluating his other work, and ends with an appraisal of the poet's final position. In a concluding chapter, the effect of the Romantic dilemma in determining the direction of nineteenth- and twentieth-century English poetry is briefly traced.

2: WORDSWORTH

❦❦❦❦❦❦❦❦❦❦❦❦❦❦❦❦❦❦❦❦❦❦❦❦❦❦❦❦❦❦

I. HIGH ARGUMENT

THE most ambitiously conceived poem in Romantic literature was *The Recluse*. As early as 1798, and perhaps earlier, Wordsworth had determined "to compose a philosophical poem, containing views of Man, Nature, and Society." By 1814, when he published *The Excursion*, he had dreamed of the poem as consisting of three parts. He had completed the first book of Part I in 1800, and in the preface to *The Excursion* he quoted the concluding lines of this book "as a kind of *Prospectus* of the design and scope of the whole poem." Beyond this, all that we know of the plan of the first and third parts is the statement in the preface that "they will consist chiefly of meditations in the Author's own person."

In preparation for writing the philosophical epic, he had undertaken, as he explained in the preface, "to record, in verse, the origin and progress of his own powers, as far as he was acquainted with them." He was referring, of course, to *The Prelude*. But Wordsworth's conception encompassed more than *The Prelude* and *The Recluse*. All of his writings he saw as contributory to and integrated with the philosophical structure of *The Recluse*. Indeed, through the famous simile in the preface, he suggests that his poems from the beginning were composed according to a consistent and unwavering plan, and that quite literally they could be considered the parts of one great epic poem. *The Prelude* and *The Recluse*, he says,

. . . have the same kind of relation to each other if he may so express himself as the ante-chapel has to the body of a gothic church. Continuing this allusion, he may be permitted to add that his minor pieces, which have been long before the Public, when they shall be properly arranged, will be found by the attentive Reader to have such connection with the main Work as may give them claim to be likened to the little cells, oratories and sepulchral recesses, ordinarily included in these edifices! [1]

But at this point, with the publication of *The Excursion,* work on *The Recluse* abruptly stopped. There the poem stands, a huge, unfinished edifice. It is even impossible to tell if *The Excursion* is to be considered the completed second part. As Harper says, "There is no apparent reason why it should end where it does." [2] The last lines in Book IX would indicate that Wordsworth had arbitrarily and conveniently stopped the poem on the note of high Panglossian optimism struck by the Pastor in his windy sunset prayer. On a superficial reading the impression is conveyed—indeed quite deliberately fostered by the rhetoric—that the Pastor's affirmations are the summing up of an invincible religious system that has triumphantly silenced the Solitary's doubts. But the main business of the poem has been left unfinished— the conversion of the Solitary. He may have been silenced, but he has not been refuted. Symbolically as well as structurally, his conversion is needed to complete the poem.

The ironic fact is that, long before he wrote the preface to *The Excursion,* Wordsworth had become incapable of realizing his epic dream. *The Excursion* itself, in spite of its determinedly optimistic tone, reveals a progressive impoverishment and exhaustion of ideas. The imaginative power and grandeur of expression so apparent in the lines from *The Recluse* have faded into turgid rhetoric, except notably in passages written before 1806, the year when the poem was taken up in earnest. Indeed, the reader stumbling through *The Excursion* with the lines from *The Recluse* retreating like a mirage before his eyes becomes ever more painfully aware of how far below their bold conception the poem has fallen. The lines were composed probably as early as February, 1798, when Wordsworth first determined to write a philosophical epic, and they became the conclusion to Book I of *The Recluse* in the spring of 1800.[3] They stand, therefore, at the beginning, as the publication of *The Excursion* stands at the end, of Wordsworth's significant activity. That he could in 1814 present these lines without discomfort "as a kind of *Prospectus* of the design and scope of the

[13]

whole poem" indicates how confused and shallow had become his intellectual commitments, how dulled his artistic sensibilities. To trace through the poetry between 1798 and 1814 the convolutions that led from the promise of *The Recluse* to the dreary end of *The Excursion* is to uncover the rationalizing mind in the process of crippling and destroying its own perceptions.

II. THE GRAVITATIONAL BOND

The great perception that set Wordsworth (in the poems of 1797–1800) apart from his eighteenth-century predecessors and his contemporaries was his "sense" of the gravitational bond between man and nature.[4] The interaction of man and nature was to him not merely an intellectual and abstract concept but something sensuously apprehended, physically experienced. Some of the most powerful passages in the first two books of *The Prelude* express this interaction with stark literalness. Wordsworth's basic experience, stripped of its civilized abstractions, is an elemental primitive rite in which he absorbs nature into himself by eating and drinking it:

> . . . and I would stand,
> Beneath some rock, listening to sounds that are
> The ghostly language of the ancient earth,
> Or make their dim abode in distant winds.
> Thence did I *drink* the visionary power.[5]
> [*Prel.*, II.326–30. My italics]

When he was but ten years old, he remembers, even then:

> A Child, I held unconscious intercourse
> With the eternal Beauty, *drinking* in
> A pure organic pleasure from the lines
> Of curling mist, or from the level plain
> Of waters colour'd by the steady clouds.
> [*Prel.*, I.589–93. My italics]

When first he came to Tintern Abbey:

> The sounding cataract
> Haunted me like a passion: the tall rock,
> The mountain, and the deep and gloomy wood,
> Their colours and their forms, were then to me
> An appetite. . . .
> [*Tintern Abbey,* lines, 76–80]

[14]

In the context of these passages, the tired, familiar lines in *To My Sister* and *Expostulation and Reply,* deadened by sentimental associations, leap to life:

> Our minds shall *drink* at every pore
> The spirit of the season.
>
> . . . we can *feed* this mind of ours
> In a wise passiveness.
>
> [My italics]

The last lines contain an ambiguity or contradiction that is implicit in all the poetry of this period. "Feed" suggests an active effort in conflict with "passiveness." How active or passive was Wordsworth's relationship with nature? The looseness of language indicates his indifference to the answer. What was important to him was that man was an inmate of an "active universe" in which the interrelationship was such that it was impossible to tell where one left off and the other began. It was the relationship of mother and child; and "feed" was the spontaneous instinctual act of the child. The child has no sense of distinction or separateness from nature:

> No outcast he, bewilder'd and depress'd;
> Along his infant veins are interfused
> The gravitation and the filial bond
> Of nature, that connect him with the world.
>
> [*Prel.,* II.261–64]

The blood metaphor is at the heart of many of the passages in which Wordsworth attempts to convey the sense of uninterrupted continuity and flow from nature to man. Sometimes the image is startlingly direct, as in " 'mid that giddy bliss / Which, like a tempest, works along the blood / And is forgotten." But more often it is implicit in the description of the experience as in the *Boy of Winander* or in the following passage:

> Oh! then the calm
> And dead still water lay upon my mind
> Even with a weight of pleasure, and the sky
> Never before so beautiful, sank down
> Into my heart, and held me like a dream.
>
> [*Prel.,* II.176–80]

In the word "heart" is often contained the suggestion of the total action, as in the apostrophe:

[15]

The Romantic Ventriloquists

Thou Soul that art the eternity of thought!
That giv'st to forms and images a breath
And everlasting motion! Not in vain,
By day or star-light thus from my first dawn
Of Childhood didst Thou intertwine for me
The passions that build up our human Soul,
Not with the mean and vulgar works of Man,
But with high objects, with enduring things,
With life and nature,
. . . until we recognize
A grandeur in the beatings of the heart.

[*Prel.*, I.429–37, 440–41]

The universe of the first two books of *The Prelude* and of *Tintern Abbey* is one of "everlasting motion" which has often the appearance of stillness, and indeed the motion and stillness are for Wordsworth ultimately the same thing, or two aspects of the same thing, like the beat and pause of the heart. The four incidents of the first book are all linked together by the word "motion"; they are illustrative of the way in which the child became conscious of the world outside him as a living, moving force, during each of the four seasons of the turning year. In the first, when the boy in autumn has stolen the bird from another's trap:

I heard among the solitary hills
Low breathings coming after me, and sounds
Of undistinguishable *motion,* steps
Almost as silent as the turf they trod.

[*Prel.*, I.329–32]

In the second, when in spring he hangs alone on the ridge:

With what strange utterance did the loud dry wind
Blow through my ears! the sky seem'd not a sky
Of earth, and with what *motion* mov'd the clouds!

[*Prel.*, I.348–50]

In the third, when in summer he has rowed out in the stolen boat, from behind the craggy steep of the shore

. . . a huge Cliff,
As if with voluntary power instinct,
Uprear'd its head. I struck, and struck again,
And growing still in stature, the huge Cliff
Rose up between me and the stars, and still,
With measur'd *motion,* like a living thing,
Strode after me.

[*Prel.*, I.406–12]

Wordsworth

For many days after he had seen this spectacle

> . . . huge and mighty Forms that do not live
> Like living men *mov'd* slowly through the mind
> By day and were the trouble of my dreams.
> [*Prel.*, I.425–27]

And in the last incident, when in winter he is skating

> And all the shadowy banks, on either side,
> Came sweeping through the darkness, spinning still
> The rapid line of *motion;* then at once
> Have I, reclining back upon my heels,
> Stopp'd short, yet still the solitary Cliffs
> Wheeled by me, even as if the earth had roll'd
> With visible *motion* her diurnal round. . . .
> [*Prel.*, I.480–86. My italics throughout]

In these four incidents, and particularly in the last, Wordsworth is describing experiences that are more or less auditory or optical illusions by means of which he is able to apprehend sensuously a fundamental scientific truth about the universe. In the last, for example, the movement of the cliffs is an optical illusion; but as part of the earth revolving in space the cliffs are literally in constant movement, and Wordsworth visually experiences a fact that otherwise—and for most men—is only a dry scientific abstraction. Similarly, the fact that matter is in constant motion, that the "surface of the universal earth" literally works like a sea, is revealed to him through the illusion of the mountain striding after him, or the sounds of low breathings among the solitary hills.

How primitive is Wordsworth's sense of the power instinct in the inanimate objects of nature, how indifferent he is to the sophisticated scientific abstractions is shown by the animism of the apostrophe that follows the skating episode:

> Ye Presences of Nature in the sky
> And on the earth! Ye Visions of the hills!
> And Souls of lonely places! can I think
> A vulgar hope was yours when Ye employ'd
> Such ministry. . . .
> [*Prel.*, I.490–94]

F. R. Leavis has pointed out how Wordsworth's use of the word "presences" for the mother in Book II of *The Prelude* is related to his use of the word in the central passage of *Tintern Abbey*.[6] And it is

[17]

evident in the passages above that Wordsworth has transferred to nature the parental role, and into the individual objects projected the maternal "presence."

The conception of natural objects not only as instinct with life but as bearing familial relation to himself receives its climactic expression in "Home at Grasmere" (Book I of *The Recluse*),[7] written under the excitement of the return from Germany with his sister and the renewal of the boyhood associations so nostalgically explored in Books I and II of *The Prelude*. The tone becomes intimate and unrestrained in a way unusual in Wordsworth; there is an abandonment of self-reserve, perhaps because this is no recollected emotion, but the immediate experience:

> Embrace me then, ye Hills, and close me in;
> Now in the clear and open day I feel
> Your guardianship; I take it to my heart;
> 'Tis like the solemn shelter of the night.
> But I would call thee beautiful, for mild,
> And soft, and gay, and beautiful thou art,
> Dear Valley. . . .
>
> [*Recluse*, lines 110–16]

The intensity of his address owes something to the intensity of the love he feels for his sister. His feeling for her affects everything he sees and is responsible for the excited happiness that pervades the book. This "calmest fairest spot of earth / With all its unappropriated good" is "not mine only" but hers:

> Ay, think on that, my Heart, and cease to stir,
> Pause upon that and let the breathing frame
> No longer breathe, but all be satisfied. . . .
>   Where'er my footsteps turned,
> Her Voice was like a hidden Bird that sang,
> The thought of her was like a flash of light,
> Or an *unseen* companionship, a breath
> Of fragrance independent of the wind.
> In all my goings, in the new and old
> Of all my meditations, and in this
> Favorite of all, in this the most of all.
>
> [*Recluse*, lines 80–82, 90–97]

How much of what he found in nature was truly there and how much was projected outward from his mind Wordsworth at this time did not know and did not particularly care. What he was primarily

[18]

Wordsworth on Helvellyn, by B. R. Haydon, 1842

concerned with was, as we have suggested, the interaction of mind and nature. In Book II of *The Prelude,* he writes of the infant as largely receiving from nature and then largely giving again:

> . . . his mind,
> Even as an agent of the one great mind,
> Creates, creator and receiver both,
> Working but in alliance with the works
> Which it beholds.
> [*Prel.,* II.271–75]

Nor did he see this as true only of the growing child; it was his present experience, as he makes clear in *Tintern Abbey* in referring to the "mighty world / Of eye and ear—both what they half create / And what perceive," and in the conclusion to Book I of *The Recluse* where he speaks of the purpose of his epic poem as being to chant the wedding of the discerning intellect of man to the goodly universe, to show

> How exquisitely the individual Mind
> . . . to the external World
> Is fitted:—and how exquisitely too . . .
> The external World is fitted to the Mind;
> And the creation (by no lower name
> Can it be called) which they with blended might
> Accomplish:—this is our high argument.
> [lines 63, 65–71, in preface to *The Excursion*]

In these poems he tended to see nature as the more important of the two, molding and shaping the mind that was a part of it. The therapeutic power of the countryside around Racedown to restore him to both physical and mental health had made a lasting impression; and the associational psychology of which Coleridge was an enthusiastic supporter in 1797, and the use of which is clearly evident in the poems, emphasized the dominance of external stimuli. Coleridge's speculations were probably the decisive factor in shaping Wordsworth's attitudes; indeed, Coleridge determined the particular expression of these attitudes in numerous significant instances. For example, in *This Lime Tree Bower* and *Fears in Solitude* he strikingly anticipates the language of *Tintern Abbey.*[8]

At the same time, in reconstructing the memories of childhood in Book I of *The Prelude,* Wordsworth is careful to insist upon an activity within himself independent of nature:

[19]

Nor, sedulous as I have been to trace
How Nature by extrinsic passion first
Peopled my mind with beauteous forms or grand,
And made me love them, may I here forget
How other pleasures have been mine, and joys
Of subtler origin; how I have felt,
Not seldom, even in that tempestuous time,
Those hallow'd and pure motions of the sense
Which seem, in their simplicity, to own
An intellectual charm, that calm delight
Which, if I err not, surely must belong
To those first-born affinities that fit
Our new existence to existing things,
And, in our dawn of being, constitute
The bond of union betwixt life and joy.

[*Prel.*, I.571–85]

And in Book II he emphasizes that "by the regular action of the world" his first creative sensibility was unsubdued. He has difficulty defining it: it is "a plastic power"; a "forming hand, at times / Rebellious"; a "local spirit of its own, at war / With general tendency, but for the most / Subservient, strictly to the external things / With which it commun'd." It is an "auxiliar light" which came from his mind and "bestow'd new splendor" on the setting sun and the other objects about him. Indeed, there were moments, as when he sat alone among the hills at dawn, when

. . . such a holy calm
Did overspread my soul, that I forgot
That I had bodily eyes, and what I saw
Appear'd like something in myself, a dream,
A prospect in my mind.

[*Prel.*, II.367–71]

In this confusion of external with internal, in this projection outward of his own ego, there is the basis for antagonism and conflict between himself and his environment.[9] He is acutely aware of his creative sensibility as engaged in a struggle to establish and maintain for him an identity apart from nature. It is therefore at times "rebellious" and "at war / With general tendency." So abnormally heightened is this sensitivity within himself that he is led to view nature with fear and terror as often as with joy.

Three of the four incidents in the first book which, as we have seen,

Wordsworth

Wordsworth used to illustrate the interrelationship of man and nature are also incidents that show nature as terrifying and potentially destructive. If she is parental love, she is also parental hostility, pursuing the boy with threat of punishment. In the third incident, the terrorizing effect is particularly stressed. Taken in themselves, the lines that describe his reaction to the experience of the cliff indicate no harmonious and beneficial relationship with nature but a nightmare of fear:

> . . . after I had seen
> That spectacle, for many days, my brain
> Work'd with a dim and undetermin'd sense
> Of unknown modes of being; in my thoughts
> There was a darkness, call it solitude,
> Or blank desertion, no familiar shapes
> Of hourly objects, images of trees,
> Of sea or sky, no colours of green fields;
> But huge and mighty Forms that do not live
> Like living men mov'd slowly through the mind
> By day and were the trouble of my dreams.
> [*Prel.*, I.417–27]

In the last book of *The Prelude,* Wordsworth says that "even to the very going out of youth," that period with which *The Prelude* ends, he had "too exclusively esteem'd that love, / And sought that beauty which . . . hath terror in it." And it is his sister, he says, who softened down this "oversternness." Certainly the element of terror is strong in his earlier poetry, as in *The Vale of Esthwaite;* and, though it has undoubtedly been aggravated by the Gothic literary convention in which it found a convenient mode of expression, it is a terror deeply rooted in his personality.[10] One of the early passages written for *The Prelude* was that in Book XI in which he relates two incidents to illustrate the "spots of time" that retain a vivifying virtue by which "our minds / Are nourished and invisibly repair'd."[11] In the first, lost on "the rough and stony moor" he stumbles on the place where a murderer had been hanged and sees his name inscribed in the green sod:

> . . . forthwith I left the spot
> And, reascending the bare Common, saw
> A naked Pool that lay beneath the hills,
> The Beacon on the summit, and more near,
> A Girl who bore a Pitcher on her head
> And seem'd with difficult steps to force her way

The Romantic Ventriloquists

Against the blowing wind. It was, in truth,
An ordinary sight; but I should need
Colours and words that are unknown to man
To paint the visionary dreariness
Which, while I look'd all around for my lost guide,
Did at that time invest the naked Pool,
The Beacon on the lonely Eminence,
The Woman, and her garments vex'd and toss'd
By the strong wind.

[*Prel.*, XI.302–16]

This is one of the most haunting and cryptic passages in Wordsworth's poetry. It has the disconnectedness of a dream. One element is
missing, the unifying element that gives meaning to these details. Why
does he remember this experience as "beneficent"? What has been revealed to him? What is the "vivifying virtue" that nourishes and re-
pairs his mind? For the impact of the description is to emphasize the
loneliness of man in an alien world. The barren moor, the naked
pool, the blowing wind, the lonely eminence—this is nature stripped of
human coloring and warmth, an indifferent, even hostile background
to the human struggle. The girl with the pitcher on her head forcing
her way against the wind, the beacon, the yearly clearing away of the
grass by the peasants to preserve the name of the murderer—are they
symbols of the human struggle for survival? On the surface these are
all pieces in a tableau on the riddle of life. Certainly there is no visibly
reassuring or comforting pattern or explanation—but instead the inexplicable details raising terrifying questions as to the ultimate meaning of things. In the child, unaware of symbolic implications, there
were only the turbulent feelings of terror and insecurity, the sense of
"visionary dreariness," and loneliness. It is one of the first moments
in which Wordsworth is conscious of his potentialities for feeling
deeply; and, though the experience is terrifying, it is paradoxically a
source of strength and confidence, as revealing and setting in motion
this power within. Perhaps Wordsworth intended to suggest that this
was the moment at which he became aware of his own identity, just as
under similar circumstances, in his meeting with the convict in the
graveyard at the opening of *Great Expectations,* Pip tells us he became
aware of the "identity of things" including his own.

When Wordsworth incorporated the incident into *The Prelude* in
1804 he added two significant passages.[12] The spots of time that possess a renovating virtue are chiefly those, he said, in which

[22]

We have had deepest feeling that the mind
Is lord and master and that outward sense
Is but the obedient servant of her will.
[*Prel.*, XI.271–73]

And, after relating the incident, he added the memory of roaming long afterward in daily presence of this scene with Dorothy and Mary Hutchinson "in the blessed time of early love." Then upon the dreary landscape fell

The spirit of pleasure and youth's golden gleam:
And think ye not with radiance more divine
From these remembrances, and from the power
They left behind? So feeling comes in aid
Of feeling, and diversity of strength
Attends us, if but once we have been strong.
[*Prel.*, XI.323–28]

There follows one of Wordsworth's most poignant apostrophes to the mystery of man. In childhood he sees something of the base on which man's "greatness stands," and he is convinced, like Coleridge,

That from thyself it is that thou must give,
Else never canst receive. The days gone by
Came back upon me from the dawn almost
Of life; the hiding-places of my power
Seem open; I approach, and then they close;
I see by glimpses now; when age comes on,
May scarcely see at all.
[*Prel.*, XI.333–39]

The added sections have increased the mystery of the incident which has obviously assumed supreme importance for Wordsworth as revealing the sources of power in the mind that transcend nature and in some obscure way become intimations of immortality; his conception of the relationship of man and nature has changed since 1798. We shall consider the significance of this change more fully later on.

The second incident also emphasizes the visionary dreariness of nature. It describes the setting in which he watches for the horses that are to take him and his brothers home for the Christmas holidays. During the holidays his father dies, and the event appears to him to be a chastisement:

. . . and when I call'd to mind
That day so lately pass'd when from the crag

I look'd in such anxiety of hope,
With trite reflections of morality,
Yet in the deepest passion, I bow'd low
To God, who thus corrected my desires;
And afterwards, the wind and sleety rain
And all the business of the elements,
The single sheep, and the one blasted tree,
And the bleak music of that old stone wall,
The noise of wood and water, and the mist
Which on the line of each of those two Roads
Advanced in such indisputable shapes,
All these were spectacles and sounds to which
I often would repair and thence would drink,
As at a fountain; and I do not doubt
That in this later time, when storm and rain
Beat on my roof at midnight, or by day
When I am in the woods, unknown to me
The workings of my spirit thence are brought.
                                    [*Prel.,* XI.370–89]

What is most immediately striking about the incident is the stern, puritanical sense of guilt; he has been too happy and so must suffer. Wordsworth's naked primitive egoism is nowhere better, because so unconsciously, displayed: his father is the victim of his desires. The puritanical fear of happiness becomes strongly marked in Wordsworth's poetry after 1802: it is notable in *Resolution and Independence,* the *Ode to Duty,* and the story of the Solitary in *The Excursion.*

The role of nature is ambiguous. It is not nature that is thought of as chastising him, as in the first book of *The Prelude,* but God. What, then, is it that he drinks afterward from these "spectacles and sounds"? In the bleakness of the scene there is an ominous warning, a constant reminder of his punishment. More than that, however, it is a scene of grim, indestructible vitality and elemental strength. It is a sign of the fundamental force that has endured and will endure; the inexplicable nature of things, relentlessly moving without hope, without despair, without protest. This strength to endure, to accept—is it this that he drank? At least, the incident contains the qualities of the stoicism that he tries so hard to cultivate in his life and poetry after 1802; and in it is the seed of the attitude that nothing can be changed except for the worse. The bleak scene is the symbol of the predestined nature of things.

[24]

III. THE WILD AND LONELY LANDSCAPE

The wild and lonely landscape, instinct with life of its own and from which man in some way is set apart, is the background for a surprising number of Wordsworth's poems. He was tremendously impressed by Salisbury Plain when he visited it in 1793, and he was haunted during the rest of his life by an imaginative experience he had had there. In Book XII of *The Prelude,* he connects this experience with his hope that as a poet he possessed a "privilege" and that a work of his,

> Proceeding from the depth of untaught things,
> Enduring and creative, might become
> A power like one of Nature's.
> [*Prel.,* XII.310–12]

This sense of potential power "once above all," he says, he experienced at Stonehenge. There, as he wandered "along the bare white roads / Lengthening in solitude their dreary line," he had a "reverie and saw the past." He saw the ancient Britons, the druidical sacrifices of human beings, and their astronomical and mathematical rites, in which knowledge was absorbed spontaneously from the forces of nature:

> I saw the bearded Teachers, with white wands
> Uplifted, pointing to the starry sky
> Alternately, and Plain below, while breath
> Of music seem'd to guide them, and the Waste
> Was chear'd with stillness and a pleasant sound.
> [*Prel.,* XII.349–53]

The abrupt juxtaposition of brutal sacrifice and benign instruction, of destructive and constructive power, reveals, more or less consciously, how unmoral Wordsworth's fundamental poetic experience was, how much he relished the display of power for its own sake. The dreary plain of Salisbury had earlier served as a background for *Guilt and Sorrow*. In the last book of *The Excursion* he repudiates the experience through the speech of the Pastor contrasting the barbarity of the druidical religion with the benignity of Christianity. In his use of the experience on Salisbury Plain one may see imaged the rise and decline of his poetic power.

In *The Recluse* there is another significant passage in which Wordsworth reveals how important in his experience are the wild and violent forms of nature:

The Romantic Ventriloquists

While yet an innocent Little-one, with a heart
That doubtless wanted not its tender moods,
I breathed (for this I better recollect)
Among wild appetites and blind desires,
Motions of savage instinct my delight
And exultation. Nothing at that time
So welcome, no temptation half so dear
As that which urged me to a daring feat.
Deep pools, tall trees, black chasms, and dizzy crags,
And tottering towers; I loved to stand and read
Their looks forbidding, read and disobey,
Sometimes in act, and ever more in thought.

[*Recluse,* lines 703–14]

Immediately afterward he tells of how with similar impulses he heard of danger met or sought with courage; even now, he says, he cannot read of two brave vessels fighting to the death without being pleased

More than a wise man ought to be. I wish,
Fret, burn, and struggle, and in soul am there;
But me hath Nature tamed, and bade to seek
For other agitations, or be calm. . . .

[*Recluse,* lines 724–27]

What nature has performed in stealth, he goes on to say, has reason sanctioned:

Her deliberate Voice
Hath said, "Be mild and cleave to gentle things,
Thy glory and thy happiness be there. . . .
All that inflamed thy infant heart, the love,
The longing, the contempt, the undaunted quest,
All shall survive—though changed their office, all
Shall live,—it is not in their power to die. . . ."

[*Recluse,* lines 734–36, 741–44]

This long passage tells us a great deal about Wordsworth's attitudes at this time (1800). Most of his childhood memories are of wild and violent landscapes, and of wild and violent emotional experiences within these landscapes. Sometimes the landscapes are an integral part of the experiences; he reacts to them with joy and pleasure; he is absorbed into them, or they are absorbed into him. More frequently, they are at odds with him; they at one and the same time tempt him on to daring feats, aggravate his passions, and threaten him with punishments. So his attitude becomes one of defiance: "I loved to stand and read / Their looks forbidding, read and disobey." Out of these

[26]

moments of opposition and self-assertion emerges the sense of personal identity and power, an awareness of himself as separate from and equal to nature. What is of primary importance to him, as child and man, is the consciousness of possessing tremendous powers. And this is accompanied by the realization that these powers are inseparable from their setting. Indeed, he thinks of himself as evoking his power from the winds, the earth, the water, like some primitive magus or mythic priest. The extent to which he saw this power as "working but in alliance with the works / Which it beholds" is graphically illustrated in the passage in Book II of *The Prelude* already referred to in which he tells of standing

> Beneath some rock, listening to sounds that are
> The ghostly language of the ancient earth
> Or make their dim abode in distant winds.
> *Thence did I drink the visionary power.*
> [*Prel.*, II.327–30. My italics]

Nature then is remembered as wild and violent, stimulating the wild and violent passions of the boy; and the moments when he recognized in himself a unique poetic power are most frequently associated with bleak and lonely landscapes. Only after he had moved to Racedown in 1795 did he come to associate nature primarily with peace, tranquillity, and joy. In *The Recluse* he says that it was nature that tamed him, and in *The Prelude* he says that it was his sister who softened down his oversternness. The most important cause, the changes that had taken place in his own psychological attitude, he treats only indirectly.

He had gone through a series of violent emotional crises, unconnected with nature: the affair with Annette and his revolutionary activities in France and at home, culminating in disillusionment with political systems and activities. When he went to Racedown, he was subdued and purged emotionally. He had undoubtedly been frightened by what he had seen of his own capacity for emotional excess. He had temporarily had enough of terror. He wanted quiet and rest. He wanted security. And he could afford security. For the first time, he had a steady financial income, thanks to the bequest left him by Calvert. And, if he felt momentarily disillusioned, he also felt enriched and fulfilled. He was confident of his poetic powers and his ability to use them. He had almost inexhaustible emotional capital to draw on: he needed no new experiences. He was ready to settle down. At this point, it was

[27]

certainly the voice of reason that preceded nature in taming him. He had decided to concentrate his efforts on poetry; he was determined to be a great poet. To that end it was necessary to control and discipline his passions. Furthermore, as he says in *The Recluse,* through poetry he could experience vicariously all his violent desires and aspirations. He therefore deliberately decided on the tranquil life as the best and wisest course for him—as the way not merely of survival but of the achievement of all that he most desired.

All things conspired to help him in achieving his end. After the man-made terrors he had experienced he turned back to nature in relief: her terrors were mild in comparison. And at Racedown the wild and terrible was subordinated to a calm and pastoral landscape: for the first time, for any extended period, Wordsworth truly found nature benign. He lived a quiet and comfortable routine, not struggling or competing or defying. He was adored and his every whim was catered to by Dorothy. In being alone with her, free of relatives and guardians, he was at last completely happy and at ease in his day-to-day life. Her excited and joyful attitudes, her pleasure in nature tempered and transformed his own attitudes. And then there was Coleridge with his extravagant enthusiasms and his equally extravagant reverence for Wordsworth.

When he came to Racedown, Wordsworth needed a faith, or perhaps it would be more accurate to say he needed a philosophical frame, a terminology in which he could articulate his faith. He could not accept Christianity, on the one hand, or, on the other, the materialism of the *Philosophes.* But he was convinced that the universe was meaningful and man a meaningful part of it, and this conviction was almost identical with his obsessive belief in his own power and importance. He knew that he was capable of great things, that he was possessed of unusual sensitivity and perception and of awesome flashes of insight; surely these were evidence of pattern and purpose in the nature of things. It was Coleridge who, if he did not provide Wordsworth with the philosophical frame, at least provided most of its materials and helped him through his conversation to hammer it together. The most important element was the concept of association and memory. Wordsworth needed none of the complicated system and jargon of Hartley—only the basic simple idea to set him off. Here was a concept sufficient to explain coherently and logically his present sense of the relation of man and nature. It was a means of accounting for his past experiences

and sensations and of subduing them to the present or at least sub-
ordinating them as steps in his growth and development toward the
present. The concept of association also provided an esthetics by which
he could draw on the experiences of the past without being disturbed
by them. Thus all things fell into place. Set within the associationistic
frame, the moments of terror could be contemplated with equanimity
and pleasure, and he could exclaim:

> Ah me! that all
> The terrors, all the early miseries
> Regrets, vexations, lassitudes, that all
> The thoughts and feelings which have been infus'd
> Into my mind, should ever have made up
> The calm existence that is mine when I
> Am worthy of myself! Praise to the end!
> [*Prel.*, I.355–61]

Through the concept of association, he achieved the freedom to express experiences which otherwise he might have felt too deeply to
articulate, or which he would have feared to relate. The sources of
his poetic power were truly made available to him.[13]

But only as long as he could maintain the easy, unworrying security
of the relationship at Racedown, the sense of present happiness without
thought of the future, could he continue in the simple faith of *Tintern
Abbey* and the first books of *The Prelude*. For it was a faith whose
logic rested on the experience of the present rather than on the
memories of the past. It placed man and nature in a moral strait jacket.
It assumed the benevolence and "geniality" of nature, and her maternal concern for man. It assumed a spontaneous interaction of man
and nature, where by precept and example nature would tame and
soften down the wilder passions and lead to virtuous action. Sometimes,
perhaps, in childhood and youth she had had to intervene directly and
sternly, but the mature individual could be expected to follow her
promptings instinctively and joyfully.

But this faith could not bear up under any close scrutiny or any
change of situation or mood. It could hold only for the particular circumstances that existed at Racedown, at Alfoxden, and during the first
year at Grasmere. Even at this time, Wordsworth recognizes how tenu-
ous and subjective is his faith. "If this / Be but a vain belief," he cries
in *Tintern Abbey,* "Yet, oh! how oft . . . in spirit have I turned to
thee." And he ends the second book of *The Prelude:*

If this be error, and another faith
Find easier access to the pious mind,
Yet were I grossly destitute of all
Those human sentiments which make this earth
So dear, if I should fail, with grateful voice
To speak of you, Ye Mountains and Ye Lakes. . . .
[*Prel.*, II.435–40]

In each case he is referring to the mystical moments when he saw "into the life of things," saw "one life and felt that it was joy." This is what happened to me, what I have experienced, he is saying. I should like to believe that it is no illusion, but a revelation of ultimate truth; but I can only claim that it works for me—I am a healthy, happy, and virtuous man, and can only account for it through my contact with nature; and it may not work for others.

In *The Recluse* he speaks quite frankly of the limited and personal quality of the experience. The sense of peace and tranquillity and virtue that he has found in the Vale of Grasmere he would not find everywhere. Even though there are a thousand nooks outwardly the same as this one,

Nowhere (or is it fancy?) can be found
The one sensation that is here. . . .
'Tis but I cannot name it, tis the sense
Of majesty, and beauty and repose,
A blended holiness of earth and sky,
Something that makes this individual Spot,
This small Abiding-place of many Men,
A termination, and a last retreat,
A Centre, come from wheresoe'er you will,
A Whole without dependence or defect,
Made for itself; and happy in itself,
Perfect Contentment, Unity entire.
[*Recluse*, lines 136–37, 142–51]

In the opening lines of the poem he says that when as a boy he first discovered Grasmere he saw it as a paradise in which it would be a "happy fortune" to live; and significantly he remembers that he had no hope, scarcely a wish, that such fortune ever could be his (another indication of his morbid fatalism as a boy; he was not intended to be happy). Ever since he has been haunted by the memory of the place. Now he returns to it as a refuge, a place of escape from the world, a dream realized. The beauty of the vale leads him "to soothe" himself with the belief that

[30]

They who are dwellers in this holy place
Must needs themselves be hallowed. . . .
[*Recluse,* lines 276–77]

He knows that this is an illusion; but it is by such illusion, he believes, that the soul becomes "words cannot say how beautiful"; and
he apostrophizes the vale for making the illusion possible:

Hail to the visible Presence, hail to thee
Delightful Valley, habitation fair!
And to whatever else of outward form
Can give us inward help, can purify,
And elevate, and harmonise, and soothe,
And steal away, and for a while deceive
And lap in pleasing rest, and bear us on
Without desire in full complacency,
Contemplating perfection absolute
And entertained as in a placid sleep.
[*Recluse,* lines 299–308]

He insists that he did not come "with romantic hope" to find the
persons like the place; he came not "dreaming of unruffled life, / Un-
tainted manners." Born and bred among the hills,

I wanted not a scale
To regulate my hopes. Pleased with the good
I shrink not from the evil with disgust,
Or with immoderate pain.
[*Recluse,* lines 349–52]

He expected the ordinary man to differ little from Man elsewhere

For selfishness, and envy, and revenge,
Ill neighborhood—pity that this should be—
Flattery and double-dealing, strife and wrong.
[*Recluse,* lines 355–57]

But immediately he argues away this realistic recognition. It is a
"mighty gain" that here the laborer is a free man; that extreme penury,
the wretchedness of cold and hunger, are unknown; that here people
can afford to be charitable and merciful:

. . . this deep Vale,—as it doth in part
Conceal us from the Storm,—so here abides
A Power and a protection for the mind,
Dispensed indeed to other solitudes,
Favored by noble privilege like this,

Where kindred independence of estate
Is prevalent. . . .

[*Recluse*, lines 375–83]

He devotes the next hundred lines to adducing evidence of the fundamental nobility of the "untutored shepherds," so that he can say:

. . . confident, enriched at every glance,
The more I see the more delight my mind
Receives, or by reflection can create.
Truth justifies herself, and as she dwells
With Hope, who would not follow where she leads?

[*Recluse*, lines 497–501]

He turns then to consider the happy and harmonious life of the animals and birds and concludes this survey of life in Grasmere by contrasting the "living and dead Wilderness / of the thronged world" with the true community "of many into one incorporate" that he finds here, a community both "human and brute." Dismissing, therefore, all Arcadian dreams, he and his sister will take at once "this one sufficient hope" that here they will not want for pleasure in the life around them, or for health of mind, or for knowledge and love; and that, feeling as they do,

. . . we shall moreover find
(If sound and what we ought to be ourselves,
If rightly we observe and justly weigh)
The inmates not unworthy of their home,
The Dwellers of their Dwelling.

[*Recluse*, lines 644–48]

And so we come full circle. What we have summarized here is certainly one of the most fascinating illustrations in literature of an artist's mind in process of working its tortuous way from desire to conviction. Wordsworth begins with a clear recognition of the distinction that must be maintained between the illusion and the reality, and through rationalizations and rhetorical subtleties he ends in delusion. He has persuaded himself—in fact, he is determined—that he will find what he wants to find, that the reality will not fall short of the dream. Rhetorically, the process is from the positive affirmation of the desire to believe that those who are dwellers in this holy place "must needs" themselves be hallowed, to the negative conviction that if we observe rightly we shall find the inmates "not unworthy" of their home. The next step in the process is unqualified conviction, and this step is taken in the preface to the *Lyrical Ballads,* written in the autumn of 1800. Here the argument and even the wording of the poem are used in developing the reasons for choosing humble and rustic life as a subject for poetry. What in the poem had applied strictly to life in Grasmere is now given universal application and becomes a fundamental law of human behavior in rural life.[14]

IV. THE FADING GLEAM

Wordsworth had committed himself to a conception of nature and rustic life that depended almost wholly upon the continuance of his sense of well-being. Beneath the placid surface of the present relationship lurked an uneasy fear and distrust of nature. She had too long been associated with alienation, insecurity, loneliness, and violent passions to be accepted as completely benign, even now. *Ruth,* written at this time, reveals that Wordsworth was reminding himself that under certain conditions nature encouraged rather than subdued the passions. And never again after 1800 does he sing the praise of nature so unqualifiedly as in "Home at Grasmere." He hedges round the praise with cautious and timid modifiers; he begins to attribute to God as apart from nature, perhaps working through nature, perhaps using her as sign and symbol, the benign power he had at first attributed to nature directly; and more and more frequently he sets God and nature at odds. The sense of well-being, of tranquillity, which he had brought to Grasmere could not and did not last long; and when he lost it he lost also his magical view of nature. His first and obsessive aim after that was to regain his security and tranquillity; since nature had been powerless to prevent the loss, it was necessary for him to look beyond her for meaning and purpose. Tranquillity was no longer something to be spontaneously possessed and enjoyed. It now could be achieved only momentarily and precariously through strenuous effort of will; through grim discipline and denial of the spontaneous; through withdrawing from the psychological and emotional response to nature which he had once cultivated; through constantly reminding himself

> That the procession of our fate, howe'er
> Sad or disturbed, is ordered by a Being
> Of infinite benevolence and power;
> Whose everlasting purposes embrace
> All accidents, converting them to good.
> *[Ex.,* IV.13–17]

Without this assurance, earthly life became for Wordsworth a meaning-less nightmare. With it, he could continue to look upon Grasmere as a little, womblike "nook of mountain ground."

Bateson argues that between 1799 and 1801 Wordsworth became aware of the potential emotional dangers in the relationship between himself and his sister.[15] Whether or not he was consciously aware of them is hard to say, but that they existed is quite evident from Dorothy's Grasmere journal and the numerous poems Wordsworth wrote to and for her until his marriage. The intense ardor of the lines quoted from *The Recluse* is unmistakable. Indeed, the feeling he expresses for nature is inseparable from a sublimation of the feeling he expresses for Dorothy; the happiness he finds in his surroundings is the result of the happiness he finds with her; it is she who transforms Grasmere into a paradise. When Wordsworth married Mary Hutchinson the intimate, passionate tone went out of his verse and was replaced by a more re-served, formal, and public tone. Even in *The Prelude,* when he resumed it in 1804, the change in tone was noticeable. In the first two books the original experiences and attitudes were truly rekindled and re-experienced, the immediacy of the emotion was expressed. But, in the later books, the distance and detachment of the author from the recol-lected experience are evident.

Whatever his reasons for marrying, it was a carefully premeditated move toward increased security and stability. It was a clear indication that he would no longer rely upon the "genial sense of youth"; it be-came a protection against the passions and emotions he had come to distrust and no longer wanted to experience. It forced him to take heed for the future. The frame of mind in which he was preparing to set out for France and settle things with Annette, and then to marry, is indicated vividly by *Resolution and Independence,* written between May and July, 1802.

The poem is an excellent example of the way Wordsworth has fused two different experiences. The encounter with the prototype of the Leech Gatherer took place near Dove Cottage in October, 1800; but the "state of feeling" described at the beginning of the poem occurred, according to Wordsworth, when he was crossing Barton Fell, pre-sumably in April, 1802, on his way to Bishop Middleham to visit Mary and arrange for his marriage to take place after his return from France. The setting in the opening lines, however, parallels closely Dorothy's description in a letter of their experience at Patterdale, where they stopped overnight on their way home from the Clarksons' upon his return. During the night there was a great storm, but by morning the storm had cleared away, and the sun was shining as they set forth.¹⁶ The sudden dejection described in the beginning of the poem was associated then with all the complex feelings involving Dorothy, Mary, and the momentous decision to marry and so alter radically the whole pattern of his life. The attitude with which he writes is like the attitude we have already noted in the "spots of time" passage on the death of his father. There is the same implication that thoughtless happiness will be punished. As he thinks of the skylark and the hare, he realizes that "even such a happy child of earth am I . . .":

> Far from the world I walk, and from all care;
> But there may come another day to me—
> Solitude, pain of heart, distress, and poverty.
> [*Resolution and Independence,* lines 33–35]

And he thinks morbidly of the usual fate of poets. Upon this background the memory of the encounter with the Leech Gatherer is quite literally superimposed, like a photographic montage, so that the old man indeed becomes

> Like one whom I had met with in a dream;
> Or like a man from some far region sent,
> To give me human strength, by apt admonishment.
> [*Resolution and Independence,* lines 110–12]

Now the significant thing is that, in this psychological crisis, nature is of no help, for to the Leech Gatherer nature is one of the hostile forces against which he must fight for survival; even the leeches have dwindled and become hard to find. The sources of his strength come obviously from within, from his faith in God. It is "with God's good help" that he finds housing by choice or chance. And as Wordsworth talks to him the sun seems to fade from the landscape, its character changes, and it becomes hostile and alien like the landscapes of childhood:

> While he was talking thus, the lonely place,
> The Old Man's shape, and speech—all troubled me:
> In my mind's eye I seemed to see him pace
> About the weary moors continually,
> Wandering about alone and silently.
> [*Resolution and Independence,* lines 127–31]

As the poem ends, Wordsworth appeals to God to be his "help and stay secure," as He has been for the Leech Gatherer. The poem dramatizes a momentous decision, a radical shift in perspective. In an important sense, the resolution of the title is the poet's resolution to abandon one way of life for another. He will no longer live "as if life's business were a summer mood," and thus vulnerable to the ills that might descend, but he will determinedly cultivate that firmness of mind, that independence of environment which will prepare him to withstand the worst that can happen. And independence means independence from nature, which in the beginning of the poem is definitely associated with the improvident and thoughtless life, and in the end with the potential ills that threaten him. The poem stands symbolically, then, as a turning point in his attitude toward and relationship with nature.[17]

The change in his relationship also concerns him in the *Ode: Intimations of Immortality.* In the first four stanzas, begun before *Resolution and Independence,* he writes as if the loss of the gleam is a recent thing or as if at least he had only recently become aware of the loss. Something has happened to disturb the spontaneous, intimate relationship described in *The Recluse.* The only clue is in stanza 3:

> To me alone there came a thought of grief:
> A timely utterance gave that thought relief,
> And I again am strong. . . .[18]

When during the following year he returns to write the rest of the poem, he is ready to impose upon the experience a rationalization, to enclose it in a theoretical system, exactly as he had imposed upon the experiences of *Tintern Abbey* and *The Prelude* a rationalization and had enclosed them in a system. The source of the gleam is apart from and beyond nature: we bring it with us at birth. As we grow the gleam gradually fades from the world about us, and at last the man perceives it die away. There is an ambiguous reference to the youth who still is "Nature's Priest" and is attended by "the vision splendid," even though daily he must travel farther from the east, that is, the heavenly source of the gleam. Within the context of the stanza, this must mean that he worships nature as transformed by the vision, as if the source of glory were in her rather than emanating from himself. But there is nothing ambiguous about stanza 6:

> Earth fills her lap with pleasures of her own,
> Yearnings she hath in her own natural kind,

And, even with something of a Mother's mind,
And no unworthy aim,
The homely Nurse doth all she can
To make her Foster-child, her Inmate Man,
Forget the glories he hath Known,
And that imperial palace whence he came.

Earth here is evidently the literal natural world in which the child
grows up, as distinct from the personified abstraction of the previous
stanza, and thus she is equivalent to the nature of the first two books
of *The Prelude* and the Vale of Grasmere in *The Recluse*. But the
shift that has taken place in Wordsworth's way of looking at her is
strikingly illustrated by placing the passage from Book II already
quoted beside the stanza from the ode. In Book II the infant is no
outcast: along his veins are interfused

> The gravitation and the filial bond
> Of nature, that connect him with the world.
> Emphatically such a Being lives,
> An inmate of this *active* universe;
> From nature largely he receives; nor so
> Is satisfied, but largely gives again. . . .
>
> [*Prel.*, II.263–68]

His mind is creator and receiver both, "working but in alliance
with the works / Which it beholds." As we have seen, the relationship
of nature to child is conceived of as that of mother to child; indeed, she
literally absorbs the function of the mother. And the creative sensibility,
source of the "auxiliar light," is augmented and sustained by the interaction with nature.

In stanza 6, however, Earth is seen not as a mother but as a homely
and not very bright nurse who, with something of a mother's mind
and with the best intentions, does all she can to make her "foster child"
forget the glories he has known. Earth then becomes an unwitting an-
tagonist, trying to substitute her own pleasures for, and to distract the
child from, the vision. The difference between the attitudes in Book II
of *The Prelude* and in the ode might be summed up in the paradoxical implication of the phrase, "the child is father of the man." In *The
Prelude,* the child is looked upon as the seed from which the man will
grow. In the interaction of child and nature are established all the potentialities of the man. The progress from child to man is one of or-
ganic growth, of evolution. In the ode, the movement from child to
man is one of retrogression; the child is almost literally the father, be-

cause he possesses an intuitive wisdom, a vision that the man lacks and can only comprehend by returning in recollection to his childhood. The difference in the attitudes reflects the difference in the conditions under which Wordsworth is writing. During the period in which he is composing the first two books of *The Prelude,* he possesses a sense of well-being, of harmony with nature and contentment with a faith and a way of life based on her alone; he has complete confidence in his powers and full and uninhibited enjoyment of them. In fact, he possesses the visionary gleam or, what is as important, the power to revive it poetically at will; in his immediate experience with nature he finds continuing reaffirmation of his childhood experience, and evidence for his hypothesis that nature shapes and stimulates the growth of power. But by the time he is writing the ode he has lost his sense of well-being, his sensuous, magical contact with nature, and his almost Epicurean happiness in the life of the moment. If he is to retain confidence in himself and his future, if he is to avoid the bleak inference that, since his power rested upon an interaction with nature, he is dependent upon unpredictable forces outside himself, he must recast his whole hypothesis and set the source of the power beyond and independent of nature.

The intensity of the tone of the ode grows out of the fact that the loss lamented has been recent and unexpected, and that the poet does not dare admit this to himself but must explain it as something occurring naturally and gradually and in such a way that the very loss becomes proof of man's superiority to nature and grounds of hope rather than despair. That he had until recently taken the visionary power for granted and had anticipated no loss is evident in *The Recluse:*

> Of ill-advised Ambition and of Pride
> I would stand clear, but yet to me I feel
> That an internal brightness is vouch-safed
> That must not die, that must not pass away.
> Why does this inward lustre fondly seek,
> And gladly blend with outward fellowship?
> Why do *they* shine around me whom I love?
> [*Recluse,* lines 673–79]

Once Wordsworth had placed the source of the power beyond nature and could find strength in "the faith that looks through death," then he could re-establish his relationship with nature almost on the old footing. But the intimacy is gone; the relationship has become formal and conventional. There is a separation between the two; he stands aloof, detached, watching and observing, not participating except in spirit. In stanza 10 he says:

> We in thought will join your throng
> Ye that pipe and ye that play. . . .

His love for nature now is not for herself, but for what she suggests to him of ultimate relationships. When he says in stanza 11 that he only has relinquished one delight "to live beneath your more habitual sway," it is within the context in which he speaks of the faith that looks through death and the years that bring the philosophic mind. Nature here is the sign and symbol of eternity; in her he sees God manifesting himself: the fountains, meadows, hills, and groves, which in themselves are remindful of mutability and the evanescence of all mortal things, become evidence of immortal power. In the *Ode to Duty,* Wordsworth addresses the eternal law to which nature testifies:

> Flowers laugh before thee on their beds
> And fragrance in thy footing treads;
> Thou dost preserve the stars from wrong;
> And the most ancient heavens, through Thee, are fresh and strong.
> [*Ode to Duty,* lines 45–48]

The "more habitual sway" beneath which he will live suggests this manifestation through nature of the laws of duty. But, much as he may wish to end on a strong and positive note, he is unable to avoid revealing in the last lines of the poem the ambivalent pull of his feelings. He cannot divorce from his intimations of immortality his awareness of mutability, or from his optimism the sense of loss. So the clouds gathering round the setting sun take "a sober colouring" from an eye that has kept watch over man's mortality. And, "thanks to the human heart,"

> To me the meanest flower that blows can give
> Thoughts that do often lie too deep for tears.

The last two lines evoke the same complex and ambiguous feelings as do the last lines of Keats' *Ode on Melancholy,* or his apostrophe to the urn: "thou doth tease us out of thought as doth eternity." For the suggestion of the "often" is that never for long can the poet move beyond tears, and that when he does it is to an experience inexpressibly poignant.[19]

The Romantic Ventriloquists

Though beginning with these poems in 1802 Wordsworth moved steadily away from a reliance on nature alone, he was nevertheless violently shocked in 1805 by the death of his brother. The circumstances under which John died awoke the old memories of wild and hostile nature and forced him to recognize how untenable his beliefs of 1798–1800 had become. In the letter to Beaumont he frankly admitted the need to believe in *"another* and a *better* world" beyond this one.[20] Only in that context did the action of nature become explicable and justifiable. In the *Elegiac Stanzas* he dramatized the change in his attitude. Once, he says, "in the fond illusion of my heart," he would have depicted the castle in a very different world from the stormy one of the painting:

> A picture had it been of lasting ease,
> Elysian quiet without toil or strife;
> No motion but the moving tide, a breeze,
> Or merely silent Nature's breathing life.[21]
> [*Elegiac Stanzas,* lines 25–28]

From now on the true, the realistic way of viewing the scene is as Beaumont has painted it, "the sea in anger, and that dismal shore." He loves to see the look with which the huge castle braves "the lightning, the fierce wind, and trampling waves." And like the castle he will

> . . . welcome fortitude, and patient cheer,
> And frequent sights of what is to be borne!
> Such sights, or worse, as are before me here.—
> Not without hope we suffer and we mourn.
> [*Elegiac Stanzas,* lines 57–60]

The *Elegiac Stanzas* are the open renunciation of the attitude toward nature which he had expressed in *The Recluse.* When he cries:

> Farewell, farewell the heart that lives alone,
> Housed in a dream, at distance from the Kind!
> Such happiness, wherever it be known,
> Is to be pitied; for 'tis surely blind . . .
> [*Elegiac Stanzas,* lines 53–56]

he seems to be ironically echoing and revoking the farewell expressed there. In *The Recluse* he had recalled how in his childhood he had "breathed . . . among wild appetites and blind desires." He had sought the wild and violent in nature and opposed it in reckless defiance. Similarly, in human affairs he had responded to passionate and

[40]

dangerous actions. "But me hath *Nature* tamed, and bade to seek / For other agitations, or be calm." And nature's influence had been sanctioned by reason's "deliberate" voice, which had said, "Be mild, and cleave to gentle things." So he proclaims portentously:

> Then farewell to the Warrior's schemes, farewell
> The forwardness of Soul which looks that way
> Upon a less incitement than the cause
> Of Liberty endangered, and farewell
> That other hope, long mine, the hope to fill
> The heroic trumpet with the Muse's breath!
> [*Recluse,* lines 745–50]

Henceforth, his life is to be tranquil, his relationship with nature joyful, and, "musing in solitude" on man, nature, and society, he will write of how exquisitely the individual mind and the external world are fitted to one another.

Now in the *Elegiac Stanzas* he bids farewell in turn to this dream, this "fond illusion" of the heart, and reverts to the view of man and nature as separate and opposite. The wild and violent aspects of nature which he had sought as a boy he again seeks, but his role in relation to them has changed. Then his attitude was one of active defiance; now it is one of passive forbearance. Then he loved to stand and read the forbidding looks of the chasms, crags, and towers—and disobey; now he stands like the castle in patient fortitude and rocklike endurance. Nature becomes a test and challenge of his stoicism, and he is eager to prove himself. The larger implication behind the last stanza is certainly that suffering or the readiness to suffer is necessary to the realization of the hope, and that the foolish attempt to live otherwise will lead to swift retribution. Though the poetic statement in the *Elegiac Stanzas* is extreme, and Wordsworth continued on in the old familiar relationship with the natural world of Grasmere, nevertheless his attitude toward nature in the large was from now on strained and formal.

V. THE UNFATHERED VAPOUR

Wordsworth's sense of the harmonious interaction of man and nature and of the benign power within nature to mold and calm the mind of man was directly undermined by the series of experiences which we have been until now considering, but the ultimate destruction of this "sense" was inherent from the very beginning in his obsessive preoccupation with the growth of his own mind. We have seen already how in the first books of *The Prelude* he emphasized a "creative sensibility" in himself, born with him and independent of nature; and how in *The Recluse* he spoke of an "internal brightness" that set him apart from others. This conviction of his own creative superiority made it impossible for him long to remain content with a view of things in which his mind was subordinate to and dependent upon nature for its power. His ego would not permit him simply to enjoy his imaginative and sensuous experiences with nature and to indulge his visionary power for its own sake, but it must brood and, in Keats' phrase, peacock over them. As it grew more arrogant, it demanded that the imaginative power be seen as something superior to and apart from nature, and allied to something transcending nature.

Wordsworth reached the point where nothing less than the conviction of his own immortality could satisfy him. There was something of the Greek hubris in this, an overweening pride that invoked its own destruction or, more accurately, the destruction of the very imaginative power whose self-sufficiency and perpetuation it wanted to insure. Wordsworth was like Antaeus, the giant whose strength came from the earth and lasted only as long as his feet were firmly grounded. The source of his power was in the sense of things which he had between 1795 and 1802; when he tried to explain the source in other terms, when he denied his dependence upon nature, then he cut himself off from this experience that nourished the roots of his poetic strength. His unwillingness to be content with what he had was one of the reasons for the loss of the vision. Instead of letting it express itself, he tended more and more to abstract generalizations from it. He became too sophisticated to retain the magic contact with the external world from which his best poetry had sprung. Ironically, his meddling intellect by dissecting his vision was in danger of murdering it.

The process we have summarized is vividly dramatized in Books III to XIII of *The Prelude*. The great psychological shift in Wordsworth's relationship to nature had already taken place when he picked up in 1804 with Book III, and thus he looked back upon his youth differently from in the first two books.[22] The emphasis now in the equation of the mind as receiver and creator is upon the latter, and nature is subordinated to the position of an agent of God. The change in attitude is accompanied by a change in tone. Gone are the doubts and qualifications, replaced by a confidence in himself and his perceptions amounting to arrogance (the kind of confidence that accompanies a hardening of sensitivity and a closing in of the circle of intellectual and imaginative experience). Very early in Book III he says in regard to his melancholy at Cambridge that he had

> A feeling that I was not for that hour
> Nor for that place. But wherefore be cast down?
> Why should I grieve? I was a chosen Son.
> For hither I had come with holy powers
> And faculties, whether to work or feel. . . .
>
> [*Prel.*, III.80–84]

Turning the mind in upon itself, he felt

> Incumbencies more awful, visitings
> Of the Upholder of the tranquil Soul;
> Which underneath all passion lives secure
> A steadfast life.
>
> [*Prel.*, III.115–18]

These are proof that he was now ascending to "community with highest truth." He turns to consider the way in which to every natural form, even the stones, he gave a moral life: "the great mass / Lay bedded in a quickening soul, and all / That I beheld respired with inward meaning." The deliberate de-emphasizing of the active power of nature is clear enough:

> I had a world about me; 'twas my own,
> I made it; for it only liv'd to me,
> And to the God who look'd into my mind.[23]
>
> [*Prel.*, III.142–44]

Henceforth when he refers to nature it is with careful qualification of her powers, even when he is referring to his early childhood, and the reminder that she is simply an agent of God is never far off. For example, in Book IV after the episode of the sunrise walk in which "vows" were made for him:

> . . . bond unknown to me
> Was given, that I should be, else sinning greatly,
> A dedicated Spirit . . .
>
> [*Prel.* IV.342–44]

he goes on to say that during the summer he experienced in himself

[43]

Conformity as just as that of old
To the end and written spirit of God's works,
Whether held forth in Nature or in Man.
[*Prel.*, IV.357–59]

In Book V he says that we should speak of books as powers only less

For what we may become, and what we need,
Than Nature's self, which is the breath of God.
[*Prel.*, V.221–22]

And in Book VIII, after describing the way in which he becomes aware of man, he cries:

But blessed be the God
Of Nature and of Man that this was so,
That Men did at the first present themselves
Before my untaught eyes thus purified,
Remov'd, and at a distance that was fit.
[*Prel.*, VIII.436–40]

The shifting perspective of *The Prelude* can be most dramatically illustrated through a consideration of the mountain episodes in Book I, Book VI, and Book XIII. In Book I the mountain is felt to be quite literally alive. The experience of the boy at the time and as relived by the mature man is one of elemental terror. The cliff,

As if with voluntary power instinct,
Uprear'd its head. I struck and struck again,
And, growing still in stature, the huge Cliff
Rose up between me and the stars, and still,
With measur'd motion, like a living thing,
Strode after me.
[*Prel.*, I.407–12]

Here is the animistic quality of primitive myth.

In Book VI Wordsworth relates how he and his companion had lost the road leading through the mountains and learned from the peasant who directed them back to it that they had already unknowingly crossed the Alps. Abruptly and with a passionate intensity for which we have been totally unprepared, Wordsworth bursts into an apostrophe to the imagination:

Imagination! lifting up itself
Before the eye and progress of my Song
Like an unfather'd vapour; here that Power,
In all the might of its endowments, came

[44]

Wordsworth

Athwart me; I was lost as in a cloud,
Halted, without a struggle to break through.
And now recovering, to my Soul I say
I recognize thy glory; in such strength
Of usurpation, in such visitings
Of awful promise, when the light of sense
Goes out in flashes that have shown to us
The invisible world, doth Greatness make abode,
There harbours whether we be young or old.
Our destiny, our nature, and our home
Is with infinitude, and only there;
With hope it is, hope that can never die,
Effort, and expectation, and desire,
And something evermore about to be.

[*Prel.*, VI.525-42]

The syntax at the beginning of this passage is tortured and confused; the references in such words as "here" and "now recovering"
are vague; indeed, the expression of the whole passage seems to have
been deliberately blurred—as if to indicate that the experience was
truly ineffable and incommunicable. However, the psychological significance of the original experience is clear enough: Wordsworth had
looked forward to crossing the Alps, anticipating imaginatively the
magnificence of the sensuous experience. But the sensuous experience
had been inconsequential, in fact had been lost. Now, as he broods
upon his disappointment in 1804, he has suddenly a mystical revelation of the meaning of the experience: the mind draws its power from
"the invisible world" beyond nature. As Keats was later to put it, the
prototype of the imaginative experience "must be hereafter."

That Wordsworth's disappointment at having crossed the Alps
without knowing it is fundamental to the experience is indicated by
the reference, immediately following the passage on the imagination,
to the "dull and heavy slackening that ensued" on the Peasant's tid-
ings. Simplon Pass, which he now descends, is described as a scene
of "visionary dreariness" with the same suggestion of mysterious and
terrifying power that infuses the description of the striding cliff:

The immeasurable height
Of woods decaying, never to be decay'd,
The stationary blasts of water-falls,
And every where along the hollow rent
Winds thwarting winds, bewilder'd and forlorn,
The torrents shooting from the clear blue sky,

The Romantic Ventriloquists

The rocks that mutter'd close upon our ears,
Black drizzling crags that spake by the way-side
As if a voice were in them, the sick sight
And giddy prospect of the raving stream,
The unfetter'd clouds, and region of the Heavens,
Tumult and peace, the darkness and the light
Were all like workings of one mind, the features
Of the same face, blossoms upon one tree,
Characters of the great Apocalypse,
The types and symbols of Eternity,
Of first and last, and midst, and without end.
                          [*Prel.*, VI.556–72]

But there has been an important shift in emphasis and tone. Where the lines in Book I are presented as evidence of an animating force in nature herself, the details of Simplon Pass became evidence of a dying and mutable nature, the imperfect physical forms through which the Godhead manifests Himself, the types and symbols of a perfection beyond itself. Nature here bears the same relationship to the higher reality that it does in the *Intimations* ode. Wordsworth has superimposed the kind of Neoplatonic distinction between the world of idea and the physical world that Shelley develops in *Adonais*. The passage owes something of its peculiar intensity to Wordsworth's more or less conscious desire in 1804 to convince himself that the revelation of a reality beyond nature was really the significance of his experience.

In the description of the ascent of Mount Snowdon in Book XIII [24] the details are sharply and clearly realized: the abrupt emergence from the mist into the clear moonlight; the prospect of a vast sea of mist extending in "headlands, tongues, and promontory shapes" into the "real" sea, with a hundred hills upheaving their dusky backs over this still ocean; and, most important, the "blue chasm" in the vapor a third of a mile away:

A deep and gloomy breathing-place through which
Mounted the roar of water, torrents, streams
Innumerable, roaring with one voice.
. . . in that breach
Through which the homeless voice of waters rose,
That dark deep thoroughfare had Nature lodg'd
The Soul, the Imagination of the whole.
                          [*Prel.*, XIII.57–59, 62–65]

When Wordsworth turns to interpret the experience, he falls, as in Book VI, into syntactical vagueness:

> A meditation rose in me that night
> Upon the lonely Mountain when the scene
> Had pass'd away, and it appear'd to me
> The perfect image of a mighty Mind,
> Of one that feeds upon infinity,
> That is exalted by an underpresence,
> The sense of God, or whatsoe'er is dim
> Or vast in its own being. . . .
> [*Prel.*, XIII.66–73]

What does "it" refer to? Is "it" the mountain, the mist, the moon, or the entire scene? Apparently the last, because he goes on to say that nature had exhibited there one function of such a mind by putting forth

> That dominion which she oftentimes
> Exerts upon the outward face of things,
> So moulds them, and endues, abstracts, combines,
> Or by abrupt and unhabitual influence
> Doth make one object so impress itself
> Upon all others, and pervade them so
> That even the grossest minds must see and hear
> And cannot chuse but feel.
> [*Prel.*, XIII.77–84]

In other words, the whole pattern and organization of the scene indicates in nature a purposive intelligence, a power to impress herself upon "even the grossest mind."

This power is the "express resemblance,"

> . . . a genuine Counterpart
> And Brother of the glorious faculty
> Which higher minds bear with them as their own.
> That is the very spirit in which they deal
> With all the objects of the universe. [*Prel.*, XIII.88–92]

Completely self-sufficient and creative, these higher minds are not enthralled by "sensible impressions,"

> But quicken'd, rouz'd, and made thereby more apt
> To hold communion with the invisible world.
> Such minds are truly from the Deity,

For they are Powers; and hence the highest bliss
That can be known is theirs, the consciousness
Of whom they are habitually infused
Through every image, and through every thought,
And all impressions; hence religion, faith,
And endless occupation for the soul
Whether discursive or intuitive;
Hence sovereignty within and peace at will
Emotion which best foresight need not fear
Most worthy then of trust when most intense.
Hence chearfulness in every act of life
Hence truth in moral judgements and delight
That fails not in the external universe.

[*Prel.*, XIII.104–19]

The subjection of nature to mind has been completed. The poet is utterly emancipated and detached, able to use her or not if and as he chooses. The triumph is symbolized by the ascent of the mountain. When he rises above the mist and surveys the world spread at his feet, he is rising above nature. Nature's organization of the scene becomes simply an "exemplum," an analogy of the way in which the superior mind functions. It becomes, in fact, evidence from which he draws the inference of the superiority of minds like his own to nature. For it is in reality his mind that is superimposing meaning and pattern upon the experience; he is the one, not nature, who is organizing the scene before him. He is surveying it as God would survey it: nature is to Wordsworth as Wordsworth is to God. Thus, at the end of his poem Wordsworth has returned to the old doctrine of correspondences which he had so successfully broken through in the early books of *The Prelude*. Furthermore, he has quite openly abandoned the pretense of universality and equality, of the "man speaking to men." He has drawn a sharp distinction between the higher and the grosser minds. The higher minds are the elect; they are truly "from the Deity." And he clearly identifies himself with the elect.

The tortuous process of absorption, transformation, and revocation of earlier attitudes continues in the lines that follow the mountain passage. In the apostrophe concluding Book II, Wordsworth had cried to the mountains and lakes of his childhood that if in youth he had been pure in heart, if he had lived removed "From little enmities and low desires," if he had retained a faith that failed not, "the gift is yours / Ye mountains! thine, O Nature!" Now he calls the "Solitudes" where he received his "earliest visitations" to witness that, "howsoe'er misled," he never in the quest of right and wrong tampered with his conscience from private aims, or was the dupe of selfish passions, or ever willfully yielded to "mean care and low pursuits":

> But rather did with jealousy shrink back
> From every combination that might aid
> The tendency, too potent in itself,
> Of habit to enslave the mind, I mean
> Oppress it by the laws of vulgar sense,
> And substitute a universe of death,
> The falsest of all worlds, in place of that
> Which is divine and true.
>
> [*Prel.*, XIII.136–43]

The opposition he sets up here is extremely puzzling, and thus the whole drift of his meaning is thrown into confusion. What is the equation or the relationship between tampering with conscience from private aims or being the dupe of selfish passions or yielding to low pursuits—between these and the universe of death? Once again, we feel that vital elements for the understanding of the passage are missing. Wordsworth is refusing to face, or at least unwilling to state directly, what he has in mind. An obscure and complicated process of rationalization is at work. The reference to the tendency "of habit" to enslave the mind to the laws of vulgar sense would identify the "universe of death" with the doctrine of associationism, and by extension with the naturalism, "the language of the sense," which Wordsworth had so fervently endorsed in *Tintern Abbey* and the first two books of *The Prelude*.[25] He is engaged now in repudiating (to himself, first of all) that endorsement; he is saying that he never meant what he appears to mean in the earlier books; he has always been motivated by the highest aims, so obviously he could never willingly have subscribed to what seems to him now so pernicious a doctrine. How cunning he is in self-persuasion is indicated by the way in which he calls upon the "Solitudes" to witness that he has always believed as he believes now.

Comparisons of this sort between the earlier and later books of *The Prelude* can be multiplied almost indefinitely. I have analyzed these passages at length because, on the one hand, when set side by side, they show a quite discernible difference in attitude and meaning between early and later books; and, on the other hand, and most importantly, they show the process by which Wordsworth was able to reconcile earlier and later attitudes without being aware that there were differences to reconcile. His terminology is so vague and ill-defined that he can superimpose his later attitudes upon the earlier, or absorb the earlier into the later, without embarrassment or pain. The terminology becomes an important element in blurring and blunting his artistic and psychological sensitivity. It explains why he was able to incorporate into later books of *The Prelude* passages (usually concrete narratives), written earlier, which clash violently with their context, as for example the "Spots of Time" passages in Book XI. It explains why he was able to prefix to *The Excursion* the passage from *The Recluse.* He not only was making a symbolic gesture of continuity in testimony that he was carrying out what had been projected so long ago, but he actually was unable to see any difference between what he said then and what he was saying in *The Excursion;* he thought that he still believed what he had believed earlier. The hypnotic magic of terminology helps explain the casual patching together of passages widely separated in time and meaning in *The Excursion,* particularly in Books I and IV, and the endless revising of *The Prelude* between 1805 and his death.

A comparative examination of earlier and later books also undermines attempts to see and justify *The Prelude* as a systematic exposition of a philosophy or even, as Wordsworth saw it, as the "Growth of a Poet's Mind." It is rather the picture of the changing mind of Wordsworth between 1799 and 1805, as reflected in his reaction to and interpretation of certain experiences in his childhood and youth. Most of *The Prelude* from Book III to the end, with the exception of the books on London and France, is expository—a reconstruction of his youth as it ought to have been and as he now liked to believe it had been, in terms of abstractions and generalizations. There is no attempt at an objective artistic reconstruction of his growth. He loses interest progressively in concrete experiences and "ruminates," to use the word Eliot applies to Tennyson. The result is that much of the poem suffers from the fault that Coleridge charitably described as occasional: "prolixity, repetition, and an eddying, instead of progression, of thought." [26]

In the last book Wordsworth attempted to impose upon the poem a logical and systematic structure. Imagination, he says, has been the moving soul of his long labor:

Wordsworth

. . . we have traced the stream
From darkness, and the very place of birth
In its blind cavern, whence is faintly heard
The sound of waters; follow'd it to light
And open day, accompanied its course
Among the ways of Nature, afterwards
Lost sight of it, bewilder'd and engulph'd,
Then given it greeting, as it rose once more
With strength, reflecting in its solemn breast
The works of man and face of human life,
And lastly, from its progress have we drawn
The feeling of life endless, the great thought
By which we live, Infinity and God.
Imagination having been our theme,
So also hath that intellectual love,
For they are each in each, and cannot stand
Dividually.

[*Prel.*, XIII.172–88]

Religiously and philosophically speaking, we are to see *The Prelude* as the record of his growth toward the faith he now holds; unrolled before us, as before him presumably, has been the progressive revelation of truth leading to his present conviction. Psychologically speaking, we are to see *The Prelude* as the record of a gradual emergence of identity from "the blind cavern," the emergence of consciousness from unconsciousness, the creation of self from the anonymous universal; until, at the end, he possesses the consciousness of who he is "habitually infused / Through every image and through every thought / And all impressions," this consciousness itself being evidence of immortality and the existence of a personal deity to whom he is dear.

When the poem is considered as a whole, however, there is no indication of such a tightly knit development of theme. In the first two books the theme has not even been conceived; the words "imagination" and "intellectual love" do not occur, and God is definitely subordinated to nature. These two books are written in a questioning or doubtful spirit; they are an inductive exploration of his childhood to see how he was molded into the man he is and to determine whether he is fitted to write the kind of poem he wishes to write. Indeed, in particular he is concerned with trying to break through the psychological block that seems to keep him from writing at all.[27] He is distressed by his procrastination and rationalization, and the first book begins in earnest when he asks:

The Romantic Ventriloquists

Was it for this
That one, the fairest of all Rivers, lov'd
To blend his murmurs with my Nurse's song? . . .

[*Prel.*, I.271–73]

There is nothing wrong in Wordsworth's using *The Prelude* as the means by which to write his way out of uncertainty and into conviction, as the process by which to discover a theme, or work his way to a faith; but it distorts the record of his growth, throws it artistically and factually into confusion to claim that the pattern with which he has emerged in the last book was one inherent in his growth, to be seen in the stages of his development. The point at which he ends *The Prelude,* indicating that the self-identification has been completed, is the same point at which he begins in self-doubt and questioning. Obviously, in Book I he did not see his childhood and youth leading to any such conviction as in the last book. What he has done from Book III on has been to superimpose back upon his growth the emergence of self-identity that took place between 1802 and 1805. Indeed, the theme appears full-born in the third book when he picks up the poem after several years. In that book he presents himself as fully aware of who he is, of his relation to God, of his creative imagination. His growth is complete in all essential respects, and dramatically, artistically, and psychologically there is nothing for him to evolve to. So from Book III until Book IX, when he begins the story of his experiences in France, there is almost no forward movement, but simply a series of more or less discursive comments on education, books, nature, and man within a frame of reference already established.[28]

VI. THE STILL, SAD MUSIC

In Books IX and X *The Prelude* as psychological history comes suddenly alive. Not only does it have narrative movement, pinned down in space and time, not only is it concrete and dramatic in its descriptions of persons and places, but it also carries us into the mind of the poet as of that time and place. Wordsworth dramatically conveys his excited response to new ideas and Utopian prospects, his growing confusion and conflict, his ultimate disillusionment and despair. The mind, quite literally, grows before our eyes. We realize that this is the heart of the poem, the real point of intellectual awakening and growth in which he becomes aware of himself and the world. This

[52]

is the experience beyond which nothing can ever be as it was before, and which alters the memory of all that preceded it. Specifically, it made Wordsworth aware of "man's inhumanity to man," of society's responsibility, not God's or nature's, for human suffering. It made him aware that man could change the conditions of society, that he was potentially capable of and could work toward eliminating social evils.

He also unfortunately saw the French Revolution begin to go bad, so that it seemed in its violence and terrorism to become more evil than that which it superseded. Perhaps it was at this point that the social pessimism and reaction that were already beginning to flourish in him in 1804 took root, the belief that any change must be for the worse. But this does not alter the fact that Wordsworth's experience and sophistication resulting from the French Revolution made impossible for him any simple explanation or resolution of the problem of human suffering. And when, in the rest of *The Prelude* and in *The Excursion*, he ignores the social causes or attempts to gloss them over, there can be no artistic or ethical justification for his act. In his handling of the story of the Soldier in Book IV of *The Prelude*, and of Margaret in Book I of *The Excursion*, we are given vivid examples of the strange, evasive process by which he corrupted the value of much that he wrote and prevented his talent from ever fully realizing itself. He was aware, if ever so obscurely, of what he was doing, as the peculiar nature of his revisions indicates. This knowledge accounts perhaps for some of the psychological unrest that seemed to grow rather than diminish under the philosophy of stoical tranquillity and acceptance.

Between his return from France and his departure for Germany in 1799, Wordsworth was almost obsessively preoccupied with the socially oppressed and outcast. Consider the sailor and the female vagrant in *Guilt and Sorrow;* almost the whole cast of *The Borderers;* numerous mad and abandoned mothers, beggars, old men and women in the *Lyrical Ballads*. The social causes of their misfortunes were not blinked, although only in *Guilt and Sorrow* were these causes given special emphasis and made the subject of moralizing sermons. What principally concerned him was the suffering of these people and the almost heroic stature they took on under suffering. He was obviously fascinated by their ability to endure and survive. All that was best and noblest in human nature seemed to emerge under these conditions, and the almost indestructible toughness of the human spirit was revealed. In each of the poems he seems to be brooding over the question he asks the Leech Gatherer: "How is it that you live and what is it you do?" What gives them the strength to survive?

In many of the poems, also, he seems to be deliberately testing to discover the breaking point of the characters. Examined in this narrow and intense way, suffering becomes a virtue in and for itself, bringing out the best in those that suffer and those that observe, and the causes of suffering are apt to be progressively subordinated and even ignored. Suffering is, whatever the causes, unavoidable; all human actions lead to it. Oswald's speech in *The Borderers* reflects Wordsworth's own attitude, for later he affixes it to *The White Doe of Rylstone* with the characteristic addition of his later years that, in the words of the *Elegiac Stanzas,* "not without hope we suffer and we mourn." [29] Oswald tells Marmaduke:

> Action is transitory—a step, a blow,
> The motion of a muscle—this way or that—
> 'Tis done, and in the after-vacancy
> We wonder at ourselves like men betrayed;
> Suffering is permanent, obscure and dark,
> And shares the nature of infinity.
>
> [*Borderers,* III.1539–44]

In the later poems, suffering is seen as a necessary condition of life which becomes proof of immortality, an ultimate reprieve and reward; it is God's test of us. Conversely for Wordsworth there was the terrible fear that he could not stand up under the test unless he had the hope of immortality.

Even in the poems of 1797–98 a neurotic element enters into Wordsworth's attitude as observer. He stands aloof and detached and draws strength and even quiet satisfaction and pleasure from his observation of the suffering of others. In *Tintern Abbey* the context of the famous line on humanity is one of serenity:

> For I have learned
> To look on nature, not as in the hour
> Of thoughtless youth; but hearing oftentimes
> The still, sad music of humanity,
> Nor harsh, nor grating, though of ample power
> To chasten and subdue.
>
> [*Tintern Abbey,* lines 88–93]

The reaction is that of one who, withdrawn, watches a tragic drama or listens to an andante by Mozart: humanity is important as a remote stimulus to make him feel more intensely, but not to disturb or torment him. Similarly, in the *Old Cumberland Beggar* the old man becomes the means by which the good in people is brought out. His presence does not distress, but rather gives a sense of well-being:

> . . . all behold in him
> A silent monitor, which on their minds
> Must needs impress a transitory thought
> Of self-congratulation, to the heart
> Of each recalling his peculiar boons,
> His charters and exemptions; and, perchance,
> Though he to no one give the fortitude
> And circumspection needful to preserve
> His present blessings, and to husband up
> The respite of the season, he, at least,
> And 'tis no vulgar service, makes them felt.
> [*Old Cumberland Beggar*, lines 122–32]

The poet himself is swept at the last into a chilling prayer:

> Then let him pass, a blessing on his head!
> And, long as he can wander, let him breathe
> The freshness of the valleys; let his blood
> Struggle with frosty air and winter snows;
> And let the chartered wind that sweeps the heath
> Beat his grey locks against his withered face . . .
> Let him be free of mountain solitudes;
> And have around him, *whether heard or not,*
> The pleasant melody of woodland birds.
> [*Old Cumberland Beggar,* lines 171–76, 183–85. My italics]

Granted that Wordsworth was motivated by the best intentions; granted that he wished to show that "none, the meanest of created things," exists divorced from good, that "man is dear to man" and "we all have one human heart"; granted that he was opposing to the terrible life in a workhouse the relatively dignified life of a wanderer; there is still a curious insensitivity about the passages quoted. The beggar himself is not consulted or thought of as a man; he is looked at from the outside as an instrument. Wordsworth assumes that the beggar wants what the poet thinks he should want: to struggle with frost and snow, to be beaten by winds, to wander deaf and blind in the woods. It is an illuminating example of selfish projection. There is no suggestion, furthermore, that this is simply the lesser of two evils; the question of why there should be beggary at all never comes up. It is true that even to the liberal leaders of the day beggars were so familiar a part of the landscape as to be taken for granted as a necessary, ineradicable evil.[30] But Wordsworth had been made vividly aware in France of all the implications of poverty and beggary. In Book IX of *The Prelude,* written in 1804, he remembered that when Beaupuy pointed to the little "hunger bitten" girl and

> In agitation said ' 'Tis against *that*
> Which we are fighting,' I with him believed
> Devoutly that a spirit was abroad
> Which could not be withstood, that poverty
> At least like this, would in a little time
> Be found no more. . . .
>
> [*Prel.,* IX.518–23]

He obviously no longer believed this, and he perhaps had convinced himself that there was a difference between English and French beggary, but this does not justify him in rationalizing beggary, no matter how eloquently, as a fundamental good. The *Old Cumberland Beggar* indicates an important stage in the process of Wordsworth's social and intellectual retreat, the deliberate limiting of the range of his perceptions about human nature. In a curious way, he acknowledges the lopsidedness of the poem in the story which he has the Solitary relate in Book II of *The Excursion,* and which we shall look at shortly.

In 1798 Wordsworth wrote the passage on the discharged soldier which he later incorporated into Book IV of *The Prelude.*[31] This in itself is one of the most moving and effective of his matter-of-fact narratives. The soldier is first seen sitting against a stone:

> He was of stature tall,
> A foot above man's common measure tall,
> Stiff in his form, and upright, lank and lean;
> A man more meagre, as it seem'd to me,
> Was never seen abroad by night or day.
> His arms were long, and bare his hands; his mouth
> Shew'd ghastly in the moonlight. . . .
>
> [*Prel.,* IV.405–11]

In his very dress appeared a "desolation," a simplicity akin to solitude. From his lips issued "murmuring sounds, as of pain / Or of

[56]

uneasy thought." The boy regarded him for a long time with mingled fear and sorrow. When he finally got up the courage to address the soldier, the man lifted to his head "a lean and wasted arm / In measured gesture," and, upon being asked his history,

> . . . he in reply
> Was neither slow nor eager; but unmov'd,
> And with a quiet, uncomplaining voice,
> A stately air of mild indifference
> He told, in simple words, a Soldier's Tale.
> [*Prel.*, IV.441–45]

When later the boy was guiding him to a laborer's cottage where he might spend the night, and could not "forbear" to ask him what he had endured "from hardship, battle, or the pestilence," he remained calm in demeanor, concise in answer:

> Solemn and sublime
> He might have seem'd, but that in all he said
> There was a strange half-absence, and a tone
> Of weakness and indifference, as of one
> Remembering the importance of his theme
> But feeling it no longer.
> [*Prel.*, IV.473–78]

Before leaving him at the cottage, the boy entreated him not to linger in the public way from now on but to ask for such help as he needed; and the soldier, "with the same ghastly mildness in his look," replied:

> . . . my trust is in the God of Heaven
> And in the eye of him that passes me.
> [*Prel.*, IV.494–95]

Then, touching his hat again with his lean hand and in a voice that seemed to speak "with a reviving interest / Till then unfelt," he thanked the boy, who returned the blessing of the "poor, unhappy Man."

> And so we parted. Back I cast a look,
> And linger'd near the door a little space;
> Then sought with quiet heart my distant home.
> [*Prel.*, IV.502–4]

This is the end of the tale, and of Book IV. The word "quiet" comes as a disquieting shock. It says both too much and too little. The tale is so powerfully evocative in its understatement, and so complex, almost inexpressible, a structure of emotion is built up, that it would certainly have been better to have no qualifying phrase at all and to allow the reader's imagination to supply the state of mind in which the boy sought his home; or else to have a much more elaborate comment at the end. For "quiet" is not an ambiguous word in the sense of suggesting a complex of meanings, but simply an inadequate and inhibiting word. It deliberately cuts off the flow of response, represses and denies the tremendous range of questions clearly evoked in the story, somewhat like stuffing a genie into a bottle and hammering in the cork. The turmoil aroused by the tale is not resolved or reconciled dramatically into a higher serenity, as in a tragedy, but simply *pronounced* resolved. A "quiet heart" can be relevant only in the sense that the boy has seen the man safely taken care of for the night; that he knows that the man will somehow survive; that he has been assured of the fundamental dignity and worth of human nature as it has been revealed in the man. But, in any final sense, his heart could not be "quiet."

The ghastly figure brought by the intensity of his suffering to a state beyond feeling, so that he becomes a kind of walking "life in death," with the universality of an Ancient Mariner or a Wandering Jew, raises questions not simply of the effects of war and social injustice, but—set against the night, the solitude, and the public road —of the ultimate meaning and role of human life. To these questions no answers are suggested by the leave-taking; rather they are made more disturbing. The meaninglessness and the needlessness of the man's suffering are underscored by the placid beauty of the moonlit night and by the simple goodness of the Laborer by which his immediate troubles are so quickly and easily resolved. Indeed, the figure of the man should, like the striding cliff in Book I, have sent the boy home "with grave and serious thoughts" and have been a trouble to his dreams, and for many days his brain should have worked "with a dim and undetermin'd sense / Of unknown modes of being."

When he comes to incorporate the episode into Book IV, Wordsworth aggravates rather than mollifies our sense of dissatisfaction. Having clamped a lid on the implications of the episode through the word "quiet," he now proceeds to wrap it in cotton batting by placing it in a context that so blurs the approach, and sets up connotations so opposite to the episode, that we are almost prevented from recognizing what is really there.

Wordsworth

The episode follows upon the famous description of the sunrise walk in which

> . . . bond unknown to me
> Was given, that I should be, else sinning greatly,
> A dedicated Spirit.
>
> [*Prel.*, IV.342–44]

Wordsworth goes on to say that the summer, though it was in great part given over to trivial pleasures and swarmed with thoughts "transient and loose,"

> . . . wanted not a store
> Of primitive hours, when, by these hindrances
> Unthwarted, I experienc'd in myself
> Conformity as just as that of old
> To the end and written spirit of God's works,
> Whether held forth in Nature or in Man.
>
> [*Prel.*, IV.354–59]

From many wanderings he says laconically he will single out one, "then pass to other themes." He describes how he stole along the silent road, his body from the stillness "drinking in / A restoration like the calm of sleep, / But sweeter far." Around him all was "peace and solitude."

> O happy state! What beauteous pictures now
> Rose in harmonious imagery—they rose
> As from some distant region of my soul
> And came along like dreams; yet such as left
> Obscurely mingled with their passing forms
> A consciousness of animal delight,
> A self-possession felt in every pause
> And every gentle movement of my frame.
>
> [*Prel.*, IV.392–99]

It is at this moment that he sees the "uncouth shape" of the Soldier. The language of this frame passage is almost obtrusively language of contentment and affirmation, reminiscent of the language of *Tintern Abbey:* "calm of sleep," "peace and solitude," "happy state," "harmonious imagery," "animal delight." Both poet and reader have been psychologically prepared to view the meeting with the soldier in a special way, anesthetized against the disturbing elements in the experience. Pain and suffering become unreal, difficult to imagine or feel, remote and transient, when set within this perspective. The

Soldier is absorbed into the peace and tranquillity of the night, and he seems to be part of the harmonious scheme of things. Surely he will be all right, and his sufferings will have been all to a good end, all part of the same benign force that pervades the solitude. And so the meeting with him becomes reassuring evidence of the "end and written spirit of God's works."

The process at work here is a dangerous one. It is hard in this context to accept the "quiet heart" as anything but the complacency growing out of a purely personal sense of well-being. And in the Wordsworth of 1804 it becomes a sign of moral and artistic rationalization by which any evil can be justified and contemplated with equanimity The revisions that Wordsworth made after 1805 bear out this charge. The language of the introduction becomes extremely elaborate and literary in the worst manner of the older Wordsworth. In place of lines 360 and following he inserts a beginning:

> When from our better selves we have too long
> Been parted by the hurrying world, and droop,
> Sick of its business, of its pleasures tired,
> How gracious, how benign, is Solitude;
> How potent a mere image of her sway;
> Most potent when impressed upon the mind
> With an appropriate human centre. . . .
> [1850. *Prel.*, IV.354–60]

And he cites the hermit, the votary kneeling alone at prayers in the cathedral, the watchman in the lighthouse,

> Or as the soul of that great Power is met
> Sometimes embodied on a public road,
> When, for the night deserted, it assumes
> A character of quiet more profound
> Than pathless wastes. . . .
> [1850. *Prel.*, IV.366–70]

The last step has been taken in the transformation of soldier from individual into abstraction. Wordsworth has achieved the "esthetic" distance that enables him to contemplate his soldier undisturbed, without pain, as the embodiment of the gracious and benign soul of solitude. The whole strange process of anesthetization is summed up in a change made at the end of the episode where the "poor unhappy" man whose blessings he returned in 1798 becomes at last simply the "patient" man.

The same process is to be seen at work in the successive revisions of the comment appended to *The Ruined Cottage,* culminating in the comment of the Wanderer when at last the poem has been incorporated into Book I of *The Excursion.* It is easy to see why both Wordsworth and Coleridge were so enthusiastic about the poem, and why Wordsworth labored over it so long and lovingly and finally made it the cornerstone of *The Excursion.* For it is the best of his poems on humble and rustic life.

He began work on it in 1795 and in the spring of 1798 had completed it almost exactly as it is to be found in *The Excursion.*[32] In its slow, meticulous accumulation of detail, it takes on the powerful movement of tragedy. There is a kind of relentless inevitability in the grinding down of Robert and Margaret—the blighted harvests, the plague of war, the long illness of Robert which consumes his little store of money, his enforced idleness until at last he breaks under the strain and deserts his wife and children to enlist as a soldier going overseas. But it is in the description of the slow disintegration of Margaret and the accompanying disintegration of the cottage that the poem becomes truly great. The greatness lies in the unflinching way in which the tale is unfolded through objective details to its logical and dramatic end, without editorializing, simplifying, or evading, and in the complete insight into Margaret's character and problem that is conveyed.

It is a remarkable psychological study and reveals that Wordsworth possessed a penetrating eye for the outward manifestations of psychological disorder. Margaret's consuming sorrow is never sentimentalized. The love for her husband is not simply personal and romantic; his presence is literally necessary for the physical and economic survival of Margaret and her children within the social pattern described; he is an integral part of her life, and her grief is spontaneous and irremediable. She does not give in to despair; she continues to work on courageously, doggedly, futilely, without comfort or aid, or prospect of either.

The last lines of the poem are unrelievedly bleak. Five years (nine years in *The Excursion*) she lingers on after her husband's desertion. "Need must it have been / A sore heart wasting." The Wanderer tells that he has heard how she sat alone through half the Sabbath day in the arbor: "And if a dog passed by, she still would quit / The shade and look abroad." And he tells how through many a summer's

[61]

day she paced spinning the hemp, and whenever a soldier or sailor mendicant passed by would stop to inquire of her husband, or if a strange horseman passed she would look wistfully into his face, and if she discovered there "aught of tender feeling" she might "dare" repeat the same sad question.

> . . . Meanwhile her poor Hut
> Sank to decay; for he was gone, whose hand,
> At the first nipping of October frost,
> Closed up each chink, and with fresh bands of straw
> Checkered the green-grown thatch. And so she lived
> Through the long winter, reckless and alone;
> Until her house by frost, and thaw, and rain,
> Was sapped; and while she slept, the nightly damps
> Did chill her breast; and in the stormy day
> Her tattered clothes were ruffled by the wind,
> Even at the side of her own fire. Yet still
> She loved this wretched spot, nor would for worlds
> Have parted hence; and still that length of road,
> And this rude bench, one torturing hope endeared,
> Fast rooted at her heart: and here, my Friend,—
> In sickness she remained; and here she died;
> Last human tenant of these ruined walls!
>
> [*Ex.*, I.900–16]

This is a disturbing poem; it provides no grounds for complacence or optimism. It arouses intense compassion for Margaret, admiration for and confidence in the fundamental worth of human beings, and a restless impatience with the conditions responsible for her suffering. For her suffering is not inevitable or necessary; it is the direct product of the social conditions of the time and is preventable by human action. The poem itself, and this is one of its virtues, is in no way didactic and propagandistic; it presents almost with detachment the details of Margaret's life, and for that reason it is the more powerful in revealing the needlessness of her suffering and forcing upon us as human beings a sense of moral involvement or responsibility. Only if we assume that the social situation is absolutely unalterable can Margaret's suffering seem unavoidable and inherent in the scheme of things: the implications in such a view are pessimistic indeed. And yet this in effect is the very view that Wordsworth forces upon the tale. He intended, of course, the opposite effect. He obviously could not bear to let the tale stand without comment; he had to transmute its negations into affirmations; he had to see it somehow *sub specie aeternitatis* as a source of consolation and encouragement.

At the end of the 1798 manuscript Wordsworth "made three different attempts at a reconciling passage for the close of the poem."[33] These are very brief passages of which the first is the most important. As he looks at the ruined cottage and its setting,

> . . . to some eye within me all appeared
> Colours and forms of a strange discipline.
> The trouble which they sent into my thought
> Was sweet, I looked and looked again, and to myself
> I seemed a better and a wiser man.

It is interesting as an indication of how close was the collaboration between Wordsworth and Coleridge, and how similar were their psychological needs, that at this very time Coleridge was having his wedding guest wake up the morning after the Mariner's tale, "a sadder and a wiser man."

But Wordsworth struck out these passages and tried again with a long and elaborate argument by the Pedlar, the core of which later became the last section, significantly, of Book IV of *The Excursion*—the culmination of the Wanderer's reply to the Solitary. The gist of the argument is that the man once taught to love "such objects" in nature as excite "no morbid passions, no disquietude / No vengeance and no hatred" must feel the "joy of that pure principle of love" so deeply that he cannot but choose to seek for objects of a kindred love in fellow nature and a kindred joy. "He seeks for good and finds the good he seeks."[34] Every day we shall enlarge our sphere of pleasure and of power, and the senses and the intellect shall "invigorate and sharpen and refine" each other:

> Thus deeply drinking in the soul of things
> We shall be wise perforce, and we shall move
> From strict necessity along the path
> Of order and of good. Whate'er we see
> Whate'er we feel, by agency direct
> Or indirect, shall tend to feed and nurse
> Our faculties, and raise to loftier heights
> Our intellectual soul.
> [Addendum to MS B, lines 92–99; *PW*, V, 402. Cf. *Ex.*, IV.1265 ff.]

The argument in this context is in keeping with the spirit of *Tintern Abbey* and the first books of *The Prelude*. The specific application to Margaret seems to be that the contemplation of the beautiful forms of nature so purges us of evil that we cannot feel other than love and sympathy for human kind; the contemplation of Margaret's sufferings intensifies our compassion and sense of identification with all human beings. Presumably, every reader of Margaret's tale will be purged of evil thoughts and bigoted attitudes and, by identifying with Margaret, will be a better and wiser man. Theoretically, if all men could be subjected to the poet's discipline, social and natural evils, the causes of Margaret's suffering, would simply disappear under the sympathy that binds men together.[35]

The danger in all this is that it relieves the individual like the Wanderer or the poet or the reader who responds to Margaret's story of any responsibility to act within the present frame of things. He can salve his conscience, free himself from any sense of guilt by saying that all men could, should, and ultimately will feel as he feels. He need only wait. And in the meantime he can gain a quiet and pleasant glow of satisfaction, even an exhilaration, from his superior awareness and sensitivity, his realization that he is in advance of his fellow men. He becomes one who, like the Wanderer, "can *afford* to suffer with those" whom he sees suffer; he can be justified in drawing strength and happiness from their suffering.

And such precisely is the delusory conclusion to which Wordsworth is led. Following the old man's argument, the poet, still much moved, turns toward the cottage to trace "that secret spirit of humanity" which " 'mid the calm oblivious tendencies" of nature still survives:

> The old Man, noting this, resumed, and said,
> My Friend! enough to sorrow have you given,
> The purposes of Wisdom ask no more:
> Be wise and chearful, and no longer read
> The forms of things with an unworthy eye.
> She sleeps in the calm earth and peace is here.
> I well remember that those very plumes,
> Those weeds and the high spear-grass on that wall,
> By mist and silent rain-drops silvered o'er,
> As once I passed, did to my mind convey
> So still an image of tranquillity,
> So calm and still, and looked so beautiful,
> Amid the uneasy thoughts which filled my mind,

That what we feel of sorrow and despair
From ruin and from change, and all the grief
That passing shews of being leave behind
Appeared an idle dream, that could not live
Where meditation was. I turned away,
And walked along my road in happiness.[36]
[Addendum, lines 117–35; *PW*, V, 403]

In affixing such a conclusion, Wordsworth has in effect repudiated the story as he has told it, denied the truth of his artistic experience. Consequently, he has made it from now on very difficult and ultimately impossible for himself to write stories like *The Ruined Cottage*. When once he can contemplate Margaret's sufferings and walk along his road in "happiness," he has symbolically turned his back on a whole range of experience. He has closed off like unused rooms various areas of his imagination.[37] Only such stories and details will tend to present themselves as will demonstrate the foregone conclusion of the Wanderer. All that threaten to disturb that conclusion will be automatically filtered out.

After 1800 Wordsworth almost stops writing of rustic life. Within narrow limits he is still capable of writing well about it until 1806; after that the stories are of little value. The stories in Books V through VII of *The Excursion* are the logical end of the psychological retreat: they are pretentious, carefully censored, and lifeless. How could they be else when the Pastor states that he intends to confine his narrative to subjects that excite

. . . love, esteem
And admiration; lifting up a veil,
A sunbeam introducing among hearts
Retired and covert; so that ye shall have
Clear images before your gladdened eyes
Of nature's unambitious underwood,
And flowers that prosper in the shade.
[*Ex.*, VI.648–54]

One last addition remained to be made to the Wanderer's comment on the story of Margaret. When Wordsworth incorporated the tale into *The Excursion,* the comment stood much as it had been written in 1798, stripped, however, of the justifying argument that led up to it. And for thirty years it remained unchanged. Then in 1845 Wordsworth, under the pressure partly perhaps of religious criticism but

[65]

in complete conformity with his own narrowing orthodoxy, revised the passage to read:

> "My Friend! enough to sorrow you have given,
> The purposes of wisdom ask no more:
> Nor more would she have craved as due to One
> Who, in her worst distress, had ofttimes felt
> The unbounded might of prayer; and learned, with soul
> Fixed on the Cross, that consolation springs,
> From sources deeper far than deepest pain,
> For the meek Sufferer. Why then should we read
> The forms of things with an unworthy eye? . . ."
>
> [*Ex.*, I.932–40]

We might charitably see this last addition as the product of artistic senility. It has nothing to do with the poem. Prayer is not mentioned in the tale; Margaret has no consolation; except for her child, she has no wish to live; she must die of sorrow, for her only comfort was in her husband. But this pious irrelevance to which Wordsworth has come is implicit in his first attempt at comment. The insensitivity he reveals here is the insensitivity that marks his manipulation of *The Prelude* and *The Excursion*. He had become progressively artistically and intellectually blind, so that he did not recognize or understand, and therefore did not respect, his earlier works. As a result he did not scruple to pervert or emasculate them, carefully undermining their integrity.

VII. THE DIM AND PERILOUS WAY

When Wordsworth first projected the larger epic of which *The Excursion* was to be the middle section, it was, as we have seen, in the spirit of the first two books of *The Prelude* and "Home at Grasmere." He intended to write the great philosophical poem of his generation, embodying a bold new constructive philosophy based on his experiences and observations, particularly of the therapeutic power in nature. It was to provide an ethics based on fundamental laws of human nature to replace the rationalistic ethics that seemed to fail so miserably in the French Revolution, and to restore the confidence of a disillusioned generation in the power of man to perfect himself and his society. Indeed, Wordsworth probably intended to present a blueprint of the way in which society could reform itself.

The first book of *The Excursion*, stripped of pious accretions added mainly after 1814, gives us some idea of what the poem might have been like if it had proceeded according to the original plan. The Wanderer's growth is presented in terms similar to those of the first two books of *The Prelude;* in fact, some of the passages written for him were later transferred to Books II and III of *The Prelude.* But the Wanderer is not simply a mask for Wordsworth. He is a truly revolutionary innovation in the tradition of the philosophical and epic hero. He is a member of the lower classes, following the lowliest of trades. His education is from nature, and his observations from the humble library of the country vicar and schoolmaster; yet his wisdom is the equal of that of the most learned. He stands as the symbol of the equality of men, living evidence of the absurdity of social hierarchies. By choosing the Wanderer as his protagonist, Wordsworth was making a perfectly clear criticism of the values of his own society and a confident prediction of the kind of classless society that must and would take its place.

The Wanderer, then, is the common man as hero. He perceives and shares in the characteristics that all men hold in common. Yet by his trade he is set apart in one important respect. He is given a detachment, freed from the cares of ordinary life and from the usual sufferings and miseries of men. He achieves a kind of selflessness and serenity by which he can enter into the sorrows of others:

> He had no painful pressure from within
> Which made him turn away from wretchedness
> With coward fears.[38]
> [lines inserted in *Ruined Cottage* MS; *PW*, V, 387]

It was in this sense that originally "he could *afford* to suffer / With those whom he saw suffer." And it is as such a man that he is given the story of Margaret to tell. Within this context, the social indictments implicit in the story are integral and important. For the Wanderer sees both the evils and the remedies not merely in eternal but in human terms. We could have expected, if Wordsworth had continued *The Excursion* in 1800, to hear from the Wanderer a direct statement of how perhaps in the future such sufferings as Margaret's could be exterminated. And we could have expected many other stories like this with their implied remedies or counterparts. It is also possible to envision what the debate between Wanderer and Solitary would have been like. The Solitary was originally intended to be a disillusioned and despondent victim of the French Revolution, perhaps as Wordsworth described himself in Book X of *The Prelude*. He would have presented the arguments for the hopelessness of any social improvement or perfectibility in man on the evidence provided by the failure of the Revolution, in which "all good had been turned to ill," and the Wanderer would have countered with the arguments for hope based on his observations of the fundamental laws of human nature in simple rustic folk; and in the end he would have restored the Solitary to confidence and social usefulness.

But the irony is that long before Wordsworth turned to the debate between the Wanderer and the Solitary, the Wanderer had been defeated by the disillusionment of Wordsworth himself. The confident and optimistic characterization of the Wanderer, the basic conception of him as the noble common man, had rested not upon reasoned convictions and principles, but on the unstable, precarious foundations of the poet's personal security and sense of well-being, his purely subjective happiness at the time in which he began the poem. And, as we have seen, these foundations began to totter as early as 1800. From then on, Wordsworth had but one aim: to shore them up as best he could in order to regain his security. The very things which the Wanderer stood for were now identified with his insecurity. So, in the same way in which he had shifted the emphasis in *The Prelude,* he transformed the Wanderer into an old Pedlar of the *status quo,* defender of the present order of things in nature and society, as much a member of the upper classes as the poet and the Pastor in attitude and behavior. And the Solitary was transformed from one disillusioned primarily by social revolution into one disillusioned primarily by nature. He became the therapeutic vessel into which Wordsworth more or less consciously poured his doubts, the kind of man Wordsworth might have become if he had not been able to fall back upon a faith beyond nature. The colloquy of the Solitary and the Wanderer becomes in one sense a psychomachia, a soul debate, in which the Solitary presents the questions that threatened Wordsworth with despair, and the Wanderer the only possible answers to those questions.

The new role of the Solitary Wordsworth never openly admitted, even to himself. To Miss Fenwick he insisted that the chief prototype of the Solitary was Joseph Fawcett, the revolutionary preacher and Godwinian who became "pretty much such a person as I have described; and early disappeared from the stage, having fallen into habits of intemperance which I have heard hastened his death." [39] The Wanderer's priggish description of the Solitary at the opening of Book II indicates that Wordsworth intended to make him a straw man for whom the reader would feel such contempt that his arguments would be immediately suspect. In Blakean terms, error was to be given form in order that it might be destroyed. Weak in character, lax in morals, plunged into despair by the sudden death of his wife and children, disillusioned by the failure of the Revolution, the Solitary had "forfeited / All joy in human nature," says the Wanderer, and retreated into the remoteness of the Lake country where now he

> . . . wastes the sad remainder of his hours,
> Steeped in a self-indulging spleen, that wants not
> Its own voluptuousness.
>
> [*Ex.,* II.310–12]

Obviously the arguments of such a self-pitying pessimist could be set up and knocked down at will. By presenting the Solitary so negatively, Wordsworth prevented his readers from examining too closely what he had to say. Similarly, he inoculated himself against the Solitary. As poet he had sufficiently discredited and dissociated himself from his creation so that he felt free to let the latter speak uncensored. Wordsworth was able to confront his doubts and fears with less inhibition through the Solitary than face on. What he could not admit to himself he felt it was safe to let the Solitary admit. The result is that the Solitary became a formidable opponent to the Wanderer, with perhaps the most powerful and effective arguments (and poetry) in *The Excursion.*

And so, when we meet the Solitary at last, he turns out to be a true Wordsworthian, sensitive to the beauty of nature, passionately aware of the still, sad music of humanity. He is comforting a child who is weeping over the death of an old man whose funeral has just taken place. To the Wanderer and the poet he tells the story of the old man, a story designed to show

> What stuff the Dwellers in a solitude,
> That seems by Nature hallowed out to be
> The seat and bosom of pure innocence,
> Are made of. . . .
>
> [*Ex.,* II.622–25]

The old man, feeble-minded and dependent upon public charity, had been taken in by a heartless housewife who exploited him as "her vassal of all labour." Sent into the mountains to gather fuel, he had been caught in a storm. A searching party, including the Solitary, found him in the ruins of an old chapel the next day and brought him home to die. The story presents a bleak counterargument to the thesis of the *Old Cumberland Beggar*. To the goodness of the housewife who though pressed by her own wants gave unsparingly, and to the benevolence of nature, is opposed not evil but indifference—the thoughtless greed of the housewife and the indifferent violence of nature which are equally responsible for the old man's death. We are made aware of his complete insignificance. Only the Solitary and the little boy will mourn him.

The Solitary then tells his auditors of a strange and wonderful experience that befell him as he was descending the mountain in the mist after finding the old man. Suddenly there was opened to his view a glorious spectacle of a "mighty city" wrought by "earthly nature"

> Upon the dark materials of the storm
> Now pacified. . . .
> That which I saw was the revealed abode
> Of spirits in beatitude: my heart
> Swelled in my breast—"I have been dead" I cried,
> "And now I live! Oh! wherefore *do* I live?"
> And with that pang I prayed to be no more!
> [*Ex.,* II.847–48, 873–77]

Once more Wordsworth has used his favorite symbol of the vision on the mountain. But what in *The Prelude* would have been used like the experience on Mount Snowdon as an affirmation of ultimate truth becomes, when given to the Solitary, a cause of despair. For the Solitary, though he is momentarily entranced and desperately wants to believe, remains acutely aware that the vision is an "apparition" wrought by earthly nature. When he says in recounting the experience, "I forget our Charge, as utterly / I then forgot him," he is implying that the vision can be held only at the expense of forgetting human suffering. But the Solitary cannot long forget: though the apparition has not faded, he descends the mountain; and he ends his story with an account of the lingering death of the old man. The ironic conjunction of the heavenly vision and the painful story of the insignificant old man symbolizes the fundamental cause of the Solitary's despondency. He cannot believe that the apparition is meaningful, or at least that it gives any meaning to human life. And ultimately he cannot reconcile belief in a purposive universe—naturalistic or Christian—with human experience.[40]

It is interesting that the Wanderer never attempts any direct answer to the Solitary's story. But in Book IV, when he is apostrophizing the benignity and bounty of nature, he refers suddenly to the vision. Three weeks ago, he says to the Solitary, you climbed these heights "on a service bent / Of mere humanity."

> And what a marvelous and heavenly show
> Was suddenly revealed! the swains moved on,
> And heeded not: you lingered, you perceived
> And felt, deeply as living man could feel.
>
> [*Ex.*, IV.471–74]

He launches, then, into a pompous exhortation to the Solitary to stop burning the midnight taper, to rise with the lark, and to be so vigorously active during the day that he will fall asleep exhausted at night —in other words, to keep so busy that he will not have time to think. This is a feeble evasion of the questions raised by the Solitary. The Wanderer is quite seriously suggesting that one of the virtues of the contemplation of natural beauty is the very thing that has distressed the Solitary—that it enables us to forget such unpleasant experiences as he has had, or at least to place them in proper perspective as of minor importance. It is nature's way of reassuring us that everything is really all right. It is a convenient means of taking our minds off questions we cannot answer, human situations we cannot do anything about.

The Wanderer very neatly illustrates his own argument by brushing aside the incident of the old man as a service of "mere humanity" —he apparently does not consider the questions of human callousness that trouble the Solitary worth bothering about, and he has really forgotten the old man in the contemplation of the larger vision. His argument here is a cruder version of the conclusion to the story of Margaret. His failure to answer the Solitary is more serious than the rationalization by which he explains away Margaret's story. For in juxtaposing the vision and the old man, the Solitary is raising the basic problems of the relationship of good and evil in man and nature, and this has to be met and answered in its own terms before any meaningful philosophy can be evolved. In refusing to cope with the problem, Wordsworth made the artistic and philosophical failure of *The Excursion* inevitable. On the other hand, it was the only way in which he could save himself from disintegration. For he had no answers, and he did not have the moral fortitude of the Solitary to accept that fact. The possibility that man might accept responsibility for human suffering and live usefully without despair in an indifferent universe was inconceivable to him.

This is made clear in Books III and IV of *The Excursion* when the alternatives between despondency and optimism are reduced pretty much to the question of human immortality. Ultimately both Solitary and Wanderer assume the futility of human activity to correct human evils. The Solitary is immobilized by his despair; the Wanderer, by his faith that whatever is, is right, and that earthly ills will be compensated for after death.

The setting for Book III (lines 50–73) is heavily symbolic.[41] The Wanderer suggests to his friends that they follow a rill to the spot where it probably issues "like human life from darkness." But the rill leads to a hidden nook into which it falls "disembodied and diffused" over the smooth surface of a lofty crag. At the foot of the precipice lies a mass of rock resembling a stranded ship, with keel upturned, that rests "fearless of winds and waves." The similarity of the image to the circumstances of the sinking of John Wordsworth's ship in 1805 is striking. Nearby stand three smaller stones, not unlike "monumental pillars," and farther on two stones supporting a flat smooth fragment like an altar. Out of a chink in the altar grows "a tall and shining holly":

> As if inserted by some human hand
> In mockery, to wither in the sun,
> Or lay its beauty flat before a breeze. . . .

But at the moment there is no breeze, no motion except the water "softly creeping" down the barrier of rock. The hidden rock, the falling water, the stranded ship, the pillars and the altar, the shining holly—these are all symbols like those in Book XI of *The Prelude* in a tableau of the riddle of human life. What is the meaning of the riddle: design or chance?

The Wanderer is ecstatically certain that the rocks bear "a semblance strange of power intelligent." He is haunted by "shadowy intimations" that they are a record

> Of purposes akin to those of Man,
> But wrought with mightier arm than now prevails.

Though he never makes clear just what he has in mind, druids or some pre-Adamic race such as Cuvier postulated, he does make clear that he finds this the perfect place for contemplation of design in the universe. Gazing upward from the "calm centre" toward the abyss "in which the everlasting stars abide," one may penetrate "wherever truth shall lead" (III.74–112).

On the other hand, the Solitary can see these rocks only as

> The sport of Nature, aided by blind Chance
> Rudely to mock the works of toiling Man.

His fancy has amused itself by naming one rock Pompey's pillar, another a Theban obelisk, and the altar a druid cromlech,

> But if the spirit be oppressed by sense
> Of instability, revolt, decay,
> And change, and emptiness . . .

then these freaks feed and aggravate "pity and scorn, and melancholy pride" just as do Stonehenge, the Pyramids, or Syria's ruins. The setting that has raised the Wanderer's mind to an exalted pitch is for the Solitary "fraught rather with depression" because it emphasizes the meaninglessness of human existence (III.116–58). Happier even than the Wanderer, he thinks, is the botanist or geologist who never bothers about the riddle. And he agrees with the poet that happiest of all is the thoughtless cottage boy whom they see mending the dam that runs his toy mill.

> Ah, what avails imagination high
> Or question deep?
> . . . if nowhere
> A habitation, for consummate good,
> Can be attained,—a better sanctuary
> From doubt and sorrow, than the senseless grave?
> [*Ex.*, III.209–10, 220–24]

It is the question that had been haunting Wordsworth since 1802, when he had lost the sense of "present" happiness and well-being and had begun to worry about the future. It is the question that lies buried beneath the optimistic rhetoric of the *Intimations* ode. It is a corollary to the question that he raises upon the death of his brother and finds so monstrous that he is driven to take the last step in orthodoxy:

Would it not be blasphemy to say that upon the supposition of the thinking principle being destroyed by death, however inferior we may be to the great

The Romantic Ventriloquists

Cause and Ruler of things, we have *more of love* in our nature than he has? The thought is monstrous; and yet how to get rid of it, except upon the supposition of *another* and a *better world*, I do not see.[42]

The Solitary's apathy illustrates what is for Wordsworth the alternative to faith. Unable to believe in anything beyond nature and finding her indifferent or capricious, the Solitary faces the comfortless thought of the river of life engulfed, "like Niger, in impenetrable sands / And utter darkness." His bitterness and hopelessness are so great that he longs for death with an almost Keatsian passion. Night is better than day, sleep than waking, death than sleep:

> Feelingly sweet is stillness after storm,
> Though under covert of the wormy ground.
> [*Ex.*, III.280–81]

After his expression of despair, the Solitary turns to describe the state of happiness that had once been his "in more genial times." Living as a "child of earth" upon earth's native energies, he forgot that his was then a condition which required neither energy nor fortitude —it was a "calm without vicissitude." And so he lived thoughtlessly in love and joy "without the aid of hope," assuming that the future would be like the present. But, as he discovered, "Mutability is Nature's bane, / And slighted Hope will be avenged." When one needs her favors he will find instead "fear—doubt—and agony."

The Solitary's "bitter language of the heart" echoes eerily the language of *Resolution and Independence*. What Wordsworth had feared in that poem has come to pass for the Solitary. The Puritan dread, implicit there and in *The Prelude* as we have seen, that one will be punished because one has been too happy and carefree, has been proved justified for the Solitary. "Tremble ye," he says, "to whom hath been assigned" a period of happiness. And when he speaks of "Nature's bane" it is with the force of "carefully calculated, deliberately planned retribution." For the Solitary living without the aid of hope, that is, without belief in God or immortality, the genial face of nature had become a mask behind which a merciless and vengeful fate lay in wait to destroy his happiness. Commenting later on the Pastor's stories, he speaks of

> . . . the dread strife
> Of poor humanity's afflicted will
> Struggling in vain with ruthless destiny.
> [*Ex.*, VI.555–57]

[74]

The story of his life which the Solitary now tells is, in part, a curious jumbling of Wordsworth's own life. His idyllic life in Devon following his marriage is markedly like Wordsworth's at Alfoxden in 1797–98. His description of the birth of the children, the seven years of domestic happiness, and the death of the children and his wife is apparently a very late insertion, after the deaths of Wordsworth's own children in 1812.[43] One would like very much to know what catastrophe Wordsworth had originally planned as the basic cause of the Solitary's dejection, but there is no reason to doubt from the passage in which the Solitary describes his despair that it was a personal loss, or perhaps, if we think of Oswald in *The Borderers,* some moral crisis:

> Then my soul
> Turned inward,—to examine of what stuff
> Time's fetters are composed; and life was put
> To inquisition, long and profitless!
> By pain of heart—now checked—and now impelled—
> The intellectual power, through words and things,
> Went sounding on, a dim and perilous way! [44]
>   [*Ex.,* III.695–701]

It is after this that the Solitary becomes a convert to the French Revolution. In rapid succession there follows disillusionment with the Revolution, with Godwinism, with democracy in America, and, last of all, with "Primeval Nature's child," the Indian whom he finds to be "a creature squalid, vengeful, and impure." He concludes on a note of stoical despair. He has found neither in man nor in nature the evidence for belief which he seeks. Yet "I exist, / Within myself, not comfortless." He compares his life at the moment to a still passage in the swift course of a mountain stream and can only hope

> That my particular current soon will reach
> The unfathomable gulf, where all is still!
>   [*Ex.,* III.990–91]

It is clear that in the Solitary's story Wordsworth is mirroring psychological crises that had arisen in his own life since he had moved to Grasmere, and in the Solitary's despair he views what might have been his own. The Solitary's view of the treachery of nature, the helplessness of man, the inevitability of suffering is in reality the view to which he himself has come. The only difference between them is the difference between the Solitary's final statement of Book III and the Wanderer's opening statement of Book IV. The Wanderer does

[75]

not try to refute the Solitary or to provide an alternate view—he simply builds his faith on the same foundation on which the Solitary has built his despair. Like a magician he transforms pessimism into the optimism of "whatever is, is right":

> One adequate support
> For the calamities of mortal life
> Exists—one only; an assured belief
> That the procession of our fate, howe'er
> Sad or disturbed, is ordered by a Being
> Of infinite benevolence and power;
> Whose everlasting purposes embrace
> All accidents, converting them to good.
>
> [*Ex.,* IV.10–17]

Once the "magical view" of the universe has been so abruptly and arbitrarily superimposed, all is up with *The Excursion.* This view of things is so utterly final that it cuts off any intellectual exploration, any argument or discussion about man, nature, and society. Whatever question is raised, whatever experience appears intolerable, this becomes the rubber-stamp answer. It cannot be developed philosophically; it can only be repeated in a variety of forms and lengths. On it is based an ethics of submission. Patience and cheerful fortitude must be cultivated, and an acceptance of the *status quo* as it is perpetuated in the "ideal commonwealth of the lakes." [45]

Indeed, the only social change or reform that is approved by the Wanderer (and no one else suggests any) is that which will restore the traditional stability. He glances in horror at the effect of the Industrial Revolution upon the lower classes and, after some prodding by the Solitary, at the debasement of the agricultural laborer. He evades facing directly the problems raised and takes refuge in generalities about moral equality and the right of a "human creature to be exempted from being considered a mere instrument." He rather uneasily deplores the bondage of the "rustic Boy . . . the slave of ignorance, and oft of want," and lamely concludes:

> But no one takes delight
> In this oppression; none are proud of it;
> It bears no sounding name, nor ever bore;
> A standing grievance, an indigenous vice
> Of every country under heaven. My thoughts
> Were turned to evils that are new and chosen,
> A bondage lurking under shape of good. . . .
>
> [*Ex.,* IX.182–88]

Wordsworth

We can see that the Wanderer—and Wordsworth—considers the
rustic slave as a relatively minor ill, to be noted, deplored, and accepted. When the Wanderer turns to the new evils, he trails off in
equally vague fashion into pious rhetoric:

> Alas! what differs more than man from man!
> And whence that difference? Whence but from himself?
> [*Ex.*, IX.206–7]

And he goes on to point out how every man is capable of appreciat-
ing the beauty of nature; how to all men, high or low, are given reason, imagination, free will, and, most important, the moral sense:

> He, whose soul
> Ponders this true equality, may walk
> The fields of earth with gratitude and hope;
> Yet, in that meditation, will he find
> Motive to sadder grief, as we have found;
> Lamenting ancient virtues over thrown,
> And for the injustice grieving that hath made
> So wide a difference between man and man.
> Then let us rather fix our gladdened thoughts
> Upon the brighter scene.
> [*Ex.*, IX.247–56]

This kind of skittishness is typical of the Wanderer's and of Wordsworth's technique in the last half of the poem. If forced to acknowledge the unpleasant, they shy away from it without even pretending
to cope with it and without bothering to stand on rhetorical ceremony.
One reason for the uneasy shiftings in this case is that Wordsworth
no longer knows quite what he believes and does not believe. Fundamentally, he no longer believes in the fine platitudes on the equality of
man to which the Wanderer pays lip service. The Wanderer himself
has denied them earlier in his comment on the Solitary's story; they
are denied by the descriptions of the brutalized laborers; they were
denied by Wordsworth himself in the last book of *The Prelude*. Nor
does he believe in political equality. He does not really want to investi-
gate social injustices too closely because this would force a tampering
with the social structure. He hopes only that the leaders, the manu-
facturers, and so forth can be brought to learn that "all true glory
rests, / All praise, all safety, and all happiness, / Upon the moral
law." (If the Industrial Revolution cannot be abolished, then allow
the workers time to go to church.) The "brighter scene" upon which
the Wanderer focuses, and this is the only concrete proposal in *The*

Excursion, is the hope that a system of national education will be provided in the future which will secure for all

> The rudiments of letters, and inform
> The mind with moral and religious truth.
>
> [*Ex.,* IX.301–2]

Look at the revolutions and upheavals in the countries around; we can prevent them by inculcating the "discipline of virtue":

> Thus, duties rising out of good possess
> And prudent caution needful to avert
> Impending evil, equally require
> That the whole people should be taught and trained.
> So shall licentiousness and black resolve
> Be rooted out, and virtuous habits take
> Their place, and genuine piety descend,
> Like an inheritance, from age to age.
>
> [*Ex.,* IX.355–62]

Such is the tone of Panglossian optimism laboriously cultivated in the last books. Wordsworth has trapped himself in the position of having to assert that this is literally the best of all possible worlds. Any qualification is a concession to the Solitary. But beyond that, by postulating the supernatural alchemist who turns all evil into good, he can easily convince himself that the genial face of nature is no mask but the projection of the true nature of things. He is not merely justified, he is duty-bound to fix his "gladdened thoughts / Upon the brighter scene," as the mirror of ultimate truth. It is hard not to believe when one lives in an earthly paradise.

The Excursion very appropriately ends with a picnic. It is a scene of sedate gaiety and complacent reverence. At sunset, the excursionists ascend a "green hill" from which they have a view of the valley, the lake, and the church. Once more Wordsworth is using his favorite setting. But now there is nothing wild or grand:

> Soft heath this elevated spot supplied,
> And choice of moss clad stones, whereon we couched
> Or sate reclined; admiring quietly
> The general aspect of the scene; but each
> Not seldom over anxious to make known
> His own discoveries: or to favorite points
> Directing notice, merely from a wish
> To impart a joy, imperfect while unshared.
>
> [*Ex.,* IX.580–87]

The whole is like a Victorian sampler; even the language is stiff with primness. There follows a description of the sunset which recalls the Solitary's description of the cloud spectacle after the storm, but with the difference that now there is no contrast with previous violence, no resolution of conflict. It is a "refulgent spectacle, diffused / Through earth, sky, water, and all visible space" with "unity sublime"—the lost vision of the *Intimations* ode regained in its pristine purity and tranquillity:

> And multitudes of little floating clouds . . .
> Innumerable multitudes of forms
> Scattered through half the circle of the sky;
> And giving back, and shedding each on each,
> With prodigal communion, the bright hues
> Which from the unapparent fount of glory
> They had imbibed, and ceased not to receive.
> [*Ex.*, IX.597, 601–6]

To this spectacle the Pastor, "in holy transport," addresses a prayer that sums up all that Wordsworth has to say from now until the end of his life. The Pastor offers thanks to "universal God" for "this effluence of thyself," this "local transitory type / Of thy paternal splendours" and of the radiant cherubim. Such as the cherubim are, the "elect of earth" shall be when "cleansed from mortal stain." Like the Solitary he now prays for an end to life:

> Accomplish then, their number; and conclude
> Time's weary course.
> [*Ex.*, IX.634–35]

But, if the end of the world is far distant, then "let thy word prevail, to take away / The sting of human life." Only in this way, through supernatural aid and intervention, can "enmity and strife, / Falsehood and guile" be eliminated and "righteousness obtain / A peaceable dominion." The extent of Wordsworth's loss of faith and interest in human nature and human action is shown by comparing this passage, in which it is suggested that only by a miracle can society change for the better, with the lines from *The Recluse* which he so blindly affixed to the 1814 preface "as a kind of *Prospectus* of the design and scope of the whole Poem."

The next portion of the Pastor's address becomes symbolically Wordsworth's renunciation of his former poetic self, of the attitudes and way of life which he had expressed in his greatest poetry and which had helped make him a great poet, and his acceptance of a way of life which cuts him off from the sources of poetic power and insures that he will never have anything new to say. It is the farewell to all his greatness. In Book XII of *The Prelude* he had described his visionary experience at Stonehenge in 1793 in which he received a sense of consecration:

> . . . that in some sort I possess'd
> A privilege, and that a work of mine
> Proceeding from the depth of untaught things,
> Enduring and creative, might become
> A power like one of Nature's.
>
> [*Prel.*, XII.308–12]

Now the Pastor "with wild demeanor" describes how the ancient Britons bowed the head

> To Gods delighting in remorseless deeds;
> Gods which themselves had fashioned, to promote
> Ill purposes, and flatter foul desires . . .
> Amid impending rocks and gloomy woods—
> Of these terrific Idols some received
> Such dismal service that the loudest voice
> Of the swoln cataracts (which now are heard
> Soft murmuring) was too weak to overcome,
> Though aided by wild winds, the groans and shrieks
> Of human victims. . . .
>
> [*Ex.*, IX.685–87, 691–97]

Of the druidic faith only a few rude monuments of mountain stone survive:

> From such, how changed
> The existing worship; and with those compared,
> The worshippers how innocent and blest!
> So wide the difference, a willing mind
> Might almost think, at this affecting hour,
> That paradise, the lost abode of man,
> Were raised again: and to a happy few,
> In its original beauty, here restored.
>
> [*Ex.*, IX.712–19]

And Wordsworth's was a willing mind. He had exorcised, along with the druids, the impending rocks and gloomy woods and wild winds; reduced the swollen cataracts to soft murmuring falls; tamed and subdued nature—and in so doing he had exorcised the passions within himself which gave life to his poetry but which he feared as destructive and evil. Having paid such a price, he wanted more than anything else to believe that the illusion, which he so blithely accepted as illusion in *The Recluse,* was the reality, and that he had found the peace he sought. All the rest of his life was devoted to shoring up the belief that to "a happy few" the earthly paradise had been almost if not quite granted in its original beauty, that all questions had been answered and the truth which gave meaning and purpose to life revealed. Increasingly his poetry was devoted, like the conclusion of the Pastor's prayer, to

> Vocal thanksgivings to the eternal King;
> Whose love, whose counsel, whose commands, have made
> Your very poorest rich in peace of thought
> And in good works; and him, who is endowed
> With scantiest knowledge, master of all truth
> Which the salvation of his soul requires.
>
> [*Ex.,* IX.732–37]

But the somber figure of the Solitary remains to give the lie to the wishful thinking of the Pastor and of Wordsworth. So long as he is unconverted, nothing has been resolved. And Wordsworth knows it, for as the poem ends with the Solitary turning off to the cottage, the last wistful lines are:

> How far those erring notions were reformed . . .
> My future labours may not leave untold.

But the poet found it better in the long run to rest content with the compromise of the picnic than to risk all in a renewed struggle. The illusion of the earthly paradise and of the perfect philosophy could be maintained only as long as he shut out the figure of the Solitary; and to reopen *The Recluse* was to renew the struggle with the Solitary. There was the lurking danger that he could never be defeated, and that he could drag his creator down with him. A letter to Landor on April 20, 1822, reveals the state of mind in which Wordsworth must have contemplated for the rest of his life the druidic monument of his unfinished epic: "*The Recluse* has had a long sleep save in my thoughts; my mss are so ill-penned and blurred that they are useless to all but myself, and at present I cannot face them."[46]

3: COLERIDGE

1. POWER WITHOUT STRENGTH

THE most memorable description of Coleridge remains Thomas Carlyle's portrait of the old man who sat on the brow of Highgate Hill "looking down on London and its smoke-tumult, like a sage escaped from the inanity of life's battle." Beneath the serene mask Carlyle saw the tragic opposition of high endowment and insufficient will:

An eye to discern the divineness of the Heaven's splendours and lightenings, the insatiable wish to revel in their godlike radiance and brilliances; but no heart to front the scathing terrors of them, which is the first condition of your conquering an abiding place there. The courage necessary for him, above all things, had been denied this man. His life, with such ray of the empyrean in it, was great and terrible to him; and he had not valiantly grappled with it, he had fled from it; sought refuge in vague day-dreams, hollow compromises, in opium, in theosophic metaphysics.

Coleridge's appearance he found the outward sign of his inward weakness:

Brow and head were round, and of massive weight, but the face was flabby and irresolute. The deep eyes, of a light hazel, were as full of sorrow as of inspiration; confused pain looked mildly from them, as in a kind of mild astonishment. The whole figure and air, good and amiable otherwise, might be called flabby and irresolute; expressive of weakness under possibility of strength.[1]

Coleridge had all of his life recognized the tragic contradiction in himself and freely, fluently, perhaps all too fluently, analyzed it (too

S. T. Coleridge, by Peter Vandyke, 1795

fluently, because the analysis stood in place of action, a justification for not doing anything about it). In November, 1796, he described himself harshly to John Thelwall:

. . . my face, unless when animated by immediate eloquence, expresses great Sloth, & great, indeed, almost ideotic [*sic*], good-nature. 'Tis a mere carcass of a face: fat, flabby, & expressive chiefly of inexpression. . . . As to my shape, 'tis a good shape enough, if measured—but my gait is awkward, & the walk, & the *Whole man* indicates *indolence capable of energies.*[2]

And in the depths of his despair just before he left for Malta in March, 1804, he wrote to Humphrey Davy, who had reiterated his faith in Coleridge's power:

There *is* a something, an essential something wanting in me. I feel it, I *know* it—tho' what it is, I can but guess. I have read somewhere that in the tropical climates there are Annuals [as lofty] and of as ample girth as forest trees. So by a very dim likeness, I seem to myself to distinguish power from strength & to have only the power . . . if it be no reality, if it be no more than a disease of my mind, it is yet deeply rooted & of long standing & requires help from one who loves me in the Light of knowledge [*CL,* II, 1102].

Power without strength was an essential characteristic of Coleridge as man, as critic and philosopher, as poet. It suggests what has made him so peculiarly fascinating to his own and every succeeding generation. From a handful of poems, scattered remarks in his notebooks and letters, isolated sentences and paragraphs in his criticism, come "gleams like the flashing of a shield," glints of genius which, if they could have been sustained, would have placed him among the very great. We see him standing at the frontier of the mind unable to advance.

To the end of his life, Coleridge dreamed futilely of realizing his power. The immense, fantastic schemes he constantly and effortlessly projected are almost too numerous to mention. "You spawn plans like a Herring," Southey said once in a fit of peevish exhaustion. There is a famous entry in the notebook Coleridge kept between 1795 and 1798 (the Gutch Memorandum Book) containing a fascinating list of "My works," interwoven with recipes for ginger wine and a boiled dinner and other miscellanea. Some thirty projected works are mentioned, including "The Origin of Evil, an Epic Poem," "Hymns to the Sun, the Moon, and the Elements," the "Egomist, a metaphysical Rhapsody" and a "Mem. To reduce to a regular form the Swedenborgian's reveries."[3] None was ever written.

Coleridge was, of course, desperately aware of the need of reducing to regular form his own reveries or of freeing himself from them. One of the entries in the notebooks is the solemn note of a projected "Poem on the endeavor to emancipate the soul from day dreams." [4] But he could no more emancipate his soul than he could write the poem. Only in his three greatest poems, *The Rime of the Ancient Mariner, Christabel,* and *Kubla Khan,* did he succeed in reducing his reveries to form. Yet it is significant that he was unable to complete two of them.

Indeed, *Kubla Khan* is a symbolic expression of his inability to realize his power as poet. It is a poem of power without strength, wanting in substance like the great tropical plants to which Coleridge compared himself, and the last lines are a quite explicit statement of frustration. But Coleridge attached a preface to *Kubla Khan* which has until recently so effectively intoxicated its readers that the poem has been little more than a colorful blur before their eyes. As the result of the preface, *Kubla Khan* has been extolled as an example of pure poetry (which for many critics seems to have meant pure nonsense), the product of an opium dream, the wonderful proof that spontaneous composition can be art, even that the source of art is the imagination freed from the censor of conscious control. Nineteenth-century critics were breathless with adoration. Swinburne is typical:

This is perhaps the most wonderful of all poems. In reading it we seem rapt into that paradise revealed to Swedenborg where music and color and perfume were one, where you could hear the hues and see the harmonies of heaven. For absolute melody and splendor it were hardly rash to call it the first poem in the language.[5]

And in the twentieth century, Lowes in his *Road to Xanadu* insisted that the poem is a phantasmagoria in which "linked and interweaving images irresponsibly and gloriously stream, like the pulsing, fluctuating banners of the North. And their pageant is as aimless as it is magnificent." [6]

But Professor Elisabeth Schneider has conclusively demonstrated that the preface is not to be trusted; that it bears all the signs of being a late concoction designed to accompany and justify the publication of the fragment.[7] The poem may very well have been "composed in a sort of reverie brought on by two grains of Opium, taken to check a dysentery," as Coleridge says in a note on the Crewe manuscript of *Kubla Khan,* but this is far from the claims of the preface that he

composed the poem "in a profound sleep, at least of the external senses
. . . if that indeed can be called composition in which all the images
rose up before him as *things,* with a parallel production of the correspondent expressions, without any sensation or consciousness of effort." [8]
The Crewe note suggests a process of composition no more unconscious or miraculous than that of *The Rime of the Ancient Mariner,*
which was originally subtitled "A Poet's Reverie," or of *Christabel,*
which owed much to the conscious recollection of dreams and of which
Coleridge said in his 1816 preface that from his very first conception
of the tale he had the whole present to his mind "with the wholeness
no less than with the liveliness of a vision."

Why then did he write so extravagant a preface for *Kubla Khan?*
Miss Schneider points out that the preface "sounds a good deal like
the self-justifying memory of Coleridge on other occasions," at work
cleaning up and in general putting the best possible dramatic face on
the past.[9] It is one of his apologies for uncompleted work: an attempt
to forestall harsh criticism or ridicule by emphasizing that the poem is
being published "rather as a psychological curiosity than on the grounds
of any supposed poetic merits." The incident as Coleridge remembers
it takes the responsibility for the incompleteness of the poem out of
his hands and at the same time becomes evidence of his singular and
superior gifts. There is a suggestion of the supernatural in his reference to "what had been originally, as it were, given to him." He must,
of course, have instinctively known that such a preface would give
the poem the special attention which he craved. And finally, at the
same time that the preface was evidence that he truly possessed the
powers of which he dreamed at the end of the poem, it effectively
diverted attention from what was too nakedly expressed there. In the
largest sense, it became a justification for his infirmities. Opium is presented as a benign anodyne, responsible for the dream; and the man
from Porlock rather than sloth or procrastination interrupts the composition.

If we put the preface aside, and read the poem as Miss Schneider
suggests, "without ulterior motive and without fixed preconceptions,
Kubla Khan has, throughout, a perfectly normal meaning, one that
is as logical and, as far as one can tell, as conscious as that of most
deliberately composed poems." [10] The description of the pleasure
grounds in the first thirty-six lines is that of an earthly paradise,
similar in details to such paradises as Milton's Garden of Eden in

Paradise Lost, Book IV, and Johnson's happy valley hidden behind Mount Amara in *Rasselas.* More importantly, Kubla's paradise is a blending of the landscapes of England, especially around Nether Stowey, and of North America as Coleridge had read about it in such books as Bartram's *Travels* and imagined it in his dream of pantisocracy. For example, "that deep Romantic chasm" is very like "that deep fantastic [originally, 'that deep gloomy'] Rift" into which Coleridge imagined his friends peering in the first version of *This Lime Tree Bower My Prison,* written in the summer of 1797. In the final version, the rift becomes

> The roaring dell, o'erwooded, narrow, deep,
> And only speckled by the midday sun;
> Where its slim trunk the ash from rock to rock
> Flings arching like a bridge;—that branchless ash,
> Unsunn'd and damp, whose few poor yellow leaves
> Ne'er tremble in the gale, yet tremble still,
> Fann'd by the waterfall! [11]
>
> [*This Lime Tree Bower,* lines 10–16]

Though in this version the verbal parallel has disappeared, the whole description anticipates the manner and tone of *Kubla Khan.* And from this English chasm is forced a fountain with properties remarkably like those of a fountain in Georgia described by Bartram.[12]

As Miss Schneider has pointed out, Coleridge in his earlier poems used his nature imagery very deliberately as sign and symbol of abstract ideas, sometimes spelling out the equivalences. Thus, in *A Wish* (1792), he compares his life to a stream, in imagery that quite directly anticipates that of *Kubla Khan:*

> Lo! through the dusky silence of the groves,
> Thro' vales irriguous, and thro' green retreats . . .
> Awhile meand'ring round its native fields . . .
> Then downward flowing with awaken'd speed
> Embosoms in the Deep!
>
> [*PW,* I, 33]

In this way, he hopes, may his life flow until dark age shall close its little day. In another poem, addressed to Charles Lloyd (1796), he describes in detail the ascent of a mountain and then glosses:

> Thus rudely versed in allegoric lore,
> The Hill of Knowledge I essayed to trace . . .
> That hill with secret springs, and nooks untrod,

Coleridge

And many a fancy-blest and holy sod
Where Inspiration, his diviner strains
Low-murmuring, lay. . . .

[*PW*, I, 157]

In *Religious Musings* he refers to the "immeasurable fount, / Ebullient with creative Deity" (lines 403-4). And many similar passages can be found.

Coleridge's early poems, then, provide us with numerous imagistic patterns anticipatory of the gardens of Kubla Khan, and with ample authority for seeing symbolic implications. The sacred river suggests the river of life arising from the ebullient fountain of creation, sinking into the sunless sea of death. Psychologically, as Richard Fogle points out, it suggests "the primordial and the irrational, whatever lies beyond the control of the rational and conscious mind." [13] Specifically, in the poem it arises from and flows through the primitive, inchoate world of nature. Upon that world the gardens have been imposed; a portion of the wilderness has been tamed and cultivated, and the fabrics of art have been erected. Man has made order from the chaos of nature. The origin and end of the river are terrifying and inscrutable, but in the midst is meaning. The description of the chasm and the violent eruption of the fountain hint that the equilibrium between the primitive forces and the cultivated gardens may be precarious and temporary; what ultimately is to prevent the savage thrust of the river from ravaging the gardens? But within the poem the only overt threat to the serenity of the gardens is in the "ancestral voices prophesying war," and Miss Schneider argues plausibly that this line points in the direction in which the poem might have developed.[14]

Otherwise, time is suspended, and a perfect balance or reconcilement—to anticipate Coleridge's description of the workings of the poetic imagination—is achieved of the primitive and the civilized, the unconscious and the conscious, the elemental passions and the rational mind, nature and art. This is the kind of balance that Coleridge sought as man and artist in his own life. Just such a balance of wilderness and cultivated garden he had dreamed of realizing in the Susquehanna Valley; and it was the juxtaposition of pastoral farms and wild hills that he delighted in at Nether Stowey and later at Keswick.

On a more complex level the first thirty-six lines are the symbolic representation of what for Coleridge was the ideal relationship of the irrational to the rational, the passions to the intellect. The savage and

[87]

demonic elements are not excluded or repressed; on the contrary they are enclosed within the walls, where they may be safely expressed and enjoyed, subordinated to the control of Kubla Khan. Kubla becomes the symbol of human reason and creative power, dominating the landscape and holding the disparate elements together. He "decrees" the pleasure dome and the girdling of the gardens with walls and towers. And he lives in splendid isolation, hearing the "mingled measure / From the fountains and the caves," encompassing and at the same time aloof from the tumult.

Such godlike omniscience and detachment Coleridge longed for and perhaps momentarily achieved in the early stages of opium addiction. In a letter to Thelwall on October 14, 1797, he says: "My mind feels as if it ached to behold & know something *great*—something *one* & *indivisible*—and it is only in the faith of this that rocks or waterfalls, mountains or caverns give me the sense of sublimity or majesty!— But in this faith *all things* counterfeit infinity!" He then quotes lines 88–93 of *This Lime Tree Bower,* in which he tells of standing "silent with swimming sense" gazing on the wide landscape "till all doth seem / Less gross than bodily," and continues:

It is but seldom that I raise & spiritualize my intellect to this height—& at other times I adopt the Brahman Creed. . . . I should much wish, like the Indian Vishna, to float about along an infinite ocean cradled in the flower of the Lotos, & wake once in a million years for a few minutes—just to know that I was going to sleep a million years more. I have put this feeling in the mouth of Alhadra my Moorish Woman [*Osorio,* V.i.37–56].

Whether or not *Kubla Khan* was written at this time, the letter expresses the mood out of which the poem grew.[15]

But such a mood is subversive of poetic action. The wonderful equilibrium he had achieved in the first thirty-six lines of the poem Coleridge was unable to sustain or build upon. Just at the point where Kubla's pleasure dome seems about to be described, the narrative abruptly breaks off, and the poet intrudes himself to explain the conditions under which he could finish what he had begun and thereby as artist reveal himself more powerful than Kubla. Once in a vision, he says, he saw an Abyssinian Maid playing on her dulcimer and singing of Mount Abora. If he could revive within himself her symphony and song, it would win him to "such a deep delight" that he could build the dome and caves with music, and all who heard should see them there and recognize him as the divinely inspired creator:

Weave a circle round him thrice,
And close your eyes with holy dread,
For he on honey dew hath fed,
And drunk the milk of Paradise.[16]

What was the "symphony and song" he had lost? We get an unexpected clue to it in a poem of 1795, *To the Rev. W. J. Hort While
Teaching a Young Lady Some Song-Tunes on His Flute.* To Hort the
poet cries:

O skill'd with magic spell to roll
The thrilling tones, that concentrate the soul!
Breathe thro' thy flute those tender notes again,
While near thee sits the chaste-eyed Maiden mild;
And bid her raise the Poet's kindred strain
In soft impassion'd voice, correctly wild.

In Freedom's UNDIVIDED dell,
Where *Toil* and *Health* with mellow'd *Love* shall dwell,
Far from folly, far from men,
In the rude, romantic glen,
Up the cliff, and thro' the glade,
Wandering with the dear-loved maid,
I shall listen to the lay. . . .

[*PW*, I. 92]

Here, in Coleridge's most sentimental, personal style, is a poem with
meters and cadences anticipating those of *Kubla Khan;* with the landscape of the pantisocratic dream foreshadowing the earthly paradise
of Xanadu; and with the decorous prototype of the Abyssinian Maid
in Sara Fricker, that "chaste-eyed maiden mild" who is bidden to
raise the poet's strain "in soft impassion'd voice, correctly wild." (This
dreadful line sums up the poetic ideal of the youthful Coleridge.)

The symphony and song which Coleridge wishes that he could revive may be then, in part anyway, the exhilaration aroused in him by
revolutionary ideals, by the prospect of Utopian living "Far from folly,
far from men / In the rude, romantic glen." Mount Abora (Mount
Amara in the manuscript) may be not simply the earthly paradise of
Rasselas or the allegoric hill of knowledge with many a holy sod
where Inspiration lay murmuring "his diviner strains," but very specifically the ground of Coleridge's pantisocratic dream. The symphony
and song may be also the hope of happiness with Sara. At any rate,
they are the lost promise and illusions of youth. If he could regain,
he is saying, that confident vision of the future, that faith in himself,

then he could as an artist be more powerful than Kubla, because he could build "with music" the dome and caves.[17] By giving form to phantasy he would be truly the omnipotent creator, working his magic not for himself alone but for all who heard, and they would recognize and fear him as a God-inspired and indeed godlike figure.

But all this—the realization of his power—is conditional, and so the conclusion of the poem is a cry of frustration. It is true that through the writing of the poem he momentarily realizes his hope and becomes what he dreams. In his description of Kubla's paradise, we are given a glimpse of his magic power, so that we know his claims are authentic, and to that extent the poem that bewails his frustration becomes a dazzling achievement. *Kubla Khan* is the perfect illustration of Freud's conception of the function of art, as expressed in *A General Introduction to Psychoanalysis.* I am not here concerned with the general validity of Freud's theory; I am interested only in its applicability to *Kubla Khan:*

[The artist] is one who is urged on by instinctual needs which are too clamorous; he longs to attain to honour, power, riches, fame, and the love of women; but he lacks the means of achieving these gratifications. So, like any other with an unsatisfied longing, he turns away from reality and transfers all his interest, and all his libido too, on to the creation of his wishes in the life of phantasy, from which the way might readily lead to neurosis. . . . But the way back to reality is found by the artist thus. . . . First of all he understands how to elaborate his day-dreams, so that they lose that personal note which grates upon strange ears and become enjoyable to others; he knows too how to modify them sufficiently so that their origin in prohibited sources is not easily detected. Further, he possesses the mysterious ability to mould his particular material until it expresses the ideas of his phantasy faithfully; and then he knows how to attach to this reflection of his phantasy-life so strong a stream of pleasure that, for a time at least, the repressions are out-balanced and dispelled by it. When he can do all this, he opens out to others the way back to the comfort and consolation of their own unconscious sources of pleasure, and so reaps their gratitude and admiration; then he has won—through his phantasy—what before he could only win in phantasy: honour, power, and the love of women.[18]

It is rather startling how completely not only in the writing of the poem but in the self-conscious comment of the coda Coleridge anticipates this conception of the relation of phantasy and art. The irony for Coleridge is that he desires to win, and knows that it is possible to win, *through* his phantasy what before he could win only in phantasy; but he is unable artistically to sustain the phantasy long enough to succeed. Such belated recognition as the poem did receive came through the further phantasy of the preface, in which attention is effectively diverted from the meaning of the poem and artistic failure is turned into the highest proof of genius.

II. THE SWELL OF DICTION

The failure of *Kubla Khan* to sustain itself is, as we have already said, symbolic of Coleridge's failure to sustain himself as a poet. The reader who makes the chronological journey through the collected poetry is emotionally numbed and finally exhausted by the striving rhetoric, the "swell of diction" as Coleridge himself called it, of most of the poems written before 1798. It is the poetry of a man whose great talents are recognizable on nearly every page, but who seems unable to develop or even to avoid misusing them. The conversational poems are exceptions, of course; but they are the relaxed, informal musings of the poet in his off hours, not professional efforts at greatness, and even they are marred by sudden disconcerting lapses. Nor do they prepare the reader for *The Ancient Mariner* and *Christabel,* which stand almost unique in style and subject and unrivaled in achievement. One comes upon them still, familiar as they are, with incredulity and excitement, almost as if they were the work of another man, spots of enchantment, to paraphrase Coleridge's description in a letter to his brother in 1798 of the effect of laudanum, in the very heart of a waste of sands (*CL, I,* 394). *The Three Graves* has something of the balladlike impersonality of *The Rime* and *Christabel,* and a similar preoccupation with the problem of evil, but it lacks the subtlety and magic of these two. And *Love* and the fragment of *The Ballad of the Dark Ladie* are inferior sentimental ballads, quite recognizably the product of the Coleridge of the chronology.

Coleridge was a skilled and painstaking craftsman who developed intricate metrical patterns, often with pedantic ingenuity. As his notes and comments to friends reveal, he prided himself upon his cadences, upon the melodic harmonies of vowels and consonants. His technical virtuosity is in fact partially responsible for the excesses of the poetry. He takes over and develops the worst characteristics of late eighteenth-century diction. His natural bent is toward the uncontrolled exclamation, the grandiose phrase, the fantastic personification. He goes far beyond Collins and Gray; almost all of the poems before 1796 have the qualities that Gifford ridiculed in the Della Cruscans.[19] The association with Wordsworth stimulated him in developing a simple and natural diction, but after 1800 he fell back more often than not into the old rhetorical pattern. The ease with which even in the conversational poems he could assume the declamatory:

> Meek daughter in the family of Christ!
> Well hast thou said and holily dispraised
> These shapings of the unregenerated mind . . .
>
> [*The Eolian Harp,* lines 53–55]

throws into doubt at crucial moments his sincerity. It becomes often very hard to know when he is expressing an honest emotion and when he is being, in Mr. Pickwick's indignant epithet, a "humbug." Or, as Stephen Potter aptly puts it in relation more to his prose than his poetry, when he is being Coleridge and when he is being S.T.C.[20]

Obviously, Coleridge's rhetoric reflects more than formal virtuosity; it reflects a quality of mind. It is necessary to try to isolate and examine this quality before going further. The extraordinary subtlety of his mind and his enormous self-consciousness made it possible for Coleridge, on the one hand, to explore his own thought processes with devastating thoroughness and, on the other hand, to build an impenetrable web of speculation, rationalization, and self-deception, by which he closed off the "hiding places" of his power and the ultimate knowledge of himself. From childhood, he possessed strong, even violent, emotions and physical appetites stimulated by his reading and by parental indulgence. He was abnormally susceptible to "vice": indolence, day-dreaming, drinking, gambling, laudanum; and, if he did not indulge in sexual promiscuity, he possessed strong sexual impulses that unrelentingly haunted his dreams.

If he was abnormally susceptible, he suffered abnormally also from a sense of guilt and remorse; and the interaction of susceptibility and remorse owed much to his religious upbringing. At recurrent intervals, shame and fear would send him running away from his excesses. At all times he was genuinely terrified by some of the characteristics he found within himself, and he tried either to pretend they were not there or to explain them away. A sign of his abnormality, one might say, was his refusal to admit that these characteristics were inextricably part of his own nature. He wanted to believe that he was fundamentally the virtuous man who was acted upon and driven to vice by some power beyond his control. At any rate, he cultivated passivity and a denial of responsibility for his behavior. The evangelicalism of the age in religion and the sentimentalism in literature and ethics enabled and encouraged him to channel his emotions into virtuous outbursts. His sense of intellectual superiority, fed by the adulation of old ladies, coffeehouse patrons,[21] and schoolmates, led to a sense of moral superiority. In spite of his frailties, it was hard not to think of himself as one of the elect, and he assumed the role of the righteous man exultingly contemplating virtue or mourning over the fallen, pouring indignant scorn upon the wicked of the world, overflowing with love for the innocent and oppressed.

This was the role that he felt was necessary and proper to the poet-seer he aspired to be; this was, therefore, the role he cultivated in the political and philosophical poems of 1794-98, in which he made his most strenuous efforts to realize his poetic powers. Specifically, he presented himself in the role of the inspired prophet, acclaiming and then lamenting the Revolution, predicting the destruction of wicked nations, and describing the millennial and apocalyptic visions divinely granted him. Unhappily, he believed that the necessary language for vision was the frenzied rhetoric for which he had so fatal a predilection; and so he cultivated it without inhibition or restraint. Indeed, in poems like *Religious Musings, Destiny of Nations,* and *Ode to the Departing Year,* he used the rhetoric as an incantatory formula through which to invoke the vision for himself as well as for the reader. It was as if he hoped that the effort to write sublimely would by some alchemy be transformed into sublime writing. But alas! too often the rhetoric soared empty and uninspired, a substitute rather than a vehicle for vision.

Ironically, intoxicated by his own incantations, Coleridge was convinced that he had earned the prophet's role. Perhaps nowhere else is his moral and esthetic self-deception so vividly illustrated as in the pious conclusions to *Ode to the Departing Year* and *Fears in Solitude.* In the ode, after the vision of England's predestined ruins, he cries:

> Away, my soul, away!
> In vain, in vain the Birds of warning sing—
> And hark! I hear the famish'd brood of prey
> Flap their lank pennons on the groaning wind!
> Away, my soul, away!
> I unpartaking of the evil thing,
> With daily prayer and daily toil
> Soliciting for food my scanty soil,
> Have wail'd my country with a loud Lament.
> Now I recentre my immortal mind

In the deep sabbath of meek self-content;
Cleans'd from the vaporous passions that bedim
God's Image, sister of the Seraphim.[22]
[*Ode to the Departing Year*, lines 149–61]

Undoubtedly, he wishes to convey the impression of the prophet-bard who has done his duty; he has warned his country and purged his soul of the agony of vision. Purified, he can return to plain living and high thinking. He does not see that instead of the impression of bardic humility he has succeeded in conveying only that of self-righteous complacency.

In *Fears in Solitude* he develops most fully the pattern implicit in the other political poems. The poem opens with the good man contemplating in solitude the beauty of nature and the joys of virtuous living, and so being led to reflect upon the turbulence of the world from which he has removed himself. Gradually he is aroused to heights of indignation and exaltation, finally to sink back into the original quiet contemplative state. Having once more done his duty in warning his countrymen of their peril from the "sensual" French, he returns to his "lowly" cot:

. . . grateful, that by nature's quietness
And solitary musings, all my heart
Is softened and made worthy to indulge
Love, and the thoughts that yearn for human kind.
[*Fears in Solitude*, lines 229–32]

Coleridge permits the reader no escape from the complacency of the conclusion.

Clearly, the attitude and "swelling diction" of these poems were those through which he believed he could and should realize his potential greatness. In particular, he believed that given the proper conditions he had the power to write great philosophical epics in which from a position of detached omniscience he could erect the imaginative structures whereby all philosophical mysteries were revealed and all human problems resolved.[23] The only philosophical poem of any length that he completed was *Religious Musings;* it was his most ambitious attempt to reconcile religion and revolution, Christianity and eighteenth-century philosophy. Upon completing it, he held it in extravagantly high regard: "I build all my poetic pretentions on the *Religious Musings*," he wrote to Thelwall in May, 1796 (*CL*, I, 205). But it remains the bombastic expression of the dream rather than the imaginative fusion of philosophical ideas.

The fundamental solipsism of Coleridge's religious attitudes is nowhere more unabashedly revealed than in the beginning of the poem. The soul is, he cries,

> From Hope and firmer Faith to perfect Love
> Attracted and absorbed; and centered there
> God only to behold, and know, and feel,
> Till by exclusive consciousness of God
> All self-annihilated it shall make
> God its Identity; God all in all!
> We and our Father one!
>
> [*Religious Musings,* lines 39–45]

And later he laments the present state of man:

> A sordid solitary thing . . .
> Feeling himself, his own low self the whole;
> While he by sacred sympathy might make
> The whole one Self! Self, that no alien knows!
> Self, far diffused as Fancy's wing can travel!
> Self, spreading still! Oblivious of its own,
> Yet all of all possessing!
>
> [*Religious Musings,* lines 149, 152–57]

God becomes the projection of the ego into an ideal self which encompasses and becomes part of all things—an ideal self which later in *Biographia Literaria* he calls the "infinite I Am." [24]

As the poet-seer, he goes on to foresee the success of the French Revolution, to be followed by the downfall of religious establishments and the coming of the millennium when the gates of paradise are thrown open and forth come

> Sweet echoes of unearthly melodies,
> And odours snatched from beds of Amaranth.
> . . . such delights, such strange beatitudes
> Seize on my young anticipating heart
> When that blest future rushes on my view!
>
> [*Religious Musings,* lines 348–49, 355–57]

In the end he has a vision of the throne of God. He addresses the "contemplant" spirits that hover over the fountain "ebullient with creative Deity," and those of "plastic power" that "roll through the grosser and material mass / In organizing surge":

The Romantic Ventriloquists

I haply journeying my immortal course
Shall sometime join your mystic choir! Till then
I discipline my young and novice thought
In ministries of heart-stirring song . . .
[*Religious Musings,* lines 409–12]

Stripped of its tortured rhetoric, the ending of the poem becomes, like that of *Kubla Khan,* a dream of power. Coleridge has been granted a vision of the millennium and the throne of God in much the same way that in *Kubla Khan* he dreams of himself as the divinely maddened poet to whom the splendors of paradise have been revealed. But between the two there is an important difference. The tone of *Religious Musings* is one of unrestrained confidence. If the total vision has not yet been revealed to him, he can nevertheless afford to wait and "discipline his young and novice thought / In ministries of heart-stirring songs." The conclusion of the poem exudes assurance of greatness to come. But *Kubla Khan* ends in uncertainty and frustration: the realization of the dream is contingent upon reviving within him the song of the Maid.

In the interim, the projected philosophical epics had remained entries in the notebooks. It may be that Coleridge, looking back wistfully to the promise of *Religious Musings,* was more or less consciously lamenting in the loss of the song the loss of his earlier vision of the millennium and the "mystic choir." At any rate he is implying that he has lost the magic music to which he could build the dome and caves. Yet, as a matter of fact, the circumstances for writing the great poems were more favorable in 1797–99 than at any other time in Coleridge's life. Under the combined influence of the relative serenity of life at Nether Stowey and the association with Wordsworth, he had achieved the sense of well-being, confidence, and intellectual power for which he yearned. The landscape calmed and soothed him and, as the conversational poems demonstrate, encouraged the honest and natural expression of thought and feeling. In its peaceful cultivated harmony, it stirred him to the "idle flitting phantasies" that so upset Sara, and to the speculations on God-in-nature that were so important in stimulating Wordsworth to *his* great philosophical poems.

Under these circumstances Coleridge did realize fully for the first time the potentialities of his poetic power—even as he was lamenting its frustration in *Kubla Khan*—but not in the way he had intended. The political and philosophical poems in which he tried to be the great poet were pompous and hollow failures. They give no evidence that he could ever have been the kind of poet he dreamed of being. The truth is that, as *The Rime of the Ancient Mariner* and *Christabel* ironically reveal, the real sources and direction of his power lay in quite other channels than those into which he had been trying to force them. In the impersonal dramatic form of the ballad the true nature of his power was suddenly realized because it could there find expression without his conscious awareness or interference.

III. THE SICKNESS OF THE HEART

Very early in his poetry, Coleridge began to worry about potential failure and brooded over the way in which he was already squandering his talents. In *Quae Nocent Docent,* written in Christ's Hospital Book, he laments:

> Oh! might my ill-past hours return again!
> No more, as then, should Sloth around me throw
> Her soul-enslaving, leaden chain!
> [*PW*, I, 7]

But at the age of seventeen he can still cheer himself by promising that he will do better as he matures: "Let follies past to future care incite."

Two years later in *Lines on a Friend Who Died of a Frenzy Fever Induced by Calumnious Reports*—this was the vicar of Ottery St. Mary, who bore the wonderfully Dickensian name of the Reverend Fulwood Smerdon—Coleridge contemplated in him a similar soul and perhaps a similar fate:

> To me hath Heaven with bounteous hand assigned,
> Energic Reason and a shaping mind
> The daring ken of Truth, the Patriot's part,
> And Pity's sign, that breathes the gentle heart—
> Sloth-jaundic'd all!
> [*Lines on a Friend,* lines 39–43]

In his revision of the *Monody on the Death of Chatterton* he adds another and more important reason for his failure. He dare no longer brood over Chatterton's death:

> Lest kindred woes persuade a kindred doom:
> For oh! big gall drops, shook from Folly's wing,
> Have blackened the fair promise of my spring. . . .
> [*Monody,* lines 135–37]

[97]

The Romantic Ventriloquists

But his soul shall dwell no more "on joys that were" or "endure to weigh / The shame and anguish of the evil day." Over the ocean he seeks the "cottaged dell" where virtue may stray and where, in a tantalizing anticipation of the imagery of *Kubla Khan:*

> . . . dancing to the moon-light roundelay,
> The wizard Passions weave an holy spell!
> [*Monody*, lines 146–47]

We have already seen how another poem concerned with pantisocracy anticipated *Kubla Khan*. And in *Kubla Khan* itself he says that, if he could revive the symphony and song, "To such deep delight 'twould win me, / That with music loud and long" he would build the dome and caves. "Delight" becomes the immediate condition for creation. Later, in *Dejection: An Ode*, he calls this condition "Joy." He uses the imagery of song again:

> . . . from the soul itself must there be sent
> A sweet and patient voice, of its own birth,
> Of all sweet sounds the life and element!
> [*Dejection*, lines 56–58]

This "strong music in the soul," this joy, is given only to the pure, and "in their purest hour." By now he has no hope of reviving the symphony and song, but can turn only to "abstruse research." [25]

The sense of guilt, the conviction that he was dooming himself as a poet because he had lost his innocence, became obsessive with Coleridge. And there is no doubt that, beyond a certain point, his despondent sense of guilt began to inhibit and block off his "shaping spirit of imagination." But we must distinguish carefully between the sense of guilt as the inhibiting cause, and the cause Coleridge gives. He asserted almost superstitiously that it was his loss of innocence, the weakening of his will by forces beyond his control, so that he sinned in spite of himself, that suspended his poetic power. But the truth is that there is never any indication to the end of his life of loss or impairment of his poetic imagination. Some short poems written in later years are equal, as I. A. Richards has insisted,[26] to any he ever wrote except for the three great poems. And, as a matter of fact, it is the loss of innocence, the experience of evil and the psychological conflict thus engendered, that are ironically responsible for the fullest development and expression of Coleridge's imagination. What truly stimulated his imagination was the uninhibited expression of energy and power which, repressed or

[98]

Coleridge

unable to find conventional social outlets, became violent, rebellious, and therefore evil. It is the power of Kubla Khan erecting his pleasure dome, the Ancient Mariner shooting the Albatross, Geraldine enslaving Christabel, that fascinates him.

Coleridge later in life praised Bishop Taylor's statement that heresy is an error not of the understanding, but of the will.[27] And here perhaps we have another clue to the symphony and song. Coleridge was in the depths of his being the heretic, the rebel. At first he found outlets in the French Revolution, in the dream of pantisocracy, in philosophical speculation in which he identified with God and constructed the universe according to his own needs and desires. But one after another these areas of expression were closed off from him, and his imagination was driven underground. Mainly responsible for this was Coleridge's strong puritan conscience. He was truly haunted by the necessity of conforming. He believed that one should label clearly what was morally good and what was morally bad, and that poetry should be the instrument of the former.[28] He believed that poetry should be affirmative.

As long as the French Revolution remained respectable among the intellectuals with whom Coleridge associated, he could satisfy both his moral scruples and the needs of the natural man. And similarly with his philosophical speculations. But once he had been made to feel guilty about them, once they had become morally taboo, what little power and conviction there was in his positive poetry faded out. He was increasingly frustrated in trying to write the kind of poetry he thought he ought to write. His imagination simply would not respond; it demanded a world more complex; left to its own devices it betrayed him by reveling in the "sensual and the dark." Horrified by what he found as he looked within, unable to control or force the imagination in the direction he wanted to go, Coleridge after 1800 almost gave up the writing of poetry. There was only one way in which he could have revived the "symphony and song," and that was through some socially heretical and anarchistic expression, but the older he became the more obviously impossible this was.[29]

Coleridge was quite aware of his own susceptibility to violence, which was mixed up with his timidity and sense of physical inferiority. In the autobiographical letters to Poole in 1797, he stresses the bullying he suffered from in childhood. His father was "very fond" of him, and he was his "mother's darling"; consequently, Molly, the nurse, who was "immoderately fond" of Frank, the brother next to him, hated him,

[99]

73468

and from her he received "only thumps & ill names"; Frank also "had a violent love" of beating him. "So I became fretful, & timorous, & a tell-tale—& the School-boys drove me from play, & were always tormenting me" (*CL,* I, 347).

This was the background against which Coleridge related to Poole the most memorable incident of his childhood (at least the one he gave in greatest detail). He was between seven and nine years old:

> I had asked my mother one evening to cut my cheese *entire,* so that I might toast it: this was no easy matter, it being a *crumbly* cheese— My mother however did it— / I went into the garden for some thing or other, and in the meantime my Brother Frank *minced* my cheese "to disappoint the favorite." I returned, saw the exploit, and in an agony of passion flew at Frank—he pretended to have been seriously hurt by my blow, flung himself on the ground, and there lay with outstretched limbs—I hung over him moaning & in great fright—he leaped up, & with a horse-laugh gave me a severe blow in the face—I seized a knife, and was running at him, when my Mother came in & took me by the arm— / I expected a flogging & struggling from her I ran away, to a hill at the bottom of which the Otter flows—about one mile from Ottery.—There I stayed; my rage died away; but my obstinacy vanquished my fears—& taking out a little shilling book which had, at the end, morning & evening prayers, I very devoutly repeated them—thinking *at the same time* with inward & gloomy satisfaction, how miserable my Mother must be [*CL,* I, 352–53]!

Without making too much of the Freudian implications of the story, we can see how it would leave an indelible impression upon Coleridge's memory—the trivial provocation, the act of violence, the running away, the prayers, the night-long suffering in the wet and cold, the rescue, the rejoicing of parents, and the prolonged aftereffects: "I was certainly injured—For I was weakly & subject to the ague for many years after." The pattern comes close to that of *The Ancient Mariner* in important respects.

The central theme of *The Ancient Mariner*—the wanton act of violence—becomes a dominant preoccupation of the poetry in 1797–98. At the time that he was writing to Poole, Coleridge had just finished and sent off to Sheridan his tragedy *Osorio,* which he later revised and called *Remorse.* The intent of the revision was primarily to make the play more fit for the stage, and in one important detail only, at the very end, was the essential conception altered. The play, at least from the perspective of the twentieth century, is a conventional and turgid melodramatic mixture of Shakespearean and German drama. The characters are stock figures; none is distinctively realized. The major action of the play is over before it opens, and its dramatic life hangs on the mercy of an incredible device of concealed identity. Coleridge's intent had obviously been to write a psychological drama, in which the action was incidental, and in a manuscript preface he indicates that he knows he has failed.

The drama is the exploration of the consequences of an act of murder or would-be murder. Osorio has planned and carried out, so he believes, the murder of his brother Albert, from love of Albert's fiancée Maria. But Albert has been spared by Ferdinand, the Moorish assassin hired by Osorio, and after much wandering returns home disguised as a Moor. Osorio, spurned by Maria, wants Ferdinand to perform some "mummery" that will convince Maria that Albert is really dead. Ferdinand refuses and sends him to a mysterious Moor who is, of course, Albert. Albert performs the rites, but substitutes a painting of his attempted murder for the portrait of Maria which Ferdinand had taken from him and which Osorio intends him to place on the altar as if by supernatural agency so that Maria will believe it a sign of Albert's death. Osorio, assuming that Ferdinand has betrayed him, lures him to a cavern and pushes him down a precipice. He then seeks to poison Albert, who as a result of the mummery has been held a prisoner of the Inquisition in a dungeon of the castle. When Albert reveals himself at last, Osorio is overwhelmed with remorse and terror.

Alhadra, wife of Ferdinand, leads the Moors into the dungeon in search of Osorio. She toys with the idea of letting him live as the greatest revenge but allows him in the end to be led off, apparently to death. In *Remorse,* however, she rushes upon him and stabs him. It is easy to see why Coleridge called the plan of the tragedy "romantic & wild & somewhat terrible" and indicated that it owed something to the Gothic novels he had been reviewing, "in all of which dungeons, and old castles, & solitary Houses by the Sea Side & Caverns, & Woods, & extraordinary characters, & all the tribe of Horror & Mystery, have crowded on me—even to surfeiting" (*CL,* I, 318).

But it is in the character of Osorio that the main interest of the play lies. In the manuscript preface, Coleridge says, in regard to the defects of the tragedy:

Worse than all, the growth of Osorio's character is nowhere explained—and yet I had most clear and psychologically accurate ideas of the whole of it. . . . A man, who from constitutional calmness of appetites, is seduced into pride and the love of power, by these into misanthropism, or rather a contempt of mankind, and from thence, by the cooperation of envy, and a curiously modified love for a beautiful female (which is nowhere developed in the play), into a most atrocious guilt. A man who is in truth a weak man, yet always duping himself into the belief that he has a soul of iron [*PW,* II, 1114].

In another manuscript he says that in Osorio he "wished to represent a man, who, from his childhood had mistaken constitutional abstinence from vices, for strength of character" (*PW,* II, 519).

These are curious remarks. They suggest that Coleridge was making a strenuous effort to explore the problem of evil in a character who, in "constitutional calmness of appetites," was the opposite of himself. But it was one thing to have an idea of the character, and another to give it dramatic life. Perhaps because he is so artificially conceived Osorio never comes off, but remains a stock Gothic villain. There is a desire to present Osorio as one who wants to be good but through both external and internal compulsions cannot be—we are told this, usually by Osorio himself, rather than shown it. When Osorio is trying to get Ferdinand to perform the mummery, Ferdinand recounts to him the circumstances under which Albert was presumably murdered. Osorio is seized by an agony of guilt:

> O this unutterable dying away here,
> This sickness of the heart! . . .
> What have I done but that which nature destin'd
> Or the blind elements stirr'd up within me?
> If good were meant, why were we made these beings?
> And if not meant—(He starts, looks wildly)
> [*Osorio,* II.110–11, 114–17]

Perhaps the most interesting scene in the play is that in which Osorio lures Ferdinand to the cavern and there, "darkly and in the feeling of self-justification," tells what he conceives of his own character and actions, speaking of himself in the third person. Like the Byronic hero—and indeed there are striking anticipations of Manfred—he was different from other men "and he despised them, yet revered himself." He found no fit companion in this world:

> Nature had made him for some other planet,
> And press'd his soul into a human shape
> By accident or malice. . . .
>   He walked alone,
> And phantasies, unsought for, troubled him.
> Something within would still be shadowing out

Coleridge

All possibilities, and with these shadows
His mind held dalliance.[30]
[*Osorio*, IV.88–90, 92–96]

The urge to murder Albert was such a fancy, which he expressed in "moody murmur" as "some talk in sleep"; the murmur was overheard by Ferdinand, who executed it. Ferdinand had then, he believes, betrayed him. Thus he builds up his courage for killing Ferdinand. Earlier Ferdinand had told him that he had dreamed of him "in a thousand hideous ways" and waked "in the act / of falling down that chasm." So Osorio maneuvers him to the chasm and pushes him in. "His dream is made out," he cries, and Coleridge affixes a manuscript note: "I think it an important instance of how Dreams and Prophecies cooperate to their own completion" (*PW*, II, 570).

In this scene Coleridge has almost turned his characters into psychological symbols.[31] Through Osorio and Ferdinand, he is exploring the helplessness of men before their own minds and the forces that made them. He is also exploring opposite aspects of himself. Osorio has been made different from and superior to other men. His phantasies come unsought, so that he is not responsible for his evil impulses; his mind has the power, in turn, of hypnotizing the weaker man into carrying out the impulses. Osorio murmurs; Ferdinand hears and executes. Ferdinand dreams of the manner of his death and so prepares the way for it—in effect, conditions his mind to it and is psychologically helpless to avoid it. Seen in this way, the relationship of Osorio and Ferdinand foreshadows the relationship of Geraldine and Christabel.

Coleridge intends us, of course, to see Osorio as using his superior intellect to rationalize his conduct; he is illustrating in him the "dangerous use which may be made of reason when a man has committed a great crime." The quotation is from Wordsworth's manuscript preface to *The Borderers,* and it points up the evident influence of Oswald on Coleridge's conception of Osorio. Several of Osorio's speeches seem direct echoes of Oswald's.[32] But fundamentally Osorio is a different kind of character. As soon as Albert reveals himself, Osorio breaks down in remorse and attempts to kill himself. And he cries to Albert, "Curse me with forgiveness." [33] Earlier Albert has said that, if Osorio could call up just one pang of true remorse, "Yet thou mayst be saved."

Coleridge's implication seems to be that once Osorio has freely acknowledged his guilt, assumed responsibility for his acts, he has set in motion the good forces within and without him which will lead to his salvation. This was a favorite theme. In his revision, *Remorse,* he emphasizes the theme by title and by a new closing speech. Obviously it was an idea comforting to Coleridge in respect to his own weaknesses. And in *The Rime of the Ancient Mariner* it is given its most dramatic development.

Another link between *Osorio* and *The Ancient Mariner* is in the emphasis on loneliness. Osorio "walked alone." Alhadra, into whose mouth Coleridge put the feeling he described in the letter to Thelwall already quoted, presents the dominating image of *The Rime* in what Kenneth Burke would call its benign aspect:

> It were a lot divine in some small skiff,
> Along some ocean's boundless solitude,
> To float forever with a careless course,
> And think myself the only being alive!
> [*Osorio*, V.53–56]

Finally, Osorio sums up one of Coleridge's preoccupations in the play which later becomes a preoccupation in both *The Ancient Mariner* and *Christabel:*

> Love—love—and then we hate—and what? and wherefore?
> Hatred and love. Strange things! both strange alike!
> [*Osorio*, III.211–12]

The preoccupation with the interrelationship of love and hatred is also strongly evident in *The Three Graves,* which Coleridge perhaps went to work on after he completed *Osorio. The Three Graves* was apparently started in collaboration with Wordsworth. A fragment of Part II of the poem has been found in a 1797 notebook of Wordsworth.[34] Part I was therefore probably his also. Barron Field records that Wordsworth told him that he gave the subject of *The Three Graves* to Coleridge, "but he made it too shocking and painful, and not sufficiently sweetened by any healing views." [35]

When Coleridge published Parts III and IV in *The Friend* and later in *Sibylline Leaves,* he said that the tale was based on fact, and that he had been led to choose it "from finding in it a striking proof of the possible effect on the imagination, from an idea violently and suddenly impressed upon it." He goes on to speak of his reading in Negro and Indian witchcraft and his intent to show "that instances of this kind are not peculiar to savage or barbarous tribes" (*PW*, I, 269). And at a later time he says that he attempted "to exemplify the effect, which one painful idea . . . might have in producing an alienation of the understanding and . . . to trace the progress to madness, step by step." [36]

In the preface to the poem in *Sibylline Leaves* he makes the same kind of apology for publishing the poem that he had made for *Kubla Khan*. It is, he says,

> . . . presented as the fragment, not of a Poem, but of a common Ballad-tale. Whether this is sufficient to justify the adoption of such a style, in any metrical composition not professedly ludicrous, the Author is himself in some doubt. At all events, it is not presented as poetry, and it is in no way connected with the Author's judgment concerning poetic diction. Its merits, if any, are exclusively psychological [*PW*, I, 267].

The unnecessarily derogatory reference to the style—which is, after all, pretty much that of *The Rime of the Ancient Mariner*—was probably evoked, whatever Coleridge says, by the compulsion to be consistent with the judgments he had made in *Biographia Literaria,* and even by the desire to take a backhanded slap at Wordsworth. As Mr. Hanson says, it does "illustrate Wordsworth's theory a great deal more successfully than Wordsworth himself was able to do." [37]

The story is unusually lurid and brutal as a subject for literary treatment, even when the Gothic tradition is taken into account. It belongs with the broadsides and periodical reports of the time. It is told by a sexton to a traveler whose curiosity has been aroused by the three graves of the mother, of the "barren wife," and of the "maid forlorn." Edward, a young farmer, falls in love with Mary, whom he meets at the home of her friend, Ellen. Just before the wedding, the mother tells Edward that Mary is unfit even to be his paramour, and offers him all her wealth if he will marry her instead. When Edward laughs at her, she falls to her knees and curses her daughter. And, as Edward leads Mary away, she ironically blesses them and says:

> May God forbid that thought of me
> Should haunt your marriage bed.
> [*Three Graves,* lines 186–87]

So far had Wordsworth carried the poem. Coleridge picks up with the marriage of Edward and Mary. From the marriage day Mary pines away, even though every day Ellen comes, "more dear than any sister," in an effort to make them more cheerful. On Ash Wednesday Ellen goes to church for the reading of the commination prayer. The mother enters her pew, kneels, and prays to the "Lord in Heaven. / Although you take my life," to curse Ellen. Ellen tries to smile and forget:

> It was a wicked woman's curse—
> God's good, and what care I?
> [*Three Graves,* lines 342–43]

But she too pines. Edward, who loved both Mary and Ellen alike "in the moment of his prayers," is torn by "inward strife." The two women cling to him; Edward and Mary weep; Ellen cannot, but turns her face and looks as if "she saw some frightful thing."

In Part IV Ellen gradually wastes away. Once she flung her arms around Mary's neck and felt "upon her tongue" words she had no power to smother:

> And with a kind of shriek she cried,
> 'O Christ! You're like your mother!'
> [*Three Graves,* lines 446–47]

One Sunday morning they go to a bower in the woods. Edward's health has been failing; he has passed a restless night, and now he drops into a fitful sleep. Ellen and Mary discuss the reflection of the sun on the leaves in lines that have the eeriness of lines in *Christabel* or *The Ancient Mariner*:

> 'Tis in the leaves, a little sun,
>   No bigger than your ee;
> A tiny sun, and it has got
>   A perfect glory too;
> Ten thousand threads and hairs of light,
> Make up a glory gay and bright
>   Round that small orb, so blue.
> [*Three Graves,* lines 509–13]

We are reminded of the "bloody" sun which stands right above the mast at noon, "no bigger than the moon," in *The Ancient Mariner,* and of the moon which, though at the full, "looks both small and dull" at the opening of *Christabel*. For Coleridge the tiny sun or moon is the prelude to catastrophe. In the *Three Graves,* as the two women argue whether the rays of the reflected sun are green or amber, Edward awakes and mutters, "A mother too!"

> He sat upright; and ere the dream
>   Had had time to depart,
> 'O God forgive me!' (he exclaimed)

[106]

Coleridge

'I have torn out her heart.'
[*Three Graves*, lines 530–33]

And the fragment ends with Coleridge's pathetic little Latin tag: "*Carmen reliquum in futurum tempus relegatum.* Tomorrow! and Tomorrow! and Tomorrow!"

The superiority of Coleridge's portion of the poem to Wordsworth's is marked; and the difference in conception and development is notable, too. Here we can watch the emergence of the distinctive characteristics that come so quickly to perfection in *The Rime*. Obviously, Coleridge's imagination was set afire by the religious and sexual ambiguities in the poem. The power of evil in a universe of good preoccupies him here as in the later poems. He develops, for example, the implication of the curse. In Part II, when the mother curses Mary, Wordsworth says, "She drank perdition on her knees" and forgot the God in Heaven. In Part III, when she curses Ellen, she prays to "the Lord in Heaven," and the ironic tie between her curse and the commination prayer is stressed. Ellen is made to say:

> It was a wicked woman's curse—
> God's good, and what care I?

Yet each of the innocent is being destroyed by the curse not simply through psychological "suggestion," which in fact is very little emphasized in the poem, but through inexplicable compulsion. As in *Christabel,* the evil seems to be remorselessly triumphing, and the power of good is too weak to counteract it. The implication of Edward's dream at the end is that he has been driven to will the death of the mother. There is no way of knowing whether or not Coleridge intended to have him murder the mother, but it is clear that the evil of the mother has bred evil in him.

Coleridge also develops the sexual ambiguities of the tale. The mother's lust had been stressed in Part II, but the relationship between Ellen and Mary, on the one hand, and between Edward and the two women, on the other, is developed in Part III. Ellen and Mary are more dear to each other than sisters, and Edward loves them equally in his prayers. Coleridge did not consciously intend, probably, any sexual implications; nevertheless, the intimacy among the trio is abnormal and contributes to the morbid atmosphere of the poem. It reflects the sentimental relationships of the time in which the participants either could not or would not recognize the sexual element: relationships such as

[107]

those of Wordsworth, Dorothy, Mary and Sara Hutchinson, and Coleridge; or such as the relationship Coleridge hoped to establish among himself, his wife, and Sara Hutchinson. In such fundamentally unhealthy relationships the repressed sexual element will assert itself in dreams or poetry if in no other way. In *The Three Graves,* the sexual element is objectified in the frustrated lust of the mother, which slowly destroys husband, wife, and friend. By their peculiar nature or their response to the curse, Coleridge makes them all share in the guilt of the mother.

When Wordsworth said that Coleridge made the poem too shocking and painful, and not sufficiently sweetened by any healing views, he was probably thinking of the passivity and helplessness of the young people before the curse of the mother, and the absence of any comforting moral sentiments to offset the pervading tone of evil. (It is interesting to speculate on how Wordsworth would have sweetened the poem.) It looks very much as if Coleridge's imagination had carried him into the same impasse in which he was to find himself later in *Christabel,* unable to devise an ending in which good prevailed, unwilling to permit the triumph of evil, and so incapable of finishing the poem.

IV. THE RAVEN AND THE ALBATROSS

In March, 1798, Coleridge published in the *Morning Post* a poem called *The Raven,* which is interesting if only because it is about the vengeance of a bird. It had been written over a year earlier, for Lamb refers to it in a letter of February, 1797, as "Your Dream" (*PW,* I, 169). It was supposed to be a humorous poem, written in archaic diction and prefaced by a letter which begins, "I am not absolutely certain that the following Poem was written by Edmund Spenser and found by an Angler buried in a fishing-box." When the poem was published in *Sibylline Leaves* the archaic diction was omitted, and rather disconcertingly it was subtitled "A Christmas Tale, told by a School-boy to his little brothers and sisters." The poem displays a curiously morbid kind of humor and a grotesque morality. The Raven's young ones are killed when the Woodsman cuts down a tree, and the ship made from the wood sinks in a storm with all on board while the

> . . . auld Raven flew round and round, and caw'd to
> the blast. . . .
> The Raven was glad that such fate they did meet,
> They had taken his all and Revenge was sweet.
> [1st version; *PW,* II, 1049]

Coleridge

The Raven would seem to be the kind of poem which Coleridge claimed to Mrs. Barbauld that *The Ancient Mariner* ought to be. It appears to have

> . . . no more moral than the Arabian Nights' tale of the merchant's sitting down to eat dates by the side of a well, and throwing the shells aside, and lo! a genie starts up, and says he must kill the foresaid merchant because one of the date shells had, it seems, put out the eye of the genie's son.[38]

Nevertheless, there is a suggestion of some connection between the destruction of the Raven's family and of the ship, if only in the Raven's sense of revenge, the implication of a primitive "eye-for-an-eye" morality in which even the chance act of violence sets punitive forces in action.

In 1817 Coleridge timidly added at the end two lines (following "Revenge was sweet"):

> We must not think so; but forget and forgive,
> And what Heaven gives life to, we'll still let it live.

And in a manuscript he affixed the troubled note:

> Added thro' cowardly fear of the Goody! What a Hollow, where the Heart of Faith ought to be, does it not betray? this alarm concerning Christian morality, that will not permit even a Raven to be a Raven, nor a Fox a Fox, but demands conventicular justice to be inflicted on their unchristian conduct, or at least an antidote to be annexed [*PW*, I, 171].

The note tells us more of Coleridge than of the "unco guid" whom he feared: it reveals how insecure was his own heart of faith, and how seriously he now viewed the poem, as if he half feared it to be true. In fact, Coleridge's additions in 1817 are all in the direction of connotative camouflage to prevent any unobstructed and close reading of the poem: the subtitle; a note that "seventeen or eighteen years ago an artist of some celebrity was so pleased with this doggerel that he amused himself with the thought of making a Child's Picture Book of it"; and of course the last two lines. The whole is a remarkable example of Coleridge's deviousness in regard to his own poems.

The "eye-for-an-eye" morality of *The Raven* is fundamental to *The Ancient Mariner,* and, if *The Raven* seems to be a half-humorous exaggeration of the doctrine of necessity, *The Ancient Mariner* is a deadly serious exaggeration of the remorseless series of consequences set in motion by a casual violation of the harmony of nature. In the shooting of the Albatross, Coleridge was given (by Wordsworth) the perfect symbol for the act of violence—trivial, motiveless, deliberate yet invol-

[109]

untary. It is the act of the anonymous man; nowhere does the Mariner describe himself or leave clues to his character. Lamb's reply to Wordsworth's charge that the Mariner "has no distinct character" is the best statement of the matter; the Mariner "undergoes such trials as overwhelm and bury all individuality or memory of what he was—like the state of a man in a bad dream, one terrible peculiarity of which is, that all consciousness of personality is gone." [39]

From lines in the poem and comments by Coleridge on the poem we catch glimpses of the nature of the act, though to try to define it is to risk distortion. It is most narrowly a deliberate act of sadism and lawlessness. In the argument to the poem in the 1800 edition of the *Lyrical Ballads,* Coleridge was quite explicit: "How the Ancient Mariner cruelly and in contempt of the laws of hospitality killed a Seabird. . . ." And the gloss states, "The ancient Mariner inhospitably killeth the pious bird of good omen." It is an act of blasphemy, of defiance against superstition (against the bird as one of "good omen"), of rebellion against God and the Christian universe. It is therefore an act of pride, an assertion of superiority.

The Mariner's contempt is not simply for law but for the bird. Later on, when the men have died, he "despiseth the creatures of the calm, And envieth that they should live, and so many lie dead." It is when he forgets himself and is totally absorbed in their beauty and happiness and blesses them "unaware" that the Albatross drops from his neck and his redemption begins. In his pride he is like Osorio, who justified his act by his superiority to other men and by the insignificance of the individual life:

> What if one reptile sting another reptile,
> Where is the crime? The goodly face of Nature
> Hath one trail less of slimy filth upon it.
> Are we not all predestined rottenness
> And cold dishonor? Grant it that this hand
> Had given a morsel to the hungry worms
> Somewhat too early. Where's the guilt of this?
> [*Osorio*, III.213–19]

On the borders of the conscious and unconscious, it is an act of power, like Kubla Khan's building of the Pleasure Dome. Although the one is a grandiose act of construction, and the other a trivial act of destruction, they are both godlike, or at least god-attracting, acts within the frame of the reverie. Coleridge in 1800 subtitled *The Rime,*

"A Poet's Reverie," to Charles Lamb's great annoyance. And it is the poem's dreamlike quality, its rightness as a dream experience, that is mainly responsible for its irresistible appeal. The shooting of the Albatross is the perfect dream act. Though the Mariner has no distinct character and is primarily passive, yet he is the dream "I," the shadowy id who is the focus, through his act, of universal attention. He dominates the poem. The supernatural powers who control this world concentrate upon his punishment and his redemption.

Two hundred men drop dead because of his act, but he is condemned and privileged to live on. They had become accomplices in his crime, but how unimportant they are in themselves, how inferior to the Mariner, is shown by their deaths. Within any philosophical or religious frame, the punishment of the men is absurd, but within the dream frame their fate is right and inevitable, and as readers identifying with the Mariner we accept it without question.[40] Like the figures in a dream, they have no identity apart from the dreamer. We have no awareness of them as living human beings; we watch their deaths without surprise and without feeling, except insofar as they affect the Mariner. When, dying, the men fix their eyes upon the Mariner, the effect is not only to intensify his sense of guilt but to emphasize his importance.

The blessing of the snakes is also an act of power. The Albatross falls. It rains. The angels and the polar spirit are impressed into service to bring the Mariner home. And in the end, in order to perform his penance, he is himself given supernatural powers. He passes like night from land to land; he has strange powers of speech; he is immortal. Insofar as he is to be identified with Coleridge he is, as Robert Penn Warren points out,[41] the *poète maudit;* but as such he has the power to tell his tale which Coleridge longed for in *Kubla Khan.* And, as the figure of power, he dims the moral at the end of the poem. His act may have been a sin, but it made him important to gods and men alike; in a sense he was rewarded rather than punished. To suffer, to be damned even, as long as he was given the power to express his suffering, as long as he could be recognized as apart and superior, Coleridge could endure; to suffer without power, that was the intolerable thing.

Perhaps what stands out most starkly is the fact that the act was one of inexplicable and uncontrollable impulse. This is the impression the Mariner gives as he relates the act. He is, even now as he remembers, horrified and baffled. He describes the coming of the Albatross with affection and even reverence:

> As if it had been a Christian soul,
> We hailed it in God's name.
> [*RAM*, lines 65–66]

The ice splits, the south wind springs up, and each day the Albatross comes for food or play, and each night it perches for vespers nine. It is evident that all the men, including the Mariner, look forward to the bird's visits. And it is at this point that the wedding guest cries out:

> 'God save thee, Ancient Mariner!
> From the fiends, that plague thee thus!—
> Why look'st thou so?'—With my crossbow
> I shot the ALBATROSS.
> [*RAM*, lines 79–82]

The Mariner has done the opposite of what he might have been expected to do—he has killed instead of protected the bird. We are reminded of the conclusion to Part II of *Christabel*, in which Coleridge describes the father's reaction to the child dancing before him:

> And pleasures flow in so thick and fast
> Upon his heart, that he at last
> Must needs express his love's excess
> With words of unmeant bitterness.
> [*Christabel*, lines 662–65]

As we have already observed, Coleridge was intensely interested in the paradox of the love that expresses itself in violence, of the good intent that is somehow twisted to evil. In later years, he attributed the "barbarous" mistreatment of those he loved most, his "unnatural" cruelty to his children, to opium. But all his life, as his letters show, he was prone to vicious little jabs at those for whom he professed the greatest affection, sometimes in the midst of eulogizing them. His excessive expressions of affection, as for example to his wife while he was in Germany, conceal an indifference, a hostility, often an active dislike which he does not admit to himself. As his autobiographical letters to Poole show, his childhood demonstrated his capacity for unpremeditated violence. Behind the Mariner's act lies this self-observation, this troubled realization of the sudden unpremeditated impulse to hurt. Kenneth Burke is right, I think, in seeing it as a symbolic act, the execution of a desire Coleridge had felt.[42] It is the objectification of a primitive animal drive, of what Coleridge called the lower or bestial states of life. All of his later philosophy centered on an effort to deny the power of this drive—in effect to explain away the Mariner's act.

H. N. Fairchild calls *The Rime* on one level "an allegorical tract on universal benevolism and the religion of nature . . . the killing of the albatross is a sin against the great sentimental principle that the Universe is one loving Whole." [43] Certainly the killing of the bird is the ultimate artistic transformation of a favorite theme of the sentimental poets—the killing of birds and animals. How extraordinary Coleridge's achievement is may be seen by glancing at some typically gruesome specimens of the tradition, like this one from Thomson's *Seasons:*

> Oh, let not, aimed from some inhuman eye,
> The gun the music of the coming year
> Destroy, and harmless, unsuspecting harm,
> Lay the weak tribes, a miserable prey,
> In mingled murder fluttering on the ground!
> [*Autumn,* lines 983–88]

Or this from Cowper's *Task:*

> I would not enter on my list of friends
> (Tho' grac'd with polish'd manners and fine sense,
> Yet wanting sensibility) the man
> Who needlessly sets foot upon a worm.
> . . . when, held within their proper bounds,
> And guiltless of offense, [creatures] range the air,
> Or take their pastime in the spacious field:
> There they are privileg'd; and he that hunts
> Or harms them there is guilty of a wrong,
> Disturbs th' economy of Nature's realm,
> Who, when she form'd, design'd them an abode.
> [VI.560–63, 574–80]

Or, for that matter, Coleridge's own *To a Young Ass.*

The Mariner's act, then, is the unforgivable sin of the sentimentalist. Perhaps one reason why it became so quickly a byword is that deep in his heart every sentimentalist longed to kill a bird. As the Marquis de Sade had been busily demonstrating, the almost inevitable reflex of sentimentalism is sadism.

But the universe the Mariner defies is not the sentimentalist universe: it is the Christian universe, governed by supernatural forces. Undoubtedly, "the Mariner's more specifically Catholic piety is merely dramatic"; [44] but the presentation of an authoritarian, punitive universe is part of the basic conception of the poem. It is a universe of order, but hardly one of sentimental benevolence. Its punishment of violators is swift, severe, sustained. Such a conception is foreign to the necessitarian philosophers like Godwin, Priestley, and Hartley, on the one hand, and to the idealists like Berkeley and the Neoplatonists, on the other. Its most striking affinity is with medieval Catholicism, seventeenth-century Puritanism, or the lurid Calvinism of the evangelicals. It reminds us of the nightmarish experiences of Cowper. The Mariner's blessing of the snakes is like the evangelistic moment of conversion:

> A spring of love gushed from my heart,
> And I blessed them unaware. . . .
> [*RAM*, lines 284–85]

And though, like the religious conversion, this reveals the Mariner as one of the elect and promises his ultimate salvation, it does not free him from pain and penance. He remains subject, like an evangelical, to an unrelenting sense of guilt, a compulsion to confession, an uncertainty as to when his penance will end.

The universe of the Mariner has another disturbing characteristic: the precise punishment of the Mariner and his shipmates depends upon chance. The specter crew of Death and Life-in-Death gamble for them.

> The naked hulk alongside came
> And the twain were casting dice;
> 'The game is done! I've won! I've won!'
> Quoth she and whistles thrice.
> [*RAM*, lines 195–98]

Now certainly these are loaded dice. As in a dream in which chance enters we have no doubt of the outcome, indeed we know what the outcome will be, so here we as readers accept the outcome of the throw as inevitable. As a matter of fact, critics are so accustomed to taking for granted the relentless logic of crime and punishment in the poem that they pass over without comment the astonishing implications of the dice game. Surely it knocks out any attempts to impose a systematic philosophical system, be it necessitarian, Christian, or Platonic, upon the poem. Whether we consider it as part of the ideological content of the poem, or as the Mariner's interpretation of the fact that the men died and he lived on (a product of his delirium, as it were), or simply as dramatic machinery, the dice game makes caprice the decisive factor in the Mariner's punishment. It throws into question the moral and intellectual responsibility of the rulers of the universe.

From another point of view the dice game reveals Coleridge's fundamental uncertainty and doubt about the universe of love and law which he as philosopher so confidently affirmed. He had recently been concerned, in the concluding act of *Osorio,* with the alternative punishments of Death and Life-in-Death. Osorio, remorseful over the death of Ferdinand, wants to die:

> Let the eternal Justice
> Prepare my punishment in the obscure world.
> I will not bear to live—to live! O agony!
> And be myself alone, my own sore torment.
> [*Osorio,* V.263–66]

When Alhadra rushes in to kill him and Maria begs for his life, she argues that "to let him live— / It were a deep revenge!" But she decides to let her followers put him to death anyway. Life-in-death is thus the worst punishment of which Coleridge can conceive; and he makes his human avenger Alhadra less irresponsible and ruthless than his supernatural agents in *The Rime.*

The total impression, then, which we get of the universe in *The Rime* is of unpredictable despotic forces. The punishment is not only out of all proportion to the crime, but it is also as primitive and sadistic as the Mariner's act. He kills the bird and two hundred men die, just as in *The Raven* the Woodsman fells the tree and the ship sinks in the storm. There is a hierarchy of divinities in the tale. When the Mariner blesses the snakes unaware, but through a force superior to himself ("Sure my kind saint took pity on me"), he is heard by the holy Mother who sends "the gentle sleep from Heaven" and the rain that refreshes him when he awakes. And "by the invocation of the guardian saint" the angelic spirits enter the bodies of the ship's crew. The "lonesome Spirit from the south-pole," who is certainly less a Neoplatonic daemon than a kind of primitive totem force, is subservient to the angelic forces and is pressed into carrying the ship as far as the line. But he has power enough to demand and receive penance "long and heavy" for the Mariner. However we look at it, there is something arbitrary and less than merciful in the way in which the higher powers defer to the polar spirit; particularly is this inconsistent with the view of the poem as "an allegorical tract on universal benevolism and the religion of nature."

The arbitrary exhibition of power continues in the sinking of the ship and in the woeful agony that wrenches the Mariner when he asks the Hermit to "shrieve" him. The Hermit is powerless to give absolution to the Mariner, to forgive him in the name of the church or God (as is implied in the word "shrieve"). As the gloss says ominously, "the penance of life falls upon" the Mariner from above. The conclusion of the poem is oppressively puritanical. The Mariner passes "like Night from land to land"; he tells the Wedding-Guest that it is sweeter far than a marriage feast with a goodly company "to walk together to the Kirk" and pray; he leaves his listener because the "little vesper bell" bids him to prayer; and the Wedding-Guest, turning from the bridegroom's door,

> . . . went like one that hath been stunned,
> And is of sense forlorn:
> A sadder and a wiser man,
> He rose the morrow morn.
> [*RAM*, lines 622–25]

We are confronted at the end of the poem by the eternally alienated Mariner alienating in his turn the Wedding-Guest, for the Guest is robbed of his happiness and the spontaneous participation in the marriage feast and forced to share the disillusioned wisdom and guilt of the Mariner. Within this context the Mariner's pious moral becomes inescapably ironic:

> He prayeth best, who loveth best
> All things both great and small;
> For the dear God who loveth us,
> He made and loveth all.
> [*RAM*, lines 614–17]

Lifted from context as they generally are, these lines seem to be the statement of a universal love and charity, of which the Mariner is the recipient and in which he shares. They suggest a benevolent and vaguely egalitarian universe in which "every Thing has a Life of its own, & . . . we are all *one Life*" (*CL*, II, 864). But, by the moral principles of such a universe, the prolonged punishment of the Mariner should have been unthinkable. The God who loved man as well as bird should have been merciful and forgiving. The God of the poem, however, is a jealous God; and in context the moral tag carries the concealed threat that even the most trivial violation of His love will bring ruthless and prolonged punishment. The way to avoid conscious or unconscious sin is to withdraw from active life to humble ourselves in prayer. At best, the "love" of God is the love of the benevolent despot, the paternal tyrant, the "great Father" to whom each bends. We love not through joy and spontaneous participation in the "one life" but through fear and enforced obedience. The little moral tag has the same ambiguous implications as Geraldine's remarks in Part I of *Christabel*, which are the prelude to the enslavement of Christabel:

> All they who live in the upper sky
> Do love you, holy Christabel! . . .
> [*Christabel*, lines 227–28]

Yet there is no reason to believe that either the Mariner or Coleridge intended any irony in the pious assertion. This was the faith which Coleridge wanted desperately to hold to throughout his life, and he had to assert it here with particular flatness in order to conceal from himself the full enormity of the world created by his imagination, or at least to make the contemplation of this world endurable. Indeed, he had to assert it in order to justify allowing his imagination to create such a world in the first place. So conditioned have most readers been to accept the same pious platitude that even to this day they make the stock response expected of them and automatically reconstruct the poem to fit the moral, blotting out whatever seems to contradict it.[45]

In part, the sweeping affirmation of the moral reflects the excited relief and gratitude of both Mariner and Coleridge at having reached even so partial a resolution of the Mariner's problem as the conclusion of the poem presents. The Mariner is allowed to live and to return to his own country; he is condemned (and privileged) to tell his tale; he has power and importance, a certain freedom of will and movement, a hope of salvation. He has arrived, at least, at a *modus vivendi*. And perhaps one reason why Coleridge was able to finish *The Rime* is that he had been able to work his way through within the structure of the narrative to a more or less positive resolution.

The Three Graves and *Christabel* remain unfinished, in one sense, because he could not do this. There are other reasons, of course, why he was able to finish *The Rime*. It was the culmination of a number of attempts at the ballad and at collaboration with Wordsworth—*The Three Graves*, the Ossianic *Wanderings of Cain*, *The Ballad of the Dark Ladie*, possibly the first part of *Christabel*. Under the stimulus of the association with Wordsworth his imagination became intensely active; each abortive attempt fanned it the more and freed it of limiting inhibitions, and it was obvious that given the proper subject it was capable of sustained and remarkable achievement. The great sweep of the voyage and the theme of crime, punishment, and gradual redemption, which interlock to give a peculiar inevitability to the structure of *The Rime,* provided exactly the stimulus necessary to release Coleridge's pent-up and thwarted creative energy. And on this one occasion Wordsworth was of incalculable aid in providing perhaps the most critical actions of the plot: the killing of the Albatross, the persecution by the "tutelary spirits" of the pole, and the navigation of the ship by the dead men. The last suggestion in particular may have been the means of getting Coleridge past the middle of his poem, the point at which he showed signs of bogging down.

V. THE VISION OF FEAR

He was never able to repeat the achievement of *The Rime.* He was never again able to find the magic formula for reconciling the split between the pull of his imagination toward the dark and evil and the demand of his rationalizing mind for an affirmative view of things. If he had been able to allow his imagination free play, all might have been well; but he stood over it in moral horror and thus dammed it up. Specifically, it was in the writing of *Christabel* that he came to an artistic impasse. At perhaps the most critical point in his artistic life, in 1800, he poured into the effort to complete the poem the energy and imagination that otherwise might have gone into the creation of poems equally splendid but less inhibiting. The failure to complete *Christabel* marks the collapse of Coleridge as a significant poet.

In its dramatization of the unequal conflict between the active aggressive evil and the helpless paralyzed good, invaded and violated without cause or warning, the poem parallels quite closely what Coleridge saw as the pattern of his own life. This is immediately evident when we place "The Conclusion to Part I" of *Christabel,* which recapitulates the thematic development of the poem up to that point, side by side with *The Pains of Sleep,* his frankly autobiographical account of the horrors of "withdrawal," of trying to break the opium habit, which he wrote in 1803 and significantly enough published with *Christabel* in 1816.

In the "Conclusion," Christabel is first described as she looked while praying at the old oak tree, "her face resigned to bliss or bale." Abruptly, in the next section she is shown

> With open eyes (ah woe is me!)
> Asleep and dreaming fearfully,
> Fearfully dreaming, yet, I wis,
> Dreaming that alone, which is—
> O sorrow and shame! Can this be she,
> The lady, who knelt at the old oak tree?
> [*Christabel*, lines 292–97]

In the opening section of *The Pains of Sleep,* Coleridge tells how, though it is not his custom to pray, he composes his spirit to love:

> In humble trust mine eye-lids close,
> With reverential resignation,
> No wish conceived, no thought exprest,
> Only a sense of supplication;
> A sense o'er all my soul imprest,
> That I am weak, yet not unblest,
> Since in me, round me, everywhere
> Eternal Strength and Wisdom are.
> [*Pains of Sleep*, lines 6–13]

As Christabel's prayers are followed by the embrace of Geraldine and the evil dreams, so in the second section of *The Pains of Sleep* the fiendish dreams inflict themselves upon Coleridge:

> Desire with loathing strangely mixed
> On wild or hateful objects fixed.
> Fantastic passions! maddening brawl!
> And shame and terror over all! . . .
> For all seemed guilt, remorse or woe,
> My own or others still the same
> Life-stifling fear, soul-stifling shame.
> [*Pains of Sleep*, lines 23–26, 30–32]

And in the conclusion of the poem Coleridge is driven to ask the question that Christabel might ask:

> Such punishments, I said, were due
> To natures deepliest stained with sin. . . .
> But wherefore, wherefore fall on me?
> To be beloved is all I need,
> And whom I love, I love indeed.
> [*Pains of Sleep*, lines 43–44, 50–52]

The Romantic Ventriloquists

"Shame" is the word that links Christabel's dream and Coleridge's own. And, as Christabel dreamed of Geraldine, so Coleridge dreamed recurrently of loathly ladies. The notebook entry for "Friday Night, Nov. 28, 1800, or rather Saturday morning" reads:

———a most frightful Dream of a Woman whose features were blended with darkness catching hold of my right eye & attempting to pull it out—I caught hold of her arm fast—a horrid feel—Wordsworth cried out aloud to me hearing my scream—heard his cry & thought it cruel he did not come / but did not wake till his cry was repeated a third time—the Woman's name Ebon Ebon Thalud—when I awoke, my right eyelid swelled—[*Notebooks,* Vol. I, entry 848].

And nearly two years later he writes:

My Dreams uncommonly illustrative of the non-existence of Surprize in sleep . . . I was followed up & down by a frightful pale woman who, I thought, wanted to kiss me, & had the property of giving a shameful Disease by breathing in the face / & again I dreamt that a figure of a woman of a gigantic Height, dim & indefinite & smokelike [possibly snakelike] appeared—& that I was forced to run up toward it—& then it changed to a stool—& then appeared again in another place—& again I went up in great fright—& it changed to some other common thing—yet I felt no surprize [October 3, 1802; *Notebooks,* Vol. I, entry 1250].

These dreams become a key to the ambiguous sexual implications of the poem. The relationship between Christabel and Geraldine is the relationship between Coleridge and the dream women and might very well have had its origin in one of his dream experiences. Coleridge's statement in the preface of 1816 that the first conception of the tale had come "with the wholeness, no less than the liveliness of a vision" takes on literal meaning.

More than once, in discussing his dreams, Coleridge comes to the brink of Freudian discoveries. And in *The Three Graves* and *The Rime of the Ancient Mariner,* as well as in *Christabel,* evil manifests itself in sexual imagery that parallels the dream imagery. In *The Three Graves,* the evil is openly identified with the aggressive lust of the mother. In *The Ancient Mariner,* the sexual elements are more ambiguous, but Life-in-Death is described in terms of the Loathsome Lady, and there are shadowy sexual implications in the shooting of the Albatross and the reaction to the water snakes, as Burke and others have pointed out.[46] The blessing of the water snakes, the overcoming of repugnance to them, suggests the transcendence of sexual feelings or their absorption into feelings of benevolence; at the moment when the

Mariner can pray, the Albatross falls from his neck and the "holy Mother" sends the sleep and rain. In the end, it is significant that the Mariner draws so sharp a distinction between marriage and the church, placing the emphasis on sexual abstinence.

Finally, Geraldine's evil is also sexual: she is the beautiful woman with the loathsome body whose touch is paralyzing and enervating. In the fatal embrace that enslaves Christabel she slumbers "as a mother with her child," so that she takes on the connotation of the lustful mother; and throughout the poem she is contrasted with Christabel's mother. Christabel's fearful dreams give way to a "relaxed sleep" and the vision of her mother. The pattern is twice repeated the next day when "the vision of fear" is followed by prayer and the "vision blest" of her mother. It is dangerous to generalize, but it seems evident that evil and sexual aggression by women are identified in Coleridge's mind, and sexual relations become, for him, a perversion of the mother-child relation. Experiences, probably with prostitutes, while at Christ's Hospital, referred to in the notebooks, may have been partly responsible.[47] And undoubtedly the compulsory nature of the marriage to Sara and the deterioration of the marital relationship aggravated his disgust.[48]

But the symbol of the aggressive woman implies further that the real evil is that the sexual desire itself constantly turns to lust and perversion. For Coleridge, who aspired to intellectual and moral purity, the greatest degradation must have been the powerlessness of his mind to prevent its violation by the "bad passions." If he closed his waking mind to them, he was haunted by them in his dreams. There was no escape. They threatened to usurp his mind, to drive him to psychological destruction. At the end of his life Coleridge defined madness as

. . . the sleep of the spirit with certain conditions of wakefulness; that is to say, lucid intervals. During this sleep or recession of the spirit, the lower or bestial states of life rise up into action and prominence. It is an awful thing to be eternally tempted by perverted senses. The reason may resist—it does resist for a long time; but too often, at length, it yields for a moment, and the man is mad forever [*Table Talk*, pp. 84–85].

The eternal temptation was inherent within man and therefore inherent in the order of things. And thus it was hard to avoid the conclusion, implicit in Geraldine's remarks to Christabel, that divine love contains within it the perversion of lust. Or, to put it another way, God's love contains an element of sadism which forces those who love

[121]

him into involuntary submission to, or commission of, evil, thwarting their efforts at good or rewarding them with torture. The only hope of salvation is through abstinence and prayer, and the effort to sublimate lust into the benevolent love of all things.

Sexual lust, viewed in this way, becomes a terrifying example of necessitarianism. In a notebook entry of December 28, 1803, Coleridge wrote:

I will at least make the attempt to explain to myself the Origin of Moral Evil from the *streamy* Nature of Association, which Thinking = Reason, curbs & rudders / how this comes to be so difficult / Do not the bad Passions in Dreams throw light and shew of proof upon this Hypothesis?—Explain those bad Passions, & I shall gain Light, I am sure [*Notebooks,* Vol. I, entry 1770].

Coleridge's observation of the "streamy Nature of Association" in himself undoubtedly had much to do with the almost hysterical hostility to the "pernicious doctrine of necessity" which he had begun to manifest as early as 1798, and with the desperate urgency of his efforts to refute it from 1800 on.[49] For to accept a necessitarian doctrine was to acknowledge the logical possibility that the universe was dominated by a principle that was evil as well as good, or, worse still, that the primary laws of his own nature were the evil passions of which his mind was the hopeless victim. To avoid despair, it was necessary to assert and if possible demonstrate that the will was subduing and controlling the passions, and to prove that evils were inflicted upon men by eternal wisdom for ultimately beneficial ends.

In his formal philosophizing, his efforts toward a system, Coleridge largely ignores the problem of evil, or contents himself with general assertions about universal harmony, or becomes involved in a theological quibble on original sin, which results in the rather ambiguous and disingenuous implication that evil is the product of human will acting contrary to the divine will. In the *Aids to Reflection,* he says, for example:

A moral evil is an evil that has its origin in a will. An evil common to all must have a ground common to all. . . . Now this evil ground cannot originate in the Divine Will: it must, therefore, be referred to the will of man. And this evil ground we call Original Sin. It is a *mystery,* that is, a fact which we see, but cannot explain.[50]

The truth is that he was never able to give a convincing refutation of the doctrine of necessity because his own will was never able to triumph over the bad passions and evils within himself; and to the end of his life he automatically pictured himself in necessitarian terms as the helpless and passive victim of forces beyond his control.

Both *The Rime of the Ancient Mariner* and *Christabel,* written during the years in which Coleridge was turning so violently against Hartley, are dramatizations of the psychological hell implicit in the doctrine of necessity. In each, the victim is as helpless and lost as the young Coleridge or the little child of *Dejection* who wanders

> Upon a lonesome wild,
> Not far from home, but she hath lost her way:
> And now moans low in bitter grief and fear,
> And now screams loud, and hopes to make her mother hear.
> [*Dejection,* lines 122–25]

The Mariner is helpless from the moment he kills the Albatross. Even the blessing of the snakes is "unaware." The agony that forces him to tell his tale is compulsive. How responsible ultimately is he, then, for his act of evil? Within the pattern of the poem, it stands as an inexplicable and unpremeditated act as "unaware" as the blessing of the snakes. Even though it appears momentarily to be a deliberate, defiant gesture of rebellion and free will (*"I* shot the Albatross"), it is a Kafka-like act that strips away the illusion of freedom and lets the Mariner see just how helpless he is. From any point of view it reflects the same pride and capricious sadism as the remorseless forces of retribution it sets in motion. The evil that is in the Mariner is in his universe. In *Christabel* there is no doubt that the evil is imposed from without. Christabel is utterly helpless and innocent before the apparently motiveless sadism of Geraldine which is forcing her to imitate its own evil characteristics. And Geraldine, in turn, seems to be the instrument of some inscrutable divine plan, a spirit, as Derwent Coleridge says, "executing her appointed task with the best good will." [51]

The fatalism of *Christabel* is the fatalism of Coleridge viewing his own compulsion to moral evil. Just as Christabel's supreme effort of will, at the end of Part II, in entreating the Baron to send Geraldine away simply makes Geraldine's triumph more complete, so Coleridge saw his efforts to prevent the dreams as driving him to fresh errors. The self-examination in the notebook entry of January, 1805, is a remarkable mixture of acute observation and dangerous rationalization:

It is a most instructive part of my Life the fact, that I have been always preyed on by some Dread, and perhaps all my faulty actions have been the consequence of some Dread or other on my mind / from fear of Pain, or Shame, not from prospect of Pleasure. . . . [Then follows a revealing list of causes of dread from childhood on, concluding,] And finally stimulants in the fear and prevention of violent Bowel-attacks from mental agitation / then (almost epileptic) night-horrors in my sleep & since then every error I have committed, has been the immediate effect of the Dread of these bad most shocking Dreams—anything to prevent them . . . [*Notebooks,* Vol. II, entry 2398].

The "stimulants" are undoubtedly opium and laudanum; in a number of letters he specifically blames fear of mental and physical pain for his turning to opium. And in a letter to John Morgan on May 15, 1814, he combines this explanation with imagery strikingly similar to that of *Christabel* and his dreams:

Often have I wished to have been . . . trodden & spit upon, if by any means it might be an atonement for the direful guilt that (like all others) first *smiled* on me, like Innocence! then crept closer, & yet closer, till it had thrown it's serpent folds round & round me, and I was no longer in my own power! *Something* even the most wretched of Beings (*human* Beings at least) owes to himself—& this I *will* say and *dare* with truth say—that never was I led to this wicked direful practice of taking Opium or Laudanum by any desire or expectation of exciting *pleasurable* sensations; but purely by *terror,* by cowardice of pain, first of mental pain, & afterwards as my System became weakened, even of bodily Pain [*CL,* III, 491].[52]

Perhaps the most important phrase in the letter is the parenthetical "like all others," which indicates that Coleridge recognizes in his experience with opium a familiar pattern. He describes the drug as if it were a force external to himself which under the cover of a specious appearance of good maliciously entraps him. In the next sentence, he admits his responsibility but implies that he turned to opium with the best of intentions or at least with innocent motives, out of terror of "mental pain," and therefore is finally not to blame for the consequences of his act. In another letter to Morgan, written the day before, he describes the effects of the drug in terms of paralysis not of the "will" but of the "volition." The distinction seems to be drawn between the desire to do good and the power to act upon the desire, between Christabel's awareness of Geraldine's evil and her helplessness before it:

I know, it will be vain to attempt to persuade Mrs. Morgan or Charlotte, that a man, whose moral feelings, reason, understanding and senses are perfectly sane and vigorous, may yet have been *mad*— And yet nothing is more true. By the long long Habit of the accursed Poison my Volition (by which I mean the faculty *instrumental* to the Will, and by which alone the Will can realize itself— it's Hands, Legs & Feet, as it were) was completely deranged, at times frenzied, dissevered itself from the Will, & became an independent faculty; so that I was perpetually in the state, in which you may have seen paralytic Persons, who attempting to push a step forward in one direction are violently forced round to the opposite [*CL,* III, 489].

A few weeks earlier in a letter to Cottle he had said, "My case is a species of madness, only that it is a derangement, an utter impotence of the *Volition,* & not of the intellectual Faculties" (*CL,* III, 477). The letter to Morgan continues with the introduction by way of the familiar snake imagery of a new and significant theme—the changes for the worse effected in Coleridge's character and personality by the addiction to opium:

> But tho' there was no prospect, no gleam of Light before, an indefinite indescribable Terror as with a scourge of ever restless, ever coiling and uncoiling Serpents, drove me on from behind.—The worst was, that in *exact proportion* to the *importance* and *urgency* of any Duty was it, as of a fatal necessity, sure to be neglected: because it added to the Terror above described. In exact proportion, as I *loved* any person or persons more than others, & would have sacrificed my Life for them, were *they* sure to be the most barbarously mistreated by silence, absence, or breach of promise. . . . What crime is there scarcely which has not been included in or followed from the one guilt of taking opium? Not to speak of ingratitude to my maker for the wasted Talents; of ingratitude to so many friends who have loved me I know not why; of barbarous neglect of my family; excess of cruelty to Mary and Charlotte, when at Box and both Ill—(a vision of Hell to me when I think of it!) I have in this one dirty business of Laudanum an hundred times deceived, tricked, nay, actually & consciously LIED. And yet *all* these vices are so opposite to my nature, that but for this *free-agency-annihilating* Poison, I verily believe that I should have suffered myself to have been cut to pieces rather than have committed any one of them [*CL,* III, 489–90].

It is in relation to this tangled pattern of behavior that Coleridge has recorded that we can best interpret the symbolic action of the poem. Geraldine is an incarnation of sadism, much like the women of Coleridge's dreams. To paraphrase his description of opium in his letter to Morgan, she first smiled on Christabel, then crept closer and closer until she had trapped her victim in her serpent folds. But this sadism is accompanied by a sense of shame and dread and, particularly in Part I, by an implied feeling of love and pity for the victim. In the light of the attitudes toward evil we have been tracing, all these characteristics are quite compatible with, in fact conducive to, the conception of Geraldine as the instrument used by "Eternal Strength and Wisdom" to torture and test Christabel for its own inscrutable purposes. Geraldine's reluctant seduction of Christabel can then be seen as the product of an "excess" of divine love. Such an interpretation throws into ironic new perspective Derwent Coleridge's statement, which must have come from hints dropped by his father, that Geraldine was "no witch or goblin, or malignant being of any kind, but a spirit, executing her appointed task with the best good will, as she herself says:

All they who live in the upper sky,
Do love you holy Christabel, etc."

To say that Geraldine is not a malignant being is nonsense, except in terms of ultimate motivation. Within the context of the poem, within human terms, she is as evil as opium or Coleridge's dreams. Significantly enough, she becomes more unrelievedly malevolent as the poem progresses; the ambiguity that characterizes her in Part I has almost disappeared by the end of Part II. Of course we are seeing her increasingly from the perspective of Christabel, haunted "by the vision of fear, the touch and pain," condemned to silence, and forced to take on the snakelike characteristics of Geraldine, even to the point of passively imitating her look of "dull and treacherous hate." At the end of Part II Christabel is utterly helpless and abandoned, and no way of escape from the spell is visible short of supernatural aid in the form, perhaps, of her mother's spirit. The departure of Bard Bracy represents the loss of her only friend, and it is only in the anticlimax of Gillman's summary that we are justified in seeing Bracy as a source of aid. Indeed, the whole pull of the pattern of the poem is toward the further enslavement of Christabel under the spell of Geraldine. There is even the possibility inherent in the vampire legend which Coleridge was undoubtedly drawing on that she would be mentally and morally corrupted, or at least that she would be driven to unnatural behavior like that of which he accuses himself.

The poem sticks at the point at which Coleridge himself is stuck. Until he solved the problem of evil in his own life, it was hardly likely that he could finish it. To attempt to continue with the poem would have been only to torture and exacerbate his feelings by confronting the hopelessness of finding any solution to Christabel's situation or his own. To the end of his life Coleridge was haunted by the unfinished poem. In a notebook of 1823–24 he records on his birthday that he feels so well, having bathed in the sea and "felt the benefit," that "were I free to do so I feel as if I could compose the third part of *Christabel* or the song of her desolation." [53] The entry is significant in its revelation of how closely he associates *Christabel* with his own life, of how dependent he makes the completion of the poem on a sense of well-being. Ten years later in the Table Talk of July 6, 1833, he recorded this last sad remark:

The reason of my not finishing *Christabel* is not that I don't know how to do it—for I have, as I always had, the whole plan entire from beginning to end in my mind; but I fear I could not carry on with equal success the execution of the idea, an extremely subtle and difficult one [*Table Talk*, p. 259].

Very likely he gave Gillman such a summary as Gillman reports: one suspects that he gave out a number of such glib summaries. The summary is a bit of wishful thinking that reduces the poem to a silly Gothic ballad and Geraldine to a rather moronic witch, and resolves everything meaninglessly through the *deus ex machina* trick. The ease with which the whole nightmarish problem is defeated into thin air suggests the miraculous ease with which Coleridge doggedly continued to hope that his own emancipation from the faults and evils in himself would take place.

In *Beyond the Pleasure Principle*, Freud makes the assumption as a result of his observation of shell-shocked patients that there is in the psychic life a repetition compulsion whose intent is the developing of fear. The war patients would reconstruct over and over again in dreams the bad situation which had precipitated their neuroses in order that the failure to meet it might be recouped; there was an attempt to meet the situation, to make a new effort of control.[54] It may be that some similar psychic process motivated Coleridge's dreams and his writing of *Christabel*. The central situation as we have seen is the symbolic representation of a central situation in his life, his helplessness before the hosts of temptations that tyrannized over him—sexual desires, gambling, drink, opium, and so forth. The relationship may even be more literal; there may have been an initiatory situation that precipitated the dream. At any rate, Coleridge can be said to be "reconstructing the bad situation" in art in order that the failure to meet it may be recouped—in order even that he may find a solution that he can transfer to life. This is why the completion of the poem is so important to Coleridge as man and artist—why he insists so upon having the whole poem in mind. This is why no solution is adequate in which Geraldine is not vanquished in direct combat by the power of good and her role in the scheme of things exposed. Any other solution such as the one reported by Gillman is a makeshift substitute and an evasion of the central problem.

The Romantic Ventriloquists

But for the sake of his own well-being it was necessary for Coleridge to pretend to a solution, even a trivial one, and to ignore the relation of the poem to himself. Thus, he could pretend that he had everything well in hand, including his own affairs, that he could solve his own problems if he put his mind to them as easily as he solved the problem of the poem.

When Coleridge published the poem, in an apparent effort to round off Part II in the same way as Part I he tacked on as a "Conclusion" some lines not to be found in any of the manuscripts of *Christabel,* but appearing previously in a letter to Southey on May 6, 1801, in connection with some remarks about Hartley Coleridge. In the letter the lines are accompanied by the comment, "A very metaphysical account of fathers calling their children rogues, rascals, and little varlets, etc." (*CL,* II, 728). Coming to the lines in the course of reading the poem one is startled by their apparent irrelevance, by the jangling discordance of the opening lines abruptly breaking in upon the scene of unalleviated horror at the end of Part II:

> A little child, a limber elf,
> Singing, dancing to itself.

They seem to stand as some kind of obscure comment or cryptogram on the meaning of the poem, perhaps even a clue to the ultimate resolution.

The cryptic nature of the lines is borne out by an attempt to analyze them. The passage that begins so lightly becomes increasingly somber and complex until it ends on a note of pessimism as profound as that at the end of the poem. Simultaneously, the expression becomes so congested and ambiguous that it is almost impossible to unravel the exact meaning. A rough paraphrase of the lines will demonstrate these points. The happy child "that always finds and never seeks" so causes his father's heart to overflow with pleasure that at last he "must needs express his love's excess / With words of unmeant bitterness." Perhaps it is "pretty" to force together thoughts so unlike each other (does he mean "love" and "bitterness"?), to dally with wrong that does no harm. Perhaps it is tender, too, and "pretty" (the word "pretty" is a strange word to use and then repeat in this context) to feel within at each wild word a "sweet recoil of love and pity." And what if "in a world of sin" such giddiness of heart (the "sweet recoil of love and pity"?) comes usually only from rage and pain, and "so talks as it's most used to do"?

The last line is the most tortured and obscure. But it would seem to imply that in a world of sin the natural, normal way for love to express itself may be through "wild words"; that, worse still, rage and pain may be the customary feelings, and the feeling of love in its intensity dependent upon and even produced by them. The anguished parenthetical cry, "O sorrow and shame should this be true!" makes clear that this is no trivial or transitory matter, but a profoundly disturbing question about the ultimate relationships of good and evil, love and hate in human nature.

It is this question in particular that seems to me to make the generally accepted suggestion of E. H. Coleridge unsatisfactory or at least insufficient. He says:

> The nexus between this so-called Conclusion and the closing lines of the Second Part is to be found in the implied comparison between Sir Leoline's wrath, the excess of love transformed into the excess of bitterness, and the mock resentment of love playing at wrath, which is none the less "a fault and corruption" of this world of sin.

He then goes on to suggest that the lines may have been intended for the third part.[55] Now it was perhaps Sir Leoline's wrath that recalled these lines to Coleridge. An entry in the notebooks written in the spring of 1803 indicates that he intended to comment specifically on Sir Leoline's behavior: "A kindhearted man obliged to give a refusal, or the like, that will give great pain, finds relief in doing it roughly & fiercely—explain this, & use it in Christabel" (*Notebooks,* Vol. I, entry 1392). He is obviously not here referring to the lines on Hartley already written, but to lines he intends to write. However, when he decided to tack on the "Conclusion," he may have recalled the Hartley lines because of a similarity of phrasing, particularly in rhyme words, to lines at the end of the poem—a kind of mechanical association to which Coleridge was prone, as Lowes demonstrates. The giddiness of "heart and brain" which comes seldom save from "rage and pain" echoes eerily the lines:

> Within the Baron's heart and brain
> If thoughts, like these, had any share,
> They only swelled his rage and pain,
> And did but work confusion there.
> [*Christabel,* lines 636–39]

But between Sir Leoline's "rage and pain" and that of the "Conclusion" there is at best only a superficial similarity. The basic situations are radically different. Just before she made the supreme effort to ask her father to send Geraldine away, Christabel

> . . . passively did imitate
> That look of dull and treacherous hate!
> And thus she stood, in dizzy trance,
> Still picturing that look askance
> With forced unconscious sympathy
> Full before her father's view.
>> [*Christabel*, lines 605–10]

The last line needs, perhaps, to be emphasized. Sir Leoline's reaction is conditioned by this look of hate; he quite literally sees Christabel as motivated by "more than woman's jealousy." He has been "dishonour'd by his only child," and his hospitality brought to a "disgraceful end." His is the conventional motivation for "rage and pain."

But what Coleridge is somewhat obliquely and hesitantly, even disingenuously, describing in the "Conclusion" is a habitual and abnormally painful-pleasurable experience that is a kind of sadism. The "rage and pain" have no external motivation; they are an expression of pleasure or "love's excess," and they result in "a sweet recoil of love and pity." The link between the conclusion and the poem is a more fundamental, if obscure, association than Sir Leoline's wrath. "O sorrow and shame . . . ": this is the key phrase. "This mark of my shame, this seal of my sorrow," are the words with which Geraldine refers to the physical sign of her evil. "O sorrow and shame!" is the phrase in "The Conclusion to Part I" with which Coleridge refers to the dreams of Christabel asleep in the arms of Geraldine. And "O sorrow and shame should this be true!" he exclaims at the recognition in himself of the dependence of love and pity upon rage and pain. Thus by the phrase he links himself with both Geraldine and Christabel.

The conclusion becomes Coleridge's indication of how intimately he saw the action of the poem related to his own experience; how personal a poem it is. It is a cryptic attempt to suggest that *Christabel* is no mere Gothic tale but the dramatic exploration of the nature of evil and its ambiguous interrelation with good. It is also a cryptic sign that he had gone as far as he could or would go. It ends with a question to which he could give no answer. It is his baffled acknowledgment that the sources of evil are inherent, not extraneous, and that the poem is, therefore, in a sense an "interior" drama, the projection into Gothic trappings of psychological states.

The part of the description that seems disingenuous is the suggestion that the wild words, the cruelty, are spontaneous, unintended products of unselfish love and pleasure in another's happiness. Obviously, Coleridge ignores or evades the psychological insecurities, leading to resentment or envy and a desire to hurt, which are contributing sources of cruelty. He still must insist upon the inexplicability of the sadistic act, as he had in *The Ancient Mariner*. But he admits the compulsive nature of the act, the delight (though he rationalizes it) in hurting, and the paradoxical shame and pity which accompany and result from the act—all characteristics that he shares with Geraldine.

Coleridge's biography furnishes ample evidence of the way in which from childhood he made those who loved him and those upon whom he was dependent suffer. Often, as in his behavior to the Wordsworths and Sara Hutchinson in the years following his return from Malta, he seems intent on hurting them as a means of testing and proving their love. The more they suffered on his behalf, the more he loved them.[56] And of course his behavior to others was the reflex of his own suffering. Just as he believed that forces beyond his control tormented him, so he tormented those he loved. In other words, Coleridge could observe in himself the characteristics both of Geraldine and of Christabel—in opposition, yet reciprocal; provoking and reflecting; reacting against each other, inextricably entangled. *The Pains of Sleep* and the "Conclusion to Part II," taken together, suggest the ambiguous relationship between Coleridge's sufferings and his treatment of those he loved. In *The Pains of Sleep* he is the unwilling masochist, helpless, "strengthless," asking for love but resigned to, even expecting, pain; and in the "Conclusion" he is the unwilling sadist, inflicting pain to express his love's excess. The relationship might be summed up in the last lines of *The Pains of Sleep:*

> To be loved is all I need,
> And whom I love, I love indeed.

There is no reason to suppose that Coleridge had here any intent other than to stress the purity and intensity of his love, but the emphatic beat of the last line inevitably carries a threat of force of love to be imposed without restraint and recalls the irony of Geraldine's statement to Christabel just before she enslaves her:

> All they who live in the upper sky
> Do love you, holy Christabel!

And you love them, and for their sake
And for the good which me befel,
Even I in my degree will try,
Fair Maiden to requite you well.
[*Christabel*, lines 227–232]

VI. THE SOLE RESOURCE

The "Conclusion" is a symbolic gesture of frustration, a concession of defeat. It stands for the failure to resolve the personal problems thwarting not just the completion of the poem but any sustained and significant poetic activity from 1800 on. As we have seen, the pattern projected in *Christabel* becomes ever present in Coleridge's life, so that he is obsessively aware of it, and the hope of escape becomes day by day more glimmering. The creation of poetry was for Coleridge a highly introspective process. It forced him to look deep into himself, in a self-contemplation that became finally too painful to bear because it contradicted all that he wanted to believe about himself and his universe.

In *Dejection: An Ode* he lamented his loss of feeling and attributed it to the loss of joy which is given only to the pure. And then, in a quick shift of emphasis (he seems totally unaware of it and writes as if he were continuing the previous argument), he says that there was a time when this joy within him "dallied" with distress, for hope grew round him, but now afflictions bow him down to earth. He cares not that they rob him of his "mirth"—the joy, presumably, of which he had earlier lamented the loss:

But oh! each visitation
Suspends what nature gave me at my birth,
My shaping spirit of Imagination.
For not to think of what I needs must feel,
But to be still and patient, all I can;
And haply by abstruse research to steal
From my own nature all the natural man—
This was my sole resource, my only plan. . . .
[*Dejection*, lines 84–91]

Thus he satisfies his conscience by implying that his loss of joy results from his loss of innocence, and then by the shift in emphasis immediately absolves himself of blame by implying that the loss of joy (and therefore of innocence) is finally the result of afflictions beyond his control.

[132]

Coleridge

The *Christabel* pattern is clearly present. He is the helpless victim of afflictions which are "visitations" robbing him of joy and innocence and suspending his shaping spirit of imagination. Though the agony is real enough, the rest of the poetic argument is at best a half truth and at worst an evasion of the fundamental causes of his distress. The poem itself is evidence—if evidence is needed—that he had not lost the power of feeling or that his shaping spirit of imagination was not seriously affected, except insofar as the increasing use of opium suspended it. What he really means is that he is unable to feel what he thinks he should feel, and write what he thinks he should write, and he finds it both too terrifying and too painful to give his imagination its bent.

The heart of the matter is in the phrase, "not to think of what I needs must feel." The more desperate his own condition, the more Coleridge insisted that his imagination express itself in unqualified optimism. But this could lead only to fundamentally meretricious verse. In December, 1801, Coleridge published in the *Morning Post* an *Ode to Tranquillity* of which the last three stanzas read:

> Who late and lingering seeks thy shrine,
> On him but seldom, Power divine,
> Thy spirit rests! Satiety
> And Sloth, poor counterfeits of thee,
> Mock the tired worldling. Idle Hope
> And dire Remembrance interlope,
> To vex the feverish slumbers of the mind:
> The bubble floats before, the spectre stalks behind.
>
> But me thy gentle hand will lead
> At morning through the accustomed mead;
> And in the sultry summer's heat
> Will build me up a mossy seat;
> And when the gust of Autumn crowds,
> And breaks the busy moonlight clouds,
> Thou best the thought canst raise, the heart attune,
> Light as the busy clouds, calm as the gliding moon.
>
> The feeling heart, the searching soul,
> To thee I dedicate the whole!
> And while within myself I trace
> The greatness of some future race,
> Aloof with hermit-eye I scan
> The present works of present man—

The Romantic Ventriloquists

A wild and dream-like trade of blood and guile,
Too foolish for a tear, too wicked for a smile!
[*PW*, I, 360–61]

If this were simply a magazine effusion, made to order for the *Post*, it might be considered a harmless if smugly complacent stock poem. But Coleridge obviously thought well of it: he sent a version of it to the Beaumonts and reprinted it in *The Friend* and all editions of *Sibylline Leaves*. The subjective tone is clear, and the pattern of the poem follows closely that of the highly personal poems he wrote in the nineties. There is the same self-righteous separation of himself from the "tired worldling"; the same withdrawal as in the *Ode to the Departing Year* or *Fears in Solitude* into hermitlike aloofness from the "present works of present man." In the light of Coleridge's psychological crises, the calm assertion of his own tranquillity leaves the reader a little numb. The most charitable explanation would be that this was truly an opium poem, produced while under the benign and tranquilizing influence of the drug. But there are too many such poems for this explanation to hold; the reader has to face the fact that Coleridge possessed an almost Falstaffian capacity for make-believe, for persuading himself that he really possessed the characteristics he wanted to possess.

In September, 1802, he published in the *Morning Post* the *Hymn before Sunrise in the Vale of Chamouni*. This too was republished in *The Friend* and *Sibylline Leaves,* and a version was sent to Sir George and Lady Beaumont in 1803.[57] The poem is one of Coleridge's last and most desperate efforts to write the great poem of affirmation. Here is an agonizing attempt to "feel" as well as to "see" the beauty of nature; to recapture joy; to awaken the shaping spirit of the imagination —and the failure is terrible. It is significant that Coleridge would silently build his poem upon the translation of Frederika Brun's "Ode to Chamouni" and in his preface imply that it was based upon first-hand impressions of the vale of Chamouni, a place he had never seen. The effort to arouse feeling and to invoke conviction through frenzied rhetorical chant is evident in such passages as:

Hand and voice,
Awake, awake! and thou, my heart, awake!
Awake ye rocks! Ye forest pines, awake!
Green fields, and icy cliffs! All join my hymn!
[*Hymn*, as published in the *Morning Post*, lines 23–26; *PW*, I, 572]

[134]

or in the series of questions to the ice falls: Who made you glorious as the gates of heaven? Who spread garlands of gentians at your feet?— followed in the *Morning Post* version by

> God! God! the torrents like a shout of nations
> Utter! the ice plain bursts, and answers God!
> God, sing the meadow-streams with gladsome voice,
> And pine-groves with their soft, and soul-like sound,
> The silent snow-mass, loos'ning, thunders God.
> [*Hymn*, lines 56–60; *PW*, I, 573]

The frenzied tone of the passage is somewhat softened down in later versions, though no essential change is made. The poem ends with the poet raising his head, which had been bowed low in adoration, and, with dim eyes suffused with tears, invoking the mountain as if by magical incantation:

> Rise, like a cloud!
> Rise, like a cloud of incense, from the earth! . . .
> Great hierarch! tell thou the silent sky,
> And tell the stars and tell yon rising sun
> Earth, with her thousand voices, calls on God.
> [*Hymn*, lines 72–73; 76–78; *PW*, I, 573]

Coleridge is trying to perform the same act of power as in *Kubla Khan*, more directly, less subtly. The symbols are similar: the caves of ice and the pleasure dome are transformed into the ice fields and the mountain peak. And he tries to demonstrate his own godlike power by commanding the mountain to testify to the existence of God. He fails because of a lack of inner conviction; he does not "feel" the assurance he asserts; he can give only a facile display of technical virtuosity on a theme furnished by another.

He rarely tried to write, after this, poems of such oversimplified assertion. As a poet he could no longer generate at will a mood of euphoria. He could not escape what Keats called "the journey homeward to habitual self." Most of his poems after 1803 became cries of impotence and despair over his failure as man and poet and the frustration of his love for Sara. After the publication of *Sibylline Leaves* in 1817 he gave up poetry almost altogether. In a letter to Collins in 1818 he repeated more simply and starkly what he had said fifteen years before in *Dejection: An Ode*: "Poetry is out of the question. The attempt would only hurry me into that sphere of acute feelings from which abstruse research, the mother of self-oblivion, presents an asylum" (*CL*, IV, 893).

4: KEATS

I. MNEMOSYNE AND MONETA

KEATS began the first version of *Hyperion* in September or October, 1818, and laid it aside in April, 1819. He was at work on the second version in August, 1819, though he may have begun earlier, and on September 21, 1819, he wrote Reynolds, "I have given up Hyperion."[1] Brown in his life of Keats said that during November and December Keats spent the evenings remodeling *Hyperion* "into the form of a vision."[2] But a letter to Woodhouse that accompanies the one to Reynolds contains excerpts from the "induction" and the opening of Book II of the second *Hyperion,* indicating that he had already remodeled the fragment and that whatever he did after that was in the nature of revision (*Letters,* II, 171–72). At any rate, the writing of the two *Hyperions* frames the year in which Keats wrote his greatest poetry, and with the abandoning of the second *Hyperion* his poetic activity in effect ceases.

Between the two *Hyperions* lies a fundamental shift in attitude. The profound difference in the conceptions of the two poems is dramatically represented by the difference between the two goddesses, Mnemosyne and Moneta. In the first *Hyperion,* Mnemosyne is presented as one who has watched over the growth of the young Apollo and has aided in the development of his gifts. He had dreamed of her, and awoke to find the lyre upon which he composed music to which "all the vast / Unwearied ear of the whole universe / Listen'd in pain and pleasure." This is an evident dramatization of one of Keats' most passionately held convictions: "The imagination may be compared to Adam's dream—he awoke and found it truth" (*Letters*, I, 185). The implication is plain: eternal beauty is revealed to the poet in his dreams; he awakes to find the means and power of communicating what he has seen, and the universe listens.

Mnemosyne has cast her lot in with the new gods. She tells Apollo:

> Show thy heart's secret to an ancient Power
> Who hath forsaken old and sacred thrones
> For prophecies of thee, and for the sake
> Of loveliness new born.[3]
> [*Hyperion*, III.76–79]

In her face Apollo reads the knowledge that will make him superior to Hyperion. As he suffers the agonies of transformation, Mnemosyne holds up her arms "as one who prophesied." If she is eternal beauty and truth, it is the beauty and truth always to be attained. She sanctions the struggle toward an ultimate perfection. If Keats is seeing himself as Apollo, then Mnemosyne symbolizes the knowledge that will make him immortal as a poet. She prophesies his future.

On the other hand, Moneta looks to the past. She is the goddess of eternal sorrow. She weeps for the beauty that has been destroyed by the new gods:

> This temple, sad and lone,
> Is all spar'd from the thunder of a war
> Foughten long since by Giant Hierarchy
> Against rebellion: this old Image here,
> Whose carved features wrinkled as he fell,
> Is Saturn's: I, Moneta, left supreme
> Sole priestess of his desolation.
> [*Fall of Hyperion*, I.221–27]

When she parts the veils that conceal her, the poet sees

> . . . a wan face
> Not pin'd by human sorrows, but bright blanch'd
> By an immortal sickness which kills not;
> It works a constant change, which happy death
> Can put no end to: deathwards progressing
> To no death was that visage.
> [*Fall of Hyperion*, I.256–61]

Before revealing her face, she has told the poet:

My power, which to me is still a curse,
Shall be to thee a wonder; for the scenes
Still swimming vivid through my globed brain,
With an electral changing misery,
Thou shalt with these dull mortal eyes behold,
Free from all pain, if wonder pain thee not.
                    [*Fall of Hyperion*, I.243–48]

Later, however, when the poet is given the power to see as a god sees, he finds "the load of this eternal quietude" almost unbearable and prays for death.

Moneta becomes, then, a terrifying incarnation of death-in-life, of beauty eternal decaying. Like the Grecian urn she preserves the record of a vanished perfection, but without hope or comfort. The temple of Saturn symbolizes a golden age destroyed. The triumph of the rebel gods represents not a "fresh perfection" but a falling off, a bringing of death into the world. Where in this retelling of the myth is there place for Apollo? So far as the fragment goes, there seems to be none. His role has been taken over by the poet who has been given the power through Moneta to see as a god sees. But the poet is simply the spectator, not a participant in the drama, except insofar as he identifies with the experience of the Titans. If Apollo was intended to appear, it was possibly as a reluctant participant in the rebellion, as a tragic figure who realizes that only evil can come of the overthrow of Hyperion—certainly not as a triumphant victor. For obviously Moneta has found in the rule of Apollo no consolation or solace for her loss.

Perhaps Kenneth Muir is right in saying that in *The Fall of Hyperion* Keats intended to dramatize some such conception as that sketched in the "vale of soul-making" letter.[4] The whole point of the vision, in the light of Moneta's castigation of the dreamer, seems to be to reveal to him the knowledge that will transform him into a poet able to mitigate and ease the suffering of mankind, to aid in "soul making." But, if so, then something has gone wrong. The poem has got out of hand. For the power Moneta gives the dreamer results in so overwhelming a realization of irretrievable loss that the effect is a paralyzing sense of futility or hopelessness. It is hard to see how the knowledge the dreamer gains through Moneta will aid in easing the suffering of mankind: it seems designed to confirm him in his morbid fear of his own utter inutility.

The reason for giving up the poem which Keats offers Reynolds, that "there were too many Miltonic inversions in it—Miltonic verse cannot be written but in an artful or rather artist's humour" (*Letters,* II, 167), is not very satisfying and sounds like a rationalization to conceal more significant reasons that he did not wish to admit, perhaps even to himself. In the entry for the same day in the journal letter to George and Georgiana, he says without mentioning *Hyperion* that life to Milton "would be death to me. Miltonic verse cannot be written but in the vein of art" (*Letters,* II, 212). The significant phrases in these letters are "artful or artist's humour" and "vein of art." They reveal that it was not simply a trick of style, but rather a point of view, an esthetics, which he was rejecting.

The dialogue between Moneta and the dreamer, who is clearly the self-centered artist, confirms this. The dreamer is condemned; only the selfless laborer for mortal good or the physician poet is praised. Through Moneta, Keats is condemning in himself the "artist's humour"; if he is to be a poet, he must write without thought of art. Yet *Hyperion* is an artist's vision, artificial and remote, the kind that "vexes the world," and that presumably the dreamer is to transcend by coming to the altar. In saying, then, that he gave up the poem because of its "Miltonic inversions," Keats was indicating by a kind of synecdoche his awareness that he had failed to write the kind of poem he had intended to write, the only kind by which he believed he could justify his continuance as an artist.

The reference to Milton becomes a way, conscious or not, of diverting attention from the fact that *The Fall of Hyperion* is Keats' boldest and most complex experiment in his own poetic idiom. It is also his most heroic effort to reconcile the esthetic and utilitarian functions of poetry, to resolve the conflicting desires in himself of escaping from the world through the poetic vision and of doing the world "some good." *The Fall of Hyperion* is first of all a "dream." The introduction is a painfully graphic account of the psychological process—the ascent into dream—which for Keats had always been an integral part of poetic creation. The poem then develops into a desperate attempt to justify the dream by its utility; to demonstrate that through the dream is revealed the truth by which the poet may pour "balm upon the world." But at the crucial point of the vision Moneta, who is to be the means of revelation, attacks the dreamer with vitriolic contempt, and, by asserting that the true laborers for mortal good, including poets, are no dreamers, she dooms the vision to failure. Instead of reconciling the functions of dreamer and poet, Keats impales himself on an apparently insoluble dilemma. He concedes that he can no longer justify the dream experience as a means of realizing the function of the poet, but he is incapable of proceeding in any other way to realize that function. The dialogue between the dreamer and Moneta indicates a crisis within Keats so severe as to threaten to paralyze him as an artist, regardless of his approaching illness.

II. ADAM'S DREAM

The crisis reflected in *The Fall of Hyperion* is the logical culmination of a dramatic struggle that begins with Keats' decision to abandon surgery for poetry and may be traced in its growing complexity through most of his poems and letters. The key to the struggle is in the dreamer's plea to Moneta:

> . . . sure not all
> Those melodies sung into the world's ear
> Are useless: sure a poet is a sage;
> A humanist, Physician to all men.
> [*Fall of Hyperion*, I.187–90]

Whatever his reason for marking these and the next twenty lines for revision or rejection,[5] we can be sure that it was not because Keats had changed his mind on this point. The series of equations in these lines is the most simple and direct statement of a faith to which he had clung from the moment he had thought of himself as a poet. A compulsive desire to prove the utility of poetry was common to all the poets of his generation, but Keats gave it an unmistakably personal emphasis. It is likely that he never got over a sense of guilt at abandoning surgery and that he felt called upon to justify his choice of poetry by transferring to it all the therapeutic powers of medicine. The common assumption is that he disliked his apprenticeship, and very probably he also disliked the routine and sordidness of the hospitals. There is plenty of testimony to the fact that Keats paid little attention to his instruction and that during lectures "his thoughts were far away in the land of Faery." [6] But a conscience so well developed as his must have ached at the decision to reject a career for which Abbey had spent in educating him more than his share of the estate, a career that furthermore was inescapably the quickest way "of doing the world some good." The uneasiness that accompanied his decision is reflected in the *Epistle* to his brother George, written in August, 1816, when he

was making up his mind. He recounts at length the satisfaction of the
dying poet as he thinks of the good his poetry will do for posterity, and
then unexpectedly he sighs:

> Ah, my dear friend and brother,
> Could I, at once, my mad ambition smother,
> For tasting joys like these, I should be
> Happier, and dearer to society.
>
> [*Epistle*, lines 109–12]

In the two major poems of the 1817 volume he stresses the specifically healing powers of poetry. The nuptials of Endymion and Cynthia
in *I Stood Tiptoe* were responsible for ethereal and pure breezes that

> . . . crept through half-closed lattices to cure
> The languid sick; it cool'd their fever'd sleep
> And soothed them into slumbers full and deep.
> Soon they awoke clear eyed; nor burnt with thirsting,
> Nor with hot fingers, nor with temples bursting. . . .
>
> [*I Stood Tiptoe*, lines 222–26]

And in *Sleep and Poetry* he chides poets like Byron for

> . . . forgetting the great end
> Of poesy, that it should be a friend
> To soothe the cares and lift the thoughts of man.
>
> [*Sleep and Poetry*, lines 245–47]

A little further on he says:

> And they shall be accounted poet kings
> Who simply tell the most heart-easing things.
>
> [*Sleep and Poetry*, lines 267–68]

In *Endymion*, Keats continues to emphasize the health-giving power
of the beauty which the poet contemplates. "A thing of beauty is a joy
forever" chiefly because it will always keep

> A bower quiet for us, and a sleep
> Full of sweet dreams, and health, and quiet breathing.
>
> [*Endymion*, I.4–5]

This is a motif clearly developed and varied through the poem, and
indeed some of the major episodes, like those of Adonis in Book II
and Glaucis in Book III, are concerned with the ultimate implications
of the motif—the restoration of life. The implications of the latter
episode are particularly plain. Endymion performing the magic ritual

and scattering the fragments of the scroll over the dead lovers is certainly the symbol of the life-giving poet.

In the light of this, the vicious attack in Blackwood's *Edinburgh Magazine* must have hurt Keats to the quick in the contrast it drew between apothecary and poet. As apothecary, said the reviewer, his talents would have made him a useful citizen; as a poet he was a sick man, even to the point of insanity, as shown by the "calm settled imperturbable drivelling idiocy" of *Endymion*. The contemptuous brutal conclusion of the review struck where Keats would have felt the most vulnerable:

> It is a better and a wiser thing to be a starved apothecary than a starved poet so back to the shop Mr. John, back to "plasters, pills, and ointment boxes." But for Heaven's sake, young Sangrado, be a little more sparing of extenuatives and soporifics in your practice than you have been in your poetry.[7]

This must have seemed to Keats the mocking echo of his own worst fears. In his castigation of himself in the second *Hyperion* as a sick dreamer, "a fever" of himself, who "venoms" all his days, we hear the far-off reverberations of this attack.

The immediate effect of such an attack was to aggravate the attitude of defiance and indifference to the public which Keats had assumed from the time of his rejected preface to *Endymion,* though he probably originally adopted the attitude under the influence of Hunt or Byron as the proper one of the young poet in revolt—the "public" then being for Keats conventional society and the conservative reviews. But because he cared so much what the public thought, because he needed so much to believe in his poetry as a public good, the attitude became an intensely personal defense mechanism, a protection against rejection and failure. Even as he was trying to subscribe to a theory of detachment, to an esthetic acceptance of beauty for its own sake, he continued in his poetry to emphasize the health-giving power of beauty. In *Hyperion,* Oceanus warns the Titans that, just as they show beyond heaven and earth a thousand signs "of purer life," so they will be followed by "a power more strong in beauty, born of us / And fated to excell us," and he uses the image of the soil that feeds the trees that tower above it. Let this truth, he says, "be your balm." In *The Eve of St. Agnes* the contrast is drawn between the young lovers, on the one hand, and the benightmared Baron and the dying Angela and beadsman, on the other. The song of the nightingale transports Keats momentarily beyond a world of sickness. The beauty of the urn rests partly in the transcendence of human frailty and suffering. But in the odes the tone of conviction turns to questioning as he is haunted by the awareness of the mutability of beauty, and in poems like the *Ode on Melancholy* and *Lamia* the perception of beauty becomes a source of vexation rather than of balm. And this loss of faith in the therapeutic power of beauty, and therefore in the kind of poetry he had been writing, helped precipitate the crisis of the second *Hyperion*.

The therapeutic power of poetry was for Keats inseparable from the psychological experience that accompanied or resulted in the creation of poetry. All of Keats' friends from Cowden Clark on testify to his abnormally intense concentration when reading or thinking of poetry. In May, 1817, Keats wrote Leigh Hunt that he had quit the Isle of Wight because he "thought so much about Poetry so long together that I could not get to sleep at night," and that he "was too much in Solitude, and consequently was obliged to be in continual burning of thought as an only resource" (*Letters,* I, 138–39). Dilke in commenting on this passage says: "He could at any time have 'thought himself out' mind and body. Thought was intense with him and seemed at times to assume a reality that influenced his conduct and I have no doubt helped to wear him out." [8]

Keats' intensity of concentration frequently approached a state of trance or autohypnosis. He very early described this as the condition for the creation of poetry, as in the *Epistle* to George:

> But there are times, when those that love the bay,
> Fly from all sorrowing far, far away;
> A sudden glow comes on them, naught they see
> In water, earth, or air, but poesy.
>
> [*Epistle,* lines 19–22]

The frank admission that the trance is a means of escape from "sorrowing" is significant. Contemporary records relate in horrifying detail the conditions of the hospitals and the terrible suffering of the patients with all of which Keats was intimately acquainted.[9] All accounts of him as a medical student agree with Stephens that "he seemed to sit apart and to be absorbed in something else as if the subject suggested thoughts to him which were not practically connected with it. He was often in the subject and out of it, in a dreamy way." Stephens also says that he had resigned himself to medicine as a career by which to live in a workaday world, "without being certain he could keep up the strain of it."[10] Brown writes that Keats assured him:

. . . the muse had no influence over him in his determination, he being compelled, by conscientious motives alone, to quit the profession, upon discovering that he was unfit to perform a surgical operation. He ascribed his inability to an overwrought apprehension of every possible chance of doing evil in the wrong direction of the instrument. "My last operation" he told me, "was the opening of a man's temporal artery. I did it with the utmost nicety; but, reflecting on what passed through my mind at the time, my dexterity seemed a miracle, and I never took up the lancet again." [11]

Though the assurance that the Muse had nothing to do with his decision seems a rationalization, the rest of the statement rings true. The almost morbid revulsion against surgery revealed by these comments undoubtedly aggravated the frequency and intensity of his withdrawal into dreams and thus became one of the major factors in the rapid acceleration of his poetic powers. By way of the vision he could shut out the ugliness and suffering of the life around him and at the same time promise himself that he would find an easier and better way of alleviating the misery of men.

The extent to which Keats staked the justification for his decision to devote himself to poetry on the dream experience is revealed in the vision of the charioteer in *Sleep and Poetry*. "O for ten years, that I may overwhelm / Myself in poesy," he says:

> First the realm I'll pass
> Of Flora and Old Pan: sleep in the grass,
> Feed upon apples red, and strawberries,
> And choose each pleasure that my fancy sees. . . .
> And can I ever bid these joys farewell?
> Yes, I must pass them for a nobler life,
> Where I may find the agonies, the strife
> Of human hearts: for lo! I see afar,
> O'ersailing the blue cragginess, a car. . . .
>
> [*Sleep and Poetry*, lines 101–4, 122–26]

The need now is not to fly from suffering but to find the agonies and strife of human hearts that evoke the vision. But significantly the charioteer's magic is hidden from the poet. The secret of the "wond'rous gesture" with which he talks to the trees and mountains, and which calls forth the "shapes of delight, of mystery and fear," is not revealed. Nor does the poet know what the charioteer learned from the figures and writes "with such a hurrying glow." No, he has only a kind of euphoria; it is enough to know that the truth about "human hearts" can be revealed in this way. The experience ends ominously:

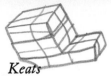

Keats

The visions all are fled—the car is fled
Into the light of heaven, and in their stead
A sense of real things comes doubly strong,
And like a muddy stream, would bear along
My soul to nothingness. . . .

[Sleep and Poetry, lines 155–59]

Here, in crude outline, is a pattern of the visionary journey that is fundamental to the theme and structure of so many of Keats' poems, and that culminates in *The Fall of Hyperion*—the intense sensuous experience preceding and perhaps inducing the visionary ascent or flight, the often momentary revelation of truth, and the sudden harsh return to "real things." The visionary journey suggests also the psychological pattern of exhilaration followed by exhaustion and depression which is a familiar accompaniment of creation, and which was particularly characteristic of Keats. At this time, he is not much disturbed by the aftermath of the vision; he will "strive / Against all doubtings," he says, by keeping alive the thought of the chariot and its journey; he is sustained, that is to say, by the confidence that at will he can renew the vision. And obviously he believes that by repetition of the experience he will ultimately acquire the power of the charioteer, become himself the charioteer, so that the vision will become the reality and there will be no annihilating aftermath. His confidence is given its most exuberant expression in the statement to Bailey, made in part as a comment on *Endymion:* "The imagination may be compared to Adam's dream—he awoke and found it truth."

Endymion is Keats' most elaborate and optimistic development of the dream pattern. Endymion's account to his sister of his first vision of Cynthia follows very closely the pattern in *Sleep and Poetry*. There is first the magic bed of "sacred ditamy and poppies red." Then he falls asleep and in "airy trance" soars on "visionary pinions" into the sky. He watches the moon, which gives way to the vision of Cynthia. Abruptly the vision fades, and he awakens to find that

> . . . the poppies hung
> Dew-dabbled on their stalks, the ouzel sung
> A heavy ditty, and the sullen day
> Had chidden herald Hesperus away,
> With leaden looks. . . .
> Away I wander'd—all the pleasant hues
> Of heaven and earth had faded: deepest shades
> Were deepest dungeons; heaths and sunny glades

Were full of pestilent light; our taintless rills
Seem'd sooty, and o'er spread with upturn'd gills
Of dying fish; the vermeil rose had blown
In frightful scarlet, and its thorns out-grown
Like spiked aloe.

[*End.,* I.682–86, 691–98]

This cycle of experience is repeated in crucial episodes throughout the poem. The most complex variation is in the last book when Endymion and the Indian Maid are carried skyward by the winged horses. Soon the purple mist of Sleep curls around them. In a strained conceit, Sleep is presented as journeying to the wedding of Endymion and Cynthia of which he (Sleep) had dreamed. Now Endymion dreams that he is in heaven and that he sees his goddess, and immediately he awakes and

Beheld awake his very dream: the gods
Stood smiling; merry Hebe laughs and nods;
And Phoebe bends towards him crescented.

[*End.,* IV.436–38]

Endymion is torn between Phoebe and the Indian Maid who is sleeping by his side. He kisses the Indian Maid, and the goddess melts away. The Maid awakes, and he pledges himself to her. The horses emerge from the mists of Sleep; they fly toward the rising moon, and now the Indian Maid fades, leaving Endymion to descend to earth alone. Before he does he passes into the Cave of Quietude, the state of utter despair and exhaustion. It is also the state of dreamless sleep, and therefore "the dark Paradise" where the soul is renewed (*End.,* IV, 513–548). When Endymion leaves it and returns to the earth, he renounces the dream and vows to devote himself to the Indian Maid. But she tells him she may not be his love: he decides to become a hermit, and she a priestess of Cynthia. The upshot is, of course, that the Indian Maid is transformed into Cynthia. The cycle has been broken; dream and reality are at last one.

Keats is evidently attempting in this involved and overextended sequence to chart the exact relationship between dream and reality—to trace the process by which one comes to a revelation of the unity of dream and reality. One must take a preoccupation with reality, the "agony and strife" of human hearts (the Indian Maid), into the dream, he indicates; perhaps, even, one must renounce the dream for the reality in order to realize it. Somehow, at any rate, renunciation and

[146]

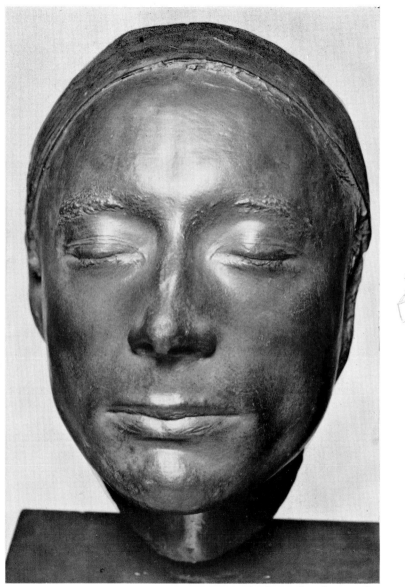

Life mask of Keats, by B. R. Haydon, 1818

suffering are necessary if the dream is to come true. If the last part of
the fourth book seems labored and blurred, it is partly because Keats
is working out what he fervently hopes to experience rather than what
he has experienced; he does not know how the poem should end; he
desperately wants to present a profound revelation of truth but is reduced to substituting ingenuity for insight. Significantly, the most
powerful passage is the description of the Cave of Quietude—that
psychological hell "made for the soul to wander in and trace / Its own
existence" to which Endymion descends when it seems that he has lost
both Cynthia and the Indian Maid. The sharp detail of the description
leaves no doubt of the fullness of Keats' experience here, and the
potential threat to his creativity is evident.

Nevertheless, the over-all tone of *Endymion* is one of confidence.
And the completion of the poem gave Keats renewed faith in himself
and in the intrinsic worth of his poetic experiences. Even if the ultimate
truths were still concealed from him, he could enjoy for its own sake
the beauty that contained them. It was in this mood of happy confidence that

> . . . several things dovetailed in my mind, and at once it struck me what quality
> went to form a Man of Achievement, especially in literature, and which Shake-
> speare possessed so enormously—I mean *Negative Capability,* that is, when a
> man is capable of being in uncertainties, Mysteries, doubts, without any irritable
> reaching after fact & reason.

The great poet is content with half-knowledge for with him "the sense
of Beauty overcomes every other consideration, or rather obliterates all
consideration" (*Letters,* I, 193–94).[12] Keats could afford to enunciate an
attitude so sweepingly contrary (on the surface at least) to his previous
statements and practice because of his faith in his "favorite speculation"
that "what the imagination seizes as Beauty must be truth" (*Letters,*
I, 184). For the moment he felt set free from the need to justify poetry
in terms of its immediate utility.

But the happy confidence reflected in this speculation did not last
long. During the following months a number of factors provoked a
mood of deepening melancholy and doubt. The growing seriousness
of Tom's illness and the gloomy weather of Devonshire seem to have
been the immediate causes of the reflections that conclude the verse
epistle to Reynolds for March 25, 1818. Keats is distressed by the kind
of dreams he has had recently, by the direction taken by his observations and meditations. If only, he sighs, our sleeping and waking

dreams would take their colors from the sunset, "rather than shadow our own soul's daytime / In the dark void of night." He implies that he has been unable to avoid an irritable reaching after fact and reason and that this has shaken his confidence:

> It is a flaw
> In happiness to see beyond our bourn—
> It forces us in Summer skies to mourn:
> It spoils the singing of the Nightingale.
> [*Epistle to Reynolds*, lines 82–85]

From the perspective of these lines, the great advantage of "negative capability" would be in providing an escape from philosophy, specifically a refuge from doubt. It could be used as an argument for not thinking. But Keats had too stern a conscience, too keen an intellectual curiosity, to be content for any length of time with half knowledge. In the epistle he goes on to tell Reynolds of a quiet evening by the sea when he should have been "most happy":

> . . . but I saw
> Too far into the sea; where every maw
> The greater on the less feeds evermore:—
> But I saw too distinct into the core
> Of an eternal fierce destruction. . . .
> The shark at savage prey—the hawk at pounce,—
> The gentle Robin, like a pard or ounce
> Ravening a worm. . . .
> [*Epistle to Reynolds*, lines 93–97, 103–5; *Letters*, I, 259–63]

The "sense of real things" has for the moment swept aside the vision of harmony and love to reveal a nightmare of cruelty and destruction. The truth in the beauty seized by the imagination can be evil as well as good, destructive as well as therapeutic. The doubt has been instilled which is from now on to "venom" all Keats' days.

At first he hopes that, by increase of knowledge, the mystery can be penetrated and the apparent evil explained. On May 3, 1818, he develops for Reynolds his comparison of human life to a mansion of many chambers, in which the simple evolutionary concept expressed in *Sleep and Poetry* is expanded and enriched. He describes the intoxicating pleasures of the Chamber of Maiden Thought and continues:

However among the effects this breathing is father of is that tremendous one of sharpening one's vision into the heart and nature of Man—of convincing one's nerves that the world is full of Misery and Heartbreak, Pain, Sickness and oppression—whereby This Chamber of Maiden Thought becomes gradually darken'd and at the same time on all sides of it many doors are set open—but all dark— all leading to dark passages.—We see not the ballance of good and evil. We are in a Mist.—*We* are now in that state—We feel the "burden of the Mystery. . . ."

Wordsworth's genius, Keats believes, "is explorative of those dark passages," and in this respect he has gone beyond Milton. This does not prove that Wordsworth is a greater philosopher than Milton, but that "there is really a grand march of intellect" (*Letters*, I, 281–82).

It is the idea of progress expressed in this letter that the first *Hyperion* is apparently intended to dramatize. The grand march of intellect, led by the poets, which would explain the dark chambers and illuminate the mystery, and the grand march of beauty, envisioned by Oceanus, are certainly for Keats one and the same. In *Hyperion*, Keats makes his most sweeping claims for the visionary experience as the way to knowledge and progress. Apollo is the poet-dreamer; Mnemosyne is more than memory—she is the creative mother of the Muses. As we have pointed out, after Apollo first dreams of her he awakes to find the lyre to which, as he plays, all the universe listens. And the "wondrous lesson" that he reads in the face of the goddess and that transforms him is the lesson Keats longed to learn from the writing of the charioteer.

> Knowledge enormous makes a God of me,
> Names, deeds, gray legends, dire events, rebellions,
> Majesties, sovran voices, agonies,
> Creations and destroyings, all at once
> Pour into the wide hollows of my brain
> And deify me. . . .
> [*Hyperion*, III.113–18]

This is the high-water mark of Keats' expression of confidence in the dream; here, in the transformation of a poet into a god, is his most extravagant symbolic act. But it is significant that with the gesture he stops—before the lesson is revealed and before we can see the effect upon Apollo. What has happened is that, even as he was writing *Hyperion*, Keats was losing faith in its basic assumptions—perfectibility through beauty, and the truth of the poetic vision. He could not go on with *Hyperion* partly because his vision failed him just at the moment of revelation.

III. COLD PHILOSOPHY

The record of Keats' changing attitudes, his growing uncertainty and anxiety, is to be found in his letters. In the famous letter to Woodhouse of October 27, 1818 (*Letters,* I, 386–88), written before or just after he began *Hyperion,* he distinguishes sharply between the function of poetry and his ambition "of doing the world some good." [13] Embittered by the vicious reviews, shaken by Tom's suffering, disturbed probably by further glimpses into the "core of an eternal fierce destruction" and his failure to find the illumination he had been seeking through poetic vision, he falls back upon the conception of "negative capability" and develops it as a defense against hurt and disillusionment, as a justification for the writing of poetry for its own sake. Turning his back on the attitudes he had expressed to Reynolds in May, he draws a harsh distinction between the poetical character "of which, if I am anything, I am a member" and the Wordsworthian or egotistical sublime. The ideal poetical character "has no character—it enjoys light and shade; it lives in gusto, be it foul or fair, high or low, rich or poor, mean or elevated. It has as much delight in conceiving an Iago as an Imogen. What shocks the virtuous philosopher, delights the Cameleon Poet."

Here he deliberately divorces the poet and the philosopher. And he goes on to divorce poetry from utility:

I am ambitious of doing the world some good: if I should be spared that may be the work of maturer years—in the interval I will assay to reach as high a summit in Poetry as the nerve bestowed upon me will suffer. . . . All I hope is that I may not lose all interest in human affairs—that the solitary indifference I feel for applause even from the finest Spirits, will not blunt any acuteness of vision I may have. I do not think it will—I feel assured I should write from the mere yearning and fondness I have for the Beautiful even if my night's labours should be burnt every morning and no eye ever shine upon them. But even now I am perhaps not speaking from myself: but from some character in whose soul I now live.

And, certainly, he was. To say this is not to question Keats' sincerity in his "speculation"—the sincerity is evident—but to point out that, within the context of his work at the time, his claim that he possessed this detachment was a rationalization, a protection against the potential failure of his poetry to realize the demands he made on it. *Hyperion,* which the letter indicates he was contemplating if not actually writing, refutes it. He was vitally interested in human affairs; he was athirst for fame and "applause"; and he was almost desperately ambitious that his poetry should do the world some good. And, though he undoubtedly lived "in gusto," he was depressed by the mean, the low, the poor, and particularly the evil.

The clash between theory and practice becomes critical in three long "speculations" in the journal letter to George and Georgiana for February–May, 1819: the quotations from Hazlitt (March 12), the passage on "disinterestedness" (March 19), and the observations on "perfectibility" (between April 15 and 30).

The discussion of "disinterestedness" carries to its logical conclusion the distinction between poetry and philosophy that Keats had drawn for Woodhouse. Disinterestedness he equates with "a pure desire of the benefit of others." Few men have arrived at complete disinterestedness; he can remember but two, Socrates and Jesus, and he realizes how far he is from it. "Yet this feeling ought to be carried to its highest pitch as there is no fear of its ever injuring society—which it would do I fear pushed to an extremity." And to illustrate his point he returns to the imagery of the verse letter to Reynolds: "The Hawk would loose his breakfast of Robins and the Robin his of worms." Most men make their way "with the same instinctiveness as the hawk." To observe the similarity between man and hawk or man and field mouse "makes the Amusement of Life—to a speculative Mind." And he is led to the much-discussed, ambiguous conclusion:

> May there not be superior beings amused with any graceful though instinctive attitude my mind may fall into, as I am entertained with the alertness of a Stoat or the anxiety of a Deer? Though a quarrel in the streets is a thing to be hated, the energies displayed in it are fine; the commonest Man shows a grace in his quarrel—By a superior being our reasoning may take the same tone—though erroneous they may be fine—This is the very thing in which consists poetry; and if so it is not so fine a thing as philosophy—For the same reason that an eagle is not so fine a thing as a truth [*Letters*, II, 79–80].

Most critics, commenting on this passage, find various ingenious reasons for not believing that Keats meant what he said in the distinction he drew between "philosophy" and "poetry." Recently, for example, Muir has said hopefully, "He probably meant merely that poetry, to be great, must be an image of truth." [14] But an "image of truth" is exactly what Keats said that poetry is not concerned with being if truth is to be defined, as he obviously defined it, as the good or beneficent. There is indeed no reason to doubt that he made his distinction deliberately, with full awareness of its implications. It grows out of the distinction he has been carefully—if not too clearly—drawing between disinterestedness and what might be called detachment or negative capability. The amused observation of behavior, the perception of beauty in action, cruel or erroneous—these are proper functions of the poetical character as he described it to Woodhouse. And from this point of view poetry, which enjoys without desiring to change the state of things, is not so fine as philosophy, which is moved "by a pure desire of the benefit of others."

In drawing this distinction, Keats has been strongly influenced or at least confirmed in his opinion by the long passage from Hazlitt's letter to Gifford which he had so painstakingly copied a few days before. It undoubtedly meant much to Keats: he did not need to fill up space in his letters; he had plenty of his own "speculations," and there was no point in copying several pages unless he felt they were saying something important.[15] In fact, his enthusiastic approval is obvious. He introduces it as "this fine passage," and he concludes: "The manner in which this is managed: the force and innate power with which it yeasts and works up itself—the feeling for the costume of society; is in a style of genius—He hath a demon, as he himself says of Lord Byron."

In the copied passage Hazlitt is defending himself against Gifford's charge that in his *Characters of Shakespeare's Plays* he slandered Shakespeare in saying that the playwright seemed to have had a leaning to the arbitrary side of the question and "to have spared no occasion of baiting the rabble" in *Coriolanus*. Hazlitt had tried to account for this leaning by showing that "the cause of the people is but little calculated for a subject for Poetry or that the language of Poetry naturally falls in with the language of power." Hazlitt's reply to Gifford is worth quoting at some length to bring out its relevance to Keats' later remarks on disinterestedness.

I affirm, Sir, that Poetry, that the imagination, generally speaking, delights in power, in strong excitement, as well as in truth, in good, in right, whereas pure reason and the moral sense approve only of the true and the good. I proceed to show that this general love or tendency to immediate excitement or theatrical effect, no matter how produced, gives a Bias to the imagination often inconsistent with the greatest good, that in Poetry it triumphs over Principle, and bribes the passions to make a sacrifice of common humanity. . . . "Do we read with more pleasure of the ravages of a beast of prey than of the Shepherd's pipe upon the Mountain?" [Gifford] No but we do read with pleasure of the ravages of a beast of prey, and we do so on the principle I have stated, namely from the sense of power abstracted from the sense of good; and it is the same principle that makes us read with admiration and reconciles us in fact to the triumphant progress of the conquerors and mighty Hunters of mankind, who come to stope the shepherd's Pipe upon the Mountains and sweep away his listening flock [*Letters,* II, 74-75].[16]

Now, though Keats claims for poetry a detachment that Hazlitt does not, nevertheless his conception of poetry as consisting in the presentation of graceful and instinctive attitudes, regardless of whether they are morally good (the quarrel in the streets) or true (our reasonings), is clearly related to Hazlitt's conception of poetry as delighting in power. The images Keats uses are what Hazlitt would call images of power. And the rating of poetry below philosophy takes on fresh significance from Hazlitt's statement that poetry delights primarily in power whereas pure reason and the moral sense approve only of the true and the good.

Keats must also have been struck by Hazlitt's allusion to "the triumphant progress of the conquerors and mighty Hunters of mankind, who come to stope the shepherd's Pipe," for the implications are exactly opposite to the implications of *Hyperion*. In the light of Hazlitt's and Keats' arguments, Oceanus' generalization, "Tis the eternal law / That first in Beauty should be first in might," takes on ironic overtones. The first in beauty need not be the true or good, but only the most powerful. What one saw in "wild nature" was the triumph of the hawk over the robin, the robin over the worm, the hunter over the shepherd. What justification was there for presenting the triumph of Apollo, as Keats had conceived him, over Hyperion?

From still another point of view Keats had lost faith in perfectibility. A month after the disinterestedness passage he writes of his reactions to two books, Robertson's *America* and Voltaire's *Siècle de Louis XIV*:

The whole appears to resolve into this—that Man is originally "a poor forked creature" subject to the same mischances as the beasts of the forest, destined to hardships and disquietude of some kind or other. . . . The most interesting question that can come before us is, How far by the persevering endeavors of a seldom appearing Socrates Mankind may be made happy—I can imagine such happiness carried to an extreme—but what must it end in?—Death—and who could in such a case bear with death. . . . But in truth I do not at all believe in this sort of perfectibility the nature of the world will not admit of it—the inhabitants of the world will correspond to itself. . . . The point at which Man may arrive is as far as the parallel state in inanimate nature and no further . . . [*Letters*, II, 101].

These passages written in March–April, 1819, reveal carefully thought-out and consistent attitudes that would make the continuation of *Hyperion* difficult or even impossible. *Hyperion* was a philosophical poem; and Keats, during the whole period of its composition from October to April, was trying to convince himself that the function of poetry should be different from and inferior to philosophy. More important, perhaps, was the fact that he could no longer accept or believe in the philosophy of the poem. The evolutionary creed of Oceanus was too simple, too naïve for the Keats of the journal letter. *Hyperion* was an epic about gods, but very plainly its philosophy was for men. And the history of neither gods nor men supported so optimistic a faith.

The progress from Hyperion to Apollo was a progress in power whose beauty was to be admired but not rationalized by the poet. Furthermore, *Hyperion* failed to take into account the limitations of nature and human life, of which Keats had now become acutely aware. Above the gods, as above men, was "a heaven with its stars," and the beauty of the gods was subject to decay and death. There was a point beyond which beauty could not progress, and this point was constant and eternal, known to every generation. In fact, there could be no "fresh perfection" of beauty; there could be only the cyclic growth and decay within the order of nature. From the perspective of the journal letter, Hyperion would be as beautiful as Apollo. It was probably Keats' awareness of this that caused him to shift the emphasis in the third book from Apollo's beauty to the knowledge acquired through suffering and vision. But in doing so he altered the theme of the poem, and he may very well have decided that, rather than revise the first two books to fit in with his new conception, it would be better to start over again.

Finally, as we have earlier pointed out, Keats stopped the poem abruptly just on the verge of revelation—just as "the burden of the mystery" was to be lifted. The manner in which Apollo is to be transformed—through gazing upon the face of Mnemosyne—symbolizes Keats' unquenchable hope: that knowledge can be gained spontaneously, intuitively, as in Adam's dream. But what is the knowledge that is to transform Apollo? The journal letter indicates that Keats did not know and that he had come to doubt that it could be discovered by way of poetry. The writing of the charioteer is still hidden from him; the mood in which he abandons *Hyperion* is probably best caught by the statement in his speculation on disinterestedness, that he is "straining at particles of light in the midst of a great darkness— without knowing the bearing of any one assertion, any one opinion."

IV. BEAUTY AND TRUTH

In spite of the speculations of the journal letter, it was impossible for Keats as an artist to accept the conclusion that poetry was inferior to philosophy; or, more specifically, that the beauty "seized" by the imagination was not necessarily truth (in the sense in which he always uses the word "truth"—as an aspect of an eternal good, beneficent to man). His restless perplexity and troubled vacillation, the swiftness with which his attitudes swung from confidence to doubt, from questioning to acceptance, are revealed by considering the great odes, written in April and May, in relation to one another. Like variations on a theme in music, they reflect the changing, conflicting moods with which Keats contemplates the artistic experience.

Most in keeping with the attitude of the speculations is the earliest written, the *Ode to Psyche,* which was sent as part of the journal letter. Keats said of it significantly that it was the only poem with which he had taken "even moderate pains . . . I think it reads the more richly for it and will I hope encourage me to write other things in even a more peaceable and healthy spirit." And the happy, confident tone of the ode is evidence of the peaceable and healthy spirit. Psyche symbolizes specifically the Ideal Beauty in whose name the artist creates:

> Yes, I will be thy priest, and build a fane
> In some untrodden region of my mind! . . .
> [*Psyche*, lines 50–51]

But, as the lines suggest, she lives only through the creative activity of his imagination, and thus the poem becomes a serene statement of the self-sufficiency of the artist's vision. The mind creates its own religion, its own beauty, which it worships for its own sake.[17]

The *Ode on Indolence* carries the mood of the *Ode to Psyche* to its ultimate implications. In a setting similar to that of *Psyche,* it celebrates a state of suspended thought, of absorption into the immediate sensuous experience so complete that even poetic activity is a destruc-

tive intruder. This is the ideal state of detachment, self-sufficient and
self-justifying, in which questions of value lose all meaning or are forgotten in the intensity of the experience, in the worship of Psyche, as
it were. But from the outset it is threatened by the figures of Love,
Ambition, and Poetry. The poem dramatizes the struggle between the
desire to shut out the figures:

> O, why did ye not melt, and leave my sense
> Unhaunted quite of all but—nothingness?
> [*Indolence,* lines 19–20]

and the almost irresistible temptation to pursue them, even as they
fade:

> To follow them I burn'd
> And ached for wings because I knew the three. . . .
> [*Indolence,* lines 33–34]

In the end Keats resists them and tries to banish them or absorb them
back into the dream by rhetorical incantation:

> Fade softly from my eyes, and be once more
> In masque-like figures on the dreamy urn;
> Farewell! I yet have visions for the night,
> And for the day faint visions there is store;
> Vanish, ye Phantoms! from my idle spright,
> Into the clouds, and never more return!
> [*Indolence,* lines 55–60]

Within the poem, he has preserved his dream world inviolate and
fought off the temptations to leave it. He has his "store" of visions and
can get along without the "phantoms." And yet the concluding command rings hollow; he seems to be making a half-whimsical gesture,
conceding defeat as he makes it. He can command, but he is powerless
to make the phantoms obey.

The mood of *Indolence* was not one, as a matter of fact, with which
Keats could be contented long, if only because his "demon poesy" was
excluded. The magnificent momentary resolution of his dilemma, in
which the artist's vision becomes on its own terms "as fine a thing as
philosophy," is achieved in the *Ode on a Grecian Urn.* The setting is
again like that of *Psyche,* but now it is contemplated as it has been
transferred to and preserved in the work of art, or as it would be preserved (for the urn is the creation of Keats' imagination, like the
"dreamy urn" of *Indolence*). Where in *Indolence* the figures on the

urn, and therefore the creation of art itself, threaten his happiness, in this ode the urn becomes the means of fulfillment by objectifying the artist's vision, giving it form and permanence, so that it becomes an enduring source of comfort not only to himself but to generations of men. Thus the artist's escape into indolence and vision is justified.

The urn raises questions to which no answers can or need be given; the observer is made "capable of being in uncertainties, Mysteries, doubts," of remaining content with half knowledge in the contemplation of the "graceful, though instinctive attitudes" pictured on the urn. In the journal letter Keats had considered poetry not so fine as philosophy because of its concern with attitudes, but now within the context of the ode he finds in the ritualized presentation of attitudes the great virtue and vindication of art. Nature and human life have been caught at the points of highest potential happiness—spring, youth, love about to be consummated—all freed from the evils and sorrows of mutability. These become the reflection and anticipation of an eternal principle and symbolize all that man knows or needs know of truth on earth. Keats' most fervent hope has become triumphant assertion, growing inevitably out of the process of creating the poem and demonstrated by the completed poem. The urn—through the poem that creates it—will perform by its silent existence the disinterested function of "doing the world some good." It will remain,

> . . . in midst of other woe
> Than ours, a friend to man, to whom thou say'st,
> "Beauty is truth, truth beauty."
>
> [*Urn,* lines 47–49]

I. A. Richards has said of the concluding lines in *Mencius on the Mind:* "Urns induce states of mind in their beholders; they do not enunciate philosophical positions—not in this kind of poetry—and *say'st* here is used by a metaphor which should not be overlooked." [18] In other words, he sees the urn's statement as what he has called pseudo-statement, "a form of words which is justified entirely by its effect in releasing or organizing our impulses and attitudes" and whose scientific truth or falsity is irrelevant to its purpose. [19] Eliot, though he professed to find the statement meaningless, was "sure that Keats would have repudiated any explanation of the line which called it a pseudo-statement." [20]

Actually, Keats would very likely have agreed with Richards. His speculation in the journal letter, written only a few weeks before the ode, shows that he had come very seriously to doubt that "what the imagination seizes as beauty must be truth" in any absolute sense. Indeed, he had gone so far as to imply that the enjoyment of beauty had nothing to do with truth or goodness. But in the excitement of speculation he had undoubtedly been swept further than he would willingly go.[21] The attitude by which as artist he wanted to live is the attitude of the urn. It is worth emphasizing again that the urn and the poet raise questions that they do not pretend to answer. Neither urn nor poet claims to reveal ultimate truth. When contemplated within the universal frame, the silent form of the urn does "tease us out of thought / As doth Eternity." It does nothing to reveal the mystery, rather by its existence intensifies it. But, within the frame of human life, it is a friend to man whose message is all that he knows or needs know. The truth on the urn is relative. What the urn has provided is a series of idealizations of earthly life—a "magical view of life" that gives purpose and meaning to human life in the midst of suffering. The urn becomes, in Richards' definition of pseudo-statement, an instrument by which "we order our attitudes to one another and to the world."

Yet this triumphant vindication of the poetic vision can be only a momentary consolation, for it is attained in the poem through transcending the "agonies and strife" of human hearts. The urn is a "silent form," a "cold pastoral"; it is, in itself, lifeless; and the truth it presents has in it the "transcendental chill" of death.[22] Outside the poem, within the larger context of Keats' life, the message of the urn is at best but a half truth, to be lost in the return to the misery of everyday living. It is the *Ode to a Nightingale* that expresses what is at this time probably Keats' most frequent experience. The pattern of the poem follows that pattern of ascent through the sensuous experience into the dream and the abrupt return to reality which we have traced in *Sleep and Poetry* and *Endymion*. It is important to note that here for the first time Keats uses the dream experience as a self-contained form. Theme and structure are one.

The ode begins with the intense sensuous enjoyment of the song of the bird, so intense that the senses seem drugged. The poet longs for the draught of vintage that will enable him to join the bird, but it is finally on "the viewless wings of Poesy" that he flies to him. Quite frankly now, he wants not to find the agony and strife of human hearts but to escape from them, to "quite forget the weariness, the fever and the fret." Furthermore, the world of the nightingale is one of "embalmed darkness," a place of life-in-death, where death becomes the eternal prolongation of the dream:

> Still wouldst thou sing, and I have ears in vain—
> To thy high requiem become a sod.
> [*Nightingale,* lines 59–60]

This is the world of the *Ode on Indolence,* but it is also the world of the *Urn.* Sensuous annihilation becomes imperceptibly and paradoxically the eternal suspension of life at the present point of heightened consciousness. The song of the bird, like the scenes on the urn, gives meaning and continuity to mortal life; it charms the "magic casements" and reveals the beauty of faerylands to the imagination of the poet. But the moment of revelation is the moment of despair: the faerylands are "forlorn," with no reality except in the dream of the poet. The recognition "tolls" him back to his "sole self." The fancy, he says wistfully, "cannot cheat so well / As she is fam'd to do"; he cannot for long escape from the "sense of real things"; it is useless for him to pretend that he can live in the world of the bird. Or does he mean even more— that it is useless to pretend any longer that the song of the bird has an ultimate meaning? As the "plaintive anthem" fades and at last is "buried" in the next valley glades, he desperately keeps alive the hope that it does have ultimate meaning:

> Was it a vision, or a waking dream?
> Fled is that music:—Do I wake or sleep?
> [*Nightingale,* lines 79–80]

In the *Ode on Melancholy,* Keats neither questions nor attempts to flee the world of mortality. Instead he accepts and even savors the paradox that the full enjoyment of beauty is inseparable from an awareness of mutability. This is the mood which from now on becomes dominant. Even within the poem, the delicate balance of the paradox is threatened by the overemphasis upon mutability. In the months that follow there is a steady deepening of the mood, until it becomes tinged with bitterness and cynicism. The nagging sore throat and his almost certain awareness of what it forewarned may have been partly responsible for his increasing dejection. In fact, he may already by May have been suffering from the debilitating effects of tuberculosis. Two other elements—the terrible, almost inexpressible complexity of his feeling for Fanny Brawne, and a growing conviction that, in Hazlitt's words, "the necessary advances of civilizations . . . are unfavorable to the spirit of poetry"—helped to undermine his confidence in the dream and poison his will to write.

Keats' love for Fanny Brawne had turned out to be far different from the love he had so blithely envisioned in *Endymion.* Fanny's beauty gradually takes on sinister connotations; it enslaves him and threatens to destroy him. He resents what he considers the irresponsible cruelty of the possessor of the beauty, who makes it impossible for him to think of anything else and yet gives him no happiness. It was inevitable that with his intense idealism Keats would fall violently in love and demand what no one could return. It was inevitable that he would discover thereby the darker side of love, no matter who the woman was.

In April, he had given perfect poetic expression to this discovery in *La Belle Dame sans Merci,* which he sent as part of the journal letter. The ballad follows the familiar pattern we have been tracing but with terrifyingly different results. It becomes an ironic comment on Endymion's dream and the speculations in the letter to Bailey. The love of the "faery's child" leads to a vision of those who have been destroyed by her, and the knight awakes to find the vision true. Whether or not the poem grew out of personal disillusionment, it anticipates strikingly the attitude of the letters to Fanny in July, 1819:

Ask yourself my love whether you are not very cruel to have so entrammelled me, so destroyed my freedom [*Letters,* II, 123].

All my thoughts, my unhappiest days and nights have I find not at all cured me of my love of Beauty, but made it so intense that I am miserable that you are not with me; or rather breathe in that dull sort of patience that cannot be called life. I never knew before, what such a love as you have made me feel, was; I did not believe in it; my Fancy was afraid of it, lest it should burn me up [*Letters,* II, 126].

Love had proved to be no spiritualization, but an enslavement; and Fanny a Circe instead of a Cynthia.

Sometimes he identifies his possession of her love and of death in the same way that he identifies the song of the nightingale and death, as a means of escape from the world:

I have two luxuries to brood over in my walks, your Loveliness and the hour of my death. O that I could have possession of them both in the same minute. I hate the world: it batters too much the wings of my self-will, and would I could take a sweet poison from your lips to send me out of it [*Letters,* II, 133].

But this bitter dream was as forlorn as that inspired by the nightingale's song; all that he could know was the torture of frustration. It is not strange, then, that he also identified his love for her with his resentment of the public. He had come to Shanklin in the summer of 1819 with the intention of writing for immediate profit. His resentment against the circumstances that forced him to write for money, of which the faint hope of being able to marry Fanny was one, led to violent attacks on the public and to claims of his indifference to public approval. To Taylor he wrote defiantly on August 23, "I have confidence that if I choose I may be a popular writer; that I will never be; but for all that I will get a livelihood—I equally dislike the favour of the public with the love of a woman—they are both a cloying treacle to the wings of independence" (*Letters*, II, 144). This statement was made during the time when Keats was composing the last part of *Lamia*, and it must owe something of its violence to his personal involvement in the situation of the poem. It is significant that on September 5 he tells Taylor he has finished *Lamia* and sends him as "a good sample of the Story" the savage lines, omitted in the printed version, describing the guests at the feast (*Letters*, II, 157–59). These lines are obviously intended to satirize the "public."

His conflicting attitudes toward Fanny Brawne are at least partially responsible for the ambiguity in the portrayal of Lamia which has bothered so many critics. He is consistently sympathetic in his treatment of Lamia, but in the first part of the poem she clearly stands primarily for the power and desire in women to enslave men by their beauty and to make them forget everything except sensual love. She is no Cynthia who wishes to "ensky" Endymion, no dependent Indian Maid, but " a real woman" metamorphosed from a serpent. The sinister connotations of the source of her power cannot be obliterated, no matter how beautiful as serpent and as woman Keats makes her.

In the second part, however, at the point when Lycius determines upon a public wedding in order to show her off in spite of her tearful protests, Keats' conception of her begins to change or perhaps to enlarge. She takes on the connotation of an ideal or dream love. Lycius is ultimately responsible for the catastrophe by his desire to display her. Had he been willing to keep her to himself, he might never have lost her. The implication is plain that only through utter withdrawal from the world can the visionary beauty and love retain reality.

In the end Lamia very definitely comes to symbolize Keats' "demon poesy." She is the poet's dream, the beauty his imagination seizes as truth, and she is destroyed by philosophy, by superior knowledge. There is no doubt as to this; the famous insertion is quite specific:

> Do not all charms fly
> At the mere touch of cold philosophy?
> There was an awful rainbow once in heaven:
> We know her woof, her texture; she is given
> In the dull catalogue of common things.
> Philosophy will clip an Angel's wings,
> Conquer all mysteries by rule and line,
> Empty the haunted air, and gnomed mine—
> Unweave a rainbow, as it erewhile made
> The tender-person'd Lamia melt into a shade.
>
> [*Lamia*, lines 229–38]

Once again the particular form of his argument was probably suggested to Keats by Hazlitt. His impassioned generalizations bear the same relationship to certain matter-of-fact statements in "Poetry in General" as the speculations in the journal letter bear to the *Letter to Gifford*. Hazlitt says:

. . . poetry is one part of the history of the human mind, though it is neither science nor philosophy. It cannot be concealed, however, that the progress of knowledge and refinement has a tendency to circumscribe the limits of the imagination, and to clip the wings of poetry. The province of the imagination is principally visionary, the unknown and undefined; the understanding restores things to their natural boundaries, and strips them of their fanciful pretensions. Hence the history of religious and poetical enthusiasm is much the same; and both have received a sensible shock from the progress of experimental philosophy. . . . There can never be another Jacob's dream. Since that time, the heavens have gone farther off and grown astronomical. They have become averse to the imagination, nor will they return to us on the squares of the distances. . . . It is not only the progress of mechanical knowledge, but the necessary advances of civilization that are unfavorable to the spirit of poetry. . . . Society, by degrees, is constructed into a machine that carries us safely and insipidly from one end of life to the other, in a very comfortable prose style.[23]

Now Hazlitt, though he concedes that poetry will be circumscribed by the advancement of science, emphasizes in the rest of his essay that it remains an important and necessary part of human experience. He is at pains to point out that poetry has a validity which cannot and should not be measured by scientific criteria, and which cannot be destroyed: "poetry is one part of the history of the human mind, though it is neither science nor philosophy." His position is not far from that of

Keats in the journal letter and the *Ode on a Grecian Urn*. But Keats is no longer content with that position. As the context of the passage shows, he is thinking of the rainbow not as a physical phenomenon but as a sign of divine power, symbol of the "magical view" of the universe. And, because science has made belief in the symbol impossible, he cries out in bitter resentment that the beauty of the rainbow has been destroyed also. The extent of his disenchantment is marked by the fact that it is Lamia's fate which suggests to him the larger question.[24]

Lamia, if not simply the serpent Apollonius calls her, is, nevertheless, a snake-woman who, stripped of her "fanciful pretensions," vanishes under the scrutiny of the understanding. Her beauty is delusory, the "purple-hued palace of sweet sin" is a magic trick, and Lycius has been seduced from his search for knowledge into erotic indulgence. Keats makes no effort to protect or rationalize Lamia as he might have. In fact, he accepts Apollonius' values and concedes her destruction. But as he does so he is filled with an almost unbearable bitterness. Lamia is beautiful and harmless. Why should Lycius not be permitted to enjoy her? Accepting her for what she appears to be, he is happy; the shock of discovering what she is and of losing her kills him.

In equating the rainbow with Lamia, Keats is abandoning all effort to defend poetry or the poetic vision as truth. He seems to be reduced to the impossible demand that the poet be left alone to believe in beautiful illusions; in fact, to be protected from disillusionment. In equating Apollonius and philosophy, he implies that both are villains who deliberately set out to destroy the poet's dream, and that, if all philosophers could be banished, the dream could be restored as truth.[25]

Within the context of the poem Apollonius becomes a nightmarish caricature of the philosopher who, by his irritable reaching after fact and reason, destroys both beauty and the Keatsian individual who lives by his dream of beauty. But obviously the destructive element in which the poem is immersed is Keats' own mind. Even if he could protect his illusions against the withering scrutiny of the Apolloniuses among his contemporaries by withdrawing into himself,[26] he could not protect them against his own skepticism. For, ironically, if he was Lycius he was also Apollonius; it was his own "speculations" that turned such a pitiless gaze upon the beauty which his imagination had seized as truth.

The conclusion to *Lamia* suggests, I think, that Keats had reached a point of extreme crisis in his thinking about poetry. He could no longer pretend to be content with beauty for its own sake; he could not bear the thought of poetry as escape into a dream world, beautiful but irrelevant or useless. The poet's vision, if it was to be justified, had to stand as truth under the scrutiny of the philosopher; it had to be "as fine a thing as philosophy" in its usefulness to society. But nothing he had done so far could stand this test; he had to find what hitherto had remained hidden from him. Even, therefore, as he was completing *Lamia,* he was at work on the recasting of *Hyperion* as a vision that would refute the implications of *Lamia,* resolve the conflict between Lycius and Apollonius, and demonstrate once and for all that poet and philosopher can be one:

> . . . sure not all
> Those melodies sung into the world's ear
> Are useless; sure a poet is a sage;
> A humanist, Physician to all men.[27]
> [*Fall of Hyperion,* I.97–100]

V. IMMORTAL SICKNESS

The vital importance that Keats attached to the writing of *The Fall of Hyperion,* the sense of deadly urgency that possessed him, is indicated by the induction. The dreams of fanatic or savage die for lack of "melodious utterance": "Poesy alone can tell her dreams." But the distinction obviously goes deeper than this. The dream of the fanatic is false, unworthy of preservation; the dream of the poet, true. But, since every man "whose soul is not a clod" has visions and would express them, no living person is in a position to judge another and say, "You are no poet—you have no right to tell your dreams." Only posterity can judge.

> Whether the dream now purpos'd to rehearse
> Be poet's or fanatic's will be known
> When this warm scribe my hand is in the grave.
> [*Fall of Hyperion,* I.16–18]

Inasmuch as the dream in its unfolding contains a judgment of all his past activity, becomes therefore the culminative, decisive poetic experience, Keats is staking his poetic future upon the poem.

The journey to the height of vision that follows is no spontaneous flight but a laborious, tortured climb in which the poet almost loses his life. The whole process has been reduced, as it were, to slow motion, so painful and accumulated is the detail in which it is presented. The way into the vision, as in the earlier poems, is through the drugging of the senses. In *Hyperion,* Apollo reads knowledge in the face of Mnemosyne and is deified as if he had drunk some "blithe wine"; in the *Ode to a Nightingale,* the poet longs for the draught of vintage but finally joins the nightingale on the viewless wings of poesy. Here in the Garden of Eden in which he finds himself at the opening of *The Fall:*

> . . . appetite,
> More yearning than on earth I ever felt,
> Growing within, I ate deliciously;
> And after not long, thirsted, for thereby
> Stood a cool vessel of transparent juice,
> Sipp'd by the wander'd bee, the which I took,
> And pledging all the Mortals of the world,
> And all the dead whose names are on our lips,
> Drank. That full draught is parent of my theme.
> [*Fall of Hyperion,* I.38–46]

The magic draught for which he longed in the ode he has at last obtained; the very literalness of the experience is an indication of how desperate have become his will and need to be transported into a vision-ary world with a reality apart from himself. It is worth noting also that the dream garden is remarkably like the wonderland of the nightingale; the potion thus becomes the magic ritual by which he is carried beyond the world of the nightingale to a higher reality to which the only entrance in the ode was death. Indeed, the place in which he awakes is the eternal world of Greek myth, the "transcendental ground" of the Grecian urn. It is no place of escape from the miseries of the world, like the wonderland of the nightingale, but on the contrary is a place attainable only by

> . . . those to whom the miseries of the world
> Are misery, and will not let them rest.
> [*Fall of Hyperion,* I.148–49]

It is a place of suffering where the intruder must pass the ordeal of the steps or die. It is the place where will be revealed to him the knowledge the active laborer for mortal good knows intuitively or perhaps does not need to know. The meaning is perfectly plain. As dreamer, he broods over the misery of the world, but does nothing about it, and therefore is inferior to the active benefactors of humanity who "have no thought to come" to the altar. He is there because he is "less than they." "What benefit canst thou do, or all thy tribe, / To the great world?" Moneta asks scornfully. Obviously, he has been allowed to come to the altar to learn how to be of benefit; only in this way can he as a dreamer learn. And the implication is that if he learns he will never need or want to return.

Through the contemptuous words of Moneta, Keats is with deliberate brutality calling into question the value of all his past poetic activity. He is as ruthless to himself as Apollonius was to Lycius:

> Thou art a dreaming thing;
> A fever of thy self—think of the Earth;
> What bliss even in hope is there for thee?
> What haven? every creature hath its home;
> Every sole man hath days of joy and pain,
> Whether his labours be sublime or low—
> The pain alone; the joy alone; distinct:
> Only the dreamer venoms all his days,
> Bearing more woe than all his sins deserve.
> [*Fall of Hyperion*, I.168–76]

He had indulged, Moneta seems to say, in a selfish dream which if not false was without benefit to the world. He had become discontented with things as they were but was powerless to escape them. And so the dream itself was poisoned for him. Even his joy in the things of the earth that contain or reflect the beauty of which he dreams becomes pain as he is consumed with awareness of their mutability. We remember the *Ode on Melancholy* and the "Beauty that must die":

> And Joy, whose hand is ever at his lips
> Bidding adieu; and aching Pleasure nigh,
> Turning to Poison while the bee-mouth sips:
> Ay, in the very temple of Delight
> Veil'd Melancholy has her sovran shrine. . . .
> [*Melancholy*, lines 22–26]

The complexity and the confusion of Keats' state of mind in *The Fall* is revealed by the fact that he describes the Moneta who castigates him as if she were the "Veil'd Melancholy." And indeed she is the product of his envenomed dreaming, of his awareness of mutability. But somehow she is to show him how foolish and unnecessary his brooding has been and give him the knowledge that will emancipate him and enable him to live like those "who came not here":

Keats

Therefore, that happiness be somewhat shar'd,
Such things as thou art are admitted oft
Into like gardens thou didst pass erewhile,
And suffer'd in these Temples. . . .
              [*Fall of Hyperion,* I.177–80]

The dreamer's stilted and obscure reply indicates how uncertain Keats is of what he means at this point; he has taken refuge in rhetoric. I rejoice, he says,

That I am favoured for unworthiness,
By such propitious parley medicin'd
In sickness not ignoble. . . .
              [*Fall of Hyperion,* I.182–84]

The reply is significant, however, in revealing the extent to which Keats thinks of his psychological problem as a sickness.

The reply is followed by the controversial lines which, Woodhouse notes, "Keats seems to have intended to erase": [28]

'Majestic shadow, tell me: sure not all
Those melodies sung into the world's ear
Are useless: sure a poet is a sage;
A humanist, Physician to all men.
That I am none I feel, as Vultures feel
They are no birds when Eagles are abroad.
What am I then? Thou spakest of my tribe:
What tribe?'—The tall shade veil'd in drooping white
Then spake, so much more earnest, that the breath
Mov'd the thin linen folds that drooping hung
About a golden censer from the hand
Pendent,—'Art thou not of the dreamer tribe?
The poet and the dreamer are distinct,
Diverse, sheer opposites, antipodes.
The one pours out a balm upon the world,
The other vexes it.' Then shouted I
Spite of myself, and with a Pythia's spleen
'Apollo! faded, farflown Apollo!
Where is thy misty pestilence to creep
Into the dwellings, thro' the door crannies,
Of all mock lyrists, large self-worshipers,
And careless Hectorers in proud bad verse.
Tho' I breathe death with them it will be life
To see them sprawl before me into graves. . . .'
              [*Fall of Hyperion,* I.187–210]

[167]

The distinction between poet and dreamer which Moneta draws is quite consistent with the preceding dialogue and indeed the logical climax to it. Undoubtedly, these lines need revision, but so it seems to me does the whole passage which contains them, from the moment the dreamer stands before Moneta. None of the argument is clearly thought out or clearly expressed. There are evidences throughout of haste and carelessness. The tone is feverish and almost hysterical; the attack upon the dreamer is violently masochistic. There is none of the control, the ability "to envisage circumstance, all calm," which Keats sought. It is hard to escape the conclusion that he had come close to psychological breakdown at the time he wrote the passage—not simply because the distinctions he draws are fundamentally unsound, but because his despair and self-contempt are out of all proportion to his circumstances and to what he had accomplished during the last year. De Selincourt's suggestion that Keats probably added in November and December "some of those lines that express the bitterest self-recrimination, and altered some to fit more closely to his mood of growing despair," is extremely plausible and accounts convincingly for the characteristics we have mentioned.[29] If Keats intended to erase the lines marked by Woodhouse, it was certainly not because he saw them as contradicting what he had said before, or as "not true of himself." It is more likely that he saw them as the pivotal lines upon which the whole argument of the poem hinged, and therefore as inadequate or insufficient as they stood and in need of expansion, replacement, or integration into the earlier passage on the dreamer.

The only lines that are irrelevant, or at least do not grow naturally out of the distinction drawn by Moneta between poet and dreamer, are those in which the dreamer anticipates with vindictive glee the death before his own

> Of all mock lyrists, large self-worshipers,
> And careless Hectorers in proud bad verse.

They are purely self-indulgent lines and reveal vividly Keats' unhealthy state of mind. They are usually supposed to refer to Byron, and certainly his letters during this period indicate how much he detested Byron. But they may very well refer to several of his contemporaries whose success he had come to resent. Byron would be, of course, the "careless Hectorer." But Moore, even Hunt, could be the "mock lyrist." Wordsworth, whom he had earlier called the "egotistical sublime," is perhaps the "large self-worshiper." At any rate, Keats found satisfaction in the thought that, even if he is not the poet he wanted to be, he is better than his contemporaries; and he gloats in fantasy over seeing them shown up for what they are and sprawling into graves before him.

But, understandable though the feeling is, this personal attack, this cry of hurt pride, has no place here. Perhaps Keats' realization that he had given in to irrelevant personal spleen is one reason why he intended to erase the lines of which these are part. However, it is worth noting that the particular pattern of association is similar to that in *Sleep and Poetry*, when the vision of the charioteer is followed by an attack on the followers of Boileau, and to that in the introduction of Book IV of *Endymion*, where Keats laments the low state of poetry in his own age. By setting these passages side by side, the healthy invective of the earlier poems against the morbid spleen of *The Fall*, we can see how complete and swift had been the change from confidence to despondency.

From the point of view of the general movement of the dialogue between the dreamer and Moneta, the main reason for revising or erasing the morbid passage would be that the distinction between the dreamer and the poet is drawn so sweepingly in a moment of despair that it would preclude any possibility of dreamer's becoming poet. It is a question not, as some critics seem to think, of whether we as readers are convinced that Keats was a poet, but of whether he thought himself one, and by his own terms he did not. Obviously, the context demands a more extended discussion of how one becomes a poet, with the promise of some hope to the dreamer. Moneta, after all, has assured him that he has been admitted to the altar in order that "happiness be somewhat shar'd." And certainly the only justification for the dreamer's experience is that he will learn how to be a poet. The trouble is that within the context of the conflict we have been describing Keats himself did not know how dreamer could be transformed into poet. He could only hurry on in the desperate hope that through the poetic action he could reveal what he could not explain. When, therefore, the dreamer abruptly asks for an explanation of the temple, and Moneta turns to the story of the Titans, we become oppressively aware as readers that we are watching and participating in a painful process of poetic creation in which the final revelation is as much hidden from Keats as it is from us. We feel that Keats' poetic life, as well as the dreamer's happiness, hangs upon the knowledge that is to be revealed by Moneta's story.

[169]

This is why the remaining fragment of the poem seems almost unbearably tragic.

For the drama Moneta begins to unfold is one of desolation, of the destruction of a golden age. It is a story of death. So far as it goes, there is nothing to suggest in what way the dreamer will be made happier or will learn how to be a poet or a disinterested man of action. The description of Moneta indicates that the whole of her story would be as tragic as the beginning. At first glance, the original *Hyperion* would fit in better with the introduction than the second. The theme of perfectibility would provide a basis of hope for the dreamer. But, as we have seen, Keats' experience had deprived him of belief in perfectibility and would not have permitted him to use the theme with conviction. The truth is that no form of *Hyperion* could finally be the proper story to follow the introduction. What the dreamer needs is a story of men, not gods. He needs to know what the charioteer of *Sleep and Poetry* wrote; to have revealed the agonies and strife of human hearts; to find how miseries may be alleviated and happiness shared. He needs a dramatization of Keats' conception of soul-making. In other words, the introduction demands a Shakespearean drama rather than a Miltonic epic.

It may be that one of the reasons for abandoning the poem was a growing awareness of this. But obviously the introduction had been conceived with the myth of Hyperion in mind. Keats had set out to demonstrate that the poetic experience was as valid and useful as that of the scientist-philosopher. In fact, he had set out to vindicate the poetic vision, to justify the dreamer. The form of the poem is proof enough of that. It is within the frame of the vision and as part of the vision that Moneta attacks the dreamer. Undoubtedly, the tale she is to tell is intended to prove that "not all / Those melodies sung into the world's ear / Are useless," and that the dreamer is poet-sage-physician. For, though it is Moneta who tells the tale, it is the dreamer-Keats who records it, and so it is to be his triumphant vindication. Only such a vision as *Hyperion* will do, for *Hyperion* symbolizes the peculiarly poetic experience (as a Shakespearean drama does not) which Keats believed he must defend against the Apollonius in himself.

When he comes finally to relate the story of the Titan, however, he reveals how forlorn had been his hope. He has had no new revelation, no triumphant vindication of the poet's vision, but instead a confirmation of his worst forebodings. He sees only a dying world. It is as if he had made this last desperate ascent into the dream to discover that the dream had faded into the desolation of its aftermath; that the eternal reality was not the vision of the charioteer but "the sense of real things" that threatened to bear his soul to nothingness, not Endymion's vision of heaven but the cave of quietude into which he had been plunged afterward. There is something of the dread inevitability of the nightmare in the way the veiled Moneta is revealed as eternally dying: "deathward progressing / To no death was that visage." In retrospect we can see that, from the moment she is introduced, Moneta is a subversive force within the vision dooming it to failure. Keats had become too much of a skeptic to be able to transcend his doubts through vision —they stand in the form of Moneta at the very heart of his dream. In projecting his conception of Ideal Knowledge, he gives her the destructive arguments of his own reason and clothes her in the funereal robes of mutability. Inevitably, therefore, instead of alleviating the misery of the dreamer, Moneta can only increase it by showing him the futility of his dream. What he learns from her can never enable him to pour out "a balm upon the world" but only enable him to vex it.

The story Moneta unfolds symbolizes the exhaustion and despair that have resulted from the effort to discover truth through vision. The dying world of Moneta and Saturn is Keats' world of poetry doomed to destruction by the grand march of intellect, by science and progress. He probably gave up the poem so abruptly because to continue had become pointless. There are irony and pathos in his abandonment of the poem with the magnificent description of Hyperion's wrath. It is the kind of thing Keats did uniquely well. It is a description of the man of action whom Keats envied and longed to be. It gives the impression of artistic confidence and of central and clear knowledge of where he is going. And yet it is the description of the impotent wrath and feeble action that are prelude to inevitable defeat. More or less consciously, I think, Keats suspends his poem at just such a moment as those described on the Grecian urn—a moment of perfect beauty. "On Hyperion flares," forever triumphant and undefeated.[30]

VI. THE POSTHUMOUS EXISTENCE

On September 22, the day after the letter to Reynolds in which he speaks of giving up *Hyperion,* Keats writes to Dilke, announcing his decision to try to earn a living "by temporary writing in periodical works." He writes in an elaborately cynical tone, as if he were being driven to prostitution: "It is fortunate I have not before this been tempted to venture on the common." A year or two ago, he says, "I should have spoken my mind on every subject with the utmost simplicity"; but now "I am confident I shall be able to cheat as well as any literary Jew of the market and shine up an article on anything without much knowledge of the subject, aye like an orange." But a little further on, in reference to the *Examiner* that Dilke had sent him, he says: "Notwithstanding my aristocratic temper I cannot help being verry [*sic*] much pleas'd with the present public proceedings. I hope sincerely I shall be able to put a Mite of help to the Liberal Side of the Question before I die" (*Letters,* II, 179–80). And to Brown he states specifically: "I will write, on the liberal side of the question, for whoever will pay me" (*Letters,* II, 176).

Keats had many impelling reasons for this abrupt decision, of which the most immediate were George's need for money and his own desire to be self-sufficient and independent of his friends (and probably to be in a position to marry Fanny Brawne). But the feverish urgency of the letters, the emphasis upon writing on the "liberal side of the question," the insistence to Brown that it is time he "set himself doing something and live no longer upon hopes," the fear that he is getting into "an idle-minded, vicious way of life"—these reflect the dialogue between Moneta and the dreamer. The decision is evidence of his bitterness and discouragement. It is an impetuous, futile gesture toward the immediately practical and useful. For, though he spent two weeks in the lodging that Dilke got him, he apparently did nothing; and after he returned to Hampstead he gave up the pretense of writing for the journals. By now he was incapable of any sustained activity. The only poetry of any consequence that he wrote after his return, with the exception of whatever additions or revisions he made to *The Fall of Hyperion,* was *The Cap and Bells.*

Placed within the perspective of the conflict we have been tracing, *The Cap and Bells* becomes a travesty on the theme of the dream, specifically the Endymion theme. The ill-tempered diminutive faery prince and princess are in love with mortals and long to escape from faeryland into an impossible union with flesh and blood. Says Elfinan:

> Alas! my wearied heart within me sinks
> To think that I must be so near allied
> To a cold dullard fay—ah, woe betide!
> Ah, fairest of all human loveliness!

Keats

Sweet Bertha! What crime can it be to glide
About the fragrant plaitings of thy dress,
Or kiss thine eyes, or count thy locks, tress after tress?
[*Cap and Bells*, stanza 19]

Much of the poem, like this section, is a tasteless and labored parody
on Endymion's (and Keats') longing for union with the ideal. It is
hard to avoid seeing an act of self-desecration in the cynical manipulation of materials that had once embodied Keats' deepest beliefs. The
reduction of the dream world to a trivial and vulgar satire on English
court life, the needless insistence upon the faeries' love for mortals (the
poem would certainly be more effective as satire if confined strictly to
faeryland), the irrelevant and flippant use of *The Eve of St. Mark* are
examples. It is true that Keats was deliberately imitating Byron and
perhaps Pope with an eye to making money, but his bitter comments
on Byron in his letters and the attack in *The Fall of Hyperion* would
indicate that this imitation was in itself a cynical gesture.[31] Keats had
none of the Byronic temperament, none of the Byronic gift for burlesque, as the labored and leaden wit of *The Cap and Bells* shows. The
poem is the busy work of a tired and disillusioned man who not merely
has come to doubt the usefulness of his talents but who takes a
masochistic pleasure in debasing them.

To speculate on Keats' future as a poet if he had lived is foolish but
irresistibly tempting. By the end of 1819 so many powerful factors had
converged to inhibit and finally silence his poetic creativity that it is
impossible to see his final work in clear perspective. The most important
of these factors were, of course, his still apparently latent tuberculosis
and his self-consuming passion for Fanny Brawne. Undoubtedly the
hidden disease was a contributing cause of lethargy and despondency
as was his fatalistic anticipation of death. It is not improbable that he
had developed a hypochondriac fear of the disease and an awareness of
its presence long before he made the dramatic announcement to Brown
in February, 1820. As for Fanny Brawne, he is implying by the middle
of October that his hopeless desire for her has made him incapable of
any activity.[32] It is puzzling that this effect should have occurred when
and as it did because he had been tremendously active throughout the
summer, although his letters indicated the same intense morbidity of
desire as in October. The obsessive passion for Fanny Brawne is at any
rate symptom and result rather than cause of a more profound psychological disturbance.[33] He had reached a point where he could no longer

[173]

write with conviction the kind of poetry in which he had hitherto excelled. Any poetry that he wrote from now on might, even if health and love had been favorable, have been anticlimactic unless he had been able to resolve the dilemma posed by the dialogue between Moneta and the dreamer.

There were two possible solutions suggested by his own theory and practice. The simpler was to accept things as he saw them, to enjoy the beauty that he perceived for its own sake, without regard to its ultimate truth or falsity, and to make the description of it the end and purpose of his poetry. He had done all this in *To Autumn*. He had presented the songs of autumn, the season of decay, as being as important and beautiful as the songs of spring, the season of growth. And he had presented them "without any irritable reaching after fact and reason," content to enjoy them as he found them at the moment. But, as we have seen, Keats could never long remain content with such enjoyment; he saw the poetry of detachment that simply observed and recorded as inferior, and he was driven constantly by the desire to "moralize" his song and thus elevate it. He wanted poetry to be an active, dominant power for good, affecting immediately the society into which it entered—as tangible a force as surgery. It is not likely that he could ever have been content simply to write poems like *To Autumn* and the opening of *The Eve of St. Mark*.

The other solution was, forgetting metaphysics, to turn his attention directly to the world of men and women, to search out the agonies and strife of human hearts not through the dream but through observation and experience. This is the course of action Keats proposes for himself in one of the last letters in which he discusses his poetic ambitions— the letter of November 17, 1819, to Taylor. The letter reflects the attitude with which the dialogue between Moneta and the dreamer was written; in fact, it develops logically out of Moneta's remarks. "I have been endeavoring to persuade myself to untether Fancy" and write a poem about the marvelous, Keats says wistfully, but

I and myself cannot agree about this at all. Wonders are no wonders to me. I am more at home amongst Men and Women. I would rather read Chaucer than Ariosto—The little dramatic skill I may as yet have however badly it might show in a Drama would I think be sufficient for a Poem—I wish to diffuse the colouring of St. Agnes Eve throughout a Poem in which Character and Sentiment would be the figures to such drapery—Two or three such Poems, if God should spare me, written in the course of the next six years, would be a famous gradus ad Parnassum altissimum—I mean they would nerve me up to the writing of a few fine Plays—my greatest ambition—when I do feel ambitious. I am sorry to say that is very seldom. The subject we have once or twice talked of appears a promising one, the Earl of Leicester's history [*Letters*, II, 234].

The kind of poem Keats describes is the kind Moneta should relate to the dreamer instead of *Hyperion*. If the dreamer is to be a poet he must learn to become "more at home amongst Men and Women" than among wonders. The letter lends support to the speculation that Keats may have abandoned the second *Hyperion* because he came to realize that his introduction demanded a different kind of poem. But we may question if Keats was really more at home among men and women than among wonders, if he was not substituting the wish for the fact.

Certainly he had wanted from the beginning to be thus at home. But it is noticeable that, though in his letters he shows fine perceptions of human nature and considerable dramatic skill in describing scenes and people about him, he does not as a poet think naturally in terms of human beings. He tends almost involuntarily to think of human life repeated in a "finer tone," most frequently in the immortal world of Greek myth. Characters are subordinated to the conceptual background, to the "abstract" ideas with which the poet is preoccupied, or to the "drapery." *Lamia* is a good example. It is perhaps the best of his attempts at dramatic narrative. The major characters are given some individuality, and there are many skillful and shrewd bits of psychological analysis. But his interest in them as characters is never very great, and in the end they become abruptly types and symbols in a drama of ideas.

The two plays, *Otho the Great* and the fragment *King Stephen*, are of little help to us one way or another. Brown's role in the writing of *Otho* effectively prevents any assessment of Keats' skill in character creation—the fact that the characters are fundamentally conventional and undistinguished may be simply the result of Keats' dependence from scene to scene upon Brown's synopsis. It is interesting, however, to note that when Keats takes over in the last act the play becomes a drama of disillusionment, similar to *Lamia,* though more violent and bitter. Ludolph becomes another Lycius, driven to madness and death by the revelation that the beautiful Auranthe is evil, another projection of Keats' own conflict over illusion and reality. The last scenes of the fifth act are, nevertheless, the most positive evidence we have of Keats' dramatic ability. The fragment of *King Stephen* does not seem to me to

justify the optimistic comments of most critics. There is nothing remarkable about the character development in the four brief scenes except, perhaps, the close following of Shakespeare's method in his
historical plays.

Both *Otho* and *Stephen* are clearly imitative of Shakespeare and the
verse tragedies of Keats' day. The conventions in regard to plot, characters, and diction were terribly limiting and finally stultifying. The
assumption that subjects should have some historical basis in the remote
past was also particularly inhibiting to a man of Keats' nature. The
suggested subject of the Earl of Leicester does not promise well. In
fact, Keats' idolatry of Shakespeare was potentially a severe handicap
to the realization of his dramatic talents. One is tempted to say that his
success would depend partly upon whether he could break free of the
Shakespearean tradition and establish his own dramatic idiom. The
odds, considered from the point of view of both the cultural pressures
of his time and his own inclinations, were against him.

In the long run, however, this consideration would be subordinated
to a larger one: whether or not he could become interested in human
beings for their own sake, independent of metaphysical speculations.
This means that he would have to come to realize that skepticism about
ultimate meanings was no cause for despair; that in fact neither the
value of art nor that of human activities in general depended upon
metaphysical certainties but, on the contrary, could be measured in
human terms alone. He would have to come to realize that what was
important was the power of human beings to realize their own dreams,
to control their own destinies, as he had suggested without perhaps
fully comprehending in *Endymion*. He would have to learn how,
within that frame of faith, to cultivate the kind of detachment he had
described to Woodhouse, to lose his own identity by entering into other
human beings and participating impartially in their potentialities for
good or evil, to conceive an Iago as readily as an Imogen. But, as we
have seen, he showed not the slightest sign of being able to cultivate
such detachment, and no great wish really to cultivate it. Finally, under
no circumstances could poetry achieve the importance or do the things
he demanded of it. There is the possibility that, finding himself unable
to write poetic drama with conviction or effectiveness, he would simply
impatiently have given up poetry except for incidental composition and
turned to writing for the periodicals, or abandoned writing altogether
like Rimbaud. It is more plausible on the basis of the characteristics

revealed by the letters to see Keats potentially as a great prose writer
than to see him as a great poetic dramatist.

Beyond doubt by the end of 1819, independent of illness and love, he
was—if only for the moment—spent as a poet. Again and again in his
letters in 1819 and 1820 he speaks with a kind of dread of the destructive fever that accompanies composition and the exhaustion that
follows. There are indications that toward the end he avoided composition because it had become so painful.

Keats early likened the psychological condition accompanying composition to a fever in terms that showed he recognized its abnormal
unhealthiness. We remember that in May, 1817, while working on *Endymion,* he wrote Hunt that he thought so much about poetry that he
could not get to sleep at night, and that he was "in continual burning of
thought." And we remember Dilke's comment that thought was intense with him "and I have no doubt helped to wear him out." In
his preface Keats refers to *Endymion* as a "feverish attempt rather than
a deed accomplished." Tom's rapidly accelerating illness (combined
probably with his reaction to the insulting attacks in the quarterlies)
aggravated the fever. To Dilke on September 21, 1818, he writes that,

. . . although I intended to have given some time to study alone I am obliged
to write, and plunge into abstract images to ease myself of his [Tom's] countenance his voice and feebleness—so that I live now in a continual fever—it must
be poisonous to life although I feel well. Imagine "the hateful siege of contraries"
—if I think of fame of poetry it seems a crime to me, and yet I must do so or
suffer [*Letters,* I, 369].

On the following day he writes to Reynolds:

I never was in love—Yet the voice and the shape of a Woman has haunted me
these two days—at such a time when the relief, the feverous relief of Poetry
seems a much less crime—This morning Poetry has conquered—I have relapsed
into those abstractions which are my only life. . . . Poor Tom—that woman—
and Poetry were ringing changes in my senses [*Letters,* I, 370].

In these two letters are jumbled together all the conflicting associations linked to the writing of poetry: it is "a continual fever . . . poisonous to life"; an escape from suffering, "a crime," a "feverous relief"
which is less a crime than love; a relapse "into those abstractions which
are my only life." The ominous conjunction of "fever and poison" recurs in a letter to Miss Jeffrey on May 13, 1819:

I have the choice as it were of two Poisons (yet I ought not to call this a Poison)
the one is voyaging to and from India for a few years [as ship's surgeon]; the

other is leading a fevrous life alone with Poetry—This latter will suit me best, for I cannot resolve to give up my Studies [*Letters,* II, 113].

Undoubtedly the fatalistic sense of urgency that drove Keats in 1819, his increasingly desperate efforts to attain the insight that would justify the abstractions and enable him to pour out a "balm upon the world," his obsessive desire for fame—these aggravated the fever. And in turn the fever was at least partly responsible for the sustained and unique excellence of the poems of 1819—it was the intense psychological heat that synthesized Keats' "abstractions" into great poetry. But, as his letters show, the fever became dangerously destructive and consuming. It resulted in periods of exhaustion and dejection, which seemed to become more prolonged and harder to recover from. The agony of the experience itself—suggested in the climb to the altar in *The Fall of Hyperion*—began to haunt Keats. Moneta's remark, "Thou art a dreaming thing, / A fever of thyself," would imply that the creative excitement had become purposeless, uncontrollable, turning in to feed futilely upon itself. *The Fall of Hyperion* taken as a whole illustrates the growing self-destructiveness of the creative process. The dreamer exhausts himself by his effort, becomes the victim of his own machinery, expends his creative energies in self-attack, and has not strength enough left to relate the vision. Significantly, as we have seen, the vision itself is of an exhausted, dying world.

Long before *The Fall of Hyperion,* Keats had become aware of the potential danger to himself in the fever. In the journal letter for February–May, he writes of the *Ode to Psyche:* "This I have done leisurely —I think it reads the more richly for it and will I hope encourage me to write other things in even a more peaceable and healthy spirit" (*Letters,* II, 106). To Reynolds on August 24, 1819, he writes that, if he had heart and lungs

. . . strong as an ox's—so as to be able [to bear] unhurt the shock of extreme thought and sensation without weariness, I could pass my Life very nearly alone though it should last eighty years. But I feel my Body too weak to support me to the height; I am obliged continually to check myself and strive to be nothing [*Letters,* II, 147].

And finally, on September 21, he writes to George and Georgiana:

Some think I have lost that poetic ardour and fire 'tis said I once had—the fact is perhaps I have: but instead of that I hope I shall substitute a more thoughtful and quiet power. I am more frequently, now, contented to read and think—

[178]

but now & then, haunted with ambitious thoughts. Quieter in my pulse, improved in my digestion; exerting myself against vexing speculations—scarcely content to write the best verses for the fever they leave behind. I want to compose without this fever. I hope I one day shall [*Letters,* II, 209].

This statement, coming on the day he was announcing to Reynolds that he had given up *Hyperion,* reveals that Keats recognized the necessity of healing himself before he could be the physician poet. And he writes hopefully as if he had already found the way. But it was too late. He had, if only momentarily, exhausted his creative powers. If *The Cap and Bells* was composed without the fever, it was as an exercise of the craftsman, reflecting, as we have said, weariness and indifference rather than any new or revitalized creative power. And after he had become invalided in February, 1820, he dared not make even the effort to compose because of the excitement it generated. Just what part the creative fever played in aggravating and bringing to crisis the physical fever it is probably impossible to say. But Keats realized that there was a relationship. To his sister he wrote on July 22, 1820: "My constitution has suffered very much for two or three years past, so as to be scarcely able to make head against illness, which the natural activity and impatience of my Mind renders more dangerous" (*Letters,* II, 309).[34]

In the end, it is perhaps irrelevant what Keats might or might not have done if he had lived. His poetic life as it stands has the completeness of dramatic tragedy. In his passionate devotion to poetry lay both the sources of his power and its potential frustration. When he spoke of "those abstractions which are my only life" he was speaking literally, and yet he could not refrain from a restless, intellectual questioning of them which was certain to undermine his belief in their validity. He knew that if his creative imagination were to find its fullest expression or even simply to survive it must be set free of the hobbles of belief. In theory he was able to sever poetry from metaphysical and ethical responsibilities. But in practice he could not, and thus he was drawn relentlessly toward a psychological impasse in which the poetic self was in danger of being reduced to silence. In *The Fall of Hyperion* the most terrifying passage is the description of himself as artist and dreamer contemplating the despair of Saturn and Thea:

A long awful time
I look'd upon them; still they were the same:
The frozen God still bending to the Earth,

And the sad Goddess weeping at his feet.
Moneta silent. Without stay or prop
But my own weak mortality; I bore
The load of this eternal quietude,
The unchanging gloom, and the three fixed shapes
Ponderous upon my senses a whole moon.
For by my burning brain I measured sure
Her silver seasons shedded on the night
And every day by day me thought I grew
More gaunt and ghostly—oftentimes I pray'd
Intense, that Death would take me from the vale
And all its burdens. Gasping with despair
Of change, hour after hour I curs'd myself. . . .

                    [*Fall of Hyperion,* lines 384-99]

In such a manner he must have contemplated the forlorn and dying
world of his art during the "posthumous" year of his illness.

5: SHELLEY

❦❦❦❦❦❦❦❦❦❦❦❦❦❦❦❦❦❦❦❦❦❦❦❦❦❦❦❦

I. THE FINAL VISION

At this point of time, when the critics are locked like the serpent and the eagle in inextricable conflict, and Shelley's reputation trembles in the balance, the one poem that has been exempted by general consent from the conflict is *The Triumph of Life*. Even the two critics who have attacked Shelley most violently have had praises for it: Eliot has said that in *The Triumph* Shelley has come closer to the spirit of Dante than any other English poet, and Leavis has admitted somewhat grudgingly that it "is among the few things one can still go back to in Shelley when he has become, generally, 'almost unreadable.' " [1] Significantly, perhaps, both hostile and friendly critics would agree that *The Triumph of Life* marks a departure from Shelley's previous manner and in Dowden's words "may have been but the starting point for a new and higher development of the writer's genius." [2] The difference between them would be that the hostile critics admit almost nothing before *The Triumph of Life* to be of the first rank.

There are a number of evident reasons for the appeal of *The Triumph of Life*. The style is firm, confident, and disciplined; the *terza rima* is handled with skill and power. The imagery is bold and vivid, integrated and tangible: "down to earth." The controlling metaphor of the triumphal procession is immediately satisfying and is strong enough to pull together and reconcile the disparate and often paradoxical ideas and images. It gives the poem so far as it goes a unified

[181]

and rounded structure, a "bounding line." The result is an ironic tension, rare in Shelley's poems and gratifying to modern formalistic critics.

As an unfinished poem, *The Triumph of Life* has irresistible attraction, enhanced in this case by the tantalizing point at which it breaks off, the particular circumstances of Shelley's death, and the inevitable speculations the poem provokes about possible changes in his attitudes and manner of writing if he had lived. The traditional critical argument has been that the poem breaks off just at the point when presumably a full explanation of the meaning of "life" will be given and an idealistic rebuttal made to the pessimistic implications of the first part of the poem. White says typically that there is nothing to indicate "that the poem, if it was to be of similar length to *Prometheus Unbound* would have been any less optimistic in conclusion." [3] Yet considered in itself it undeniably expresses a persistent tone of disenchantment, apparently at odds with the tone of Shelley's previous poetry and giving no hint of optimistic resolution.

The Triumph of Life provides, therefore, an excellent vantage point from which to survey Shelley's development as a poet particularly during his years of greatest productivity, after his arrival in Italy in 1818; to trace the course of some of his major themes and images; and to examine the wayward progress of his principal ideas and attitudes. It provides also a perfect vantage point from which to survey the present raging critical controversy and come to some conclusions about the merits of the opposing arguments.

Because critics have widely disagreed on the meaning of crucial details of the poem, a summary of the action becomes important before any general discussion or interpretation is attempted. The poem opens with a description of the coming of dawn. The poet, lying down on a slope of the Apennines overlooking the sea, falls into a trance "which was not slumber," for it simply throws a transparent veil over his surroundings, so that he remains aware of them. At the same time, he has a "waking dream" in which he sits beside a public way watching a great stream of people aimlessly hurrying to and fro. As he watches,

> . . . a cold glare, intenser than the noon,
> But icy cold, obscured with blinding light
> The sun, as he the stars.
>
> [*Triumph,* lines 77–79]

[182]

"Like the young moon" comes a chariot in which sits a female Shape,
"as one whom years deform," and over whose head

> . . . a cloud-like crape
> Was bent, a dun and faint aethereal gloom
> Tempering the light.
>
> [*Triumph*, lines 91–93]

The chariot is driven by a "Janus-visaged" charioteer whose four
faces have their eyes banded. The "wonder-winged" shapes that draw
the chariot are lost "in thick lightnings." Round the chariot rages a
throng in "fierce song and maniac dance." Chained to the chariot is a
captive multitude of those famous and infamous persons "who had
grown old in power or misery." Only the "sacred few" of Athens or
Jerusalem are not there. In the van dance youths and maidens who
"kindle invisibly" as they come together and often to their "bright
destruction," like moths attracted and repelled by light, are drawn to
the chariot and fall senseless in its path as it passes over them. Behind,
"old men and women foully disarrayed" follow in the dance, seeking
to reach the light, which leaves them always farther behind. Ghastly
shadows interpose round them and "fulfill / their work"; they sink into
the dust whence they had risen, and corruption veils them as they lie.

As the poet asks half to himself the meaning of the pageant, a voice
answers, "life," and he turns to find

> That what I thought was an old root which grew
> To strange distortion out of the hillside
>
> [*Triumph*, lines 182–83]

was one of the "deluded crew." If he can forbear to join the dance, the
grotesque figure promises to tell him what led him and his companions
to join the pageant. The figure is Rousseau, and he describes the captive company as "the wise, the great, the unforgotten," including those
who wore "wreaths of light," signs of "thought's empire over thought."
But their love did not teach them to know themselves, their might could
not "repress the mystery within." He identifies Napoleon and his own
contemporaries Voltaire, Frederick, Paul, Catherine, and Leopold. Then
he points to the phantoms of "an elder day." Plato is there, because
life had conquered his heart by love.[4] Near Plato walk Aristotle and
Alexander, followed by "the great bards of elder times." After them,
Rousseau points to the Roman emperors from Caesar to Constantine,
and to Gregory and John, and men divine, "who rose like shadows

between Man and God" until their religion, "that eclipse," was worshiped by the world for the true sun it quenched.

Now the poet returns to the question of how and why Rousseau became part of the triumph. Rousseau replies that even the poet might guess how he was brought to this pass, but why this should be, and where he was going, he does not know. Then he adds enigmatically that, if the poet should become actor or victim in the spectacle, "what thou wouldst be taught I then may learn / From thee." He proceeds to tell how in "the April prime" he was "laid asleep / under a mountain." From a cavern in the mountain flowed a rivulet filling the grove with sounds that made whoever heard them forget

> All pleasures and all pains, all hate and love,
> Which they had known before that hour of rest.
> [*Triumph,* lines 318–20]

He himself cannot remember what life had been like before he fell asleep.

He relates how he arose, and though it was now broad day the woods and waters seemed to keep a trace "of light diviner than the common sun / Sheds on the common earth," and all the place was filled with magic sounds. Amid the sun stood "a Shape all light," with her left hand flinging dew on the earth as if she were the dawn, and bearing in her right hand a crystal glass of nepenthe. She glided out of the cavern and over the water of the stream, and her feet, "no less than the sweet tune to which they moved," seemed to blot the thought of the dreamer; and soon:

> All that was, seemed as if it had been not;
> And all the gazer's mind was strewn beneath
> Her feet like embers; and she, thought by thought,
> Trampled its sparks into the dust of death.
> [*Triumph,* lines 385–88]

At last, "as one between desire and shame / Suspended," he asked her, if she came "from the realm without a name / Into this valley of perpetual dream," to show him whence he came and where he was and why.

Her reply was, "Arise and quench thy thirst." He touched with faint lips the cup she raised, and suddenly his brain became as sand. On his sight burst a new vision, "never seen before," and the fair Shape waned in the coming light. But he remained aware of the presence of the Shape; like a star, whose half-extinguished beam

> Through the sick day in which we wake to weep
> Glimmers, forever sought, forever lost;
> So did that shape its obscure tenour keep
> Beside my path, as silent as a ghost. . . .
> [*Triumph,* lines 430–33]

But neither the phantom nor the stream's "Lethean song" could keep him from being swept among the multitude following the chariot. Before the chariot began to climb the opposing steep of "that mysterious dell," the grove grew dense with shadows. Some flung "shadows of shadows, yet unlike themselves / Behind them." Some were lost in the light, some danced, some sat and chattered, some thronged about kings, lawyers, statesmen, priests, and theorists. Some fell "on fairest bosoms and the sunniest hair" and "were melted by the youthful glow / Which they extinguished." Now Rousseau became aware of their origin.

> After brief space,
> From every form the beauty slowly waned;
> From every firmest limb and fairest face
> The strength and freshness fell like dust, and left
> The action and the shape without the grace
> Of life.
> [*Triumph,* lines 518–23]

Thus, "mask after mask fell from the countenance / And form of all." Some grew weary of the dance and fell as Rousseau has fallen, by the wayside:

> Those soonest from whose forms most shadows passed,
> And least of strength and beauty did abide.
> [*Triumph,* lines 542–43]

"Then, what is life?" the poet cries. The crippled Rousseau looks after the departing chariot and answers:

> Happy those for whom the gold
> Of ——

Here the poem breaks off.

II. THE CUP OF NEPENTHE

When we pause to examine the poem in this manner we become aware of the tightly knit logic of its structure. The poem falls obviously into five parts: the introduction (lines 1–42); the description of the triumph (lines 43–179); the meeting with Rousseau and his identification of the captives in the triumph (lines 180–300); Rousseau's dream (lines 300–99); the fading of the dream, the coming of the triumph, and the description of the shadows (lines 400–544). With the exception of the introduction, each part ends with a question or series of questions, partially answered in the succeeding part, and at the end the question, "What is life?" is followed by a few lines that indicate the beginning of a new part. The deliberate and careful organization of the fragment suggests that Shelley had thought out in advance the plan of his poem and had a clear idea of where he was going.

How intricately the structure of the poem has been wrought is shown by the way in which the poet's experience at the beginning of the poem is paralleled by Rousseau's twofold vision at the end. The poet stretches out on a slope of the Apennines at dawn. Rousseau wakes "in a valley of perpetual dream" at dawn. The quality and the effect of the light are described in similar imagery, though there are important differences. The opening scene is of the "real" world, the world of nature as we daily perceive it, though the divine transforming power of the rising sun is suggested. But Rousseau awakes in a "dream" world, an earthly paradise, in which there is a diviner light "than the common sun / Sheds on the common earth," and amid the sun stands the "Shape all light."

The vision of the triumph superimposes itself upon the scene in the same way for both. The poet remains aware of the slope where he lies and remembers the dawn, but the cold glare from the chariot obscures the sun with blinding light. And beside Rousseau the Shape keeps "its obscure tenour" as he is swept into the wake of the cold bright car, though it wanes in the "light's severe excess." The settings and the light imagery suggest, in both the poet's and Rousseau's experience, contrasting states of illusion and reality; but in the transition from the poet's to Rousseau's experience there is movement to a higher and more complex level of symbol. The poet's experience seems to suggest a quite simple distinction between the reality of the opening scene and the illusion of the triumphal procession. But for Rousseau the distinctions have been blurred. The triumphal procession has become a dream within a dream. As he himself says after describing the dream valley in which he found himself,

... whether life had been before that sleep
The Heaven which I imagine, or a Hell
Like this harsh world in which I wake to weep,
I know not.

[*Triumph,* lines 332-35]

In keeping with the growing ambiguity of the light imagery is the increasing complexity of the shadow imagery, culminating in the magnificent description of the origin of the shadows that fill the air about the triumphal procession.

The most ambiguous passage in the poem, and perhaps the pivotal passage for its interpretation, is also the passage where the light-shadow imagery converges in greatest complexity. It is where the vision of the triumph bursts into the dream valley, and the ambiguity consists in the relationship of the Shape to the vision. The exact details of the passage are worth repeating, since they seem to have been generally overlooked. Rousseau asks the Shape to show him whence he came and where he is, and she tells him to quench his thirst. He touches the cup of nepenthe, and suddenly his brain becomes as sand. The new vision bursts upon his sight, and the fair Shape wanes in the coming light. The touching of the cup seems to be the cause of the vision, in other words. But what the significance of the relationship is we are never told. Presumably Rousseau does not know.

The valley of the dream with its cavern, fountain, and stream is like the paradisiacal settings for the end of *Prometheus Unbound,* and *Epipsychidion.*[5] It is presented very frankly as a lotus land of escape, of forgetfulness. Those who hear the sound of the waters must needs forget "all pleasure and all pain, / All hate and love" that they had known before, and the poet is told that there he would forget to deplore vainly "Ills, which, if Ills, can find no cure from thee." The Shape is described in terms that relate her to the vision in *Alastor,* to Asia in *Prometheus Unbound,* to Emily in *Epipsychidion,* and to the Witch of Atlas. She would seem to be another incarnation of Ideal Beauty or Love. The nepenthe she bears is also a familiar symbol. At the end of the third act of *Prometheus Unbound,* the Spirit of the Hour, describing the transformation of mankind, says that now neither pride

Nor jealousy, nor envy, nor ill-shame,
The bitterest of those drops of treasured gall,
Spoilt the sweet taste of the nepenthe, love.

[*Prom. Unbound,* III.iv.161–63]

And the Witch of Atlas is described as giving "to those she saw most beautiful"

> Strong panacea in a crystal bowl:—
> They drank in their deep sleep of that sweet wave,
> And lived thence forward as if some control,
> Mightier than life, were in them; and the grave
> Of such, when death oppressed the weary soul,
> Was a green and overarching bower
> Lit by the gems of many a starry flower.
>
> [*Witch of Atlas,* lines 594–600]

But in *The Triumph of Life* the pattern common to the other poems seems to have been deliberately inverted. Instead of coming as the culmination of the action, or as the symbol of a millennium or a release from life, the dream valley becomes the prelude to the vision of life. What, then, is the significance of the nepenthe? Does Shelley intend to use it simply as a device for answering Rousseau's questions— as a means by which the Shape shows Rousseau where he had come from? And in the end is he to be brought back to the dream valley, in a way that would reveal to poet and reader how to escape from the triumph and attain to the eternal happiness of the valley? How ironic are the implications the episode is intended to carry? Nepenthe is a drink traditionally assumed to bring forgetfulness of sorrow and pain, and it is with this connotation that Shelley hitherto has used the word. But here the drink brings the opposite. It is the means of plunging Rousseau into the procession, so that he is carried nearly to his destruction and falls at last by the wayside, stripped of strength and beauty, a cripple. Does this mean that the dream of the ideal is a delusion which, instead of emancipating us, makes us the victims of life—that it is in some way corrupting? Or does it mean, as Keats suggests in the *Ode to a Nightingale,* that escape is possible only for a moment, and that the very effort to give meaning to the dream destroys it? Rousseau asks the question which leads to his downfall. In its effect the question is like the word "forlorn" in the ode. Whatever Shelley's final intent, the tone of disillusionment, of disenchantment, is unmistakable and ineradicable. Even if Rousseau were to be restored to the valley of perpetual dream, the reader would be aware of how unsubstantial and temporary was his escape, how easily he could be thrown back into the procession. One implication of the episode seems indisputable; the dream can never long be held inviolate; the bursting in upon it of the vision of life is inevitable. And there is a suspicion raised of the ultimate truth or reality of the dream; a tone of skepticism, familiar in Shelley's prose, rare in his poetry; an implied questioning of the Platonic ideal. The whole of Rousseau's experience is a dream, and of the nature of ultimate reality he has no evidence beyond his dream. Could it be that the vision of life is the ultimate reality, and the dream of the ideal the illusion?

Rousseau himself is an ambiguous figure. He is no simple victim in the Triumph of Life. He is not one of the captives chained to the car. He seems, though crippled and aged, to have escaped destruction, to have freed himself from the procession. He shows acute self-awareness. He acknowledges his mistakes and faults. When he identifies the captives, he emphasizes the differences between them and himself. He implies that, though it has been corrupted, the spark with which "Heaven lit his spirit" sets him apart from the captives, and that, if it had been "with purer nutriment supplied," he might have escaped unscathed from the dance. He was conquered not by life, like Plato, but by his own heart alone, which nothing could "temper to its object." In contrast with the great bards of the past, he says, "I / Have suffered what I wrote, or viler pain / And so my words have seeds of misery." And in contrast with the heirs of Caesar and the religious leaders, whose power was given but to destroy, "I / Am one of those who have created, even / If it be but a world of agony."

When we isolate in this way Rousseau's comments on himself, we see how close he comes to Shelley's self-analysis in poems and letters during the last years of his life. Rousseau has been guilty of no sin, is driven by no evil impulses, has made no corrupt compromise with the world like the other great figures in the pageant. On the contrary, he seems ironically to be the victim of his idealism. He has been conquered "by his own heart alone," by the excess of his passion, his sensibility. Perhaps his fault is simply the one for which Shelley blamed himself, seeking in mortal form what is essentially ideal. Or perhaps it is the attempt to live by the ideal, to plunge into the world and try to bring it into conformity with the ideal. At any rate, the inevitable result is disillusionment. The discrepancy between the ideal and the real is unalterable. Rousseau's suffering results from his inability to "temper" his heart to its object, to accept the world as it is and live accordingly, and from his horrified awareness that the very contact with the world corrupts him and turns him into the aged cripple the poet beholds. It is worth emphasizing that it is as the cripple that Rousseau describes the vision of the ideal. The necessity of supplying the spirit with the impure "nutriment" of mortal activity, of satisfying the longing for the ideal through mortal means is the true corruption. Rousseau's great virtue is that he fought against the corruption. He created even if it "be but a world of agony," and he could boast that "there rise / A thousand beacons from the spark I bore."

In the *Defence of Poetry,* Shelley called Rousseau "essentially a poet." [6] He perhaps chose Rousseau as his protagonist in the poem because he fulfilled so well his conception of the poet, both as one who lifted "the veil from the hidden beauty of the world" and as one of the unacknowledged legislators of the world. Rousseau as the formulator of the ideals by which society was to be transformed could be seen as the prototype of the modern poet, and specifically of Shelley himself. And in his fate, and perhaps in the fate of his ideals, he symbolized the fate that confronted Shelley.

How to avoid it? In the past apparently Socrates and Christ had avoided it. The lines in which they are referred to are obscure and obviously in need of revision but suggest that they escaped because they "put aside the diadem of earthly thrones or gems"—in other words, they escaped through self-denial or, in Keats' term, disinterestedness. But the growing implications of the vision are that for the poet-spectator the only means of escape from the fate of Rousseau is through total withdrawal from the world. And even that may not save him. He may be caught up in spite of himself, as apparently Rousseau was. There is nothing to indicate that he can in any way transform the nature of the triumph. Socrates, Christ, and Rousseau have not been able to. The only slightest hint of political or social progress, of possibility of change, is Rousseau's remark that a thousand beacons rise from the spark he bore. But this hint is swept away in the gloomy vision that follows. [7] Within the context of the poem there is no glimpse of a millennium, and for the poet the logical resolution of the vision would be the ending of *Epipsychidion* or *Adonais*—retirement or death.

During the time of the writing of the *Triumph* the idea of withdrawal from the world was very much in Shelley's mind. In a letter to Mary of August 16, 1821, he makes his most sweeping statement on the matter. Though undoubtedly it reflects his revulsion to the Hoppner affair, it is consistent with the attitude frequently revealed in letters and poems of the Italian years:

> My greatest content would be utterly to desert all human society. I would retire with you and our child to a solitary island in the sea, would build a boat, and shut upon my retreat the floodgates of the world. I would read no reviews, and talk with no authors. If I dared trust my imagination it would tell me that there were two or three chosen companions besides yourself whom I should desire. But to this I would not listen—where two or three are gathered together the devil is among them. And good far more than evil impulses—love far more than hatred, has been to me, except as you have been its object, the source of all sort of mischief. So on this plan, I would be *alone,* and would devote either to oblivion or to future generations the overflowings of a mind which, timely withdrawn from the contagion, should be kept fit for no baser object! But this it does not appear that we shall do.
>
> The other side of the alternative . . . is to form for ourselves a society of our own class, as much as possible in intellect, or in feelings; and to connect ourselves with the interests of that society [*Works,* X, 315].

The few months at Lerici became for Shelley the realization of a compromise between the alternatives. Writing to John Gisborne on June 18, 1822, he describes his boat and adds:

> Williams is captain, and we drive along this beautiful bay in the evening wind, under the summer moon, until earth appears another world. Jane brings her guitar, and if the past and the future could be obliterated, the present would content me so well that I could say with Faust to the passing moment "Remain, thou, thou art so beautiful" [*Works,* X, 403].

On June 29 he writes to Horace Smith what is to be his last political and social comment. It reflects the state of mind in which he was writing *The Triumph of Life* and reinforces the interpretation that has just been given of the poem:

> It seems to me that things have now arrived at such a crisis as requires every man plainly to utter his sentiments on the inefficacy of the existing religious, no less than political systems, for restraining and guiding mankind. Let us see the truth, whatever that may be. The destiny of man can scarcely be so degraded that he was born only to die—and if such should be the case, delusions, especially the gross and preposterous ones of the existing religion, can scarcely be supposed to exalt it. If every man said what he thought, it could not subsist a day. But all, more or less, subdue themselves to the element that surrounds them, and contribute to the evils they lament by the hypocrisy that springs from them—

He writes then of the desperate conditions in England and Ireland:

I once thought to study these affairs, and write or act in them—I am glad that my good genius said *refrain*—I see little public virtue, and I foresee that the

contest will be one of blood and gold, two elements which however much to my taste in my pockets and my veins, I have an objection to out of them. . . .
    I still inhabit this divine bay, reading Spanish dramas and sailing, and listening to the most enchanting music.—We have some friends on a visit to us, and my only regret is that the summer must ever pass, or that Mary has not the same predilection for this place that I have, which would induce me never to shift my quarters [*Works*, X, 410–11].

Withdrawal from society or the world is the end toward which most of the major poetry of Shelley moves. It provides the focal climactic image for his conception of the millennium in *Prometheus Unbound*, of love in *Epipsychidion*, of death in *Adonais*. It reveals that his psychological response to each of these was the same, and that in fact they tended to blur together in his mind. The endings of these poems have usually been taken as indications of his "fundamental optimism," but certainly they show a much more complex attitude for which "optimism" is at best a shallow and misleading term.

III. THE ORACULAR VAPOUR

In Act III, scene iii, of *Prometheus Unbound*, after Jupiter has been overcome by Demogorgon, Prometheus is released by Hercules. Immediately he turns to Asia, Panthea, and Ione and says:

> Henceforth we will not part. There is a cave,
> All overgrown with trailing odorous plants,
> Which curtain out the day with leaves and flowers,
> And paved with veined emerald, and a fountain
> Leaps in the midst with an awakening sound . . .
> A simple dwelling, which shall be our own;
> Where we will sit and talk of time and change,
> As the world ebbs and flows, ourselves unchanged.
> [*Prom. Unbound*, III.iii.10–14, 22–24]

He goes on to describe the pastoral life of childlike innocence which they will live; how they will search their unexhausted spirits, "with looks and words of love," for hidden thoughts; how, like lutes touched by the wind, they will weave harmonies divine. Here will come "the echoes of the human world," and lovely apparitions will visit them:

> . . . the progeny immortal
> Of Painting, Sculpture and rapt Poesy.
> And arts, tho' unimagined, yet to be.
> [*Prom. Unbound*, III.iii.54–56]

These are the shapes and sounds of all that man becomes, and as he grows wise and kind they grow more fair and soft. Then, as if suddenly reminded, Prometheus turns to the Spirit of the Hour and tells her to take the shell Ione will give her and circle the earth, sounding the music of emancipation. After she leaves, the Earth, who apparently has not heard Prometheus' long speech, describes presumably the same cave, locating it in Greece beside a temple dedicated to Prometheus, and sends the winged Spirit of the Earth along to guide them there. It is in the forest outside the cave that the fourth scene takes place, and Prometheus receives the reports of the Spirit of the Earth and the Spirit of the Hour on the transformation of man that follows upon the sound of the shell.

As we become immediately aware, a curious thing happens to the play as a work of art upon Prometheus' release. It ceases to be a dramatic allegory and becomes a Shelleyan daydream. Jupiter's fall, as it were, releases the pent-up desires in Shelley's mind, and he simply takes over the role of Prometheus. He loses all interest in the dramatic action and even in the idea of the play. His mind leaps impatiently to *his* idea of heaven on earth, ignoring the painful yet potentially dramatic steps in man's adjustment to freedom and the application of his hard-won wisdom. All the complex connotations bound up in Prometheus as the suffering representative of mankind in the first act are forgotten, and he becomes a private individual, a spectator where he had been the protagonist. He does not even make his own tour of inspection, the least that, dramatically, he could be expected to do. In spite of the various critical efforts to justify the last scenes of the third act (by suggesting that "Prometheus' retirement into the cave signifies the uniting of man and wisdom," [8] for example), Shelley's indifference to his medium and his apparently unconscious reduction of Prometheus from symbol to individual—in short, his abandonment of his dramatic responsibilities— seem inescapable.

I have written "apparently unconscious reduction of Prometheus" because there is nothing to indicate that Shelley ceased to see him as "the emblem of the human race." It never occurred to Shelley that what he himself would do was not what the symbol of emancipated mankind would or should do; that it was eccentric and not universal to retire precipitously to a cave. The conclusion of the third act reveals perhaps Shelley's most serious limitation as artist—the switching off, as Leavis calls it, of the "critical intelligence." [9] He could not resist the temptation of leaping over the hard labor, the intellectual discipline of showing man in process of transformation, to the dazzlingly simple dream of the achieved perfection. The perfect symbol for Shelley the artist of revolution was the trumpet or shell. He wanted to be able to blow the trumpet of prophecy and by the magic of the sound spontaneously and effortlessly transform society.

This is not to say that in the poem he should have provided a blueprint. He was quite right in insisting in his preface that it was not his purpose to present "a reasoned system on the theory of human life." But he went to the opposite extreme and made no concession to dramatic logic or to what might be called the "reasonable" expectations of his audience. He made no effort "to transfer from our inward nature a human interest and a semblance of truth sufficient to procure for those shadows of imagination that willing suspension of disbelief for the moment, which constitutes poetic faith." He did not project in symbolic action the transitional steps between the fall of Jupiter and the perfection of society. And, more seriously, he shows no awareness or allows his characters no awareness that such transitional steps are necessary.

In addition, the peculiar quality of the dialogue that frames the concluding vision seriously damages the poem. It is a quality that reveals a great deal about Shelley as man and artist. It is perhaps best described as archness, and it reflects a tendency to reduce Utopia to a kind of sexless second childhood, or to a paradise in which sex would become a kind of innocent child play. As we have seen, Prometheus describes the life that he and Asia will lead as one of pastoral innocence. But it is the Spirit of the Earth who is responsible for the archness, and the evident importance of his role justifies us in seeing him as central to Shelley's conception of perfection. The Spirit is a winged child who is sent by the Earth to guide Prometheus and Asia to the cave. Panthea says that it is the "delicate spirit / That guides the earth through heaven," and that before Jove reigned it had loved Asia, made to her its childish confidences, and called her mother (though its origin is unknown). It presents the first report on the transformation of mankind, describing how it hid in a fountain in the public square of a great city and watched the masks of evil and ugliness fall from the people and pass through the air. This report is framed within an embarrassingly maudlin conversation between the Spirit and Asia. After the report, Asia says that they will never part again until his

[194]

chaste sister of the moon looks on his "more warm and equal light" and loves him. The Spirit asks, "What; as Asia loves Prometheus?" and Asia replies:

> Peace, wanton, thou art yet not old enough.
> Think ye by gazing on each other's eyes
> To multiply your lovely selves? . . .
> [*Prom. Unbound,* III.iv.91–93]

This is the note on which the Spirit of the Hour is introduced to give the final report on the transformation of man. The fault lies not merely in the attempt to allegorize as a child the gravitational principle, or whatever natural law the Spirit represents, though this is unnecessary to the drama and indeed is fundamentally irrelevant and absurd, but in the terrible coziness of the conception which threatens to reduce the theme of man's regeneration to triviality and opens the artist to the charge of intellectual frivolity. When a poet is capable of presenting such a conversation as illustration of the perfect state of things, his values immediately come into question. One becomes suspicious of his fundamental seriousness as artist and thinker. And certainly this scene is indicative of an unhealthiness of perspective, an emotional immaturity, a kind of infantilism which is prominent in much of Shelley's early writing, particularly the lyrics. It begins to fade from his poetry after *Prometheus,* but it is still noticeable in *The Witch of Atlas* and some of the conceits in the first part of *Adonais.* It is closely related to his conception and treatment of love as we shall see when we examine *Epipsychidion.* In passing, it might be pointed out that the heavy archness or whimsicality we find in Shelley is simply the most extreme manifestation of a characteristic that was becoming increasingly prominent in British culture and ended up as one of the fundamental ingredients in Victorianism. This quality was one reason for his great appeal to the Victorians, and it probably made his attitudes acceptable to many who otherwise would have rejected them. The particular form of it that we have been discussing probably reached its culmination in literature in *Peter Pan.* And today we find its counterpart in the whimsey of Walt Disney.

I want to emphasize that in thus criticizing the dramatic development of the third act of *Prometheus Unbound* I am not attacking the ideas which Shelley was attempting to dramatize. T. S. Eliot seems to me completely wrong, and guilty also of a critical *non sequitur,* when he attacks Shelley for borrowing "shabby" ideas. "I can only regret," he says, "that Shelley did not live to put his poetic gifts, which were certainly of the first order, at the service of more tenable beliefs— which need not have been, for my purposes, beliefs more acceptable to me." The "shabby" ideas that "affront" Eliot are "the ideas which Shelley bolted whole and never assimilated, visible in the catchwords of creeds outworn, tyrants and priests," the ideas of the "humbug" Godwin.[10] In other words, they are the ideas of the enlightenment. Such ideas are likely to seem "shabby" only to one who like Eliot has re-acted in violent disillusionment against his nineteenth-century heritage and reverted to zealous support of the tradition, complete with creeds outworn, tyrants and priests, that these ideas attack.

In reality, the ideas Shelley "borrowed" from the eighteenth-century philosophers are of great power and nobility. They remain potent to-day and lie at the root of all that is most viable in twentieth-century culture. They are far more intellectually acceptable than the ideas they supplanted. If we look objectively back over the last century and a half, the ideas are seen to stand up remarkably well under the impact of an almost incredibly accelerating material civilization. They have, in turn, been responsible for decisive social and political changes, and, if we can put aside the faddish traditionalism of the moment, we can see that where they have been truly tested by observation and experi-ence they have demonstrated their validity.

From the vantage point of our fuller knowledge of ourselves, the idea of the "innate goodness" of man (which few eighteenth-century thinkers held without qualification) may seem naïve, but hardly more so than the idea of "original sin," and it contained within it the stimu-lant to the psychological investigation that found it naïve. The fact that the ideas of progress and perfectibility have been abused, because they lend themselves easily to sentimental and irresponsible exploita-tion, no more invalidates them than such exploitation invalidates the ideas of freedom and equality. The basic social ideals they embody, the conception of what man and society ought to be, are logically in-controvertible; and even peripheral speculations, like Godwin's on marriage, are intellectually if not socially respectable and worthy of debate. In all cases, these ideas pointed the way to intellectual ex-plorations we are still carrying on. But, apart from that, they are bold and epic ideas, and there is no reason why they should not be powerful stimulants to the imagination of the artist, or why they should not be susceptible of convincing dramatic treatment. They should be capable of presentation in such a way as to satisfy the most unsentimental and intellectually demanding audience.

Partly because Shelley's poetry has become identified with these ideas, and partly because the modern attack on his poetry has been led by T. S. Eliot and the Formalist critics, any adverse criticism is unfortunately likely to be misinterpreted by friends and enemies of Shelley alike as an attack on the ideas. The result has been that many critics, in protection of what Shelley stands for, have extended themselves in extravagant praise or in elaborate defense, refusing to concede any faults or weaknesses in his poetry. But there is finally no denying that the poetry is vulnerable to many of the attacks leveled against it. Inevitably, the ideas will suffer, as indeed they have suffered, through association with Shelley.

One of the most misleading critical dicta on Shelley is that he is an "intellectual" poet, the implication being that there is a profound development of ideas in his poetry. But in *Prometheus Unbound* the idea of perfectibility is reduced to the most naïve and sentimental terms, in which it becomes intellectually unacceptable. For the modern reader, who is still suffering from the errors committed by the sentimental perfectibilitarians in 1914 and whose life is shadowed by the hydrogen bomb, the dramatic development at the end of the third act of *Prometheus* is ridiculous and even repellent. When Eliot says that when Shelley borrowed ideas "he muddled them up with his own intuitions," he is making a more just and perceptive criticism than in his attack on the ideas themselves.[11] Perhaps "intuitions" is too vague a word; psychological needs and desires might be better. However, if we think of the metaphysic of love, stated by Demogorgon and embodied by Asia, which frames the action of *Prometheus,* then Eliot's statement is right as it stands. For the conclusion of *Prometheus* represents the muddling of the idea of perfectibility with Shelley's own intuition of love.

When Shelley gave himself up to the contemplation of love, thinking stopped. It was his peculiar concept of love that made it possible for him to present the spontaneous transformation of society and made him oblivious to the logical contradictions in so much of his poetry. It enabled him to reconcile all opposites and rationalize his conduct. It was, of course, "muddled up" with his sexual needs and desires. It is necessary to understand this relationship, at least as it is presented in his poetry, before we can interpret the metaphysical ramifications. We find it nakedly revealed in the last part of *Epipsychidion.*

The Romantic Ventriloquists

IV. THE MUTINOUS FLESH

Epipsychidion properly comes to an end at line 388. The part that follows is in the nature of an epilogue, almost a separate poem. If the first part of the poem is concerned with the definition of the Ideal Love and the search for it, the conclusion is concerned with the vision of the ideal existence. Once again, as in the conclusion of *Prometheus Unbound,* Shelley is swept away into the dream of withdrawal from the world. The same process of association sets the dream in motion: Prometheus is released from the rock, Emily from the prison of the convent. The relationship of Emily and the poet is to be sexless:

> The day is come and thou will fly with me.
> To whatsoe'er of dull mortality
> Is mine, remain a vestal sister still. . . .
> *[Epipsychidion, lines 388–90]*

The ship is waiting in which they are to sail to an Ionian island "beautiful as a wreck of paradise." It is inhabited only by some pastoral people

> Who from the Elysian, clear, and golden air
> Draw the last spirit of the age of gold,
> Simple and spirited; innocent and bold.
> *[Epipsychidion, lines 427–29]*

The island is described in heavily sensuous imagery; it is strikingly anticipatory of Tennyson's land of *The Lotus Eaters:*

> The light clear element which the isle wears
> Is heavy with the scent of lemon-flowers,
> Which floats like mist laden with unseen showers,
> And falls upon the eyelids like faint sleep;
> And from the moss violets and jonquils peep,
> And dart their arrowy odour through the brain
> Till you might faint with that delicious pain.
> *[Epipsychidion, lines 446–52]*

But Shelley will not have it as sensuous; immediately follow the lines:

> And every motion, odour, beam, and tone,
> With that deep music is in unison,
> Which is a soul within the soul—they seem
> Like echoes of an antenatal dream.—
> *[Epipsychidion, lines 453–56]*

[198]

Shelley

The island is free from all natural evils, like earthquakes and storms, and from man-made evils such as war. Finally, in a startlingly erotic image, the perfection of the island is summed up. From sea and sky there rise and fall exhalations:

> Veil after veil, each hiding some delight,
> Which Sun or Moon or zephyr draw aside,
> Till the Isle's beauty, like a naked bride
> Glowing at once with love and loveliness,
> Blushes and trembles at its own excess:
> Yet, like a buried lamp, a Soul no less
> Burns in the heart of this delicious isle,
> An atom of th' Eternal. . . .
>
> [*Epipsychidion*, lines 472–79]

Once again, Shelley is quick to have it both ways: sensuous and ideal. The image of the veiled but naked woman is a familiar one in his poetry, appearing notably in the descriptions of the vision in *Alastor* and of Asia at the end of Act II in *Prometheus*. It is also used in the *Defence of Poetry* to describe the action of poetry: "It strips the veil of familiarity from the world, and lays bare the naked and sleeping beauty, which is the spirit of its forms." In each case, the erotic implications are heightened by the startling incongruity of the image in its context.

On the island is a strange, ruined pleasure house built in the "world's young prime" by some wise and tender ocean king for his sister and spouse. It scarcely seems now a wreck of human art:

> But, as it were, Titanic; in the heart
> Of Earth having assumed its form, then grown
> Out of the mountains, from the living stone,
> Lifting itself in caverns light and high. . . .
>
> [*Epipsychidion*, lines 494–97]

In short, Prometheus' cave. And, like Prometheus, the poet has sent books and music there, and those instruments with which "high Spirits" evoke the past and the future and make the present last

> In thoughts and joys which sleep, but cannot die,
> Folded within their own eternity.
>
> [*Epipsychidion*, lines 523–24]

Here he and Emily will sit and walk and talk together. And now in one of the most remarkable rhetorical feats in Romantic poetry Shelley

[199]

builds, beginning with a series of erotic nature images, to the consummation of their love, from a mood of calm, at first gradually and then rapidly accelerating, to a state of annihilating passion, plunging immediately into exhaustion and despair. As they walk, he says, they will ascend the "mossy mountains"—where the heavens bend

> With lightest winds, to touch their paramour;
> Or linger, where the pebble-paven shore,
> Under the quick, faint kisses of the sea
> Trembles and sparkles as with ecstasy. . . .
> [*Epipsychidion,* lines 545–48]

Or at noontime they will arrive where some old cavern "seems yet to keep / The moonlight of the expired night asleep." And here sleep, "the fresh dew of languid love," may close Emily's eyes:

> And we will talk, until thought's melody
> Become too sweet for utterance, and it die
> In words, to live again in looks, which dart
> With thrilling tone into the voiceless heart,
> Harmonizing silence without a sound.
> Our breath shall intermix, our bosoms bound,
> And our veins beat together; and our lips,
> With other eloquence than words, eclipse
> The soul that burns between them, and the wells
> Which boil under our being's inmost cells,
> The fountains of our deepest life, shall be
> Confused in passion's golden purity,
> As mountain-springs under the morning Sun.
> We shall become the same, we shall be one
> Spirit within two frames, oh! wherefore two?
> One passion in twin-hearts, which grows and grew,
> 'Till like two meteors of expanding flame,
> Those spheres instinct with it become the same,
> Touch, mingle, are transfigured; ever still
> Burning, yet ever inconsumable. . . .
> [*Epipsychidion,* lines 560–79]

If the passage is remarkable, it has in turn been responsible for some of the most remarkable rhetorical gymnastics in the history of criticism. It is difficult to believe that most critics have read it. This is self-evidently a description of sexual experience, of union with a "real" woman (as Keats would say) which is as much physical as spiritual; and the fact that it is a dream intensifies if anything the sensual nature of the experience. It may be more than this, and we shall discuss the

Platonic implications later, but to deny or ignore the sexual implications requires an immense effort at self-deception. Yet Locock speaks of the "wonderfully peaceful" conclusion. Woodberry and Baker regard the island as allegorical of the realm of ideal poetry, "where the creative soul merges with the world-soul at the highest possible level." White says, "Shelley proposed an elopement with Emilia only in spirit, but he dwelt lovingly and at length upon their spiritual union on the Ionian Island. . . . Even so, Shelley probably intended Mary, and possibly even Claire to accompany them." [12]

Obviously, for most critics the poem becomes morally and esthetically acceptable if the relationship with Emily is seen as "spiritual." Imaginative infidelity to Mary can be justified as long as no sexual union takes place, and as long as Emily is not Emily, but the mortal embodiment of the ideal. This Pecksniffian morality is understandable enough among the Victorians; even so, it is hard to accept without a flicker of skepticism the solemn comment of such a respectable clergyman as Stopford Brooke: "The one true love of human life is their ideal, not in the world of the senses at all, and cannot be realized or satisfied by anything or anyone on earth." [13] However, Brooke's comment furnishes us with a clue to the Victorian admiration of so unorthodox a poem. The Victorian intellectuals wished to believe that the transcendence or sublimation of the sexual impulse was one sign of man's evolution toward perfection, of his separation from the animals. Their attitudes owed much to the Puritan tradition of denial and repression, of course, but the sophistication resulting from the intellectual developments of the eighteenth century gave these attitudes a new and positive emphasis. The relationship between the sexes was to be not repressed but idealized, so that sexual intercourse would become unnecessary, even detrimental to the perfect relationship, to the fullest realization of our *human* desires. Shelley's "Platonics" in *Epipsychidion* and elsewhere seemed to be the perfect illustration of this belief. The proper Victorian could read *Epipsychidion* and receive vicariously all the pleasures of sexual indulgence under the illusion that they were intellectual pleasures. He was obviously able as if by some kind of magical ray to blot out in his conscious mind the sexual implications, or to translate them instantaneously into innocuous connotations.

But the modern critic could not, even if he wanted to, blot out the sexual implications. Not only have the areas of meaning the Victorians cut off been restored, but we have also been forced into awareness of the hidden or rationalized motivations underlying the choice and use of words. Nor are we disturbed by the sexual element per se. On the contrary, we would assume that the sexual experience is an inevitable part of the ideal relationship. We know that, if the artist attempts to avoid direct recognition of the sexual, it will come in through the metaphor, as in *Epipsychidion*. Why, then, do the majority of modern critics friendly to Shelley try to perpetuate the Victorian illusion? Primarily, of course, because they have inherited it and accepted it as the sign of the peculiar excellence that sets Shelley apart from other men—and poets. But also because they believe it is necessary to protect his reputation as man, philosopher, and poet against his detractors. If once they admit the sexual implications, then the careful separation between spiritual and sensual, between the Emily of the poem and Emily the "real" woman, tends to break down or become meaningless. Inevitably the sincerity as well as the profoundity of Shelley's "Platonism" is called into question. The inconsistencies in tone and ideas become glaring. Worst of all, once *Epipsychidion* is admitted to be a love poem addressed to a particular woman, Emily, the extravagant protestations that she is the incarnation of the ideal for which he has been looking all his life become inevitably a little ridiculous in the light of his brief acquaintance with her and his almost immediate revulsion against her. The comparison with Dante's *Vita Nuova* that is frequently urged, and for which Shelley is largely responsible, becomes absurd.[14] Dante's account of his love for the dead Beatrice stands in sharp opposition to Shelley's hothouse apostrophe to Emily, too soon loved and too quickly rejected.

Unfortunately, the moral muddle of Shelley's defenders simply reflects his own confused and self-deceiving statements. Much of the supporting evidence for the "Platonic" interpretations is drawn from his and Mary's comments on the poem. These comments should not be considered, as they have been, in isolation from the circumstances under which they were written. Obviously, *Epipsychidion* was the kind of poem that was likely to arouse the gossips. Shelley's attitude toward gossip was ambivalent. He constantly encouraged notoriety, and he resented it. He tended to exhibitionism in action and writing and then spun elaborate rationalizations to justify his conduct. He rather complacently wrote Byron that his intimacy with Emily had made a "great fuss" at Pisa and that if the whole truth were known Mary might be "annoyed." Furthermore, he openly and unnecessarily addressed the poem to Emily. It apparently never occurred to him to remove her name or to mask it as the Elizabethans would have done by substituting an allegorical or mythical name.

The confusion between the real and the ideal Emily, which "literalists" are always accused of stirring up, existed quite simply in Shelley's mind and was built into the poem. Under the circumstances, therefore, he had no business publishing *Epipsychidion*, even anonymously and in a limited edition; as long as it was addressed to Emily, it should have remained a private poem. In a transparent effort to justify himself, he resorted to a conventional trick of mystification by pretending that the author was a friend who had died as he was preparing a voyage to the island described in the poem. As was often the case, the simple assertion that a thing was so made it so for Shelley; the affirmation was a hypnotic ritual that transformed dream into reality or, in this instance, reality into dream. We need not doubt, therefore, his self-conviction when he writes Ollier that he desires the poem not to be considered as his own: "Indeed, in a certain sense, it is a production of a portion of me already dead; and in this sense the advertisement is no fiction. It is to be published simply for the esoteric few; and I make its author a secret to avoid the malignity of those who turn sweet food into poison." Even a hundred copies might be too many, since "those who are capable of judging and feeling rightly with respect to a composition of so abstruse a nature certainly do not arrive at that number" (*Works*, X, 236).

Shelley's confusion is again shown in the letters to John Gisborne; his two comments nearly cancel each other out. In the first, October 22, 1821, he says that "the *Epipsychidion* is a mystery. As to real flesh and blood, you know that I do not deal in these articles." But in the second, June 18, 1822, he says:

The *Epipsychidion* I cannot look at; the person whom it celebrates was a cloud instead of a Juno; and poor Ixion starts from the Centaur that was the offspring of his own embrace. . . .

Nevertheless,

It is an idealized history of my life and feelings. I think one is always in love with something or other; the error, and I confess it is not easy for spirits cased in flesh and blood to avoid it, consists in seeking in a mortal image the likeness of what is perhaps eternal [*Works*, X, 333, 401].

The last comment is one of Shelley's most perceptive on himself: he admits the highly personal basis of the poem. But he is guilty of a greater error than he recognizes, or at least than he admits: he mistakes purely mortal impulses, the fulfillment of psychological needs, for spiritual ones, infatuation for ideal love. The major error was not in seeking the eternal in a mortal image, but in projecting a dream fantasy upon a convenient object.

In his general discussion of Ideal Love, Shelley quite clearly includes the sexual as an essential element. In the preface to *Alastor* he describes the poet as imaging to himself

. . . the Being whom he loves. . . . The intellectual faculties, the imagination, the functions of sense, have their respective requisitions on the sympathy of corresponding powers in other human beings. The Poet is represented as uniting these requisitions, and attaching them to a single image.

In the poem, the appeal of the veiled maiden to the intellect, the imagination, and the senses is described in turn, and the vision culminates in a frankly sexual embrace:

His strong heart sunk and sickened with excess
Of love. He reared his shuddering limbs and quelled
His gasping breath, and spread his arms to meet
Her panting bosom . . . she drew back a while,
Then yielding to the irresistible joy,
With frantic gestures and short breathless cry
Folded his frame in her dissolving arms.
Now blackness veiled his dizzy eyes. . . .
                              [*Alastor*, lines 180–88]

In the fragment *On Love*, Shelley makes the same distinction as in the preface to *Alastor*. Here the emphasis is specifically narcissistic. "There is something within us which, from the instant that we live, thirsts after its likeness." The "invisible and unattainable point to which Love tends" is the discovery of its antitype, with an understanding and an imagination like our own, and "with a frame whose nerves . . . vibrate with the vibrations of our own" (*Works*, VI, 202).

But it is in "A Discourse on the Manners of the Antient Greeks," which he intended as an introduction to his translation of the *Symposium*, that Shelley gives most openly and fully the views on the relation of sex and love which he can be presumed to have held at the time of writing *Epipsychidion*.[15] He points out that "one of the chief distinctions between the manners of Antient Greece and modern Europe, consisted in the regulations and the sentiments respecting sexual intercourse" (Clark, p. 219b). In this matter "the modern Europeans have . . . made an improvement the most decisive in the regulation of human society," insofar as "the sexual and intellectual claims of love, by the more equal cultivations of the two sexes, converge toward one point" (Clark, p. 221a). Among the Greeks, women were degraded and simply satisfied the sexual appetite, while men became the objects of "sentimental love." In considering the contrast between Greeks and modern Europeans, Shelley is led to the following observation on the relation of sex and love. The gratification of the senses, as civilization develops,

. . . is no longer all that is sought in sexual connexion. It soon becomes a very small part of that profound and complicated sentiment, which we call Love, which is rather the universal thirst for a communion . . . of our whole nature, intellectual, imaginative and sensitive. . . . The sexual impulse, which is only one, and often a small part of these claims, serves from its obvious and external nature as a kind of type or expression of the rest, as common basis, an acknowledged and visible link. Still it is a claim which even derives a strength not its own from the accessory circumstances which surround it, and one which our nature thirsts to satisfy [Clark, p. 220b].

In the concluding section of the essay, not published until 1931, occur Shelley's most important comments.[16] "An enlightened philosophy," he says, "although it must condemn the laws by which an indulgence in the sexual instinct is usually regulated, suggests, however, the propriety of habits of chastity in like manner with those of temperance. . . . The act itself is nothing" (Clark, p. 221b). Indulgence in it may be condemned first "as it regards the complicated and arbitrary distinctions of society." The general law applicable here is "that nothing is to be done, which, including your own being in the estimate, will produce, on the whole, greater pain than pleasure. In this sense adultery, seductions, etc., until mankind shall have enough." In the last sentence he apparently means that, until men become more enlightened, one should abide by society's arbitrary laws on adultery. A canceled sentence, revealing that Shelley's fundamental principles had remained unchanged since *Queen Mab,* asserts that the high penalties attached to adultery "seem to depend on elementary feelings in animals as well as men & like revenge avarice perverseness and pride, are found weak in proportion to the extent in intellectual cultivation." Another canceled sentence indicates that the elementary feelings in man are to be defined as "a reluctance that his female companion should be the source of pleasure to another (simply a narrow and envious motive)." [17] These sentences show clearly that Shelley meant physical as well as spiritual love in the famous passage in *Epipsychidion* beginning:

> I never was attached to that great sect,
> Whose doctrine is, that each one should select
> Out of the crowd a mistress or a friend,
> And all the rest, though fair and wise, commend
> To cold oblivion, though 'tis in the code
> Of modern morals. . . .
>
> [*Epipsychidion,* lines 149–54]

Sexual indulgence may also be condemned if it violates "the indestructible laws of human nature." These laws are three:

1st. That the person selected as the subject of this gratification should be as perfect and beautiful as possible, both in body and in mind; so that all sympathies may be harmoniously blended, and the moments of abandonment be prepared by the entire consent of all the conscious portions of our being; the perfection of intercourse consisting, not perhaps in a total annihilation of the instinctive sense, but in the reducing it to as minute a proportion as possible compared with those higher faculties of our nature, from which it derives a value.

2nd. Temperance in pleasure. This prevents the act which ought always to be the link and type of the highest emotions of our nature from degenerating into a diseased habit, equally pernicious to body and mind. . . .

3rd. This act ought to be indulged *according to nature* . . . [Clark, p. 222a. Shelley's italics].

Shelley's horror at the thought of physical perversion is quite genuine. He makes a strained effort to present the Greek view of love sympathetically. He is persuaded that the action by which the Greeks expressed the homosexual passion "was totally different from the ridiculous and disgusting conceptions which the vulgar have formed on the subject." In his desire to find an acceptable substitute, he is led to an ambiguous suggestion which nevertheless becomes a revealing comment on the process at work in the conclusion of *Epipsychidion*:

If we consider the facility with which certain phenomena connected with sleep, at the age of puberty, associate themselves with those images which are the objects of our waking desires; and even that in some persons of an exalted state of sensibility, that a similar process may take place in reverie, it will not be difficult to concieve [*sic*] the almost involuntary consequences of a state of abandonment in the society of a person of surpassing attractions, when the sexual connection cannot exist, to be such as to preclude the necessity of so operose and diabolical a machination as that usually described. This is the result apparently alluded to by Plato [in the *Phaedrus*] [Clark, p. 222b].

But Shelley's conclusion is that,

. . . represent this [homosexual] passion as you will, there is something totally irreconcilable in its cultivation to the beautiful order of social life, to an equal participation in which all human beings have an indefeasible claim, and from which half of the human race, by the Greek arrangement, were excluded [Clark, p. 223a].

The "Discourse" presents a much more honest consideration of love, and a more illuminating commentary on *Epipsychidion,* than have most interpreters of the poem. Shelley's basic attitudes revealed in the "Discourse" may be summed up thus: sexual love is an inseparable part of Ideal Love, which is the universal thirst for a communion of our whole nature; the sexual act ought always to be the *link* and *type* of the highest emotions, from which it derives a strength and value not its own; the sexual impulse serves, he puts it again, "as a kind of type or expression of the rest" (Clark, p. 220b). This statement implies that he would take for granted the use of sexual imagery in his poetry as the symbol or metaphor for Ideal Love. He is not opposed in principle to sexual love for more than one woman; he insists only on chastity and temperance in sexual relations (Clark, p. 221a). By chastity he obviously means, in the literal sense of the word, purity, and by extension sincerity. There should be complete reciprocity, "equal participation" between man and woman. This would undoubtedly be, though Shelley does not say it in so many words, the *sine qua non* for sexual love. One's sexual relations would be regulated by the occasions on which one met the person with whom there was complete empathy or communion, "all sympathies harmoniously blended."

But, though the sexual gratification is essential, Shelley insists repeatedly that it becomes "a very small part of that profound and complicated sentiment, which we call love." The paradox to which he is obviously attracted is that the perfection of sexual intercourse consists "not perhaps in a total annihilation of the instinctive sense, but in the reducing it to as minute a proportion as possible, compared with those higher faculties of our nature, from which it derives a value." [18] In other words the perfect sexual experience is one in which the sexual act itself is almost eliminated or forgotten. The act then truly becomes unimportant, and all necessary sexual gratification can be achieved without it—through what the post-Freudian mind recognizes as the dangerously neurotic substitute of the dream fantasy.

Shelley seems to be suggesting such a substitute in his sentence on the sublimated homosexual experience. Whether or not he was aware of it, the process he describes there is the process by which he presents sexual gratification and the achievement of Ideal Love in his poetry. It is the process responsible for the peculiar imagery and tone so appealing to the Victorian and so repellent to the modern mind. The key phrase to the understanding of the conclusion of *Epipsychidion* is: "in some persons of an exalted sensibility . . . a similar process [of gratification] may take place in reverie." [19]

Among the most familiar images in Shelley's poetry are those of blending or intermingling, which might be grouped together under the heading of the "embrace," and which take on specific significance in the light of the above discussion. The passages quoted from *Epipsychidion* on the touching of mountain and sky, of sea and shore, are examples. The central image of the conclusion is that of a blending into one, which begins by the lovers' looking upon one another:

> And we will talk, until thought's melody
> Become too sweet for utterance, and it die
> In words, to live again in looks. . . .
> Our breath shall intermix, our bosoms bound,
> And our veins beat together.
> > [*Epipsychidion,* lines 560 ff.]

The most famous example of this imagery is in the lyric, *Love's Philosophy:*

> The fountains mingle with the river
> And the rivers with the Ocean,
> The winds of Heaven melt together
> With a sweet emotion:
> Nothing in the world is single;
> All things by a law divine
> In one another's being mingle
> Why not I with thine? [20]

The sexual basis of the imagery is emphasized by the stanza which may have been intended to conclude the poem, but which was not included in the version sent to Sophia Stacey or in the one published by Hunt:

> Follow to the deep wood, sweetest,
> Follow to the wild-briar dingle,
> No eye thou there meetest

When we sink to intermingle,
And the violet tells no tale
To the odour-scented gale,
For they two have enough to do
Of such work as I and you.²¹

The images of flowers and odors are frequent and curious. Odor
aroused in Shelley a blending of sexual pain and pleasure, as the image
in *Epipsychidion* suggests (lines 451–52). In a letter to Peacock, March
23, 1819, he writes of "radiant blue flowers . . . which scatter through
the air the divinest odour which as you recline under the shade of the
ruin, produces a sensation of voluptuous faintness, like the combina-
tions of sweet music" (*Works*, X, 39). Writing to Claire, January 16,
1821, of his health, he says:

The *relapse* which I now suffer into a state of ease from one of pain, is attended
with such an excessive susceptibility of nature, that I suffer equally from pleasure
and from pain. You will ask me naturally enough *where I* find any pleasure?
The wind, the light, the air, the smell of a flower affects me with violent emotions [*Works*, X, 229].

Wind, light, air, odor, music, the fall of rain—these are often used,
interchangeably, to suggest sexual union. In *The Witch of Atlas,* we
are told that the Sun had never beheld so fair a creature as the
mother of the Witch

> . . . as she lay enfolden
> In the warm shadow of her loveliness;—
> He kissed her with his beams, and made all golden
> The chamber of gray rock in which she lay—
> She, in that dream of joy, dissolved away. . . .
> [*Witch of Atlas*, lines 12–16]

She is supposed to have changed into first a vapor, then a cloud, then a
meteor, then a star. Within the cave

> . . . a dewy splendour hidden,
> Took shape and motion: with the living form
> Of this embodied Power, the cave grew warm.
> [*Witch of Atlas*, lines 30–32]

This is the Witch "garmented in light from her own beauty."
In the fourth act of *Prometheus Unbound* all of these images are
used to describe the love of Earth and Moon. The Moon sings to the
Earth:

> Some spirit is darted like a beam from thee,
> Which penetrates my frozen frame.
> And passes with the warmth of flame,
> With love, and odour, and deep melody
> Through me, through me!
> [*Prom. Unbound,* IV.327–31]

As she gazes on him, she feels "green stalks burst forth, and bright flowers grow," and clouds soar "dark with the rain new buds are dreaming of: / Tis love, all love." Similarly, in Act II, scene i, Panthea describes to Asia the effect upon her of looking at Prometheus:

> . . . the overpowering light
> Of that immortal shape was shadowed o'er
> By love; which from his soft and flowing limbs,
> And passion-parted lips, and keen, faint eyes,
> Steamed forth like vaporous fire; an atmosphere
> Which wrapped me in its all-dissolving power,
> As the warm aether of the morning sun
> Wraps ere it drinks some cloud of wandering dew.
> I saw not, heard not, moved not, only felt
> His presence flow and mingle through my blood
> Till it became his life, and his grew mine. . . .
> [*Prom. Unbound,* II.i.71–81]

And in the last scene of the second act, the "voice in the air, singing," describes the effect upon Prometheus of the apotheosis of Asia in similar imagery.[22]

The narcissistic implications, the self-creating, self-consuming quality of this love are everywhere evident. In the song, Prometheus apostrophizes Asia:

> Light of Life! thy lips enkindle
> With their love the breath between them.
> [*Prom. Unbound,* II.v.48–49]

The Moon sings of the Earth in Act IV:

> Thou art folded, thou art lying
> In the light which is undying
> Of thine own joy, and heaven's smile divine. . . .
> [*Prom. Unbound,* IV.437–39]

And again the Earth underlines the sexual implications in the famous stanza, not nearly so interesting for the obvious scientific allusion always emphasized as for the erotic simile:

Plaster cast of medallion of Shelley, posthumous, attributed to Marianne Leigh Hunt

Shelley

> I spin beneath my pyramid of night
> Which points into the heavens dreaming delight,
> Murmuring victorious joy in my enchanted sleep;
> As a youth lulled in love-dreams faintly sighing,
> Under the shadow of his beauty lying,
> Which round his rest a watch of light and warmth doth keep.
>
> [*Prom. Unbound,* IV.444–49]

The description of the flowers in Part I of *The Sensitive Plant* is the most extended development of the narcissistic implications. The flowers

> Shone smiling to Heaven, and everyone
> Shared joy in the light of the gentle sun;
> For each one was interpenetrated
> With the light and the odour its neighbor shed,
> Like young lovers whom youth and love make dear
> Wrapped and filled by their mutual atmosphere.
>
> [*Sensitive Plant,* I.64–69]

The narcissi, "fairest" among them, "gaze on their eyes in the stream's recess, / Till they die of their own dear loveliness." And we remember the "downward gazing" flowers with which the poet longs to deck his hair in *Alastor,* and of which Asia sings in *Prometheus.*

Though in the essay Shelley states that the perfection of intercourse consists not, perhaps, in a total annihilation of the instinctive sense but in reducing it to as minute a proportion as possible, compared with the higher faculties of our nature, the tendency in his poetry is toward an annihilation of all faculties, toward complete dissolution in the love experience. Instead of transcending the senses, he is submerged in them. The concluding passage of *Epipsychidion* is the perfect example of this, with its mingling of the lovers climaxing in

> One life, one death,
> One Heaven, one Hell, one immortality
> And one annihilation.
>
> [*Epipsychidion,* lines 585–87]

Shelley is unwilling to admit to himself (or to his reader) the essential sexual nature of the experience, and so he introduces words and phrases of opposite connotation which conceal it and delude him into believing that he had turned it to something else: "passion's golden purity"; "one / Spirit within two frames"; "flames too pure and light . . . Which point to Heaven"; "One hope within two wills, one will beneath / Two overshadowing minds." But, though he asserts, he does not reveal any spiritual or intellectual transfiguration. What the pattern of words reveals, as in the metaphors within which words like "spirit" are set, is identical with the orgasmic experience as described, for example, by D. H. Lawrence.

The role Shelley usually assigns to himself (or to the "I" of the poems) in the love experience is one of passivity and masochism. The experience he undergoes is one of gradual loss of strength and power. Shelley's conception of love was undoubtedly shaped by his deliberate cultivation of narcissistic reverie, his desire to experience the fullness of the sexual relationship without the sexual act. The passive role of the lover of the ideal is stressed in the most vivid section of *Epipsychidion*. The Moon leads the poet to a cave and puts him to sleep:

> And all my being became bright or dim
> As the Moon's image in a summer sea,
> According as she smiled or frowned on me;
> And there I lay, within a chaste cold bed. . . .
>
> [*Epipsychidion*, lines 296–99]

Into this cavern floated the Sun goddess:

> And called my Spirit, and the dreaming clay
> Was lifted by the thing that dreamed below
> As smoke by fire, and in her beauty's glow
> I stood, and felt the dawn of my long night
> Was penetrating me with living light. . . .
>
> [*Epipsychidion*, lines 338–42]

The Moon and the Sun are the

> Twin spheres of light who rule this passive Earth,
> This world of love, this *me;* and into birth
> Awaken all its fruits and flowers, and dart
> Magnetic might into its central heart. . . .[23]
>
> [*Epipsychidion*, lines 345–48]

As the imagery in the last quotation rather startlingly suggests, not only is the poet's role passive, but it is the traditionally feminine role. Partly responsible is Shelley's conception of the relation of man to the ideal, as symbolized in *Alastor,* where the dream maiden bends above the supine poet and folds "his frame in her dissolving arms." But, even in the love lyrics to Emily, Sophia Stacey, and Jane Williams, he takes the subordinate role. The loved one is made the aggressor, the seducer, as in:

Shelley

I fear thy kisses, gentle maiden,
Thou needest not fear mine.

Or in the lines *To Sophia:*

If the fainting soul is faintest
    When it hears thy harp's wild measure,
Wonder not that when thou speakest
Of the weak my heart is weakest.

As dew beneath the wind of morning,
    As the sea which whirlwinds waken . . .
Is my heart when thine is near it.
        [*To Sophia*, lines 15-20, 24]

The images with which he describes himself are feminine images:
the cave, sea, wave, cloud. The role he takes might be likened to that
of Danae, fainting beneath the shower of gold, or Semele, consumed by
the lightning in which Zeus appeared to her.

The role is also that of the child, as in the image of the Moon
Goddess bending over him in his chaste cold bed, or of the sensitive
plant who was the earliest

Up gathered into the bosom of rest;
A sweet child weary of its delight,
The feeblest and yet the favorite,
Cradled within the embrace of Night. . . .
        [*Sensitive Plant*, I.111-14]

But it is the role of a precocious child, who possesses a knowledge of
sexual love and enjoys innocently the pleasures of sex. The passage
we have discussed at the end of Act III in *Prometheus* and the love
duet between Earth and Moon in Act IV are examples. Frequently, the
connotations of child and passive lover are blended, as in *Epipsychidion.*

The physical and psychological reaction that Shelley associated with
love was enervation. In fact, it was his reaction to every major emotional and sensuous experience. It was, whatever its ultimate cause,
perhaps the basic pattern of his nature. His most consistently held
conception of himself is of the strong man drained of his strength. He
contemplates this portrait with pity, and yet with pride. Sometimes, as
in the *Ode to the West Wind,* he sees himself as one "tameless and
swift, and proud" who has been chained and bowed by the heavy
weight of hours, and specifically by the persecution of society. And

sometimes he sees the loss of power as a sign of his sensitivity, as the price he must pay for having gazed on "Nature's naked loveliness," as the inevitable result of the pursuit of the ideal. It becomes the mark of his superiority to other men. The self-portrait in *Adonais* is the most striking illustration of this attitude. He is

> . . . a Power
> Girt round with weakness;—it can scarce uplift
> The weight of the superincumbent hour;
> It is a dying lamp, a falling shower,
> A breaking billow;—even whilst we speak
> Is it not broken?
>
> [Adonais, lines 282–86]

More often than not, languor and faintness, the movement toward dissolution, are the images of highest potential pleasure. The reaction of the poet in *Alastor* is the fundamental Shelleyan reaction: "His strong heart sunk and sickened with excess / Of Love." For Shelley the ideal situation is, as we have seen, the embrace, the gradual dissolving of self-identity in "the sea of love," in the fusion of two beings into one. It is the eternal suspension on the verge of annihilation, like the suspension of the poet's boat on the edge of the whirlpool in *Alastor*, or, as his death on the edge of the precipice as the horns of the moon sink beneath the horizon suggests, an imperceptible fading into oblivion. But for Shelley the dreamer love is a kind of hypnotic trance in which he, the weaker, is suspended or is constantly revived by the "magnetic might" darting into him from his lover.

The idea of a "living light" radiating from the ideal is found in Shelley's poetry almost from the beginning. But in 1820, through Medwin, he became interested in "animal magnetism" and discovered that he could be easily hypnotized. The reaction to hypnosis may be partly responsible for the particular imagery we have noticed in *Epipsychidion* and the later lyrics. Jane Williams was adept at giving Shelley "magnetic" treatments, and his poems to her directly reflect this relationship. In *The Magnetic Lady to Her Patient* (1822), he has her say that, though she does not love him and cannot be his:

> Like a cloud big with a May shower,
> My soul weeps healing rain
> On thee, thou withered flower!
> It breathes mute music on thy sleep:
> Its odour calms thy brain!

Shelley

Its light within thy gloomy breast
Spreads like a second youth again.
By mine thy being is to its deep
Possesst.
[*Magnetic Lady*, lines 28–36]

In the unfinished poem *Music* (1821) the erotic implications are plain. Here the portrait of the lover fainting toward extinction under the weight of love and kept alive by the power that weakens or drugs him is given its most extravagant expression:

I pant for the music which is divine,
    My heart in its thirst is a dying flower;
Pour forth the sound like enchanted wine,
    Loosen the notes in a silver shower;
Like a herbless plain, for the gentle rain,
    I gasp, I faint, till they wake again.
[*Music*, lines 1–6]

Similarly, in the lines to Sophia quoted earlier he cries that "the fainting soul is faintest / When it hears thy harp's wild measure."

Though Shelley could induce reverie and all the accompanying sensations as easily as he could be hypnotized, he needed to be able to contemplate the ideal in the form of a "real" woman in order to sustain them. In spite of what he says, he did not search for the woman to love; proximity and accident provided them. His worship of these women was, in a way, ritualistic; they were "magnetic" beings by whose presence or look or touch he absorbed restorative powers (a "second youth"), and through dream union with them he realized momentarily his illusions of the Ideal Love. *The Indian Serenade* neatly dramatizes this sexual ritual. The poet arises from dreams of the loved one and is led somnambulistically to her chamber window. The wandering airs faint on the stream; the odors fail like thoughts in a dream; the nightingale's complaint dies upon her heart as the poet must upon that of his beloved—in other words, all nature languishes in a swoon of dissolution. And in the last stanza the beloved must perform the magic ritual of restoration, though the poet implies that it is too late; his heart will break at last, but contentedly. It was this sort of suggestion of the power of the woman and the weakness of the male that I suspect was responsible for much of the tremendous appeal that Shelley had for the Victorian woman.

But the dream union could never be sustained for long under any

[215]

circumstances. There is a different kind of hysterical despair in the last few lines of *Epipsychidion* from that in the love lyrics. When, at the very climax of the ecstatic union, he says that the winged words on which his soul would pierce into the height of love's rare universe are chains of lead—"I pant, I sink, I tremble, I expire!"—he means a number of things. Overtly he is referring to the futility of finding words to express the ideal relationship, and to his belief that, "when composition begins, inspiration is already on the decline." In addition, he realizes that he has been carried too far (for prudence) by the winged words, and so he stops abruptly and tries to avoid the obvious implications by suggesting that the words have kept him from going far enough.

In reality, within the pattern of the dream he has gone as far as he could go; the words have done their duty magnificently. With "annihilation" the union is complete; there is no more that can be said. What follows is the inevitable aftermath of physical and mental exhaustion. But in this case there is more than exhaustion; there is frustration and defeat. He becomes aware, with the climactic words, of the futility of the dream experience; he knows that the union can never be realized (at least with Emily), and he is tolled back "to his sole self." No more than with Keats can his words make the dreams come true. Like Keats in the *Ode to a Nightingale* he learns that "the fancy cannot cheat so well / As she is famed to do." What he has dreamed of is no "abstract" ideal whose prototype is hereafter, but the perfect human love within the perfect earthly setting. And the desolation of his awakening is the greater as he realizes that this is what is unattainable. When he fails to pierce love's universe, his collapse is immediate and complete. Like Icarus he falls to his death. There is no struggle except the convulsive reflex. He makes no effort to live in the imperfect world. He simply gives up. Perhaps Shelley's greatest weakness is revealed in the lack of embarrassment with which he describes his weakness, the unawareness finally that it is a weakness.

Against this background it is now possible to interpret the broader implications of Shelley's view of love and evaluate its effectiveness in his poetry. His basic conception is of a flowing together, a dissolving of identities into one harmonious whole. All things are drawn together, whether human beings or elements of nature, as by a magnetism or gravitational attraction. But only the good and beautiful parts are so drawn, pulled away from the evil, ugly, painful, and violent. The pull is toward a suspension of activity in an intensity of feeling. Shelley's ideal, therefore—whether of man, love, or the universe—is highly simple and limited. Almost all human activities are eliminated except love. And from human love all variety and action are to be removed; it is to be reduced to passive, trancelike faintness from which even the sex act has been eliminated or forgotten, and in which the sexual feelings are purged and purified until adults love each other as innocently as children. All conflict is eliminated from nature, and the universe dissolves into a sea of love. Human relations are reduced, as in the fourth scene of the third act of *Prometheus Unbound,* to familial relations in a pastoral setting and a perpetual state of sentimental affection. Almost all masculine characteristics and activities have been subordinated; the point of view at the end of the third act is primarily female—the final description of the transformation of man is by the Spirit of the Hour who is female. Indeed, Shelley's conception of the ideal society, as of the universe, is by the very nature of his conception of Intellectual Beauty strongly matriarchal. The simplest symbol of the ideal state is that of the lady and the garden in *The Sensitive Plant.*

In sum, his conception of universal and social love is simply the projection of his own extraordinarily intense and limited desires. It was impossible for Shelley as a poet to imagine "perfectibility"; he could imagine only the sharp and immediate change from imperfection to perfection. For him the experience of love was just that: an immediate falling away of evil and pain, and with them a falling away of identity. And when as a poet he contemplated the transformation of society, it was in these terms. All intellectual distinctions—between political and social progress and moral regeneration, between Godwinism and Platonism, between sexual and ideal love, between millennium and heavenly paradise—eddy and dissolve into the reverie. Not the least of Shelley's faults is his unawareness that he is blurring them together, that he is talking of one as if it were another or instead of another, or that he is not now talking of the same thing as a moment ago, that his reverie is not a resolution of the ideas into one transcendent metaphysical concept but a dissolution of them into undifferentiated feelings.

What results is an utterly arbitrary picture of man and nature. When Shelley abandons himself to the dream of love it is as if he drank of the cup of nepenthe, and the world of actuality is blotted out, and he awakes into a world of completely different laws and principles. He suffers poetic amnesia. He does not know what has happened and is unaware that he has left one world for another but takes for granted that his dream world has objective existence. There is here a confusion of identities that borders on delusion and has its counterpart in Shelley's hallucinations. At any rate, the picture he presents at the end of the third act of *Prometheus* becomes so completely personal that it loses the very effect of epic sweep and grandeur for which it strives and conveys instead the effect of eccentricity and distortion. As the cultural conditions that led to a sympathy with the peculiar emotions Shelley expressed and to a yearning to believe that *Prometheus Unbound* was the great epic poem on perfectibility recede in time, the poem's status as work of art is likely to recede proportionally. F. R. Leavis' judgment that it is impossible to go on reading *Prometheus Unbound* at any length with pleasure is too harsh; but in the future the poem is likely to be read as much for its fascination as a psychological document as for its merits as a work of art.[24]

V. THE BITTER PROPHECY

The world presented at the end of *Prometheus,* like that presented at the end of *Epipsychidion,* is a dream world, and it is obvious that it can never be attained through any evolution of human nature or human society as Shelley knew it and as he had the Furies show it to Prometheus. Indeed, the end of *Prometheus* suggests a morbid antipathy and revulsion against society in any form. There is an indifference to, even a dislike of, human beings as the novelist or dramatist would be interested in them.[25] In the famous last lines of Act III men are systematically reduced to the virtuous abstraction, man, by a series of negative adjectives. This basic, partly unconscious revulsion is vividly revealed in the *Revolt of Islam,* as well as the realization that the perfect existence is attainable only in dream or death. In spite of the superficial optimism of the preface and many of the speeches within the poem, in spite of the momentary success of the bloodless revolution, the poem is a narrative of suffering and failure. Laon and Cythna in the end give themselves up to martyrs' deaths on behalf not of the people, but of each other. They are consumed in a funeral pyre which is very clearly a love-death:

> She smiled on me, and nothing then we said,
> But each upon the other's countenance fed
> Looks of insatiate love; the mighty veil

Shelley

Which doth divide the living and the dead
Was almost rent, the world grew dim and pale—
All light in Heaven or Earth beside our love did fail.
[*Revolt of Islam,* XII, stanza 15]

They awake in the paradise of *Kubla Khan* (Coleridge's influence is evident here) and *Alastor:*

> . . . on the waved and golden sand
> Of a clear pool, upon a bank o'ertwined
> With strange and star-bright flowers, which to the wind
> Breathed divine odour; high above, was spread
> The emerald heaven of trees of unknown kind,
> Whose moonlight blooms and bright fruits overhead
> A shadow, which was light, upon the waters shed.
>
> And round about sloped many a lawny mountain
> With incense-bearing forests, and vast caves
> Of marble radiance, to that mighty fountain. . . .
> [*Revolt of Islam,* XII, stanzas 18, 19]

To them comes the silver-winged child who is their daughter but who has been raised by the tyrant. After their death she dies of the plague. She tells them how before she died a man rose before the multitude and told them that those had been killed "who might have made this life's envenomed dream / A sweeter draught than ye will ever taste," and that there is lent to man "the wisdom of a high despair, / When such can die, and he live on." For the speaker "the world is grown too void and cold, / Since Hope pursues immortal Destiny / With steps thus slow." So he plunges a dagger into his heart.

The speech echoes the conclusion of *Alastor* and anticipates the conclusion of *Adonais.* It shows that Shelley had no real conviction that mankind could be changed; life is the "envenomed dream." What attracts him here as in *Alastor* and *Adonais* is the unabashed dream fantasy of the superior individual who is either persecuted and martyred or driven to his death by the unappeasable demands of his own nature (in either case, he is "too good for this world") and who looks down from his dream world upon mankind, whose lot he could have improved, and which is so much the poorer now that he is gone, and which somehow will come to realize and regret his death. *Prometheus* is simply the dream with a happy ending, in which the martyred hero saves mankind *in spite of itself,* through his suffering.

After telling them of the man who kills himself, the child carries

[219]

The Romantic Ventriloquists

Laon and Cythna in her boat down the river until they enter a "windless waveless lake."

> And in the midst, afar, even like a sphere
> Hung in one hollow sky, did there appear
> The Temple of the Spirit. . . .
> [*Revolt of Islam*, XII, stanza 41]

Drawn by the sound that issued from the temple, the boat approached and found its haven there. The similarity of the pattern here to the conclusions of *Epipsychidion* and *Adonais* is evident.

In *Hellas*, written in the same years as *Adonais*, we have a last illustration of Shelley's conflicting attitudes on human perfection. *Hellas* is a more complex, mature, and interesting poem than *Prometheus*, in spite of the obvious carelessness with which it was written. Like *The Triumph*, it shows a more controlled and disciplined use of structure, a more varied and subtle imagery in the lyrics, and a more objective and intellectually consistent conception than do the earlier poems. It is obscure and difficult, partly because of the unnecessarily involved and rhetorically strained reports of Hassan and the messengers, but also because of the highly complex yet concentrated symbolism. Hellas, for example, stands for ancient Greece, for the independent state which the modern Greeks are fighting to restore, for America, for the regenerated state of mankind, for the Golden Age of the future, and for the "intellectual empire" of ancient Greece which is

> Built below the tide of war,
> Based on the crystàlline sea
> Of thought and its eternity
> [*Hellas*, lines 697–99]

and which will be the eternal ideal, inspiring men in the fight for liberty.

In the interaction of the characters, Shelley throws into sharp juxtaposition the main cultures of Western civilization: Greek and Christian in the Chorus of Captive Women; Byzantine and Moslem in Mahmud and Hassan; and Jewish in Ahasuerus. The dramatic conflict of the poem builds by opposing the physical victories of the Turks to the moral victories of the Greeks. Mahmud is presented as possessed of a fatalistic despair, convinced that the present victories are the prelude to ultimate defeat. But the action of the poem ends with the implications of defeat instead for the Greek cause, in the announce-

ment of the refusal of Austria, Russia, and France to intervene and of
England's intervention on the side of the Turks. The final semi-
choruses concede this defeat and turn their hope for freedom to islands
in the western sea:

> Darkness has dawned in the East
> On the noon of time:
> The death-birds descend to their feast
> From the hungry clime.
> Let Freedom and Peace flee far
> To a sunnier strand,
> And follow Love's folding-star
> To the Evening land!
>
> .   .   .   .
>
> Through the sunset of hope,
> Like the shapes of a dream
> What Paradise islands of glory gleam!
> [*Hellas*, lines 1023–30, 1050–53]

These lines and the phrase "kingless continents sinless as Eden"
(line 1047) suggest America, but within the context the reference is
general rather than specific, a symbol of hope rather than of prophecy.
It is simply Shelley's dream paradise given a "local habitation and a
name." A significant change in attitude has taken place, however; he is
more cautious and subdued. "The final chorus is indistinct and obscure,"
he says in a note, "as the event of the living drama whose arrival it
foretells. Prophecies of war . . . may safely be made . . . in any age;
but to anticipate however darkly a period of regeneration and happiness
is a more hazardous exercise of the faculty which bards possess or
feign" (*Works*, III, 57). In the last stanza of the chorus the vision of
the "brighter Hellas" is cut off, and the poet breaks into agonized
pleading:

> O, cease! must hate and death return?
> Cease! must men kill and die?
> Cease! drain not to its dregs the urn
> Of bitter prophecy.
> The world is weary of the past,
> Oh, might it die or rest at last!
> [*Hellas*, lines 1096–1110]

It is as if he suddenly saw the Hellas of the future destroyed in its
turn like the Hellas of the past, or perhaps never capable of being
realized at all.

The Romantic Ventriloquists

The note of doubt, even despair, upon which the poem ends is consistent with the point of view expressed by Ahasuerus earlier, which is in turn consistent with the attitude of *Adonais*. It is the point of view that dominated Shelley's thinking during the last years of his life and in fact was implicit in his temperament from the beginning. Ahasuerus is an interesting contrast to Prometheus. He is "so old / He seems to have outlived a world's decay." He dwells in a sea cavern, Hassan tells Mahmud:

> 'Mid the Demonesi, less accessible
> Than thou or God! He who would question him
> Must sail alone at sunset, where the stream
> Of Ocean sleeps around those foamless isles. . . .
> [*Hellas*, lines 164–67]

Hassan says that he may have attained to his knowledge of things which others fear and know not

> . . . by dreadful abstinence
> And conquering penance of the mutinous flesh,
> Deep contemplation and unwearied study. . . .
> [*Hellas*, lines 155–57]

When they meet, Ahasuerus advises Mahmud to talk no more of themselves or of past and future, but to look on that which cannot change—"the One, / The unborn and the undying." This physical universe, this whole

> Of suns, and worlds, and men, and beasts, and flowers,
> With all the silent or tempestuous workings
> By which they have been, are, or cease to be,
> Is but a vision:—all that it inherits
> Are motes of a sick eye, bubbles and dreams;
> Thought is its cradle and its grave, nor less
> The Future and the Past are idle shadows
> Of thought's eternal flight—they have no being:
> Nought is but that which feels itself to be.
> [*Hellas*, lines 776–85]

The physical universe, then, derives its reality from thought. But the moment thought is incarnated in physical or mortal form it begins to decay and degenerate. Life is not healthy thought, but a morbid dream, "motes of a sick eye" or, as Shelley cries in *Adonais,* a stormy vision where we keep

[222]

Shelley

With phantoms an unprofitable strife,
And in mad trance, strike with our spirit's knife
Invulnerable nothings—*We* decay
Like corpses in a charnel. . . .

[*Adonais,* lines 346–49]

The view of history that Ahasuerus presents and that dominates the conclusion of *Hellas* is cyclic. Man eternally dreams of perfection, momentarily moves toward it, and loses it in war and hate and death. As Mahmud hears the cries of victory that interrupt the prophecy of the phantom of Mahomet, he says:

Come what may,
The Future must become the Past, and I
As they were to whom once this present hour,
This gloomy crag of time to which I cling,
Seemed an Elysian isle of peace and joy
Never to be attained.

[*Hellas,* lines 923–28]

And the chorus, as it hears the cries, says that if Greece must be a wreck its fragments shall reassemble and build themselves

In a diviner clime,
To Amphionic music on some Cape sublime,
Which frowns above the idle foam of Time.

[*Hellas,* lines 1005–7]

The tone of *Hellas* is somber and ironic like that of *The Triumph.* Its point of view is ambiguous but not necessarily confused or contradictory. Perfection can be achieved only in thought—in the eternal ideal or its reflection in mortal minds like those of the ancient Greeks. Any mortal efforts to achieve it are doomed to failure. It would seem, then, that the only possible way of life for the one who sought perfection would be that of Ahasuerus, the life of contemplation. But there is the further implication that the effort toward perfection is important and must be encouraged, that from the effort comes a moral strength which weakens psychologically the corrupt *status quo* (as Mahmud is weakened) and makes possible a change for the better. Maybe the change will not take place, but the poet has a duty to do everything he can to make men aware of the possibilities.

Shelley's immediate intent in *Hellas* seems to be to catch the conscience of the English by pointing out to them that in effect the fate of the Greeks and the "brighter Hellas" is in their hands and that by

[223]

their shameful foreign policy they have betrayed their trust. At any rate, in *Hellas* he comes closer than in any other major poem to a realization of his ideal of the poet "as the unacknowledged legislator." He is projecting his attitudes into a concrete and contemporary situation that is capable of being handled both literally and symbolically. He shows greater awareness both as poet and thinker of the problems he must solve than in any earlier poems. He keeps distinct the dream and reality. He avoids soaring off into the intoxication of unfounded optimism or of the love reverie. He keeps himself out of the poem. But in the very last stanza he reveals the bitterness and despondency that lie close to the surface of Ahasuerus' philosophy and that supply the dominant tone of *Adonais*.

VI. THE SHELTER OF THE TOMB

The generally accepted critical view of *Adonais* is that, beginning as a lament, it is transmuted in the last stanzas into a poem of affirmation in which death is "victory, an awakening from the feverish dream of Life into the unstained radiance of Eternity. This [is] an elegy not voicing the grief of the heart so much as the exaltation of the soul." [26] But to read the poem in this way is to be blind to the imagery and deaf to the tone of renunciation. For *Adonais* voices an almost Swiftian revulsion against human life. The conditions of life are presented as utterly corrupt and noisome (*"We* decay / Like corpses in a charnel . . . cold hopes swarm like worms within our living clay"). The struggle for survival is a madman's dream (we keep "with phantoms an unprofitable strife"). The ruling social order, symbolized by the critic, is irredeemably loathsome. There is no pretense here of perfectibility; the only escape from the nightmare of life is death. A distinction is drawn between the hideous dream of human life and the beauty of the physical universe, which is the outward manifestation and expression of the ideal with which Adonais becomes one at his death. At the end, therefore, the poem becomes an hypnotic exhortation to self-destruction:

Die,
If thou wouldst be with that which thou dost seek!
Follow where all is fled!—Rome's azure sky,
Flowers, ruins, statues, music, words, are weak
The glory they transfuse with fitting truth to speak.

Why linger, why turn back, why shrink, my Heart?
Thy hopes are gone before; from all things here
They have departed; thou shouldst now depart!
A light is passed from the revolving year,
And man and woman; and what still is dear
Attracts to crush, repels to make thee wither.
The soft sky smiles—the low wind whispers near:
Tis Adonais calls! oh, hasten thither,
No more shall Life divide what Death can join together.

[*Adonais,* lines 464–76]

Logically examined, the concluding section clashes with contradictions. Man and nature are set against one another. Human life is illusion, but the physical world is real. The separation of man and nature is a familiar Romantic attitude, but here, precisely because of the Platonic emphasis, it seems particularly arbitrary. If man is illusion, then his world must be also. Adonais' immortality is presented as both impersonal and personal. There is an evident shift in perspective between stanza 43, where Adonais is considered as a portion of the Ideal Beauty, and stanza 45, where he is one of the inheritors of unfulfilled renown. In the latter, his immortality consists in part at least in his "transmitted effluence," the preservation of his words among mankind, so that now human life is being taken for granted as real enough. Only the force of feeling fuses these contradictions. And this feeling is simply the feeling of *Epipsychidion,* intensified and freed of the trammels of erotic love.

When Shelley turns in stanzas 36 through 38 from the lament by the shepherd poets over the bier of Keats to the violent castigation of the critic who has been responsible for his death, one can almost see in the movement of the syntax at the beginning of stanza 38 how suddenly it occurs to him that there is no cause for lament: "Nor let us weep that our delight is fled. . . ." At first, the particular nature of death is a matter of indifference: "He wakes or sleeps with the enduring dead." The important thing is that the critic cannot "soar where he is sitting now"; the pure spirit shall flow back to the eternal burning fountain whence it came while the critic's cold embers choke the sordid hearth of shame. And, as if kindled by the image, Shelley bursts into the impassioned contrast between life and death in which the formal elegiac trappings are forgotten. Keats has awakened to the peace and rest, to the freedom from "envy and calumny and hate and pain," for which Shelley has so often yearned. In stanza 40, the references become very personal. Keats has died young and can never mourn "a heart grown cold, a head grown gray in vain." He can never experience the corruption, frustration, and failure of age. How emotional, how unpremeditated the Platonic imagery of the poem is, is shown by the use of the burning spirit image in the last lines of stanza 40 to suggest, instead of immortality, the mortality of the spirit, dying simply through age. Adonais can never,

> . . . when the spirit's self has ceased to burn,
> With sparkless ashes load an unlamented urn.
> [*Adonais,* lines 359–60]

In stanzas 41–42 Shelley sees Adonais as made one with nature. The conception is vaguely pantheistic, reminding us of the early poems of Wordsworth and Coleridge and the bold claim of Byron in *Childe Harold,* Canto III: "I live not in myself, but I become / Portion of that around me." But, as Beach puts it succinctly, "it is not obvious why he is more one with her [nature] being dead than while he was living and actively dealing with her." [27] Part of the answer is in the imagery of the stanzas. Shelley has imagined Keats transported to the paradise to which he himself was always yearning to withdraw. "Ye caverns and ye forests," "Ye faint flowers and fountains"—these are the familiar elements of the dream retreat. The image at the end of stanza 41 is in the same "symbolic cluster" as the image describing the island in lines 470–71 of *Epipsychidion.* What has been omitted is, significantly enough, the erotic connotation.

Though, philosophically, the conception of stanzas 40–43 should be that of a loss of individual identity or personality in nature or in the power "which has withdrawn his being to its own," the imagery clearly emphasizes a retention of that identity. "His voice" is heard in all of nature's music; "he is a presence to be felt and known" wherever that power may move which "wields the world with never-wearied love"; "he doth bear / His part, while the one Spirit's plastic stress / Sweeps through the dull dense world." Keats as an individual has, in other words, been made one with the Intellectual Beauty or Ideal Love for which the poet in *Alastor* sought. He has achieved that union which could be achieved only in dream or in death. And through it he has achieved the power which he could not have in life; *he* is heard and felt and known as a portion of that spirit which molds the world and

[226]

bursts "in its beauty and its might / From trees and beasts and men into the Heaven's light." It is at this point that the fantasy of the "inheritors of unfulfilled renown" occurs, and only within this emotional context does it seem to be a natural and relevant development rather than an abrupt shift in perspective or conception. Not only has Keats achieved power, but he has achieved in death the recognition denied him in life.

In short, Keats has achieved the fulfillment of self that Shelley had futilely sought through the dream of perfectibility in *Prometheus Unbound* and the dream of love in *Epipsychidion*. So, inevitably, Shelley is led to an uncontrollable longing for death for himself. As W. B. Yeats says, in the last stanzas "he sings of Death as of a mistress." [28] In *Epipsychidion* he had written of the one passion in twin hearts growing:

> Till like two meteors of expanding flame,
> Those spheres instinct with it become the same,
> Touch, mingle, are transfigured; ever still
> Burning, yet ever inconsumable;
> In one another's substance finding food,
> Like flames too pure and light and unimbued
> To nourish their bright lives with baser prey,
> Which point to Heaven and cannot pass away. . . .
> [*Epipsychidion*, lines 576–83]

Now, discarding the earthly love which was intermediary between him and the ideal, he writes:

> . . . that sustaining Love
> Which through the web of being blindly wove
> By man and beast and earth and air and sea,
> Burns bright or dim, as each are mirrors of
> The fire for which all thirst; now beams on me,
> Consuming the last clouds of cold mortality.
> [*Adonais*, lines 481–86]

In the concluding stanzas of *Adonais* the will to die is expressed with a frightening sense of immediacy. The reader is swept into the conviction that as Shelley writes the breath *does* descend upon him and his spirit's bark *is* being driven toward the abode of the eternal. Momentarily, the distinction between life and death has faded for him, as the distinction between the dream and life had been lost in other poems.

The Romantic Ventriloquists

There are in Shelley's other late poems and in his actions abundant indications of an increasingly morbid obsession with death. Two stories told by Trelawny have particular pertinence in relation to the conclusion of *Adonais*. In the one, Shelley expressed a desire to learn to swim. When Trelawny proposed to teach him, Shelley jumped into the pool, plunged immediately to the bottom, and made no effort to rise. After Trelawny had rescued him, he said: "I always find the bottom of the well, and they say Truth lies there. In another minute I should have found it, and you would have found an empty shell. It is an easy way to get rid of the body." In the other story, he took Jane Williams and her children sailing at evening in the Bay of Lerici. As they drifted farther from the shore he cried, "Now let us solve the great riddle together." [29] To Medwin he talked of suicide. [30] On June 18, 1822, he wrote Trelawny for prussic acid: "I need not tell you that I have no intention of suicide at present, but I confess it would be a comfort to me to hold in my possession that golden key to the chamber of perpetual rest" (*Works*, X, 405). [31]

There is no doubt that in certain moods, and not always moods of dejection, Shelley was "teased out of thought" by the lure of death, irresistibly attracted to the exploration of what lay on the other side of life. Between the death wish and the wish to withdraw from the world (which Shelley expressed, for example, in the letter of August, 1821, to Mary) exists no difference in kind but simply one in degree of intensity. [32] Both are expressions of his intense emotional revulsion against his present life rather than products of reasoned philosophical convictions. They reveal the extent of his disillusionment, bitterness, and weariness. They reflect an almost pathological desire to escape into a dream world, if not on earth, then in death. [33]

It is in this perspective that the Platonism of *Adonais* should be considered. Philosophically it only serves, as Beach drily comments, "to confuse the issues involved in the question of immortality." [34] Actually, Shelley's reasoned opinions on immortality in his letters and essays were primarily skeptical. By and large he was inclined to doubt the possibility of the survival either of the individual personality or of the mind. [35] But, as he pointed out in the preface to *Prometheus Unbound*, he did not consider it the province of poetry to present "a reasoned system on the theory of human life." On the contrary, the function of poetry was to embody "beautiful idealisms," imaginings, feelings and

[228]

intuitions, longings, and dreams. *Adonais,* like *Epipsychidion,* was an expression of pent-up attitudes released by a particular situation. And the Platonic imagery was the natural, indeed inevitable medium for conveying attitudes toward immortality which he longed to hold, and which momentarily he was swept into accepting as truth. There was no effort to express a logically consistent philosophy or even a statement of faith which he would find intellectually defensible, as so many critics seem determined to believe.

The attitude of mind he was trying to articulate he explained in the essay *On Life* in the course of telling why he had rejected the philosophy of materialism:

> I was discontented with such a view of things as it afforded; man is a being of high aspirations, "looking both before and after," whose "thoughts wander through eternity," disclaiming alliance with transience and decay; incapable of imagining to himself annihilation; existing but in the future and the past; being, not what he is, but what he has been and shall be. Whatever may be his true and final destination, there is a spirit within him at enmity with nothingness and dissolution. This is the character of all life and being.

He is presenting here no metaphysical speculations, but the desires of man which he feels must be taken into account. In *Adonais* this "spirit" at enmity with dissolution is given expression. Again in *On Life* he says that there are some people who are always children: "Those who are subject to the state called reverie, feel as if their nature were dissolved into the surrounding universe, or as if the surrounding universe were absorbed into their being" (*Works,* VI, 194–95). This is the state of reverie which he objectifies in his presentation of Adonais as "one with nature."

But perhaps the most significant comment on the attitude with which Shelley wrote *Adonais,* and the attitude with which he would want it read, is in a note affixed to the first chorus in *Hellas:*

That there is a true solution of the riddle [of immortality], and that in our present state the solution is unattainable by us, are propositions that may be regarded as equally certain: meanwhile, as it is the province of the poet to attach himself to those ideas which exalt and ennoble humanity, let him be permitted to have conjectured the condition of that futurity towards which we are all impelled by an inextinguishable thirst for immortality. Until better arguments can be produced than sophisms which disgrace the cause, this desire itself must remain the strongest and the only presumption that eternity is the inheritance of every thinking being [*Works,* III, 56].[36]

The conception of the poet's function suggested here, together with the theory of composition that Shelley describes in *A Defence of Poetry,* is responsible unfortunately for most of the faults in his poetry. In both theory and practice Shelley carried the implications of Romantic poetic theory to their ultimate extreme. No more dangerous set of beliefs could have been devised for a man of his temperament than those he expounds in the *Defence;* they encouraged him to indulge his weaknesses at the expense of his virtues.

The writing of poetry came easily, as the immense amount of juvenile verse shows. And, because it did, Shelley was careless and impatient in technical matters such as syntax and punctuation—even, general critical opinion to the contrary, in structure and metrics. In fact, he was until the last few years somewhat contemptuous of poetry as a craft. Poetry he saw as a spontaneous art, not a trade to be learned, and there is nothing to indicate that he served any vigorous apprenticeship. He possessed, indeed, a remarkably retentive mind, and he absorbed as if by osmosis the tricks and mannerisms of the poets good and bad whom he admired. From childhood he had a kind of uncritical veneration for the poet as a superior individual who spoke a superior language; and so he cultivated a strained and high-flown diction in the worst manner of the eighteenth century.

Undoubtedly, he conceived of the nature of poetry as fundamentally the spontaneous overflow of powerful feelings, and its success was to be measured by the extent to which it provoked a corresponding overflow in the reader. "It is the business of the Poet," he said in the preface to *The Revolt of Islam,* "to communicate to others the pleasure and the enthusiasm arising out of those images and feelings in the vivid presence of which within his own mind consists at once his inspiration and his reward" (*Works,* I, 240). He prided himself upon his sensitivity and deliberately cultivated it. Godwin had written to praise Shelley's prose writings and to censure *The Revolt,* and to urge that his powers lay in the direction of prose rather than of poetry. In reply, Shelley said:

I am formed, if for anything not in common with the herd of mankind, to apprehend minute and remote distinctions of feeling, whether relative to external nature or the living beings which surround us, and to communicate the con-

[230]

ceptions which result from considering either the moral or the material universe as a whole [*Works*, I, 410].[37]

He was led willfully and mistakenly through this belief not only to separate reason and feeling, but to set them in opposition to one another. Reason was not only unnecessary to poetic creation, but actually detrimental. Poetry, he proclaims boldly in the *Defence*, "differs in this respect from logic, that it is not subject to the control of the active powers of the mind, and that its birth and recurrence have no necessary connection with the consciousness or will" (*Works*, VII, 138). In one respect, then, the sign of true poetry is its freedom from logic or, as Shelley would certainly see it, its superiority to logic. Indeed, the poet under the intense pressure of composition does not dare and is perhaps unable to stop for logical considerations. The slightest hesitancy, and he will have perhaps fatally impaired the communication of his super-rational imaginative experience, which is the all-important matter. Shelley's remarkable description of the creative process must be quoted in full:

> Poetry is not like reasoning, a power to be exerted according to the determination of the will. A man cannot say, "I will compose poetry." The greatest poet even cannot say it; for the mind in creation is as a fading coal, which some invisible influence, like an inconstant wind, awakens to transitory brightness: this power arises from within, like the colour of a flower which fades and changes as it is developed, and the conscious portions of our nature are unprophetic either of its approach or its departure. Could this influence be durable in its original purity and force, it is impossible to predict the greatness of the results; but when composition begins, inspiration is already on the decline, and the most glorious poetry that has ever been communicated to the world is probably a feeble shadow of the original conception of the Poet. I appeal to the great poets of the present day, whether it be not an error to assert that the finest passages of poetry are produced by labour and study [*Works*, VII, 135–36].

Though Shelley has undoubtedly been carried away by enthusiasm into extravagant claims which in calmer moods he would alter or modify, nevertheless the statements in the *Defence* can be assumed to represent fundamental convictions, growing out of his own experience and in turn governing and molding his practice. As Albert Guerard observes, this essay "is the classic defense of automatic writing. . . . For Shelley as for Blake, the poet was a passive medium through which the divine afflatus worked." [38] The invitation to self-indulgence in such a view, to a suspension of self-criticism, is evident. The poet is encouraged to accept unquestioningly whatever he writes as he writes it; he is unwilling and finally unable to discriminate among the parts of a composition; he discards nothing. Shelley revised a great deal; some of his manuscripts are so marked up as to be nearly illegible, but most of these revisions were done in the heat of composition and consist largely of interpolations or alterations of words and phrases. As Leavis says, "the critical part of Shelley's creative labour was a matter of getting the verse to feel right." [39] He almost never deleted or excised; instead he added. The dialogue between the Spirit of the Earth and Asia in the third act of *Prometheus Unbound* which we discussed earlier was added, for example. Keats hit with his uncanny acuteness upon Shelley's failings:

You, I am sure, will forgive me for sincerely remarking that you might curb your magnanimity, and be more of an artist, and "load every rift" of your subject with ore. The thought of such discipline must fall like cold chains upon you, who perhaps never sat with your wings furled, for six months together . . . I am in expectation of *Prometheus* everyday. Could I have my own wish for its interest effected, you would have it still in manuscript—or be but now putting an end to the second act.[40]

With his conception of the creating mind as a fading coal, Shelley was committed to the belief that the more headlong and rapid the composition was, the better. Only thus could even "a feeble shadow of the original conception of the poet" be communicated. In his preface to *The Revolt of Islam* Shelley said:

I would willingly have sent it forth to the world with that perfection which long labour and revision is said to bestow. But I found that, if I should gain something in exactness by this method, I might lose much of the newness and energy of imagery and language as it flowed fresh from my mind [*Works*, I, 247].

In practice, rapidity of composition led to the paradox of prolixity. All of Shelley's major poems suffer from the "repetition and eddying, instead of progression, of thought" which Coleridge found so annoying in Wordsworth. In *Prometheus Unbound* and *Epipsychidion,* some of the difficulty in reading comes from the wearying variations on a few basic images, and the repetition of vague words. It is quite revealing that Shelley was tremendously impressed with the performances of Sgricci, the *improvvisatore,* at the end of 1820, and particularly with his improvisations on the model of Greek poetic drama.[41] Blunden suggests that *Epipsychidion* "has a hurry and flow, together with some want of determined and distinctive language, which suggest that he was trying to do what he had heard Sgricci do. It has the air of a glittering improvisation." [42] And Shelley himself called *Hellas* "a mere improvise" (*Works*, III, 7).

But improvisation suggests too much the clever exhibition of professional skill, too casual an attitude toward the creative act, to account adequately for Shelley's practice. We have to turn back and pick up Guerard's reference to the poet as the passive medium for the "divine afflatus." For in the *Defence of Poetry*, at least, Shelley sees poetry as the product of a kind of vatic trance. The poet is the inspired seer, the intoxicated oracle through whom the divine voice speaks. The oracular image is one that Shelley frequently uses, most spectacularly perhaps in Act II, scene iii, of *Prometheus Unbound* where Panthea cries that the sound has borne Asia and her to the mighty portal of Demogorgon's realm:

> Whence the oracular vapour is hurled up
> Which lonely men drink wandering in their youth,
> And call truth, virtue, love, genius or joy,
> That maddening wine of life, whose dregs they drain
> To deep intoxication; and uplift
> Like Maenads who cry loud, Evoe! Evoe!
> The voice which is contagion to the world.
> [*Prom. Unbound*, II.iii.4–10]

With the oracular function is associated, it may be noted, the cup; some of this association undoubtedly clings ironically to the cup of nepenthe offered Rousseau in *The Triumph*.

On various occasions Shelley speaks of the excitement or the "unbounded and sustained" enthusiasm with which he composed. In the letter to Godwin he says significantly that much of *The Revolt of Islam* was written "with the same feeling—as real, though not so prophetic—as the communications of a dying man" (*Works*, I, 410). Of many of his major poems the same thing could be said. In the last months of his life, Shelley mentions several times with a kind of fatalistic resignation his loss of incentive to write. To Gisborne he says:

I write little now. It is impossible to compose except under the strong excitement of an assurance of finding sympathy in what you write . . . I do not go on with "Charles the First." I feel too little certainty of the future, and too little satisfaction with regard to the past, to undertake any subject seriously and deeply. I stand, as it were, upon a precipice, which I have ascended with great, and cannot descend without *greater* peril, and I am content if the heaven above me is calm for the passing moment [*Works*, X, 403–4].

Shelley's emphasis on the need to think of his poems as "public" as he composes, to have in mind an audience outside himself, is revealing.

The incantatory tone is strongly evident in all of Shelley's poetry. It is obvious that he could easily induce and compose in a state of intense excitement such as his contemporaries strove for in theory but could not so readily achieve in practice. His abnormal sensibility is shown by his hallucinations; his susceptibility to hypnosis; his Platonic love-making; his violent response to the reading of poetry, as in the famous story of his response to *Christabel;* his somnambulism; and so on. He had what the modern psychologist calls a "low threshold." He seemed to move quite involuntarily in response to certain stimuli from the conscious control of the ego to almost (but never quite) uninhibited expression of the id. And, because he believed that such should be the process of poetic creation, he came to cultivate voluntarily "the switching off of the intelligence." [43] It was, at any rate, the switching off of self-consciousness, and an encouragement to pour out his "full heart / In profuse strains of unpremeditated art."

This attitude and practice are partly responsible for the constant self-portraits and the autobiographical abandonment of poems like *Julian and Maddalo* and *Epipsychidion.* They are portraits and revelations of the artist, who is compelled to express them by the obscure forces that drive him. Shelley sees the poet as a mythic being, as semidivine or at least more than human under the influence of his inspiration, whose experiences—particularly whose sufferings and trials—become of universal interest and importance. The self-pity grows out of the fact that he has been chosen through no will of his own to bear the burden of revelation, on the one hand, and to be hated and persecuted by mankind in consequence, on the other. There is a curious suggestion of religious predestination in this conception—he is the sacrificial victim possessed of vision which is both blessing and curse, but mainly curse for him as a human being: it condemns him to a life of suffering. The narcissism in this attitude is staggering, but it cannot be summarily dismissed as simple egotism. For Shelley stood genuinely in awe of his own powers and of his own personality; he described himself often in a naïvely detached manner, as if he were watching the mirror image of himself (the mirror image, in fact, recurs frequently in his poetry). There is a kind of clinical realism, an effort at psychological honesty and completeness, in poems like *Alastor, Ode to the West Wind,* and *Adonais.* The trouble was that Shelley tended to be absorbed by the mirror image to the exclusion of the truth he was to reveal. Furthermore, in mistaking the neuroses of the man for the infirmities of genius, he was led into an extravagant indulgence in the neuroses which was almost fatal to the poet. It is this self-delusion that is responsible for what the modern reader finds the most unpleasant and graveling characteristics in the poetry.

Shelley's conception of the role of the poet is in part responsible also for the frequent contradictions in his poetry between tone and meaning that stir up in us as we read such curiously confused reactions. D. G. James puts the basic cause of confusion neatly: "It is the language of enthusiasm where we might have expected the language of dismay."[44] He points to the concluding passage in Act III of *Prometheus Unbound* as an example. Probably the most notable example is in *Adonais.* But all the major poems with the exception of *The Triumph of Life* in one way or another illustrate it. James calls Shelley's practice "a kind of disingenuousness." But this is, I think, too harsh; the explanation is once again not quite so simple.

Shelley believed, as we have seen, that the poet in his public function was seer or oracle. And his language was therefore the language of the divine speaking through the man, a highly ritualistic and "daedal" language of incantation. Furthermore, the purpose of the poet was to uplift, to present "beautiful idealisms of moral excellence." And in the *Defence of Poetry,* which is itself a prose poem, at least in its latter pages, and presents as fact what Shelley longed to believe and "in the intervals of inspiration" could not bring himself to believe and indeed feared to be false, he is led to the sweeping assertion: "Poetry is the record of the best and happiest moments of the happiest and best minds." This, especially the "happiest" (whether we take it as "most felicitous," "most fortunate," or "most joyful"), was patently not true of the greater part of Shelley's own poetry. What he means, as the paragraph goes on to make clear, is that poetry *should be* the records of those moments in which those "of the most delicate sensation and the most enlarged imagination" are granted glimpses of eternal truth. "The enthusiasm of virtue, love, patriotism, and friendship is essentially linked" with the emotions aroused by these moments.

[235]

Poetry thus makes immortal all that is best and most beautiful in the world . . .
turns all things to loveliness; it exalts the beauty of that which is most beautiful
and it adds beauty to that which is most deformed . . . it strips the veil of
familiarity from the world, and lays bare the naked and sleeping beauty, which
is the spirit of its forms [*Works*, VII, 137].

As these familiar phrases echo through our minds, we realize that
Shelley was passionately sincere in his belief that poetry should be
intensely positive and optimistic in tone. The exalted rhetoric and the
phrenetic affirmation which came naturally to him, he in turn cultivated as the manner proper and even necessary to poetry; and soon he
fell into it automatically whenever he assumed the role of the poet. The
language was therefore a very limited and inflexible instrument in
Shelley's hands. It was inevitably often at odds with the feeling he
was trying to express and tended to veil or falsify that feeling even
for the poet himself. And it was also inevitably at odds with the increasingly frequent intrusions of intellect into composition. These
factors, along with the mad rush of composition, account for many of
the logical shifts and contradictions we have noticed.

The contradiction between tone and idea is particularly evident in
the poems on the social order. The tone leads us to expect the imminent
triumph of the new society and the regeneration of man. But, in *The
Revolt of Islam,* hero and heroine fail in their efforts (society seems
utterly unregenerate); they are martyred and find their hope in
heaven. In the famous concluding lines of Act III of *Prometheus* the
soaring apostrophe to perfected man contains qualifications that almost
cancel out what have previously been asserted as permanent benefits of
Prometheus' release. Throughout the play we are confronted with a
bewildering variety of suggestions as to the origin and nature of evil,
the cause of Jupiter's triumph, and the relation of Jupiter's overthrow
to the elimination of evil—all culminating in the completely confusing
answers of Demogorgon to Asia, presented in a tone of revelation, of
one releasing top-secret information. This scene, perhaps, shows the
effect of the contradiction at its worst, coming uncomfortably close to
double talk. And in *Hellas* we have seen how remote, perhaps how
unattainable, except again in eternity, is the new society; and yet the
hasty reader could easily get the impression (as hasty readers have for
generations) that not only Greek victory but the millennium was
almost *fait accompli*. Finally, through all the poetry runs the fundamental contradiction: the use of the tone of affirmation to express a

sweeping renunciation of the world and society and the yearning for withdrawal into self or love or death—a philosophy of negation.

The best picture that has been left us of Shelley composing is by Trelawny. In the spring of 1822, Shelley disappeared from home one morning, and Mary sent Trelawny in search. At last he came to a deep, dark pool in the woods, surrounded by stunted and twisted trees. A little farther on in the lee of a pine that had toppled over the pool he found Shelley gazing abstractedly into the water. He had been at work on a poem. When Trelawny looked at the manuscript he found the writing so scrawling, the paper so blotted and smeared that it reminded him of a marsh overgrown with bulrushes in which the blots appeared as wild ducks. Shelley told him:

> When my brain gets heated with thought it soon boils, and throws off images and words faster than I can skim them off. In the morning, when cooled down, out of the rude sketch, as you justly call it, I shall attempt a drawing. If you ask me why I publish what few or none will care to read, it is that the spirits I have raised haunt me until they are sent to the devil of a printer. All authors are anxious to breech their bantlings.

The poem on which he was at work was *With a Guitar: To Jane.*[45] The story is almost too good to be true. Here are all the props of Shelley's poetry: the deep wood, the dark pool, the stunted and fallen trees, and Shelley gazing trancelike at his mirror image; and here is the manuscript composed in boiling inspiration. But there is also something new: a good-humored, direct, realistic account of his manner of composition and his desire for publication. The tone may owe something to Trelawny, but the attitude of detached self-awareness is increasingly evident in Shelley's poetry and actions in the last year of his life.

VIII. THE CRYSTALLINE SEA

The examination we have been making of the poetry of Shelley's Italian years suggests that these were years of intellectual and artistic growth toward a maturity which he was on the verge of achieving at the time of his death, and of which *The Triumph of Life* is an indication. They were years of painful experiences and discoveries, violent enthusiasms and violent disillusionments, leading him toward greater stability, self-knowledge, and discipline as an artist.

Each of the three poems we have discussed most fully expresses an uncontrolled dream of self-fulfillment: *Prometheus Unbound,* through social revolution; *Epipsychidion,* through love; and *Adonais,* through death. In a sense each poem marks a step in his development to which Shelley need not return. Each becomes a symbolic action by which, through the extreme expression of the dream, he purges himself of it and is enabled to see life more steadily and think more calmly. One feels on the basis of *The Triumph* that gradually his perspective—his mirror vision of life—was becoming more detached and complex. There was the danger, of course, that the series of sustained shocks which his enthusiasms had received, the exhaustion they left him in, and in particular the ever stronger pull of his Platonism toward withdrawal from human society would lead him into a poetic cul-de-sac. Certainly, with each major poem he left himself with fewer reasons for writing the kind of poetry he felt he ought to write; he had steadily less conviction about human perfectibility and therefore less to say as public oracle.

This does not mean that he would have been reduced to silence, except as a result of a moment of extreme despair in which he was led to suicide, or of such an accident as did befall him and in which psychological compulsion played an unanalyzable part. His need to give verbal outlet to his emotions was too great; writing poetry was for him one of the functions of life. But his poems might well have become more private and limited in subject, more pessimistic and negative in tone. Paradoxically, he would probably have become a better poet. Many of his last poems, including *The Triumph,* show that as he became less concerned with his public function he became more concerned with poetry as a craft, with conscious elaboration of images and symbols, with pattern and structure. There are, for example, the images of the pool in *The Pine Forest of the Cascine near Pisa* and of the night fisher in *Lines Written in the Bay of Lerici,* and the startling impressionism of *Evening: Ponte al Mare, Pisa,* and *The Boat on the Serchio.*[46] Both in his withdrawal into self and in his preoccupation with images, Shelley moves more nearly in the direction of the symbolist poetry of the end of the century than any of his contemporaries, except possibly Keats.

His last poems also reveal characteristics that might have counteracted the pull toward narcissism and negation, or at least have given, again as in later symbolist poetry, variety in theme and vitality in style. They reveal an increasing effort to express in informal, economical language a detached and even ironic contemplation of men and things as they are—and in this possibly they reflect the influence of Byron. Shelley had always possessed the gift for trenchant, concrete expression. He possessed also a gift for epigrammatic delineation of character and an ear for natural speech rhythms. But he had obviously refused to cultivate these gifts because he did not think them proper for poetry of the highest order. He saw them as fitting only for satire or the political song or the informal epistle. And so we find them in *Peter Bell, Oedipus Tyrannus,* or the *Letter to Maria Gisborne.*

They are also used with great effectiveness in the first third of *Julian and Maddalo.* Here we can see vividly the distinction Shelley drew between the two kinds of poetic language; or at least we can see the process of "switching off the intelligence" most spectacularly at work. The opening lines are firm, informal, realistic; the description of Venice, the character sketches, the dialogue between the two men are finely realized. But Shelley uses them simply as setting and contrast for the madman's speech. With the appearance of the madman, Shelley unleashes the Muse, and the language takes off into frenzied incoherence. The introduction is the frame of external reality for the interior monologue which is, for Shelley in this poem, the true reality. It is interesting that Shelley's first drafts for *Epipsychidion* were in a conversational, detached, half-humorous style similar to the opening of *Julian and Maddalo* or the *Letter to Maria Gisborne.*[47] In the poems of 1821 and 1822 are indications that he had come to take his gift for informal language seriously and was deliberately cultivating it as a vehicle for poetry.

In *The Triumph of Life,* the vitality and strength of the poetry, the intellectual control of pattern and symbol, and the over-all detachment in the conception weigh against the nihilistic implications of the poem. They reflect the intellectual curiosity pulling against the emotional Platonism that led toward excess and despair. In opposition to the death wish stands Shelley's urge to wage contention with his time's decay. The question upon which *The Triumph* remains suspended, "Then what is life?" is a question that one can never imagine his voluntarily ceasing to ask. Perhaps the role that he envisioned for himself and that he intended to describe in the latter part of *The Triumph* was the role of the philosophic poet—withdrawn from society, remaining a detached spectator, giving the benefits of his reflections, adding to the thought which from the days of the Greeks has shown mankind the way of regeneration. In naming those of Athens or Jerusalem who escaped *The Triumph,* he implies on the one hand the need of a stoical, ascetic personal life, and on the other hand benevolent, disinterested concern for mankind. The same implications are joined in the conception of Ahasuerus in *Hellas. Hellas,* perhaps, points better than *Adonais* to the kind of solution to the dilemma posed by *The Triumph of Life* which Shelley might have attempted. Certainly, there could be no return to the simple optimism of *Prometheus.* Peacock's haunting conclusion to his *Memoirs of Shelley* perhaps comes closest to the truth:

> I can conceive him, if he had lived to the present time [1860], passing his days like Volney, looking on the world from his windows without taking part in its turmoils; and perhaps like the same, or some other great apostle of liberty (for I cannot at this moment verify the quotation), desiring that nothing should be inscribed on his tomb, but his name, the dates of his birth and death, and the single word, DÉSILLUSIONNÉ.[48]

6: BYRON

🜂🜂🜂🜂🜂🜂🜂🜂🜂🜂🜂🜂🜂🜂🜂🜂🜂🜂🜂🜂🜂🜂🜂🜂🜂🜂🜂🜂🜂🜂🜂🜂🜂

I. THE HUMBLER PROMONTORY

AFTER Byron's death, Count Gamba and the eager Trelawny, rifling through the papers in his room at Missolonghi, found the manuscript of the opening fifteen stanzas (one of them canceled) of Canto XVII of *Don Juan*.[1] According to his custom, Byron had carefully marked down the date at which he had begun the canto—May 8, 1823—and it is likely that the fifteen stanzas had been written then. He had carried them with him, therefore, for nearly a year, as if he had intended to resume the writing of the canto whenever he found the time and had never found it. As a matter of fact, he had written almost no poetry since leaving Italy, partly as a point of principle—he was trying very hard to be a convincing leader and man of action—and partly because he was really bogged down in the daily administrative routine, confusion, and intrigue. The stanzas stand for a poetic career abruptly interrupted, thrust aside by the press of circumstances rather than by premeditation.

There are no signs in those last stanzas, or in the cantos leading up to them, of flagging energy or imagination. Perhaps there is a too frequent carelessness and roughness, a lack of the epigrammatic wit and startling ingenuity of rhymes so noticeable in the early cantos—resulting almost inevitably from a too habitual use and familiarity with the form. But there is no indication of psychological crisis or weariness. On the contrary, the last cantos of *Don Juan* show if anything a gather-

[241]

ing momentum, a building up toward a more complex utilization of theme and form than in any of the previous cantos, a steady expansion of Byron's range and proficiency as an artist.

For a while after he got Don Juan to England, Byron did give the impression—particularly in Cantos XI and XII—of marking time. The narrative was suspended, indeed it almost disappeared, and the digressions threatened to take over. The poem seemed in danger of trailing off into a garrulous monologue. Byron's comment toward the end of Canto XII helps to explain why. Juan, he says, was received into the best society where his talent, good humor, and distinction exposed him to temptation:

> But what, and where, with whom, and when, and why,
>   Is not to be put hastily together;
> And as my object is morality
>   (Whatever people say), I don't know whether
> I'll leave a single reader's eyelid dry. . . .
>   [*DJ*, XII.86 (stanza)]

Here ends, he goes on, the twelfth canto of our "introduction." When the "body" of the book is begun, you'll find it of a "different construction" from what some people say it will be: "The plan at present's simply in concoction." In other words, Byron has temporarily run out of inspiration—he does not know quite how to get his narrative of English life under way.

But from the very opening sentence of Canto XIII—"I now mean to be serious"—he obviously has his poem firmly in hand again. He has decided on his strategy; he knows, at least in general, where he is going. He moves briskly to introduce Lady Adeline Amundeville, and, though he is immediately sidetracked, he gets determinedly back to her after ten stanzas and gives us a tantalizing glimpse of the far-off denouement, a preview as it were of his long-range plan. She was

> The fair most fatal Juan ever met,
>   Although she was not evil or meant ill;
> But Destiny and Passion spread the net
>   (Fate is a good excuse for our own will),
> And caught them. . . .
>   [*DJ*, XIII.12]

Then, as he proceeds to characterize Lady Adeline and her husband, Lord Henry, to lay the groundwork for the house party, to describe Norman Abbey and to introduce the guests assembled there, he leaves

George Gordon, Lord Byron, by Count Alfred D'Orsay, 1823

no doubt that he has found the right means of utilizing his memories and experiences of English society. He has managed to get the proper distance and detachment from them and to integrate them within the larger perspective of the poem.

At first he proceeds leisurely and even tentatively, but the characters are being drawn with noticeably more care and detail than in the past. The analysis of Lady Adeline and Lord Henry develops bit by bit through the last four completed cantos and gathers complexity as it goes. Their characters are also progressively revealed through manners and action, and their relationship to each other is skillfully exposed. Significantly, a great deal of time is devoted to developing a portrait of Juan. For the first time, he begins to emerge as an individual from out of the stereotype which until now he has been.

In Canto XIV, the Duchess of Fitz-Fulke, a "fine and somewhat full-blown blonde / Desirable, distinguished and celebrated," is introduced, lightly sketched, and set to flirting with Juan. Adeline's indignation and determination to warn Juan give Byron an opportunity to explore her character further and to fill in the background of her marriage to Lord Henry. In Canto XV, Adeline's effort to get Juan interested in marriage and to find him a proper wife enables Byron to introduce Aurora Raby, the most cryptic of all his women characters:

> Early in years, and yet more infantine
>   In figure, she had something of sublime
> In eyes which sadly shone, as seraphs' shine.
>   All youth—but with an aspect beyond time;
> Radiant and grave—as pitying man's decline;
>   Mournful—but mournful of another's crime,
> She look'd as if she sat by Eden's door,
> And grieved for those who could return no more.
>
> She was a Catholic, too, sincere, austere,
>   As far as her own gentle heart allow'd,
> And deem'd that fallen worship far more dear
>   Perhaps because 'twas fallen: her sires were proud
> Of deeds and days when they had fill'd the ear
>   Of nations, and had never bent or bow'd
> To novel power; and as she was the last,
> She held their old faith and old feelings fast.
>
> She gazed upon a world she scarcely knew,
>   As seeking not to know it; silent, lone,

As grows a flower, thus quietly she grew,
    And kept her heart serene within its zone.
There was awe in the homage which she drew;
    Her spirit seem'd as seated on a throne
Apart from the surrounding world, and strong
In its own strength—most strange in one so young!

[*DJ*, XV.45–47]

Though Adeline cannot stand her, Juan is attracted and succeeds so far in charming her that she smiles and talks to him at the Escoffierian dinner that concludes the canto. Now the characters have been assembled, the stage has been set, and Byron is ready to begin his comedy in earnest. Canto XVI moves as rapidly as the previous cantos have moved slowly, in a series of vividly staged episodes. First there is Juan's encounter with the ghost of the friar. Then the breakfast scene in which the reaction of each of the ladies to Juan's distracted manner is neatly given:

She [Adeline] look'd, and saw him pale, and turn'd as pale
    Herself; then hastily look'd down, and mutter'd
Something, but what's not stated in my tale.
    Lord Henry said, his muffin was ill-butter'd;
The Duchess of Fitz-Fulke play'd with her veil,
    And look'd at Juan hard, but nothing utter'd.
Aurora Raby with her large dark eyes
Survey'd him with a kind of calm surprise.

[*DJ*, XVI.31]

Lord Henry in condolence is quite naturally led to introduce the subject of the black friar, and Adeline's song on the subject gives Byron another chance to contrast his three ladies in terms of their literary and artistic interests. Adeline had "a twilight tinge of 'Blue'" and was not ashamed to deem Pope a great poet. Aurora was more Shakespearean:

The worlds beyond this world's perplexing waste
    Had more of her existence, for in her
There was a depth of feeling to embrace
Thoughts, boundless, deep, but silent too as Space.

Not so her gracious, graceful, graceless Grace,
    The full-grown Hebe of Fitz-Fulke, whose mind,
If she had any, was upon her face.

[*DJ*, XVI.48–49]

[244]

Once she had been seen reading the "Bath Guide" and "Hayley's Triumphs." But mainly she liked sonnets to herself, or *"bouts rimés."* There follows the scene in which Lord Henry performs his duties as a squire, and Byron with Hogarthian skill and vitality pulls into order and focus an extraordinary range of activities. He conveys the sprawling confusion and at the same time through his stanzaic organization enables us to grasp and encompass it: to hold simultaneously in mind, framed as in a picture, the art dealer and the architect; the lawyers; the prize pig, plowman, and preachers; and the country girl in the scarlet coat waiting in the great hall for Lord Henry in his role of justice of the peace. A hint of one of the themes Byron may have intended to develop in later cantos is given in the description of Lord Henry as politician.

This is a "public day," during which the country gentlemen may drop in "without cards" for dinner, and so the canto moves on to the description of the public feast:

> Quite full, right dull, guests hot, and dishes cold,
> Great plenty, much formality, small cheer,
> And everybody out of their own sphere.
>
> [*DJ*, XVI.78]

Once again Byron is able to play the three ladies off against one another and Juan: Aurora looking at Juan's confusion with a "quiet smile of contemplation, / Indicative of some surprise and pity"; Adeline playing the grand role of the squire's and politician's wife, "watching, witching, condescending" so well that Juan began to feel "some doubt how much" of her "was real"; and Fitz-Fulke very much at ease, her eyes seizing on the foibles of the guests and storing them up for "mischievous enjoyment."

After the guests have departed everyone except Juan and Aurora joins in the dissection of their absurdities. Aurora looks at him with approval, mistaking his silence for charity, and Juan is grateful to the ghost for enabling him to gain esteem "where it was worth the most." Momentarily the mask of irony slips, and Byron, contemplating the fundamental idealism of Juan, reveals his own:

> And certainly Aurora had renew'd
>   In him some feelings he had lately lost,
> Or harden'd; feelings which perhaps ideal,
> Are so divine, that I must deem them real:—

[245]

The Romantic Ventriloquists

The love of higher things and better days;
The unbounded hope, and heavenly ignorance
Of what is call'd the world, and the world's ways;
The moments when we gather from a glance
More joy than from all future pride or praise. . . .
[*DJ*, XVI.107–8]

But immediately the mask is readjusted, as "full of sentiments, sublime as billows / Heaving between this world and worlds beyond," Juan retires. But not to sleep. Again the "sable friar" appears. At first paralyzed by fright, Juan regains his poise as the ghost retreats, and, "eager now the truth to pierce," he follows and discovers when he pins the ghost to the wall:

In full, voluptuous but not o'ergrown bulk,
The phantom of her frolic grace—Fitz-Fulke!
[*DJ*, XVI.123]

Thus Canto XVI ends, and the opening stanzas of Canto XVII carry us no further than the tantalizing description of Juan and the Duchess showing up, last of all the guests, at breakfast the next morning—Juan's "virgin face" is described as wan and worn, with eyes that hardly "brook'd" the light that shone through the Gothic window, and her Grace, with "a sort of air rebuked,"

Seem'd pale and shiver'd, as if she had kept
A vigil, or dreamt rather more than slept.
[*DJ*, XVII.14]

Here the poem breaks off, but it is not difficult for the reader to carry on in imagination a little further, at least, for example, to speculate on the possible ways in which the complex relationships Byron has established might work themselves out. Now that Fitz-Fulke has seduced Juan, what will Adeline do? How will "destiny and passion spread the net" and catch them? Or will one or the other escape? (At the end of Canto XIV Byron suggests that he has not made up his mind: "It is not clear that Adeline and Juan / Will fall; but if they do, 'twill be their ruin.") How will Lord Henry react to all this? And, not least, what will be the effect upon Aurora Raby? There are almost inexhaustible potentialities for comedy and ultimately tragic comedy in the basic situation, which Byron, on the evidence of previous cantos, was fully capable of realizing.

[246]

Byron

Miss Boyd thinks that,

> . . . without condemning any individual in this story as utterly black, Byron is going to show the rottenness of the social system to which they belong. They will wreck Juan with their scheming, contriving, and cross interests, and then, herding together hypocritically, they will expel him with all the blame concentrated upon him. It is too bad that Byron could not have completed this section of his poem; it would have been a more satisfactory revenge and apologia than any burned memoirs.[2]

Now this is to limit too severely both the achievement and the promise of these last cantos. Certainly, Byron had as one of his aims—and it was probably his primary aim when he began these cantos—to write a satire exposing the rottenness of the social system that had ruined and ostracized him, and thus to have his revenge. And in building his characters he drew naturally upon his own memories and experiences. But the extent of his psychological and artistic growth is measured by the detachment with which he used them.

Not one of the characters is taken directly from life, deliberately to be identified with individuals he had known; each is an independent creation. In some instances, as for example, Lord and Lady Amundeville, he fashions a composite portrait, picking characteristics from several of his old acquaintances. Probably he derived a certain malicious pleasure from this Frankensteinian kind of creation. Lord Henry sometimes reminds us of Wedderburn Webster, of Lord Holland, or of Hobhouse, but mainly perhaps of William Lamb. Lady Adeline has touches of all Byron's loves between 1811 and 1812—she is in this sense the typical Regency grand lady. But in particular she suggests Lady Byron. We can see how far Byron has come from the strictly autobiographical when we compare her with Donna Inez in Canto I. In presenting Donna Inez he drew without scruple upon easily identifiable interests of Annabella, such as her interest in mathematics, and upon a well-known episode of their marriage—her efforts to find out if he were mad. But in presenting Lady Adeline he is preoccupied with getting at a central characteristic of Lady Byron without any personal satiric purpose.

Lady Adeline is described as completely poised and self-possessed, confident of her own virtue and wisdom:

> Her chief resource was in her own high spirit,
> Which judged mankind at their due estimation.
>
> [*DJ*, XIII.31]

She is repressed and cold; her passions have never been touched, but they are the more intense and powerful for that. In a grotesque but effective conceit, Byron compares her to champagne frozen except for the very center where about a liquid glassful will remain: "Stronger than the strongest grape / Could e'er express in its expanded shape." And he comments, "your cold people are beyond all price, / When once you have broken their confounded ice." They are a Northwest Passage to the "glowing India of the soul" (XIII.37–39).

When she sees Juan being pursued by Fitz-Fulke, Adeline—motivated as she believes by friendship—begins "to ponder how to save his soul." In such a woman "intense intentions are a dangerous matter," and Byron's implication is that her efforts to get Juan married will lead to her own as well as Juan's undoing. The parallel with Lady Byron is clear. To Lady Blessington in the spring of 1823, during the time he was writing Canto XVI, he had talked at length of the character of Lady Byron. She had, he said,

. . . a degree of self control that I never saw equalled. I am certain that Lady Byron's first idea is, what is due to herself; I mean that it is the undeviating rule of her conduct. I wish she had thought a little more of what is due to others. Now my besetting sin is a want of that self-respect—which she has in *excess;* and that want has produced much unhappiness to us both. But though I accuse Lady Byron of an excess of self-respect, I must in candor admit, that if any person ever had an excuse for an extraordinary portion of it, she has, as in all her thoughts, words, and deeds, she is the most decorous woman that ever existed and must appear—what few, I fancy, could—a perfect refined gentlewoman, even to her *femme de chambre.* This extraordinary degree of self-command in Lady Byron produced an opposite effect on me. When I have broken out, in slight provocations, into one of my ungovernable fits of rage her calmness piqued and seemed to reproach me; it gave her an air of superiority that vexed and increased my *mauvais humeur.*[3]

Earlier he told Medwin of how after she had rejected his first proposal she had revived the correspondence between them a year later.

The tenor of her letter was that although she could not love me, she desired my friendship. Friendship is a dangerous word for young ladies; it is Love full-fledged, and waiting for a fine day to fly. She married me from vanity, and the hope of reforming and fixing me. She was a spoiled child, and naturally of a jealous disposition.[4]

However inaccurate the reporting of Lady Blessington and Medwin might be, the characterization rings true and is confirmed by the letters from Annabella to Byron before the marriage. That she was also a person of intense emotion ruthlessly repressed and unacknowledged is evident from all the documents on the separation. But what is most interesting to us at the moment is the way in which Byron has used his knowledge of Lady Byron to create a similar character functioning in a different situation—as the wife of a cold and proper man attempting to save a young friend from an unscrupulous woman. Thus freeing himself from emotional involvement, he is able to delineate without bitterness or condemnation and indeed with sympathy.

How deliberately Byron was striving for detachment and complexity in his creation of characters is shown by the way in which he makes Lady Adeline the central figure in an ascending trinity of women. At one extreme he sets the Duchess of Fitz-Fulke, who comes closest to being a stereotype and represents the kind of Lustful Lady with whom he was altogether too well acquainted (in her mischievousness, amorality, and instability she suggests particularly the not so full-blown Caroline Lamb). At the other extreme he places Aurora Raby, his most complex representation of his dream heroine, the pure and wise child-woman whose prototype he never found in actual life.

To say, therefore, as Miss Boyd does, that Byron does not condemn any of the individuals as "utterly black" is not to give him the credit he deserves. He goes out of his way to avoid condemning them. He presents them not as caricatures but as recognizable human beings. Lord and Lady Amundeville are not evil or stupid; they are well-intentioned, fundamentally good people whose flaws are described humorously and sympathetically. Aurora Raby possesses an eerie, almost saintlike, purity and detachment. The Duchess of Fitz-Fulke is, it is true, utterly amoral, ruthless, dangerous, and empty-headed; we are told that she is a "pretty, precious plague," haunting a lover with caprices, making a quarrel when she can't find one, bewitching, torturing and—worst of all—she "won't let you go" (XIV.63). But she is presented with Chaucerian gusto and evident enjoyment. None of these characters is a hypocrite. Byron quite possibly intended Juan to be wrecked and expelled with all the blame upon him, but in not so simple a fashion as Miss Boyd suggests. All of the central characters, even including the Duchess, are likely to be hurt as much as he. Only the shadowy peripheral figures—the guests described in Canto XIII, the young ladies from whom Adeline wants to choose a wife for Juan, the local squires and their wives—only these remain caricatures; they are the hypocrites who will herd together. Otherwise, satire is being transformed into tragicomedy.

Byron is still as much preoccupied by the relationship between appearance and reality as he had been when he began *Don Juan,* but his conception has grown deeper and richer. He delights as much as ever in pointing out ridiculous clashes and contradictions, the incongruity between our pious protestations and impious actions. He continues to stress the ironic situation, the external juxtapositions, the direct and simple relationships—as for example between Juan's sentimental farewell to Spain and Julia, and his seasickness. His laughter is tinged with moral judgment; his contempt for the self-deceptions, rationalizations, and hypocrisies of his characters is often evident.

But in the earlier cantos he was inclined to see too much of human behavior simply in terms of the pretended (noble and idealistic) motivation versus the real (petty and selfish) motivation. In the last cantos his view of human behavior is much more complex. He realizes that the distinction between the appearance and reality is often not clear or at least cannot always be clearly drawn. He becomes absorbed now in discovering just what the motivations of his characters are. He is more concerned with understanding than with judging. He is interested in his characters as individuals and in their psychological complexities. As his interest grows, his tolerance, sympathy, and even respect grow also. It is less easy to place the blame and ridicule than when he began. In his attitude he grows less like Swift, more like Shakespeare, or perhaps Cervantes. There is a digression on Don Quixote at the beginning of Canto XIII that shows how much Cervantes meant to him at this time. For my part, he says, I am but a mere spectator and, much like Goethe's Mephistopheles, gaze impartially at palace or hovel:

> But neither love nor hate in much excess;
> 　Though 'twas not once so. If I sneer sometimes,
> It is because I cannot well do less,
> 　And now and then it also suits my rhymes.
> I should be very willing to redress
> 　Men's wrongs, and rather check than punish crimes,
> Had not Cervantes, in that too true tale
> Of Quixote, shown how all such efforts fail.

Byron

Of all tales 'tis the saddest—and more sad,
    Because it makes us smile: his hero's right,
And still pursues the right;—to curb the bad
    His only object, and 'gainst odds to fight
His guerdon: 'tis his virtue makes him mad!
    But his adventures form a sorry sight;—
A sorrier still is the great moral taught
By that real epic unto all who have thought.

Redressing injury, revenging wrong,
    To aid the damsel and destroy the caitiff;
Opposing singly the united strong,
    From foreign yoke to free the helpless native:—
Alas! must noblest views, like an old song,
    Be for mere fancy's sport a theme creative,
A jest, a riddle, Fame through thick and thin sought!
And Socrates himself but Wisdom's Quixote?

[*DJ*, XIII.8–10]

Immediately after this Byron returns to Lady Adeline in the stanza already quoted, predicting that she will be "the fair most fatal Juan ever met, / Although she was not evil or meant ill." Byron is clearly adopting here the perspective he has attributed to Cervantes. Adeline is the good woman whose good intentions threaten to ruin both Juan and herself. Indeed, Byron presents her as a kind of female Quixote, pursuing the right, her only object "to curb the bad," and, in spite of her superficial sophistication, utterly naïve and lacking in self-understanding. One of Byron's nicest touches comes at the end of Canto XIV when he says that he will discuss in a later canto whether Juan and Adeline became friends:

Whether they rode, or walk'd, or studied Spanish
    To read *Don Quixote* in the original,
A pleasure before which all others vanish.

[*DJ*, XIV.98]

In Canto XVI occurs the best example of Byron's increasingly subtle handling of human behavior. The canto is framed in a parody of the Gothic novel which furnishes on one level a relatively simple juxtaposition of illusion and reality. The exposure of the monk as her frolic Grace recalls the revels of the merry monks of Newstead and pokes skeptical fun both at superstition in its grosser form and at religious belief (although the stanzas that introduce the theme of the ghost

[251]

reveal Byron's typical uneasiness before the thought of the supernatural; he is not sure that all ghosts can be explained away as this
one is). But the ultimate irony grows out of the analysis of Juan's
experience at the end of the canto. He has been genuinely moved by
Aurora Raby to idealistic feelings and retires full of sublime sentiments. At this point the ghost appears, and Juan is terribly frightened,
"for immaterialism's a serious matter." But he soon becomes ashamed
and, "eager now the truth to pierce," runs after the ghost. He thrusts
at it and, his arm apparently going through it, hits the wall; thrusts
again and presses "upon a hard and glowing bust." The upshot of the
matter is clear enough though Byron never gets beyond the coy equi-
vocation at the beginning of Canto XVII:

> Whether his virtue triumph'd—or, at length,
> His vice—for he was of a kindling nation—
> Is more than I shall venture to describe:—
> Unless some Beauty with a kiss should bribe.

> I leave the thing a problem, like all things. . . .
> [*DJ*, XVII.12–13]

However that may be, just when Juan is filled with his noblest sentiments he is brought to earth with a thump; Romantic Platonism and
supernaturalism give way to sex and empiricism. The man who dreams
of Aurora one moment thrusts his arm upon the bust of Fitz-Fulke
the next. Now Byron is not cynically forcing a choice between the
illusory and the real. He is not saying that the sentiments aroused in
Juan by Aurora are false and hypocritical. On the contrary, they are
presented as completely genuine. Byron, however, could not subscribe
to the attitude assumed by his Romantic contemporaries—at least in
their poetry—that the gross and sensual must be transcended by the
ideal love, or absorbed into it, or ignored. For Byron both are real and
very strong, and there is nothing contradictory in their existing side
by side. In order to avoid delusion, human beings have to be constantly
reminded of the reality and strength of the former. And so Juan is
reminded, as is the reader, of the fundamental reality of the physical
world and the physical self—that here finally for man all things begin
and end.

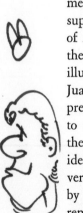

But this is not in *Don Juan* a limiting, frustrating, or dispiriting
matter. Rather it is a means of emancipation. What happens to Juan
is in the natural order of things—it is the human experience. Once

realized and admitted, it can be observed and enjoyed in endless variety. The exploration of human conduct and motivation becomes an end and sufficient justification of art. This includes the exploration and parade of self in all one's moods and speculation. Everything becomes grist to the mill. In *Don Juan*, Byron comes close ironically enough to realizing Keats' characterization of the poetical character: "it is everything and nothing—It has no character—it enjoys light and shade; it lives in gusto, be it foul or fair, high or low, rich or poor, mean or elevated. . . . What shocks the virtuous philosopher delights the Cameleon Poet." [5]

Where his contemporaries in their effort to impose their ideal upon reality, to explain all experience in terms of it, were led into narrow cul-de-sacs, were cut off from the major areas of experience, were forced into silence or distortion or evasion, Byron was free to recognize and admit all experience into his poetry. He demonstrated how poetry could be vital and meaningful in the nineteenth century and still hold its pride of place as a social instrument. One consistent, dogged conviction runs through *Don Juan*. If man can finally know nothing outside himself and is solely dependent upon his own resources for whatever he does, then it is only through as full as possible an awareness and understanding of his nature that he can control or eliminate his faults and have any hope of improving his society. Byron puts it this way in Canto XII:

> But now I'm going to be immoral; now
> I mean to show things really as they are
> Not as they ought to be: for I avow,
>   That till we see what's what in fact, we're far
> From much improvement with that virtuous plough
>   Which skims the surface, leaving scarce a scar
> Upon the black loam long manured by Vice,
> Only to keep its corn at the old price.
>
> [*DJ*, XII.40]

II. THE GOD OF THIS WORLD

How did Byron achieve this emancipation and expansiveness as an artist? What transformed him from Childe Harold into the creator of Don Juan, from romantic poseur into great artist? For at first glance there seems to be little relationship in attitude or artistry between the two; it is difficult to believe that the man who wrote *Manfred* was the man who wrote *Don Juan*. Byron himself spoke frequently and with considerable complacence of the contradictions within himself; in the seventeenth canto he makes one last self-analysis, ending with, "I almost think that the same skin / For one without—has two or three within." And it adds to our perplexity to realize that even when he was writing the last cantos of *Don Juan* he was quite capable of writing in the old heavy melodramatic manner—*The Deformed Transformed* and *The Island* were written in 1822 and 1823, respectively.

Yet, when we look more closely at the "serious" poems, we see that they do have at least one important characteristic in common with *Don Juan*—what might today be called an existentialist attitude. They are pervaded by Byron's inability to accept any of the shibboleths, traditional or Romantic, which gave comfort to his contemporaries; his oppressive sense of the meaninglessness, the futility (or fatality, which really came for him to the same thing) of human existence, looked at within the universal frame of things; his realization that man had nothing to turn to beyond himself, was responsible solely to himself, and that human society was the product of human actions, its limits set by the qualities of the human mind. What in *Childe Harold* was cause for despair and aimless rebellion becomes in *Don Juan* a cause of laughter and vigorous creative activity.

All his life Byron desperately wanted to believe in an ordered and benevolent universe, and so fluttered impulsively and erratically from one bright hope to another: from Calvinism (or "moderate Presbyterianism") to deism, to Wordsworth's pantheism, to Shelley's Platonism, to Catholicism, and back to deism—and, if there was any consistency in his wishful thinking, it was in the constant return to deism.[6] One can see from his letters and journals and from the numerous recorded conversations of his last years how hopefully he would turn to new arguments, willing to be persuaded or converted (not even in the conversations with Dr. Kennedy was he simply perverse); or how emphatically he would assert to Moore or Medwin or Lady Blessington that he really did have a positive faith, as if he had tried once more to inoculate himself, and the vaccine had finally taken.

He wanted to believe also in a benevolent and ordered society. He wanted to accept the revolutionary and Romantic faith in the perfectibility of man and society. As a matter of fact, he believed more literally and naïvely in the ideals of human conduct, in the "Christian virtues" as Knight calls them, than did contemporaries like Wordsworth and Coleridge. And, as Knight demonstrates, he lived by them to a greater extent than most of his critics are willing to concede.[7] Critics of Byron are likely to be harder and more cynical than he ever was. Professions which they applaud in Shelley and Wordsworth they are apt to call in Byron "sentimental idealism," as if somehow the ideals have turned false, or Byron's professions are insincere. Often his expression *is* sentimental or maudlin; often he falsifies when he over-simplifies a personal motivation or when he is carried away into the grand gesture (as in the lines to his wife in *Childe Harold*, Canto IV: "My curse shall be forgiveness"); often he is led into the "negative" sentimentalism of pretending that almost no one lives by these ideals except himself (as in the stanzas at the end of *Childe Harold*, Canto III)—but his acceptance of these ideals as a standard by which human conduct should be measured and, more important, his belief that these virtues actually do exist in men are honest and consistent. An aphorism in "Detached Thoughts" represents what can reasonably be considered Byron's lifelong conviction: "Man is born *passionate* of body but with an innate though secret tendency to the love of Good in his Mainspring of Mind. But God help us all! It is at present a sad jar of atoms." [8] There is plenty of evidence to indicate that from childhood to his death Byron possessed the "innate tendency" to the love of good, wanted to act by it, and left to his own devices did act by it.

But Byron possessed other characteristics that made it impossible for him to believe for any length of time in an ordered and benevolent universe, or in the necessary triumph of good over evil in human character and conduct, or in the perfectibility of human society. In the first place, though he may have been no philosopher, he had a keen and logical intelligence, quick to cut through rationalizations, contradictions, and evasions in religious and philosophical dogmas. In the second place, he had an extraordinarily acute understanding of human motivation and behavior. He was sensitive to the difference between what men professed and what they did, and to the whole range of human activities usually ignored or concealed. He was compulsively self-aware and self-observant, abnormally conscious of what he was doing, if not always of why he was doing it. He had, as Lovell puts it, a strong sense of fact; he had a sensualist's passion for the physical and empirical explanation of experience.[9]

Observable behavior of nature and man became the touchstone by which he checked the truth of religious and philosophical speculations;

he sought for the rational and common-sense answer, no matter how much he might be awed or baffled by the mystery of mental experience (like Juan with the ghost he was eager to pierce the truth). He had great intellectual curiosity and wanted to explore all of human experience—like Mephistopheles to be an observer of palaces and hovels, and like Cain to see the universe from a point in space. He was extremely sensitive to places, names, dates, the facts of history, and his memory methodically recorded enormous quantities of data. Finally, he was at bottom intellectually honest: he kept steadily in mind the whole range of his experience. He refused to ignore the unpleasant and evil, no matter how much they might contradict his aspirations and ideals, the picture he would like to hold of man and the universe. In the long run he would not delude or deceive himself about the nature of things. It is true that he often took a perverse pleasure in seeking out the unpleasant and dwelling upon it for its own sake, in reveling in evil, but this was the inevitable concomitant of the stubborn integrity that insisted upon facing and taking into account the unpalatable facts of experience even though they made all contemporary faiths untenable and indeed made the construction of any optimistic philosophy, any neat, purposeful view of life, difficult if not impossible.

Byron was haunted by two views of the universe irreconcilable both with each other and with the sentimental deism and Christianity of his day. One was the Calvinistic view and the other the scientific. The two were closely associated in his mind; one would usually recall the other. They were, in fact, frequently confused: the anthropomorphic frame of Calvinism would become the metaphorical construction enclosing the scientific view, as in *Cain*. The Calvinism of his childhood, combined with the deistic and agnostic speculations he acquired through his reading and his acquaintance with such people as Matthews at Cambridge, combined further with his observations during his travels, took care of any possibility of Byron's accepting a simple, sentimental version of Christianity. In his earliest letters dealing with religion he attacked both revealed religion and the idea of personal immortality. To Long on April 16, 1807, he wrote:

Of Religion I know nothing, at least in its *favour*. We have *fools* in all sects and Imposters in most; why should I believe mysteries no one understands, because written by men who choose to mistake madness for Inspiration, and style themselves *Evangelicals?* . . . I have lived a *Deist,* what I shall die I know not; however, come what may, *ridens moriar* [*LJ*, II, 19].

Byron

And to Hodgson, remonstrating with him on the stanzas in *Childe Harold,* Canto II, denying personal immortality, he wrote on September 3, 1811:

It is a little hard to send a man preaching to Judaea, and leave the rest of the world—Negers and what not—*dark* as their complexions, without a ray of light for so many years to lead them on high; and who will believe that God will damn men for not knowing what they were never taught? . . . I looked to death [when sick during his travels] as a relief from pain, without a wish for an after-life, but a confidence that the God who punishes in this existence had left that last asylum for the weary. . . . Talk of Galileeism? Show me the effects —are you better, wiser, kinder by your precepts? I will bring you ten Mussulmans shall shame you in all good-will towards men, prayer to God, and duty to their neighbours [*LJ*, II, 21–22].

Hodgson protested, and Byron answered more violently on September 13, 1811:

. . . the basis of your religion is *injustice;* the *Son of God,* the *pure,* the *immaculate,* the *innocent,* is sacrificed for the *Guilty.* This proves *His* heroism; but no more does away *man's* guilt than a schoolboy's volunteering to be flogged for another would exculpate the dunce from negligence, or preserve him from the Rod. . . . As to your immortality, if people are to live, why die? And our carcasses, which are to rise again, are they worth raising? I hope, if mine is, that I shall have a better *pair of legs* than I have moved on these two-and-twenty years, or I shall be sadly behind in the squeeze into Paradise. Did you ever read "Malthus on Population"? If he be right, war and pestilence are our best friends, to save us from being eaten alive, in this "best of all possible Worlds" [*LJ*, II, 35–36].

Though he considerably softened his statements in later writings, he never altered his attitudes toward the dogmas of Christianity, and even when he is being most serious in his protestations of respect he cannot resist poking fun at what seem to him the absurdities. When he speaks of himself as a Christian in his later years, it is always, as Lovell points out, with the connotation of a deist who accepts the ethics of Christ. The appeal of Catholicism for him is the appeal that it has always had for artists and for skeptics.

It is by far the most elegant worship, hardly excepting the Greek mythology. What with incense, pictures, statues, altars, shrines, relics, and the real presence, confession, absolution;—there is something sensible to grasp at. Beside, it leaves no possibility of doubt; for those who swallow their Deity, really and truly, in transubstantiation, can hardly find anything else otherwise than easy of digestion. I am afraid that this sounds flippant, but I don't mean it to be so; only my turn of mind is so given to taking things in the absurd point of view, that it breaks

[257]

out in spite of me every now and then. Still, I do assure you that I am a very good Christian [To Moore, March 8, 1822; *LJ*, VI, 39].

It is quite clear that, however wistfully drawn to the pattern of Catholicism and the certitude it promised, he is incapable of believing in it. His sense of the absurd prevents that.

The letters to Hodgson show that to Byron one of the most disturbing characteristics of Christianity was its presentation of God as a tyrant who demanded vengeance and sacrifice. It was a religion "founded on *injustice.*" Here, of course, he is reflecting his bitter reaction to Calvinism. It is difficult to say to what extent the Calvinist teachings in his boyhood were responsible for Byron's sense of sin and fatality, for his gloom and defiance.[10] All one can safely say is that by 1811 he was using Calvinism as a reason for his aversion to Christianity, as a symbol of all that he was in rebellion against; and ten years later it is the Calvinist God and creed that are presented in *Cain.*

Now one of the reasons why Byron was so affected by Calvinism is that he half believed it, or at least saw it as more nearly accounting for, or more nearly in accord with, the true nature of things than sentimental Christianity or deism, *if* one postulated a creative anthropomorphic deity. With his Voltairean eye for the inherent evils and imperfections in the scheme of nature and society, and his abnormal awareness of the ineradicable impulses toward evil inseparable from the impulses toward good within himself, he could never go along with the argument that God was purely good or benevolent. God as omnipotent must contain within himself and therefore be responsible for evil. More than that, he saw malevolence and sadism in creating creatures doomed to a life of misery and sin.

Byron's own sense of fatalism and helplessness before the evil forces in himself and his environment found dramatic confirmation in the Calvinistic doctrines of depravity and predestination. The fundamental intent of Calvinism, and of the Old Testament from which it drew, was, as he dramatized it in *Cain,* to present an "omnipotent tyrant" who deliberately set a trap for men, punished them remorselessly for falling, and demanded abject acquiescence and adoration forever after. The individual who dared look him in "His everlasting face, and tell him that / His evil is not good," was doomed to a life of alienation and wandering like Cain; but such defiance was the only way of thwarting and ultimately defeating Him. Lucifer says, in what is one of the most interesting twists on the theme of the moral sense in Romantic literature,

> *We* must bear,
> And some of us resist, and both in vain,
> His seraphs say; but it is worth the trial,
> Since better may not be without. There is
> A wisdom in the spirit, which directs
> To right.
>
> [*Cain*, I.489–94]

This spirit is obviously in opposition to and not in conformity with God. What irritated Byron with Christian apologists like Hodgson was their rationalizations of evil into good, their refusal or inability to see the hypocrisies to which they lent themselves. Perhaps the universe is to be explained as the Calvinists explain it, but let us not pretend that it is good and acquiesce in it; let us call it what it is and defy it.[11] When I say that Byron was haunted by the Calvinist view of the universe, I do not mean that he consistently saw things as he presented them in *Cain*. I mean that he saw evil as an intrinsic and possibly dominant factor in human life, dooming man to degradation and death, thwarting his conceptions of and aspirations toward good (and he wonders somewhere if perhaps the qualities of good had been given in order to make the torture the more exquisite).

As to the ultimate source and pervasiveness of the evil he wavered from poem to poem and period to period of his life. In the poems through the third canto of *Childe Harold,* he drew the more or less conventional Romantic distinction between the evil in man and the goodness in nature. But he differed from his poetic contemporaries by insisting upon the evil, not as social or as a temporary perversion of natural goodness, but as "this uneradicable taint of sin," born with man or mysteriously imposed upon him from without. In *Manfred,* the evil is more pervasive. Even nature is hostile and corrupt; Manfred's destiny is ruled by a "star condemned, / The burning wreck of a demolish'd world, / A wandering hell in the eternal space." Arimanes, equivalent to Blake's "god of this world," is similar in conception and function, as Lovell has remarked, to the tyrant Jehovah of *Cain*. The good principle is vaguely suggested as being superior to Arimanes, but all we see of it is the Spirit of Astarte, who Nemesis says is "not of our order, but belongs / To the other powers," and Manfred's final triumphant insistence upon the independence and superiority of mind. A similar emphasis upon pervasive evil runs through all the serious dramas. Only in *Don Juan* does the emphasis on evil fade away before the emphasis upon the meaninglessness or at least the inexplicability of the universe surrounding man; and this is because Byron has reached the psychological point and found the means by which he can face openly and more or less without flinching the conception of the universe which had remained hidden and undeveloped, if implicit, in the earlier poems. He had talked from the beginning of the meaninglessness of life, the apparent futility and ultimate destruction of human efforts, but he had placed his comments and attitudes within the frame of a conventional rhetoric and a traditional faith so that the edge was taken off them; they were in great part denied by their context, and Byron's readers, and perhaps Byron himself, were prevented from fully understanding them or contemplating them in their nakedness. But they were responsible for much of the power and intensity in the Byronic expression of the sense of loneliness, alienation, horror, and frustration; in the almost hysterical defiance of authority and assertion of self; and in the frantic search for some inviolable and indestructible element within the self. They were responsible in an important degree for those qualities which set Byron apart from and above the sources upon which he drew for his heroes.

Byron has often been accused of shallowness of imagination and vision, but in one respect he was more imaginative than any of his contemporaries, except possibly Blake. He perceived more clearly than any of them the implications of the universe science was constructing; or at least he was unable to insulate or protect himself as his contemporaries were. He could not keep his imagination from brooding upon the problem. He realized that an infinite universe of innumerable worlds meant the end of traditional concepts, became meaningless and in turn made human life meaningless and insignificant in any terms available to the human mind, and deprived human activity, either of the individual or of the race, of ultimate purpose or end except oblivion.

Others, notably philosophers like Holbach, had comprehended these implications intellectually and abstractly but had immediately superimposed upon them conceptions of order that reduced them to human size—the various mechanistic, rational, Platonic, or pantheistic conceptions. The poets followed suit. Wordsworth narrowed and limited his conception of nature to earth and its environs, ultimately to the microcosm of the Lake District; his relationship to it was personal, intimate, comprehensible. Only in the Solitary did he reveal the fears that gnawed at him when he allowed his imagination to roam beyond its narrow confines. Shelley in *Queen Mab* had described the infinite universe, but he had so neat an explanation of it in the conception of necessity, and was so preoccupied by his social purpose, that he was scarcely conscious of it. It existed simply as a device by which to contemplate man. Only toward the end of his life, as we have seen, did the protection afforded by the Godwinian and Platonic philosophies become insufficient. But Byron could not and would not comfort himself in any of these ways. He felt intensely and constantly the terrible "isolation of the human situation," as I. A. Richards calls it; he was imaginatively aware of "the inconceivable immensity of the universe" and the "enormity" of his own ignorance.[12] He found this awareness intolerable and tried to deny it, destroy it, or escape it by the extravagant assertion of the life force in himself, and even by the deliberate aggravation of the sense of sin—it was better to believe in God as vengeful, and oneself as damned, than in nothing.

There is a revealing letter written on June 18, 1813, to William Gifford, who had apparently remonstrated with him on the "immortality" stanzas in *Childe Harold,* Canto II. In it the Calvinist and the scientific views are interestingly associated:

I am no Bigot to Infidelity, and did not expect that, because I doubted the immortality of Man, I should be charged with denying the existence of a God. It was the comparative insignificance of ourselves and *our world,* when placed in competition with the mighty whole, of which it is an atom, that first led me to imagine that our pretensions to eternity might be over-rated.

This, and being early disgusted with a Calvinistic Scotch school, when I was cudgelled to Church for the first ten years of my life, afflicted me with this malady; for, after all, it is, I believe, a disease of the mind as much as other kinds of hypochondria [*LJ,* II, 221–22].

Byron is writing with typical exaggeration to a man whom he wishes to appease, yet "malady" and "disease of the mind" are words that probably do describe his feeling about the matter; he longed to hold the simple, positive views held (at least publicly) by his contemporaries, but he saw himself cursed with an unhealthy morbidity of mind that prevented this and drove him into perversity.

Another revealing statement is in a letter to Annabella of March 3, 1814. The correspondence between Byron and Annabella has all of the dubious fascination of an eighteenth-century epistolary novel—it is interminable, deadly dull, yet of absorbing psychological interest. Annabella tried remorselessly to draw Byron out on the subject of religion, and undoubtedly part of her charm for him was her own clear convictions. After they were engaged, he gave her carte blanche to try to convert him, and probably he hoped that through her he could come to the assurance that had so far escaped him. But before that, in this reply to one of her anxious inquiries, he gave her an honest glimpse into himself. Religion, he said, is a source from which "I never did, and I believe never can, derive comfort."

If I ever feel what is called devout, it is when I have met with some good of which I did not conceive myself deserving, and then I am apt to thank anything but mankind. On the other hand, when I am ill or unlucky, I philosophize as well as I can, and wish it were over one way or the other—without any glimpses at the future. Why I came here, I know not. Where I shall go to, it is useless to inquire. In the midst of myriads of the living and the dead worlds—stars—systems—infinity—why should I be anxious about an atom [*LJ,* III, 408]?

After the marriage, Lady Byron's humorless tolerance and solemn efforts to reform and probably convert him must have had a great deal to do with driving him into the brutality and sadism that she reports. How much of his behavior can be attributed to his sense of humor, turned almost to madness and determined to shock and outrage her, is hard to say. But undoubtedly she brought out all the perverted Calvinist in him; if she wanted a Christian, his actions seem to imply, he would show her what one really was. Years later, in 1855, she wrote to Crabb Robinson in comment on Dr. Kennedy's *Conversations on Religion in Cephalonia,* and one can still feel the thrill of horror in her tone:

Not merely from casual expressions but from the whole tenor of Lord Byron's feelings, I could not but conclude he was a believer in the inspiration of the Bible, and had the gloomist Calvinistic tenets. To that unhappy view of the relation of the creature to the Creator, I have always ascribed the misery of his life. . . . Judge, then, how I must hate the Creed which made him see God as an Avenger, not a Father. My own impressions were just the reverse, but could have little weight, and it was in vain to turn his thoughts for long from that idee fixe, with which he connected his physical peculiarity as a stamp . . . I will be pardoned for referring to his frequent expression of the sentiment that I was only sent to show him the happiness he was forbidden to enjoy.[13]

The last sentence is wonderfully ironic and pathetic coming as it does from the woman who resolutely abandoned him, even though she knew she might be ruining him, who never relented, and who spent her life consciously and unconsciously building the evidence against him. But she was never able to break the spell he exerted over her, and now near the end of her life she salves her ego by the wistful, self-righteous assertion of how much she meant to him. The final ironic twist is that she was probably correct, and Byron did say this seriously. To the end of his life, Byron's attitude toward her was ambivalent. He hated and admired her. He was always somewhat in awe of her. She represented to him, as his remarks to Lady Blessington indicate, a chastity and virtue so refined that he never really understood it, but for that very reason he aspired to it. She stood for propriety, respectability, stability, and serenity, and marriage to her meant the possibility of a happy, normal, genuinely virtuous life as an English gentleman. There is no doubt Byron wished that he were capable of such a life, and momentarily when he married Annabella he persuaded himself that he actually was.

III. THE SERVILE MASS OF MATTER

In the long run, marital happiness was "forbidden" not by any Calvinist sense of fatality, but by his too acute awareness of the nature of society, which prevented any long acceptance of a placid conventional existence, and by his sexual nature, with his accompanying feelings of isolation and difference. The sense of fatality grew partly out of his sense of helplessness before his own passions. Even when he did not indulge them, he could not get them out of his mind. Other men appeared not to suffer in this way, and so he felt himself cursed.

"Man is born *passionate* of body, but with an innate though secret tendency to the love of good in his mainspring of mind." By 1821 he had come to see as applicable to all men what he had first perceived in and thought peculiar to himself. He posits, it will be noticed, an opposition between the passions and the tendency to the love of good, which is at once the old distinction between evil and good and yet something more concrete than that. He is referring certainly to sexual passion. There has been a great deal of fruitless speculation as to whether Byron suffered from abnormal sexual energy or combined, as Fairchild puts it neatly, "an aggressively energetic imagination with a comparatively torpid body and a disorganized nervous system"; [14] but there can be no doubt that from a very early age he was obsessively aware of and disturbed by sexual desire. Nor can there be any doubt of his tremendous physical energy and magnetism; too many witnesses, male and female, have testified to the formidable power of his presence for that to be disputed. Southey, who was certainly no one to give an unnecessarily admiring opinion, told Henry Taylor in 1830 that Byron's very gentleness reminded him of a tiger softly patting with sheathed talons what had not yet angered him.[15] Undoubtedly the combination of animal grace with the crippling deformity of his foot was an important factor in making Byron excessively conscious and resentful of his body.

He possessed also strong homosexual tendencies that early manifested themselves. The homosexuality, as Knight convincingly points out, accounts for much that has been considered ambiguous and mysterious in Byron's actions and writing; it may well have played a major role in the separation from his wife, although Knight is too quick to accept as evidence the scandal-mongering *Don Leon* poems.[16] Byron's conduct toward Lady Byron was likely to have been accumulatively brutal and indecent. Knight tends to make the homosexuality the dominant characteristic, to see the heterosexual relationships as simply substitutes to which Byron was forced, and to dismiss the evidence of the incestuous relationship with Augusta as a red herring to conceal the homosexuality. But all the evidence points to Byron's sexual ambivalence. To see a conflict between the two tendencies, each equally strong, with the constant effort to sublimate the one in the other, certainly explains more about his nature than to attempt to see it in terms of one or the other alone. The homosexual tendencies would have much to do with initiating or aggravating some of his major psychological attitudes: his sense of loneliness, guilt, and remorse; his alienation from, hatred of, and rebellion against conventional society; his exhibitionism.

But homosexuality, like Calvinism, can only in part explain the harsh moral self-indictment, the melancholy amounting to despair, the overwhelming sense of sexual sin that most clearly sets him apart from his peers. Libertinism was accepted as part of the pattern of life of the Regency gentleman. Most of Byron's friends were guilty of the same kind of conduct with women and were if anything more promiscuous. And, though homosexual behavior was necessarily concealed (the penalty for homosexuality was death), the pattern of life—the purely male society of the public schools, the stag drinking parties, the all-night roamings, the hell-raking clubs—this pattern was conducive not only to Platonic friendships but to the casual act of sodomy. None of

Byron's acquaintances, including Hodgson, the Anglican priest, seemed to suffer any moral distress from their own licentious conduct; they were unimaginative or cynical enough to be able to keep their practices and principles separate, or else they were what Byron called "true" voluptuaries, those who will never abandon their minds to the grossness of reality. "It is by exalting the earthly, the material, the *physique* of our pleasures, by veiling these ideas, by forgetting them altogether, or at least, never naming them hardly to one's self, that we alone can prevent them from disgusting" (*Journal,* December 13, 1813; *LJ,* II, 377).

But Byron was never able to do this. In his "Detached Thoughts" of 1821 he tells how he felt when he went up to Cambridge: "so completely alone in this new world, that it half broke my Spirits":

> I took my gradations in the vices with great promptitude, but they were not to my taste: for my early passions, though violent in the extreme, were concentrated, and hated division or spreading abroad. I could have left or lost the world with or for that which I loved; but though my temperament was naturally burning, I could not share in the common place libertinism of the place and time without disgust. And yet this very disgust, and my heart thrown back upon itself, threw me into excesses perhaps more fatal than those from which I shrunk, as fixing upon one (at a time) the passions, which spread amongst many, would have hurt only myself.

He goes on to refer cryptically to his melancholy: the real causes that have contributed to increase this perhaps natural temperament he dare not explain "without doing much mischief" or "letting out some secret or other to paralyze posterity." A little later on he comes back tantalizingly to the subject, revealing just a bit more:

> My passions were developed very early—so early, that few would believe me, if I were to state the period, and the facts which accompanied it. Perhaps this was one of the reasons which caused the anticipated melancholy of my thoughts —having anticipated life.
> My earlier poems are the thoughts of one at least ten years older than the age at which they were written: I don't mean for their solidity, but their Experience. The two first Cantos of C. H. were completed at twenty two, and they are written as if by a man older than I shall probably ever be [*LJ,* V, 445-46, 450].

By "passions" Byron means obviously sexual passion. His melancholy is not simply the romantic melancholy of loving not wisely but too well; it is the melancholy of one to whom has been revealed the terrifying demonic power of sexual passion. He is appalled at the extent to which he is at its mercy and disgusted by what he does under its influence. It is this which seems to negate any idealistic view of man's nature; contradicts and mocks his aspirations toward good; makes the individual brutish, corrupt, and contemptible; denies the benevolence of God and any ultimate purpose or meaning to human existence. This is the melancholy at the bottom of the first two cantos of *Childe Harold;* under the melodramatic posturings there are genuine pessimism and fatalism based on observation of his own sexual nature. He is the idealist constantly disillusioned by his own behavior.

There is a considerable amount of evidence pointing to Byron's revulsion against the body and its functions. He uses the word "disgusting" frequently in the sense in which he uses it in his description of the voluptuary, to indicate "the physique of our pleasures," in other words, sexual acts. In his 1813 diary he tells of the way in which he starves himself in order to starve out the "devil"; "I will *not* be the slave of *any* appetite. If I do err, it shall be my heart, at least, that heralds the way" [*LJ*, II, 328].[17] Several times he wishes that he could leave off eating altogether. The compulsiveness of his references to eating suggests that it is a partly conscious Freudian symbol for him not simply of sexual activity, but of the physical demands and frailties that enslave and chain the mind of man. To Medwin he made a statement that carries very obvious Freudian implications: "I have prejudices about women: I do not like to see them eat. Rousseau makes Julie *un peu gourmande;* but that is not at all according to my taste. I do not like to be interrupted while writing. Lady Byron did not attend to these whims of mine." [18]

Perhaps Byron's most revealing poetic statement on the implications of man's physical nature comes in *Cain,* Act II, scene i, where Lucifer is showing Cain the abyss of space. What would you think, he asks Cain, if you found that there were worlds greater than your own, inhabited by greater things, and they themselves far more in number "than the dust of thy dull earth?" "I should be proud of thought / Which knew such things," Cain replies. And Lucifer probes remorselessly:

> But if that high thought were
> Link'd to a servile mass of matter—and
> Knowing such things, aspiring to such things,
> And science still beyond them, were chain'd down
> To the most gross and petty paltry wants,

Byron

All foul and fulsome—and the very best
Of thine enjoyments a sweet degradation,
A most enervating and filthy cheat
To lure thee on to the renewal of
Fresh souls and bodies, all foredoom'd to be
As frail and few so happy—

[*Cain*, II.i.50–59]

If it be as Lucifer has said, the stricken Cain replies,

(And I within
Feel the prophetic torture of its truth),
Here let me die: for to give birth to those
Who can but suffer many years, and die—
Methinks is merely propagating death,
And multiplying murder.[19]

[*Cain*, II.i.66–71]

Cain's answer brings us back to the familiar Byronic preoccupation with the futility of human effort. But it is worth emphasizing that what sets his preoccupation apart from the traditional and even contemporary treatments of the theme of mutability and death, what gives it immediacy, intensity, and validity, at least for the twentieth-century reader, is this combination of the Luciferian cosmic view with the agonized awareness of his body as "the servile mass of matter" to which he is chained. This provides the camera obscura, the fundamental psychological perspective through which he views the world—and all that he sees confirms him in his melancholy.

Thus, in the apostrophe to the ocean in *Childe Harold*, IV, he emphasizes the puniness and perishability of man and his works before the impersonal power of nature which the ocean symbolizes. This is his fundamental vision and is the reason why his Wordsworthian and Shelleyan pronouncements in the third canto of *Childe Harold* seem so philosophically shallow and (to the Wordsworthian) insincere. He does not really believe that "I live not in myself, but I become a portion of that around me," that is, of a benevolent and purposeful nature; nor does he believe that, when the mind is set free "from what it hates in this degraded form, / Reft of its carnal life," he shall "feel all I see," the bodiless thought, the spirit of each spot "of which, even now, I share at times the immortal lot" (III.74). He wants to believe; he makes a supreme effort to believe. Momentarily under the spell of Shelley, the Alps and his own rhetorical incantation, he persuades himself; but the very form of the rhetoric, "Shall I not feel all I see?

[267]

The Romantic Ventriloquists

Are not the mountains . . . a part of me?" reveals the basic lack of conviction. And, as soon as he was over the Alps and into Italy, he gave up the effort and reverted to his old pessimistic view.

The significance of the passages in Cantos III and IV is not in their philosophical statements. It is impossible—and to a certain extent ir-relevant—to try to extract some consistent view of nature from them. They are significant as psychological gestures, as ways in which Byron strives to express the force within him that defies his belief in the futility of human effort. They are assertions of his sense of an in-destructible identity opposed to the forces conspiring for his death and annihilation. *Childe Harold* is a series of such assertions—symbolic pro-jections of the ego into the external world, reshaping and redefining it in terms of itself—and it is this that gives it the unity and power that absorb and dissolve the contradictions. The bleaker his vision of man's fate, the more desperate is Byron's effort to make himself felt and noticed; he will somehow force even the mindless universe to pay attention to him. At times he feels that he may even cheat the ultimate annihilation and survive where others die. He cultivates his sense of a special doom; if he should prove wrong in his skepticism, and there should turn out to be a vengeful god, it is better to be damned to an immortality of punishment as a rebel like Lucifer or Cain, maintaining his independence and protesting the unjustness of the Omnipotent Tyrant, than to be one of the anonymous herd of the elect. But the most important thing is to feel that he is alive, to create the illusion of his indestructibility at all costs.

So Byron almost naïvely projects himself into the visible forces of nature. Thus, in Canto III he alone becomes "portion of that around" him, and "this is *life*," and he looks "upon the peopled desert past, / as on a place of agony and strife." He is frankly concerned with per-sonal salvation. In Canto IV he introduces the apostrophe to the man-destroying ocean by ambiguously identifying with it. He loves not man the less, but nature more, he says, from those moments in which he mingles with the universe. And he ends the apostrophe by saying, "And I have loved thee Ocean . . . For I was as it were a child of thee." Occasionally the illusion fails him, and he falls back in exhaus-tion from the attempt at identification, but triumphant in his failure because of the very audacity of his aspiration:

> Could I embody and unbosom now
> That which is most within me,—could I wreak

[268]

Byron

My thoughts upon expression, and thus throw
Soul—heart—mind—passions—feelings—strong or weak—
All that I would have sought, and all I seek,
Bear, know, feel—and yet breathe—into *one* word
And that one word were Lightning, I would speak;
But as it is, I live and die unheard,
With a most voiceless thought, sheathing it as a sword.

[*CH,* III.97 (stanza)]

The rhetoric in which the statement is couched becomes its contradiction.

Against his sense of a meaningless universe, Byron could thus oppose his sense of the life force within himself. His apparently inexhaustible energy was a fact of his existence, and he poured it out indiscriminately as a means of affirming that existence, of asserting and renewing his identity in the search for stimulation. To Annabella of all people he wrote:

The great object of life is sensation—to feel that we exist, even though in pain. It is this "craving void" which drives us to gaming—to battle—to travel, to intemperate, but keenly felt pursuits of every description, whose principal attraction is the agitation inseparable from their accomplishment [*LJ,* III, 400].

This statement helps us understand one of the apparent contradictions in Byron. He hated and feared his sexual passions, and yet he cultivated them. They were important means of feeling that he existed, and through the exploration of them and every conceivable kind of sexual experience he aggravated and intensified the feeling. They were means of knowledge, too, of discovering some of the range and potentialities of human life. They were, of course, fascinating in themselves because they were evil and forbidden and loathsome. If man is going to be damned whether he acts on them or not, Byron seems to say, he may as well know all there is to know about them and indulge them to their limits of exhaustion.

Byron's Faustian curiosity, intellectual as well as sensuous, to push to the frontiers and beyond of human experience has been too frequently ignored or shrugged off. It is this insatiable will to know, inseparable from the will to live and feel, this "fire / And motion of the soul which will not dwell / In its own narrow being, but aspire / Beyond the fitting medium of desire" that places Byron beyond good and evil in the Nietzschean sense and is responsible for the expansion of his power and range as an artist.

[269]

The Romantic Ventriloquists

IV. THE DREAM OF THE SLEEPING PASSIONS

"All convulsions end with me in rhyme," Byron told Moore when he had completed *The Bride of Abydos* (*LJ*, II, 293), and composition was always for him one of the sensations by which he felt that he existed. His attitude toward poetry was mixed and contradictory: he liked to adopt the attitude that he could take or leave it as one of the avocations of the gentleman; sometimes he spoke contemptuously and half-ashamedly of it as a poor substitute for other energies. In his diary, in understandably violent revulsion against the adulation of writers, he expressed what is a more or less constant view, and one that becomes extremely significant in the last year of his life:

> I do think the preference of *writers* to *agents*—the mighty stir made about scribbling and scribes, by themselves and others—a sign of effeminacy, degeneracy, and weakness. Who would write, who had anything better to do? "Action— action—action"—said Demosthenes: "action*s*—action*s*," I say, and not writing,— least of all, rhyme [*LJ*, II, 345].

But in spite of this writing was for him a convulsion, a passion as uncontrollable as, and in fact closely tied to, sexual passion, as Byron recognized.[20] He could not help writing, whatever he wanted to believe, and this is one reason for his ambivalent attitude toward it. In another letter to Moore (January 2, 1821), in a moment of complete frankness he says:

> I feel exactly as you do about our "art," but it comes over me in a kind of rage every now and then, like ****, and then, if I don't write to empty my mind, I go mad. As to that regular uninterrupted writing, which you describe in your friend, I do not understand it. I feel it as a torture, which I must get rid of, but never as a pleasure. On the contrary, I think composition a great pain [*LJ*, V, 214–15].

Thus he saw composition primarily as a release, direct or vicarious, of dammed-up emotions or energy. "Poetry," he wrote Annabella in November, 1813, "is the lava of the imagination whose eruption prevents an earthquake" (*LJ*, III, 405).[21] He was probably thinking specifically of *The Bride of Abydos,* which he said in his diary was written "in four nights to distract my dreams from **. Were it not thus, it had never been composed; and had I not done something at that time, I must have gone mad, by eating my own heart,—bitter diet . . ." (*LJ*, II, 321).[22] But he knew, though he only half admitted, that poetry served a more complex psychological function than simply to provide emotional release or escape:

> To withdraw *myself* from *myself* (oh that cursed selfishness!) has ever been my sole, my entire, my sincere motive in scribbling at all; and publishing is also the continuance of the same object, by the action it affords to the mind, which else recoils upon itself. If I valued fame, I should flatter received opinions, which have gathered strength by time, and will yet wear longer than any living works to the contrary. But for the soul of me, I cannot and will not give the lie to my own thoughts and doubts, come what may. If I am a fool, it is, at least, a doubting one; and I envy no one the certainty of his self approved wisdom [*Journal*, November 27, 1813; *LJ*, II, 351].

After the debacle of the separation, in the last two cantos of *Childe Harold* this view of composition is given a more positive and profound expression. In the opening stanzas of Canto III, he says that he essays perhaps in vain to sing as he once did:

> Yet, though a dreary strain, to this I cling,
> So that it wean me from the weary dream
> Of selfish grief or gladness.

He who has pierced "the depths of life / So that no wonder waits him" can tell "why thought seeks refuge" in the soul's haunted cell:

> 'Tis to create, and in creating live
> A being more intense, that we endow
> With form our fancy, gaining as we give
> The life we image, even as I do now.
> What am I? Nothing; but not so art thou,
> Soul of my thought.

Though the extravagance of this statement owes something to Shelley, perhaps, as well as to the crisis of the moment, and he later modifies it, nevertheless it expresses substantially the experience that the composition of poetry always entailed for Byron. His conception, in general, of the psychological function of poetry comes close to present-day Freudian theories; this and his description of the nature of composition justify us in assuming his fundamental sincerity as an artist: creation *was* for him a means of living more intensely.

V. THE RISE AND FALL OF THE HERO

"To live more intensely" was undoubtedly the central motivation behind the creation of the hero in the first two cantos of *Childe Harold*. The great fear of the sensationalist is that he will deaden his ability to feel, and be reduced to apathy and exhaustion. This fear Byron translates into poetic realization in the opening stanzas of *Childe Harold,* Canto I. There is a deliberate ambiguity in the presentation; the loss of passion leaves behind a residue of melancholy and remorse and intensifies the sense of loneliness but, on the other hand, brings a sense of relief. The hero has been set free to seek other pleasures. The dream nature of this is obvious. Byron both dreaded and wished for the condition of the "marble heart" in which he would be emancipated from sexual tyranny and his present state of restless frustration; and of course there is always the half-humorous, half-serious adolescent dream projection of himself as the heroic male figure irresistibly attractive to women but himself unmoved.

The implications of the word and idea of pilgrimage, says Lovell,

. . . may well be that Byron even as early as 1809 was actually going in search of some kind of spiritual cure—a cure for his ennui, discontent, restlessness, and feelings of guilt, whatever their causes may have been or however imperfectly he may have realized the fact at the time.[23]

The pilgrimage was also quite specifically a quest for new sensations to make him "feel that he existed." The tension set up by the contradiction between the portrait of the hero as "Pleasure's pall'd victim" on whose faded brow life-abhorring gloom wrote "curst Cain's unresting doom," and the evident energy and gusto with which his "joyless reveries" are presented and his adventures described; between his ennui and exhaustion, and the excitment and vitality of such scenes as the bullfight and the barbaric dances of the Albanians and such portraits as the Maid of Saragoza and Ali Pasha—this tension is responsible for much of the hypnotic appeal *Childe Harold* had for Byron's audience. The total effect is of indestructible energy and vitality "at enmity with nothingness and dissolution."

The fatalism that runs through the poem is that of one who fears that through sensual excess he has destroyed his ability and right to enjoy anything else. Implicit within this fatalism is the assumption that the excess is unavoidable, as is Harold's self-exile from society. The assumption was very much Byron's own. His was the fate or will that walked astray. In *Childe Harold* he created the instrument of his fate, became "the careful pilot of his proper woe," cunning in his overthrow. It was inevitable that one so aware of the hypocrisies and self-deceptions of society, so perversely driven to parade his own honesty and to test the mores of society to their breaking point, would sooner or later bring the world crashing about his ears. *Childe Harold* became the instrument of his fate because in it he created a hero whose excesses against the conventional mores, whose marble heart, ennui, and melancholy were just enough to attract rather than repel.

The appeal of *Childe Harold* was immediate and powerful for all classes. To the lives of a jaded, bored aristocracy, he gave meaning and glamour; through him they could see themselves in a new perspective. To the mass of people he was an exciting escape from humdrum existence. To the great Puritan middle class he was mysterious evil to be vicariously enjoyed and vigorously reformed: an exhilarating challenge. Every reader immediately identified the hero with the author and directly or indirectly with himself. Byron became overnight the expression of the English libido, so long repressed by religion, government, and war.

It was within his own social group, of course, that the adulation became fatal. To look and act the part of his hero was easy for Byron; he wanted to, and society was determined that he should. Soon there was no chance of escape. From acting the role he turned to living it, and he began to move through an increasingly dangerous series of affairs and social relationships. The tension created by his mode of life, the growing ugly and reckless mood of defiance that foreshadowed his own downfall, is revealed in the melodramatic Oriental verse narratives which he wrote at breakneck speed between 1812 and 1816. They were all probably, like *The Bride of Abydos,* safety valves which released energy that might otherwise have exploded socially. Against the background of dark and violent deeds he filled out in detail the portrait of the hero which he had begun in *Childe Harold.*

The most elaborate attempts at psychological development and analysis are made in *The Corsair* and *Lara.* In these Byron's attitude approaches most nearly to the nadir of destructive nihilism. The hero is a despairing outlaw in a meaningless world, and in *Lara* he becomes the leader, more out of misanthropic hatred than out of principle, of an abortive revolt against his own class. The portrait in *Lara* brings together the characteristics that have been slowly accumulating:

> There was in him a vital scorn of all:
> As if the worst had fallen which could befall.
> He stood a stranger in this breathing world,
> An erring Spirit from another hurled;
> A thing of dark imaginings, that shaped

By choice the perils he by chance escaped;
But 'scaped in vain, for in their memory yet
His mind would half exult and half regret:
With more capacity for love than Earth
Bestows on most of mortal mould and birth.
His early dreams of good outstripped the truth
And troubled Manhood followed baffled Youth;
And wasted powers for better purpose lent;
And fiery passions that had poured their wrath
In hurried desolation o'er his path,
And left the better feelings all at strife
In wild reflection o'er his stormy life;
But haughty still and loth himself to blame,
He called on Nature's self to share the blame,
And charged all faults upon the fleshly form
She gave to clog the soul, and feast the worm;
Till he at last confounded good and ill,
And half mistook for fate the acts of will. . . .

[*Lara*, I.312–36]

The last two lines might be taken as Byron's epigram upon his own life during this period. With the rapidity of one of his own narratives, he was driven to those acts that led to his self-exile. However we account for the separation, there is no doubt that Byron's conduct toward the end approached madness. He did everything he could, at least in words, to force society to turn on him in self-righteous hypocrisy and expel him. That he was not fully conscious of his motives, that he intended to taunt Annabella and through her the society for which she stood just up to the breaking point and no further, that he was genuinely appalled and incredulous when she turned on him and ruthlessly threatened to destroy him, is evident enough. And he was quite shaken by the violence of the social reaction. It was one thing to have anticipated in imagination the fate he had asked for; it was quite a different thing to experience it. He had been lulled into a contemptuous sense of security by the apparent willingness of society to accept his rebellious heroes. But the society in which he moved had become increasingly sullen and resentful, watchful for the first sign of weakness, ready to make him as Macaulay said a kind of ritual scapegoat "by whose vicarious agonies all the other transgressors of the same class are, it is supposed, sufficiently chastised," and thus, he might have added, to reassert triumphantly the superiority of the social order over the individual.[24]

Byron

The moment of exile was the moment in which Byron became one with his heroes. The nightmarish condition he had envisioned in the opening canto of *Childe Harold* became the reality; the life he had "anticipated" was now his own. He had become "the wandering outlaw of his own dark mind," broken by society, frustrated in the "nobler aim" he had once beheld, "one the more / To baffled millions which had gone before." His despair was acute, far beyond the despair he had imagined for the young Childe Harold. Now "all seemed over this side the tomb"; he had "outlived" himself by many a day, growing old in experiences that might have filled a century. The futility of existence and the destructiveness of human action overwhelmed him. The images of sea and desert become symbols of the psychological hell through which he aimlessly wandered. In the opening stanzas of *Childe Harold,* Canto III, he is the weed flung from the rock into the ocean; his thoughts and tears have left a "sterile track" over which the journeying years heavily "plod the last sands of life." Manfred sees himself "grey hair'd with anguish," a blasted pine "barkless, branchless, / A blighted trunk upon a cursed root"; to be thus eternally, "having been otherwise," is the ultimate of horror. And to the Chamois Hunter who pulls him back from the precipice he cries:

> . . . actions are our epochs; mine
> Have made my days and nights imperishable,
> Endless, and all alike; as sands on the shore,
> Innumerable atoms; and one desert,
> Barren and cold, on which the wild waves break,
> But nothing rests, save carcasses and wrecks,
> Rocks and the salt-surf weeds of bitterness.
> [*Manfred,* II.i.52–58]

The full extent of Byron's despair, of his *Angst,* is revealed in the poem *Darkness* written in July, 1816. Here is a dream not only of the extinction of human life, but of the death of the universe:

> The bright sun was extinguish'd, and the stars
> Did wander darkling in the eternal space,
> Rayless, and pathless, and the icy Earth
> Swung blind and blackening in the moonless air. . . .
> The World was void,
> The populous and the powerful was a lump,
> Seasonless, herbless, treeless, manless, lifeless—
> A lump of death—a chaos of hard clay.
> [*Darkness,* lines 2–5, 69–72]

Darkness was the universe. His own lonely desolation Byron sees as the ultimate nature of things.

But such black despair almost invariably gave way to defiance. The oscillation between despair and defiance is vividly illustrated by setting beside *Darkness* the poem *Prometheus,* composed at the same time. Prometheus suffers at the hands of a malevolent universe for his kindness to man:

> And the inexorable Heaven,
> And the deaf tyranny of Fate,
> The ruling principle of Hate,
> Which for its pleasure doth create
> The things it may annihilate,
> Refused thee even the boon to die. . . .
>
> [*Prometheus,* lines 18–23]

In his silent, defiant suffering he is a symbol to man of his "fate and force." Like Prometheus, man can see

> His own funereal destiny;
> His wretchedness, and his resistance,
> And his sad unallied existence.
> To which his Spirit may oppose
> Itself—an equal to all woes,
> And a firm will, and a deep sense,
> Which even in torture can descry
> Its own concenter'd recompense,
> Triumphant where it dares defy,
> And making Death a Victory.
>
> [*Prometheus,* lines 50–59]

Similarly, Byron discovered that his exile and suffering had ironically emancipated his mind and imagination, that instead of being reduced to apathy he had been stimulated to increased activity. He was free to think and do as he pleased; he was no longer under necessity of compromise. Despair itself became a source of sensation, a means of feeling that he existed.

> There is a very life in our despair,
> Vitality of poison,—a quick root
> Which feeds these deadly branches. . . .
>
> [*CH,* III.34]

As has already been pointed out, he found suffering a stimulant to artistic creation. Poetry became not simply an escape or a release, but a means of triumphing over defeat:

Byron

'Tis to create, and in creating live
A being more intense, that we endow
With form our fancy. . . .

> [*CH*, III.6]

Sometimes this creative vitality seemed to him a morbid growth, a disease—ironic confirmation of a pessimistic view of human life. For in the world about us we find no correspondence to the mind's creations. In *Childe Harold*, Canto IV, he broods over the discrepancy between the ideal and actuality of love:

Of its own beauty, is the mind diseased,
And fevers into false creation:—where,
Where are the forms the sculptor's soul hath seiz'd?
In him alone. . . .

> [*CH*, IV.122]

Our disillusionment, therefore, is swift and acute and finally destructive as the charms unwind that robed our idols, and we see "Nor worth nor beauty dwells from out the mind's / Ideal shape of such":

We wither from our youth, we gasp away—
Sick—sick; unfound the boon, unslaked the thirst,
Though to the last, in verge of our decay,
Some phantom lures, such as we sought at first—
But all too late,—so are we doubly curst.
Love, fame, ambition, avarice—'tis the same,
Each idle, and all ill, and none the worst—
For all are meteors with a different name,
And Death the sable smoke where vanishes the flame.

> [*CH*, IV.124]

Then half-unconsciously Byron shifts his perspective. Our life, he concludes, is a false nature, not in the harmony of things: sinful, poisoned, subject to "disease, death, bondage." The implication is that it is life and not the mind that is diseased.

But, in plumbing the depths of disillusionment, he found paradoxically the grounds for confidence. The mind that could create ideals could also discern, endure, and deal with the truth. And so the stanzas of disillusionment end in affirmation:

Yet let us ponder boldly—'tis a base
Abandonment of reason to resign
Our right of thought—our last and only place
Of refuge; this, at least shall still be mine. . . .

> [*CH*, IV.127]

[277]

The Romantic Ventriloquists

The mind became the fortress where Byron's will to live held firm. He remained consistently and profoundly convinced of its fundamental integrity and indestructibility; it was for him the only evidence and manifestation of something meaningful in the scheme of things.

VI. THE LAST INFIRMITY OF EVIL

Manfred is the drama in which Byron symbolically works his way through to mental sanity, to the psychological perspective that made *Don Juan* possible. It is a therapeutic drama into which Byron pours off all the pent-up, confused, and conflicting attitudes growing out of the debacle. It is truly "the lava of the imagination whose eruption prevents an earthquake." Byron himself called it a drama "as mad as Nat. Lee's Bedlam Tragedy" (*LJ*, IV, 65–66) and "of a very wild metaphysical and inexplicable kind" (*LJ*, IV, 54–55). He half-apologized for it: "it is too much in my old style . . . I certainly am a devil of a mannerist and must leave off; but what could I do? Without exertion of some kind, I should have sunk under my imagination and reality" (*LJ*, IV, 71–72).

But under the Gothic claptrap, the conscious and unconscious mystification, and the dramatic incoherence, there is a kind of systematic stock-taking. The oblivion Manfred seeks is not simply death or annihilation; even when he attempts suicide he speaks of "the power upon me which withholds / And makes it my fatality to live"— and the power is obviously his own desire to live. What he seeks is in reality the obliteration of his knowledge of past sin and his awareness of responsibility. He wants an easy kind of anesthetization that would make him "oblivious" to his own human nature and the human condition in general, that would explain away his guilt and rationalize his fears. He would like to be like other men, to have the faith or unawareness that allows them to forget themselves. But he is unwilling from the start to pay the price, to relinquish his "right of thought." When the elements of nature tell him that because they are immortal they cannot answer his question about death, he cries:

> The mind, the spirit, the Promethean spark,
> The lightning of my being, is as bright,
> Pervading, and far darting as your own,
> And shall not yield to yours, though coop'd in clay!
> [*Manfred*, I.i.154–57]

When they offer him material power—subjects, sovereignty, control over the earth and elements—gifts which for many a man have brought forgetfulness, Manfred angrily rejects them. In a sense he already possesses these gifts, and they have brought him no relief. And his calling up the spirits to demand what he knows they cannot give him insures his condemnation to self-awareness. In the spell cast upon him at the end of the scene, the elements themselves become means of awareness. In the wind is a voice forbidding him to rejoice; the night shall deny him quiet; the sun shall make him wish for its extinction. The ultimate curse is that he is compelled himself to be his "proper hell."

> Nor to slumber, nor to die,
> Shall be in thy destiny;
> Though thy death shall still seem near
> To thy wish, but as a fear. . . .
> [*Manfred*, I.i.254–57]

When the Witch of the Alps, who is a kind of Shelleyan-Wordsworthian spirit of nature and Ideal Beauty, offers to aid him if he will swear obedience to her will, he refuses as violently as he has refused the elements. To obey would be to subject his mind—symbolically, to accept the Shelleyan-Wordsworthian idealism—and this, finally, he cannot do. Similarly, he will not bow to Arimanes, the spirit of evil, or accept the comfort of the Abbot. To each he replies in the same terms. To the spirits of evil he says that he has already known

> The fulness of humiliation, for
> I sunk before my vain despair, and knelt
> To my own desolation.
> [*Manfred*, II.iv.40–42]

And to the Abbot he says that he will choose no mortal, no representative of institutionalized religion, to be his mediator with heaven; there is no prayer, or penance, or threat of hell that can exorcise the sense of guilt and remorse:

> . . . there is no future pang
> Can deal that justice on the self-condemn'd
> He deals on his own soul.
> [*Manfred*, III.i.76–78]

In the end, when the fiends come for him, he cries that he had made no compact with them. His power came solely from himself, from "superior science, penance, daring, / And length of watching, strength of mind, and skill"; and he is responsible for his own acts and their consequences:

> The mind which is immortal makes itself
> Requital for its good or evil thoughts,
> Is its own origin of ill and end,
> And its own place and time; its innate sense,
> When stripp'd of this mortality, derives
> No colour from the fleeting things without,
> But is absorb'd in sufferance or in joy,
> Born from the knowledge of its own desert.
>
> [*Manfred,* III.iv.129–36]

So the fiends disappear, leaving him to die alone, and his last words to the Abbot are: "Old man! 'tis not so difficult to die."

This line was left out at Gifford's suggestion in the first edition, and Byron wrote furiously to Murray, "You have destroyed the whole effect and moral of the poem by omitting the last line of Manfred's speaking; and why this was done, I know not" (*LJ,* IV, 157). At first glance, the line seems almost pathetically anticlimactic. Why did it loom so large for Byron? The answer would be that it represented a tremendous psychological victory, a momentous realization. Within the context of the drama as we have seen it unfolded, the line means, "It is not so difficult to die—alone—without comfort." But, within the context of Byron's own dramatic struggle, it means, "It is not so difficult to live —alone—without comfort."

The position at which Byron has arrived is similar to the existentialist position of Sartre and his followers. In his lecture, "Existentialism Is a Humanism," Sartre asserts that modern man can believe in none of the traditional supernatural faiths; he knows that he is alone in the universe:

He discovers forthwith, that he is without excuse. For if indeed existence precedes essence, one will never be able to explain one's action by reference to a given and specific human nature; in other words, there is no determinism—man is free, man *is* freedom. Nor, on the other hand, if God does not exist, are we provided with any values or commands that could legitimatize our behavior. Thus we have neither behind us, nor before us in a luminous realm of values, any means of justification or excuse. We are left alone, without excuse. That is what I mean when I say that man is condemned to be free. Condemned, because he did not create himself, yet is nevertheless at liberty, and from the moment that he is thrown into this world he is responsible for everything he does.[25]

Byron's attitude until now had been one of bitter protest against the injustice of his condition, a defiant refusal to accept it. Manfred's desire for oblivion is Byron's desire for the comforting illusion, the escape from self-responsibility. He wanted to believe in a meaningful universal pattern into which death would be an absorption. He decidedly did not want to face the prospect of death as annihilation in an indifferent universe. Manfred's desperate effort to wrest answers from the spirits is Byron's desperate effort to persuade himself that there is something beyond himself, some universal pattern concerned with man, even if it is a pattern of evil.

But Byron can no more believe in his spirits than Manfred can believe that they will tell him what he wants to know. Indeed, each episode is a ritualistic colloquy that confirms Manfred in his fear and further demonstrates what he knows: that he can look for no aid or comfort beyond himself. It is necessary to present the various alternatives, so that by his rejection of each he is forced more consciously back upon himself, and the inevitability of his self-responsibility is revealed. At the end he is forced to face it without possible escape or excuse. What he discovers through the ritualistic process is that the dreaded fate, when it cannot longer be evaded, is not so terrifying after all. It is quite possible to die as to live with the awareness of his aloneness, to accept the prospect of death as truly oblivion. It is better to face one's identity, he finds, than to try to escape it. In fact, as Manfred's reply to the fiends indicates, his acceptance of self-dependence becomes a cause of pride and satisfaction. Like Wordsworth's Solitary, Manfred has found that he can "exist within himself, not comfortless." All of these recognitions are compressed into his final statement to the Abbot: " 'tis not so difficult to die."

For Byron, Manfred's discovery meant not death but release. He could now emancipate himself from his hero and from his fear and despair. He was free to develop the larger view of himself and the world in which the defiant hero became increasingly unnecessary and even a little silly. He was in a position now to maintain a proper sense of proportion in looking at himself and at mankind in general. There was no longer anything to inhibit or restrain him in saying what he thought. He was freed of his fear of society, of obsession with his own sins and guilt and remorse. None of these seemed terribly important any more. He was psychologically prepared to relax and enjoy himself. And he obviously began to enjoy himself immensely when he found in

The Romantic Ventriloquists

Whistlecraft's (John Hookham Frere's) *The Monks and the Giants* the free-flowing comic style to match his new-found freedom and flexibility of mind and imagination. By the fall of 1817, while he was still working on Canto IV of *Childe Harold,* he was experimenting in *Beppo* with the manner that was to find its full scope in *Don Juan* in the following year.

VII. THE WANDERING OUTLAW

This is not to say, of course, that Byron abandoned the old attitudes of defiance and resentment. There were times when his "rage and fury against the inadequacy of his state to his conceptions" knew no bounds. But these moments grew rarer as they were absorbed into and to some extent neutralized by the encompassing, more persistent comic perspective. Byron did not believe in repressing his rage and fury, however; they were necessary as safety valves, and they were an integral part of the way he felt and saw the conditions of human life. Indeed, he believed that they were inevitable attitudes in anyone who was aware, and he felt that they should be encouraged. They were the prelude to a better society.

After *Childe Harold* he had written few poems in which he expressed these attitudes, but in the serious dramas that appeared as interludes within the larger drama of *Don Juan* he presented them in his protagonists. The most ambitious and important of these dramas is *Cain,* Byron's most deliberate and violent attack on the shibboleths of Christian society. For two acts it is a sustained effort to expose the absurdity of the Judaeo-Christian conception of the relation of God and man. Regardless of what Byron says, its bias and propagandistic intent are clear. It is not only Cain but the reader who is being indoctrinated by Lucifer in the second act. How much Byron had tongue in cheek it is hard to say, but certainly he was out to convert as many potential Cains as he could to revolt.

Part of the curiously ambiguous effect of the play is due to Byron's treatment of the Genesis myth as literally true. He writes a straightforward tragic drama, without satire or overt irony. All the characters, including Lucifer, accept the anthropomorphic nature of God and the personal, intimate concern of God with man. To a certain extent this was because Byron instinctively did also. He had been so indoctrinated in the literal acceptance of the Bible as a child, and this acceptance was

[282]

so integral a part of social behavior and terminology, that the Judaeo-Christian view was deeply ingrained in his pattern of thought. Even today, it is difficult for anyone brought up in strictly orthodox surroundings to break through the mold of terminology and to argue against dogma without accepting the terms and the anthropomorphic assumptions of the dogma. And so Byron, like Lucifer and Cain, accepts the reality of the tyrant God, at the same time that he is demonstrating the impossibility of His existence outside the mind of man or apart from the cultural organization that accepts and uses Him to its own ends.

The protestations of orthodoxy in Byron's preface and in his letters to Moore and Murray are to be taken neither at their face value nor as necessarily disingenuous. They are public rhetoric, intended to appease and assuage and to make his heretical potions palatable. Like many a skeptic, Byron was awed by his own audacity and refused to face directly the full implications of his thought. He also recoiled from any head-on clash with the accepted religious attitudes and automatically adopted their language and paid lip service to them. Furthermore, Byron could be swept by his own emotions and eloquence or by contact with persuasive personalities—he possessed what he called mobility or *mobilité:* "an excessive susceptibility of immediate impressions" [26]—into momentary acceptance; but as soon as he was put under pressure or forced to reflect he reverted to his fundamental skepticism. And of course he delighted in confusing and obfuscating his friends, particularly Murray. In the letter of November 3, 1821, we see all these characteristics at work—naïveté, disingenuousness, *mobilité,* obfuscation—leading finally to an intellectually honest explanation of his intent in the pivotal action of the drama:

As to "alarms," etc., do you really think such things ever led any body astray? Are these people more impious than Milton's Satan? Or the Prometheus of Aeschylus? . . . Are not Adam, Eve, Adah, and Abel, as pious as the Catechism?

Gifford is too wise a man to think that such things can have any *serious* effect—*who* was ever altered by a poem? I beg leave to observe, that there is no creed nor personal hypothesis of mine in all this: but I was obliged to make Cain and Lucifer talk consistently, and surely this has always been permitted to poesy. Cain is a proud man; if Lucifer promised him kingdoms, etc., it would *elate* him; the object of the Demon is to *depress* him still further in his own estimation than he was before, by showing him infinite things and his own abasement, till he falls into the frame of mind that leads to the Catastrophe, from mere *internal* irritation, *not* premeditation, or envy of *Abel* (which would have made him contemptible), but from the rage and fury against the inadequacy of his state to his conceptions, and which discharges itself rather against Life, and the Author of Life, than the mere living [*LJ*, V, 469–70].

It is the action of Act II that makes *Cain* an impious and—from the point of view of the orthodox—a dangerous play. For Act II superimposes the world of nineteenth-century scientific knowledge and speculation upon the anthropocentric world of the Old Testament. Although the artistic justification for this is debatable, it is undoubtedly effective in a surrealistic way. Logically the world of Act II makes the God and the world of the other acts utterly impossible. In the first act, God is presented as an anthropomorphic tyrant, directly and intimately concerned in the creation and punishment of man. The questions of Cain are directed at the inexplicable nature of His act in setting the tree of knowledge in the garden, forbidding man to eat of it, and sadistically punishing him for doing so. Earth is the center of the universe. But in Act II, when Lucifer carries Cain into the abyss of space, earth is quickly lost as a speck of light, less bright than a firefly, among the innumerable stars. There is no place for a personal deity here:

> Oh, thou beautiful
> And unimaginable ether! and
> Ye multiplying masses of increased
> And still increasing lights! what are ye? what
> Is this blue wilderness of interminable
> Air, where ye roll along, as I have seen
> The leaves along the limpid streams of Eden?
> Is your course measured for ye? Or do ye
> Sweep on in your unbounded revelry
> Through an aerial universe of endless
> Expansion—at which my soul aches to think—
> Intoxicated with eternity?
> Oh God! Oh Gods! or whatsoe'er ye are!
> How beautiful ye are! how beautiful
> Your works, or accidents, or whatsoe'er
> They may be! Let me die as atoms die
> (If that they die), or know ye in your might
> And knowledge! My thoughts are not in this hour
> Unworthy what I see, though my dust is;—
> Spirit! let me expire, or see them nearer.
>
> [*Cain*, II.i.98–117]

Lucifer tells Cain that these stars are worlds that may have their Edens also, and men "or things higher." And he carries him then to

Byron

Hades, which is the shadowy realm of dead worlds and beings. There Cain sees the forms of mighty phantoms whom Lucifer informs him were once "intelligent, good, great, and glorious things," incalculably superior to Adam, who perished from the earth when it was more glorious, before it had been crushed into its present form by a cosmic cataclysm. The picture he presents is of an eternally degenerating universe in which, he implies at one point, both he and God are latecomers. When Cain exclaims, "What! is it [this wreck of a world] not then new?" Lucifer replies:

> No more than life is; and that was ere thou
> Or *I* were, or the things which seem to us
> Greater than either.
> [*Cain*, II.i.154–56]

But Lucifer is not very clear or consistent on this point. Toward the end of the second act, when Cain asks him to point out his dwelling or Jehovah's, he says that they dwell *"here* and o'er all space," and that they represent two eternal, warring principles. Earlier he had said that, though God would have done bettter not to plant the fatal tree, ignorance of evil does not save from evil; it rolls on the same, "a part of all things." "I'll not believe it," says Cain, "for I thirst for good." Who does not? Lucifer replies:

> *Who* covets evil
> For its own bitter sake? *None*—nothing! 'tis
> The leaven of all life, and lifelessness.
> [*Cain*, II.ii.234–41]

Even in the remote and beautiful stars there is evil. And Jehovah, of course, to Lucifer and Byron represents that evil.

However fuzzy Lucifer's metaphysics may get, the basic intent and effect is clear: to demonstrate that the Biblical story explains nothing and is even irrelevant in an infinite universe. To what end, asks Cain, have you shown me these things? Did you not require knowledge? asks Lucifer ironically. Have I not taught you to know yourself? Alas, says Cain, I seem nothing. To which Lucifer replies:

> And this should be the human sum
> Of knowledge, to know mortal nature's nothingness:
> Bequeath that science to thy children, and
> 'Twill spare them many tortures.
> [*Cain*, II.ii.421–24]

But, just before he takes Cain back to earth, he balances this bleak advice with the same reassurance that Manfred had come to at his death:

> *One good* gift has the fatal apple given;
> Your *reason*—let it not be over-sway'd
> By tyrannous threats to force you into faith
> 'Gainst all external sense and inward feeling:
> Think and endure, and form an inner world
> In your own bosom—where the outward fails;
> So shall you nearer be the spiritual
> Nature, and war triumphant with your own.[27]
>
> [*Cain,* II.ii.459–66]

The third act, with its return to the anthropomorphic myth of the first act, becomes dramatically anticlimactic and logically irrelevant. As an artist Byron has tampered recklessly and perhaps fatally with dramatic illusion. Once the mythic pattern is broken, it is almost impossible to restore it and regain the willing suspension of disbelief which the reader almost automatically gives at the beginning. In a sense this disillusionment was what Byron wanted, even at the price of dramatic unity. Cain needs no trip with Lucifer to stir him up to the acts culminating in the death of Abel. They have been directly and adequately prepared for in the first act. The second act becomes a violent intrusion, the effect of which is to shatter the credibility of the myth and open the way to the intellectual emancipation of the reader.

It is in terms of social attitudes that an underlying unifying pattern is to be looked for. Byron wrote Moore that, as a consequence of his talk with Lucifer, "Cain comes back and kills Abel in a fit of dissatisfaction, partly with the politics of Paradise, which had driven them all out of it, and partly because (as it is written in Genesis) Abel's sacrifice was the more acceptable to the Deity" (*LJ,* V, 368). But these are finally one and the same reasons. The "politics of Paradise" was, as it had been for centuries, the politics of the ruling social order of Byron's day. The tyrant God with his mask of benevolence was incorporated into the social structure. The determinism implied in the story of the Fall—that the human race must forever suffer for the willful disobedience of its progenitors, except for whatever alleviation God in his mercy is willing to provide—was used to achieve acquiescence of the individual in his particular lot and to insure the preservation and stability of traditional social organization. Any probing or question-

ing of the myth became a threat to the social order and to individual
tranquillity, and so all persons combined to turn on the questioner and
silence him or drive him out. The obsequious submissiveness of Adam
and Eve and Abel as exemplified in Abel's prayer:

> Sole Lord of light!
> Of good and glory and eternity;
> Without whom all were evil, and with whom
> Nothing can err, except to some good end
> Of thine omnipotent benevolence,
>
> [*Cain*, III.231–35]

is a form of mental enslavement that carries over obviously into social
behavior.

In the first act Cain's questions expose the arbitrary and sadistic behavior that masquerades as benevolence for its own unscrupulous ends
—which are certainly not the happiness of mankind on earth. Here,
Byron suggests, is the illogical foundation upon which the assertion of
the benevolence of God rests. The full force of the exposure depends
upon the social perspective of the reader, for once the process of questioning begins it carries inevitably into all the acts and pronouncements
of society that have called themselves benevolent by analogy, and they
stand exposed in all their selfish, evil, and ugly motivations. The world
of the first act of *Cain* symbolizes, then, the accepted social order. God
stands for the very real tyranny of a social and political hierarchy that
justified its acts by appeal to divine authority, and Cain is the rebellious
intellect who insists upon questioning the justice of divine and therefore social decrees.

In the second act, Cain and the reader are carried by Lucifer to the
emancipation of mind set in motion by the questioning in the first act
—to the realization that there is no ultimate or objective sanction for
the authority attributed to God or society. The problems of evil and of
life are shown to be far too complex to be accounted for in the sim-
plified and egotistic way of the Genesis story. Both life and evil existed,
Lucifer points out, long before man existed; his limitations and his
sufferings are inherent in the eternal scheme of things. The clear intent of Lucifer's demonstration, though Lucifer never gets around to
saying this directly, is to show up the anthropocentric world of
Genesis as a man-made concoction. By revealing to Cain "mortal
nature's nothingness," the unimportance of man in the universe, with
no resources except his reason, Lucifer implies that men are free to do

what they can for themselves. Emancipated from "the mind-forged manacles" of religion and social dogmas, they have the right and indeed the duty to defy and overthrow petty tyranny based on deceit and ignorance.

To defy, however, is to provoke the wrath of those in power and risk destruction. In the third act when Cain, his eyes opened to the true nature of things, is forced into sacrifice to the "God of this World," he stands erect and reasons with Him like the nineteenth-century intellectual he has indeed become. Once again Cain's plea is as much political as religious—directed against the "politics of Paradise" and therefore of those who rule in the name of God. It is the violent rejection of his appeal to reason that arouses Cain to frustrated rage against the obsequious Abel, whose speech and actions are almost a parody of the behavior of the self-righteous, well-intentioned people who by their blind submission encourage the perpetuation of social tyranny and evil.[28] Ironically, Cain is led into the very violence he has opposed, into adopting the tactics of the tyranny he has defied. Broken and defeated, he is driven into exile as much by his parents, self-righteous supporters like Abel of the tyrant God, as by the Angel. And, at least momentarily, he abandons his right of reason, repudiates his trip with Lucifer as a "dreary dream," and intellectually submits to the values of the victor. Cain suffers the tragic fate of the enlightened man who openly challenges the anachronistic ruling dogmas of society.

But, though *Cain* is a tragic drama, it is not a drama of despair, conceding the futility of defying intellectual and social tyranny. On the contrary, it is a continuous incitement to defiance, a devastating revelation of the vulnerability of the tyrant God, so that the very manner in which His momentary triumph is presented becomes an ironic prophecy that His ultimate collapse is inevitable and that the future belongs to the sons of Cain.

Byron's general intent was undoubtedly, to borrow a metaphor from I. A. Richards, "to infect his pages with such a virulent culture of doubt" that all unthinking acceptance of dogma would wither in the minds of his readers. But that he also fully intended the play to be an attack on contemporary social and political institutions is evident from the letter which in November, 1822, he wrote Kinnaird in respect to the uproar against *Cain:*

As to myself I shall not be deterred by any outcry; your present public hate me, but they shall not interrupt the march of my mind, nor prevent me from

Byron

telling those who are attempting to trample on all thought, that their thrones shall yet be rocked to their foundations [*LJ*, VI, 140].

When he turned to *Don Juan* again with the permission of the countess in the spring of 1822 after a year's interruption (he probably resumed it and then got the countess' permission), it was with the same seriousness of intent, the same conviction that he expressed to Kinnaird in respect to *Cain*. Writing to Moore on August 8, 1822, to ask for a return of the stanzas on Wellington which were originally intended for Canto III, he says:

> I have written three more cantos of *Don Juan* and am hovering on the brink of another (the ninth). The reason I want the stanzas again which I sent you is, that as these cantos contain a full detail (like the storm in Canto Second) of the siege and assault of Ismail, with much of sarcasm on those butchers in large business, your mercenary soldiery, it is a good opportunity of gracing the poem with ***** [Wellington?]. With these things and these fellows, it is necessary, in the present clash of philosophy and tyranny, to throw away the scabbard. I know it is against fearful odds; but the battle must be fought; and it will be eventually for the good of mankind, whatever it may be for the individual who risks himself [*LJ*, VI, 101].

The difference between *Cain* and *Don Juan* or *The Vision of Judgment* is primarily one of style—of "strategy," as Burke would call it, for encompassing the situation. The effectiveness of *Cain* as a work of art is lessened by the fact that it was written, as Byron said, in his "gay metaphysical style" (*LJ*, V, 361). It is the "gay" style rather than any lack of pertinence in the theme that threatens to cut the play off today from the serious consideration that it deserves. Just at the most crucial moments, the dialogue comes perilously close to setting our teeth on edge, as Southey's recitation does Michael's in *The Vision of Judgment*. In his dramatic manner Byron typifies the difficulty the nineteenth-century artist had in breaking away from the past when he turned to drama. Like most of his contemporaries Byron seemed to lose all will and power to develop his own idiom. He struck and held a lofty pseudoclassical note. There was an immediate tightening and constriction of the Byronic muscles, and he fell into "stained-glass attitudes" like Bunthorne in *Patience*. The subject of *Cain* was particularly bad for him in this respect. It tempted him not merely into the style of tragic drama but into that of Milton and the Bible also. In brief, he couched his revolt against the traditional order in the most traditional of styles. The result was that he came close to defeating himself.

[289]

The Romantic Ventriloquists

In the last act, when Cain accepts God's authority, the rhetoric accepts also; that is, the tone is heavily weighted on the side of authority. The powerful indictment of the tyrant God becomes blurred and compromised as the play fades out on a note that seems completely to concede Cain's guilt and the justice of his punishment. What has happened is that Byron has become trapped in a style so rigid and restrictive in its Biblical connotations that it permits none of the ironic detachment that the end of the play demands.

In *The Vision of Judgment* Byron achieves that ironic detachment through the use of the "ferocious Carravaggio" style which he had developed in *Don Juan*. *The Vision* has much in common with *Cain*. Under the playful surface of the satire runs the same questioning of divine justice and the human rule based upon it. In *Cain* the honest rebel is damned; in *The Vision* the hypocritical tyrant is saved. The social implications are spelled out more carefully in *The Vision*. God saves kings but damns their underlings as well as those who rebel against them. He is, in other words, as capricious and ungrateful as earthly kings. But what makes *The Vision* so devastating is its assumption that the heavenly forces are not so much evil, as in *Cain*, as simply not very bright. The struggle for souls is presented as highly competitive. Saint Peter is pictured as a bumbling fool and Michael as a well-meaning, stuffy English gentleman. Both are terrified of and unable to cope with Satan and his followers. We discover that Satan has managed to acquire all the intelligent souls, good and bad, Tory and Whig, such as Wilkes and Fox and Pitt, George Washington and Franklin. We are left to imagine the quality of souls that get into heaven.

As in *Cain*, the myth is handled as if it were true, but here of course in such colloquial, familiar terms that it is robbed of all terror and power over our minds. How absurd it is, Byron seems to say; how is it possible to take it seriously, much less to be afraid of it? As work of art *The Vision* is ultimately more effective than *Cain* because it reduces its supernatural beings to ordinary human dimensions and thus makes them vulnerable to laughter.

It is interesting that Byron began *The Vision* in May, 1821, apparently put it aside to write *Cain*, returned to complete it in September after finishing *Cain*, and in October started his "oratorio," *Heaven and Earth*. In this way he moved back and forth between his "high" and

[290]

"low" styles with no distress, revealing how closely interwoven the themes of *Cain* and *The Vision* were in his mind.

VIII. HOCK AND SODA WATER

But the "high" style was becoming increasingly inadequate. It was too limiting and narrow in its range of expression, too inhibiting psychologically. When he returned to *Don Juan* the following spring it was with genuine eagerness, and except for two minor side excursions he devoted all his artistic energy to its development until he left for Greece in June, 1823. During that year he wrote eleven cantos (VI to XVI) and began Canto XVII, a remarkable exhibition of sustained poetic activity. The manner he had developed in *Don Juan* had set him free to express himself as uninhibitedly and informally as he talked; there was a minimum of obstruction between his thought and his expression. At the beginning of Canto XV, after chatting of the persecuted and misunderstood philosophers like Bacon and Socrates, he writes:

> I perch upon an humbler promontory,
>   Amidst Life's infinite variety:
> With no great care for what is nicknamed Glory,
>   But speculating as I cast mine eye
> On what may suit or may not suit my story,
>   And never straining hard to versify,
> I rattle on exactly as I'd talk
>   With anybody in a ride or walk.
>
> [*DJ*, XV.19]

The viewpoint *Don Juan* enables him to cultivate is Luciferian; he can hover above the world or perch on the promontory or wander "a mere spectator" like Goethe's Mephistopheles through palace and hovel, free and detached, and put down what he sees and thinks. And by now he has a great deal to say. In *Manfred* he had taken stock of himself and had come to the conclusion that man has no source of comfort or strength beyond himself; he is alone, and whatever he is he makes himself. So in *Don Juan,* at first haphazardly and then more systematically, he begins to explore and record human life's "infinite variety."

In the first five cantos, he probably had no more clearly defined purpose than "to giggle and make giggle" through a playful burlesque of the epic manner, to enjoy himself in his observations of himself and his characters, and to luxuriate in his newly found psychological equilibrium and artistic freedom. These early cantos convey something of the relieved and exuberant surprise he felt when he discovered that the situation he had come to at the end of *Manfred* was not only endurable but enjoyable. But the loud-mouthed and self-righteous outcry against the immorality of these cantos enraged him, and when he picked up the poem again he settled down in deadly earnest to expose the cant and hypocrisy of society. His references in the letters are, from now on, intensely serious. *"Don Juan* will be known by and by for what it is intended," he wrote Murray in December, 1822, "a Satire on abuses of the present states of Society, and not an eulogy of vice" (*LJ*, V, 155).

With Canto VII he began a systematic survey of abuses, beginning with war and carrying through the corruptions of the Russian court into the pious cant—literary, political, and social—of English society. He proceeded by the plan he had marked out in *Cain* and *The Vision of Judgment* of ruthlessly stripping the mystery from the sacred symbols of authority and exposing the human hands that work the machinery. He would have agreed with Blake: "All deities reside in the human breast"; all the institutions of which men have been led to stand in awe and fear have their human origins; they lend themselves to the worst human motivations and the worst ends, and most men are their deluded victims. The siege of Ismail is a meaningless horror upon which the conquering general can write a witty rhymed dispatch; the court of Catherine is an elegant façade for lust and brutality; and the members of the English ruling class are, worst of all, more stupid than vicious, as deluded by their own acts as the others they delude. And, over all, Byron emphasizes the waste of human energy and talents, not merely in the lives of the victims, but in those who rule. When he comes to the English cantos, the theme becomes pervasive, as with a kind of deadly matter-of-factness he piles up the details that reveal how utterly empty and sterile is the day-by-day existence of the aristocracy:

> Sometimes, indeed, like soldiers off parade,
>   They break their ranks and gladly leave the drill;
> But then the roll-call draws them back afraid,
>   And they must be or seem what they *were:* still
> Doubtless it is a brilliant masquerade;
>   But when of the first sight you have had your fill,

Byron

It palls—at least it did so upon me,
This paradise of Pleasure and Ennui.

[DJ, XIV.17]

That behind all this there is a driving positive conviction, more instinctive than reasoned perhaps, seems evident: once we see things as they are and realize that we are free to control them, we can make of the potentialities of human life more than we have. Byron's purpose is not to provide a blueprint for the future, but to set our adrenals flowing.

This driving conviction that until we see things as they really are, not as they ought to be, "we're far from much improvement" is responsible for the almost obsessive emphasis upon facts in the later cantos. To get at the fact becomes in and for itself a passion with Byron. It is the only means to truth, human and metaphysical, that he has. The fact is the empirical datum of the objective world gathered through the senses and tested by the reason; it is the similar datum of human motivation and action gathered through self-reflection and tested by the behavior of others. His position is ultimately one of complete skepticism:

> Nothing more true than *not* to trust your senses;
> And yet what are your other evidences?

> For me, I know nought; nothing I deny,
>   Admit, reject, contemn; and what know *you*
> Except perhaps that you were born to die?
>   And both may after all turn out untrue.

[DJ, XIV.2–3]

On the other hand, though he rejects Berkeleian idealism and intuitive knowledge, he is utterly convinced, as we have seen, of the integrity and power of human reason. In the very ability to examine and reject absolutes he finds evidence for his conviction: "O Doubt! . . . thou sole prism of the Truth's rays"; and he finds it in the demonstration that mind has given of its ability to discover new facts through its independent observation and reflection. At the beginning of Canto X he refers to the story of Newton and the apple and then very neatly compares himself and Newton, in what is one of his most revealing stanzas on how much poetry means to him:

> And wherefore this exordium?—Why, just now,
>   In taking up this paltry sheet of paper,
> My bosom underwent a glorious glow,

[293]

The Romantic Ventriloquists

And my internal spirit cut a caper:
And though so much inferior, as I know,
    To those who, by the dint of glass and vapour,
Discover stars, and sail in the wind's eye,
I wish to do as much by Poesy.

In the wind's eye I have sail'd, and sail; but for
    The stars, I own my telescope is dim:
But at the least I have shunn'd the common shore,
    And leaving land far out of sight, would skim
The Ocean of Eternity: the roar
    Of breakers has not daunted my slight, trim,
But *still* sea-worthy skiff; and she may float
Where ships have founder'd, as doth many a boat.

                                                [*DJ*, X.3-4]

As a poet he saw his purpose and function as scientific (in complete contrast with the other Romantics); he wanted to do as much by poesy as Newton by science through his scrupulous adherence to facts. Even in the first canto he playfully drew the distinction between himself and his epic brethren by saying his story was actually true, and his pride at the factual accuracy of the shipwreck glowed in almost every line. But it is with Canto VII and the introduction of the siege of Ismail that he becomes really grimly concerned with fact. In an invocation to Homer he says that to vie with him in poetry would be vain; but we can vie "if not in poetry, at least in fact; / And fact is Truth, the grand desideratum!" (VII.81). In describing the gruesome episode of the Russian officer whose heel is bitten through by the dying Moslem, he says it is the part of a true poet "to escape from fiction" whenever he can. And, when he gets Don Juan to England, then in almost every canto he reminds the reader that he is showing him his world "exactly as it goes."

Besides, my Muse by no means deals in fiction:
    She gathers a repertory of facts,
Of course with some reserve and slight restriction,
    But mostly sings of human things and acts—
And that's one cause she meets with contradiction;
    For too much truth, at first sight, ne'er attracts;
And were her object only what's call'd Glory,
With more ease, too, she'd tell a different story.

                                                [*DJ*, XIV.13]

It is noteworthy that here he makes facts synonymous with "human acts and things." In the last five cantos, he quite deliberately narrows

[294]

and concentrates the focus of the poem. In his concern to get at the facts of behavior in English society, he becomes increasingly interested in exploring and understanding human personalities rather than in attacking them, and he begins to study them with an almost clinical interest.[29]

As we have seen, in these last cantos Byron proceeded with growing assurance and firmness of purpose. He was calmly convinced that what he was writing had in it "the principle of duration." In the fragment of Canto XVII he glances at the "sad usage of all sorts of sages." The truth is never welcomed when it is first put forward. Look at Galileo:

> The man was well-nigh dead, ere men begun
>   To think his skull had not some need of caulking;
> But now it seems, he's right—his notion just:
> No doubt a consolation to his dust.
>
> [*DJ*, XVII.8]

Pythagoras, Locke, Socrates—each in his lifetime was deemed a bore. And now Byron compares himself with them; the implication is— without swagger or false modesty—that he must bear with his present state as best he can, knowing that when he can no longer share it he will have "a firm Post Obit on posterity":

> If such doom waits each intellectual Giant,
>   We little people in our lesser way,
> In Life's small rubs should surely be more pliant,
>   And so for one will I—as well I may—
> Would that I were less bilious—but, oh, fie on't!
>   Just as I make my mind up every day,
> To be a *'totus, teres,'* Stoic, Sage,
> The wind shifts and I fly into a rage.
>
> Temperate I am—yet never had a temper;
>   Modest I am—yet with some slight assurance;
> Changeable too—yet somehow *'Idem semper;'*
>   Patient—but not enamour'd of endurance;
> Cheerful—but, sometimes, rather apt to whimper;
>   Mild—but at times a sort of *'Hercules furens;'*
> So that I almost think that the same skin,
> For one without—has two or three within.
>
> [*DJ*, XVII.10–11]

This rueful and humorous shrug at his failure to achieve stoicism, this last glance at the "sad jar of atoms" that is himself, establishing his kinship with the rest of mankind, seems a fitting place for his reflections to break off. He has come the full swing of the pendulum from the defiant alienation of the young Childe Harold.

The record of *Don Juan*, then, is a record of release and growth as man and artist; canto by canto, the range of Byron's awareness expands. The amused and almost scientific detachment which includes himself as well as the rest of mankind, and which enables him to express himself in all the vagaries and caprices of moods, in all his impulsiveness and irresponsibility as a human being, at the same time that he stands aloof and controls the perspective, insures a never-flagging incentive and an almost literally inexhaustible source of subject matter. His inability to accept the transcendental sources of satisfaction in which his poetic contemporaries took refuge, his acceptance of the "nothingness of life" within the universal perspective, lead him to the discovery that "life's infinite variety" within the human perspective is a source of endless enjoyment. He could never lack for new things to say. The prediction that he makes toward the middle of Canto XII can be taken quite literally so far as Byron's potentialities as an artist and *Don Juan*'s potentialities as a poem are concerned:

> But now I will begin my poem. 'Tis
>   Perhaps a little strange, if not quite new,
> That from the first of Cantos up to this
>   I've not begun what we have to go through.
> These first twelve books are merely flourishes,
>   Preludios, trying just a string or two
> Upon my lyre, or making the pegs sure;
> And when so, you shall have the overture.
>
> My Muses do not care a pinch of rosin
>   About what's called success, or not succeeding:
> Such thoughts are quite below the strain they have chosen;
>   'Tis a 'great moral lesson' they are reading.
> I thought, at setting off, about two dozen
>   Cantos would do; but at Apollo's pleading,
> If that my Pegasus should not be founder'd,
> I think to canter gently through a hundred.
>
> [*DJ*, XII.54–55]

IX. THE POETRY OF POLITICS

Don Juan was put an end to by Byron's decision to go to Greece. Many factors entered into the decision: boredom with the emptiness and monotony of his life with the countess; irritation with the legacy Shelley's death left him of the Hunts and their little Hottentots, the *Liberal,* and Mary Shelley; melancholy and despondency occasioned by the failure of the Italian *Carbonari* movement and by the apparent collapse of any chance of meaningful political activity in Italy. Undoubtedly, too, the offer of the London committee appealed to his vanity. Rather anxiously he had seen his poetic fame declining; Murray no longer wanted his poems, and "at present I am the most unpopular writer going," he wrote Medwin in May, 1823.[30]

Though he was quite mistaken, he felt deeply his apparent neglect. There was still a lot of Childe Harold and Lara in him; he was filled with nostalgia for the happy days of his first pilgrimage to Greece; he thought sentimentally of a revival of the glories of ancient Greece; he saw himself as what he had always dreamed of being, a military hero leading—perhaps to his death—the forces of liberation. And in this way he would restore his fame, vindicate and rehabilitate himself in the eyes of his countrymen. As the Marchesa Origo emphasizes, he was obsessed with English opinion, "tremblingly alive" to the censure or opinions of persons for whom he entertained little respect, and desired above all to be accepted and acclaimed by the society that had insulted him.[31] Because he made no effort to conceal such motives, rather exaggerated and paraded them before such susceptible souls as Lady Blessington, there has been a tendency among modern critics and biographers to stress the pretensions and pose and to suspect the sincerity of his concern for the immediate cause of Greek independence —and, because furthermore he spoke frankly of the odds against the success of the revolution and flippantly of the "entusymusy" of those associated with him in the venture, to treat him even contemptuously.

But Byron's letters show that he had made a careful and deliberate decision and had committed himself with a full awareness of what he was doing. He held firmly to certain convictions. One conviction was, as we have seen, of the essential worth of man, not simply of himself. Another was of the necessity of revolution. He believed that, if the minds of men could be freed from the traditional intellectual tyrannies and they could see themselves as they were, then they might ultimately build a better society. He believed, therefore, that the social tyrannies which perpetuated the intellectual ones should be overthrown wherever possible by direct and active revolution.

He had, as we have seen, no blueprint of a future society; he identified with no political organization. When he thought of freedom, intellectual or political, it was always with the educated groups, of upper and middle class, in mind. His most concrete idea was of nationalism. Nations could be self-determining, free of foreign rule—this was the necessary prelude to other freedoms. The freeing of Italy and Greece was a symbolic action of particular importance—it could set in motion a whole chain reaction. "It is no great matter, supposing that Italy could be liberated, who or what is sacrificed. It is a grand object—the very *poetry* of politics. Only think, a free Italy!!!" (Ravenna *Diary*, February 18, 1821; *LJ*, V, 205).

So Byron became intimately involved in the *Carbonari* movement, but rather as a foreign friend than as an active participant. He wanted to be a participant, but the movement miscarried before he had a chance. And, as his journal shows, the need to act positively on behalf of something he believed became psychologically pressing when the Italian movement failed; he considered going to South America, to the United States, and finally to Greece. He had really come to the existentialist conception of *engagement:* that the man who has experienced the sense of detachment or freedom must throw himself back into the social context with the intention of changing its condition. He must act to insure his freedom by bringing to others the freedom he has visualized for himself.

Byron had reached the point where he had to act.[32] Now, more than ever, poetry had become for him a substitute for action. When the Italian movement failed, Byron wrote to Moore, April 28, 1821: "And now let us be literary. . . . 'If Othello's occupation be gone', let us take to the next best; and if we cannot contribute to make mankind more free and wise, we may amuse ourselves and those who like it" (*LJ*, V, 272). To Teresa he said, "A man ought to do more for society than write verses,"[33] and to Trelawny at Ithaca he said that he had not come to Greece "to scribble more nonsense" but would show the world that he could do "something better."[34] His letters and journals during the last years lament the waste of his energies. On his thirty-third birthday he writes, "I go to my bed with a heaviness of heart at having lived so long, and to so little purpose" (*LJ*, V, 181). These statements do not so much contradict the importance of poetry for him as assert the overwhelming moral compulsion of the Luciferian contemplator to prove himself in action. He believed that certain things should be; it became his responsibility not just to write about them, but to fight for them.

When Byron decided to go to Greece, it was in the spirit of *Don Juan*. He was determined to be hardheaded and sensible, to know exactly what he was getting into. So he set about systematically interviewing travelers returning from Greece, carefully informing himself on the complex struggles for power and the characteristics of the intrigants, valiantly trying to separate the illusion from the reality and to keep himself from being forced into the role of Childe Harold. He was surrounded by sentimentalists, and, as a protection against his own sentimentalist leanings and as a means of keeping his head above treacle, he cultivated a tone of flippancy. Lady Blessington was one of the sentimentalists, and in her expression of disappointment we have an unconsciously comic revelation of the hysterical romantic pressures against which Byron struggled:

> There is something so exciting in the idea of the greatest poet of his day sacrificing his fortune, his occupations, his enjoyments—in short, offering up to the altar of Liberty all the immense advantages which station, fortune, and genius can bestow, that it is impossible to reflect on it without admiration; but when one hears this same person calmly talk of the worthlessness of the people he proposes to make these sacrifices for, the loans he means to advance, the uniforms he intends to wear, entering into petty details, and always with perfect *sang froid,* one's admiration evaporates, and the action loses all its charms, though the real merit of it still remains. Perhaps Byron wishes to show that his going to Greece is more an affair of *principle* than *feeling,* and, as such, more entitled to respect, though perhaps less likely to excite warmer feelings. However this may be, his whole manner and conversation on the subject are calculated to chill the admiration such an enterprise ought to create, and to reduce it to a more ordinary standard.[35]

Similarly, Byron was up against various kinds of idealism—Godwinian, Benthamite, and run-of-the-mill political—in the London Committee, all of them impatient and without real knowledge of the difficulties in the way of Utopia. Byron's letters to them are models of sober reasoning and practical suggestion.

Byron was also afraid that he could not carry the job off with success. He knew that he was prepared neither by nature nor by experience for such an undertaking. He was, in spite of the legends that had accumulated about him and that he had aided through his Oriental tales and his letters, predominantly the introverted personality, and the life he had led in the last few years had aggravated this tendency toward introspection rather than action. Toward the end of the Grecian fiasco, Parry records, "He was more a mental being, if I may use this phrase, than any man I ever saw. He lived on thought more than on food." [36] Furthermore, nothing in his life had prepared him for leadership, particularly in such a nightmarish situation as this one. It is no wonder that he confided to Lady Blessington that he almost wished that he had never committed himself. "This is one of the many scrapes into which my poetical temperament has drawn me." [37] He was justifiably afraid of humiliation, of being shown up as a mock hero; but he was more afraid of making the wrong decisions, taking the wrong action, and thus leaving things in a worse mess than he had found them. But he went ahead anyway, and this should be the final proof of his courage and sincerity. The sane perspective he tried to hold is revealed in a letter to Colonel Napier on September 9, 1823, commenting on some unspecified pessimistic reports on the situation:

All this comes of . . . *"Entusymusy,"* expecting too much and starting at speed; it is lucky for me so far that, fail or not fail, I can hardly be disappointed, for I believed myself on a fool's errand from the outset, and must, therefore, like Dogberry, "spare no wisdom." I will at least linger on here or there till I see whether I *can* be of *any* service in *any* way; and if I doubt it, it is because I do not feel confidence in my individual capacity for this kind of bear-taming, and not from a disbelief in the powers of a more active or less indifferent character to be of use to them, though I feel persuaded that that person must be a military man. But I like the Cause at least, and will stick by it while it is not degraded nor dishonoured [*LJ*, VI, 257].

It was with this attitude that he went on to Missolonghi. There the situation became rapidly worse than anything he could possibly have imagined. It unfolded like a canto of *Don Juan.* He was surrounded by a motley and fantastic group of characters who seemed made to order as prototypes for the poem, and one tragicomic situation followed after another. It must have seemed to him as if his poem had come alive. But, given the handicaps of temperament and inexperience with which he had started, he managed, until he became too ill, to keep control of the situation, to command respect, to prevent deterioration into utter chaos. He demonstrated that he could act and lead. The major decisions that he made were proved to be ultimately the right ones. But he could not know this. For him, his sojourn in Missolonghi was a succession of humiliating failures. The last two months were unrelieved tragedy.

He believed that he had utterly failed in everything he set out to do. And the manner of his death was the most humiliating failure of all.

You will think me more superstitious than ever [said Byron to Lady Blessington] when I tell you, that I have a presentiment that I shall die in Greece. I hope it may be in action, but that would be a good finish to a very *triste* existence, and I have a horror of death-bed scenes; but as I have not been famous for my luck in life, most probably I shall not have more in the manner of my death, and I may draw my last sigh, not on the field of glory but on the bed of disease.[38]

Byron's deathbed scene was prolonged and terrible, but he retained his awareness of the irony. Toward the end the humor of *Don Juan* revealed itself in one last flickering remark. According to Gamba, he came out of coma to see Millingen, Fletcher, and Tita round his bed. The two first walked away weeping. "Tita also wept, but he could not retire, as Byron had hold of his hand; but he turned away his face. Byron looked at him steadily, and said, half smiling, in Italian, 'O questa è una bella scena.' "[39]

Nicolson says somewhat melodramatically, "Lord Byron accomplished nothing at Missolonghi except his own suicide; but by that single act of heroism he secured the liberation of Greece."[40] His death was suicide only in the sense that he held grimly to the course of action he had decided upon even after it seemed doomed to failure; and, in doing so, he not only secured the liberation of Greece but vindicated *Don Juan* as a way of life.

7: AFTERMATH

In *Don Juan,* Byron had found a way out of the impasse in which his contemporaries were trapped. He had achieved a point of view and method capable of encompassing the complex world in which he and they lived. It is not too much to say that he had shown a way by which poetry could survive and grow in the nineteenth century as a meaningful social art.

But the way was never followed. The Victorians were blind and deaf to the achievements of *Don Juan;* they saw only mocking desecration and heard only cynical laughter. Enthralled by the siren songs of affirmation like *Tintern Abbey, Prometheus Unbound,* and *Ode on a Grecian Urn,* they elevated the poets who sang them into prophets to whom ultimate truths had been revealed, and their poetry into a kind of apocrypha of sacred writings. If Wordsworth, Shelley, and Keats in achievement seemed to falter and fall short of their golden promise, the Victorians were confident that it was not their vision which was at fault, but simply that they had been born too soon. "What is now proved was once only imagin'd," said Blake in one of the Proverbs of Hell; and the Victorians complacently assumed that it was their destiny to prove what their predecessors had only imagined. So, committed to the Romantic affirmations, they repeated resolutely the same pattern of development, were defeated by the same obstacles, and came to the same thwarted end.

The pattern is clearly evident in the poetry of Tennyson. He aspired above all else to be the prophet-bard for his age, to cope meaningfully with its problems and to become the ringing voice of its affirmation; but the poetic concepts and constructs he had taken over scarcely provided him with the strategies for defining the problems, much less for coming to grips with them. F. R. Leavis in *New Bearings in English Poetry* makes this pertinent comment:

He might wrestle solemnly with the "problems of the age" but the habits, conventions and techniques that he found congenial are not those of a poet who could have exposed himself freely to the rigours of the contemporary climate. And in this he is representative. It was possible for the poets of the Romantic period to believe that the interests animating their poetry were the forces moving the world or that might move it. But Victorian poetry admits implicitly that the actual world is alien, recalcitrant and unpoetical, and that no protest is worth making except the protest of withdrawal.[1]

In the light of the present study, one important qualification to this statement needs to be made: the distinction between Romantics and Victorians is too sharply drawn. As we have seen, the Romantics were not able finally to sustain their beliefs, and in their poetry the same admission is implicit as in that of the Victorians. Indeed, the Victorian "protest of withdrawal" is simply the repetition of the protest that Wordsworth, Shelley, and Keats had come to make in the end.

Nowhere is this more poignantly seen than in the poetry of Arnold. As critic Arnold was aware of the dangers in the Romantic view, but as artist he was unable to overcome them. He could say of Wordsworth that "he retired (in Middle-Age phrase) into a monastery. I mean, he plunged himself in the inward life, he voluntarily cut himself off from the modern spirit."[2] Yet as poet Arnold did the same. Longing futilely to live by a "magical view" of the world, unable intellectually to accept the Wordsworthian concept of nature or emotionally to abide the new scientific concepts, repelled by the emerging Philistine society, he found himself in the unbearable position of Wordsworth's Solitary: in his own words, one who was "wandering between two worlds—one dead, the other powerless to be born." In his poetry, to quote Leavis again, he "slips away from 'this uncongenial place, this human life' to moonlight transformations, and the iron time dissolves in wistful, melodious sentiment."[3] He ends like Wordsworth in stoicism, but an even more austere stoicism, because he cannot deceive himself as to the wishful nature of his religious affirmation.

At first glance the exception to the pattern would seem to be

Browning. And it is true that through the dramatic monologues he momentarily finds a way out of the Romantic impasse. He is able to create, as Keats wanted to do, Iagos as well as Imogens, but most importantly to depict, as in *The Bishop Orders His Tomb,* a wide range of human behavior without labeling it good or evil. In fact, he is able to show as admirable the expression of desires and attitudes which mid-Victorian morality frowned upon. He has something of Byron's gusto, and he has, as every reader is immediately aware, a robust energy, inexhaustible curiosity, and lust for uninhibited living. But he can release these characteristics only within the frame of the past, particularly of the Italian Renaissance, and there is a curiously neutralizing quality in this detachment in time and space. The monologues are at bottom poems of escape, of vicarious indulgence in conduct no longer tolerated in the poet's own age of moral enlightenment. When Browning turns to the contemporary scene, his gusto and frank delight in human behavior moral or immoral congeal into complacence and hollow optimism. He becomes preoccupied with arguing the case for Christian faith and personal immortality against the scientific rationalists. He pays little attention to the economic and social upheavals of his civilization; he shuts them out, in effect. Perhaps this is the main reason why he is able to hold to the very end of his life with such strenuous confidence to the Romantic affirmation. But poems like *Childe Roland to the Dark Tower Came* and the *Epilogue to Ferishtah's Fancies* reveal what repressed terror lurks just behind Browning's confident mask.

By the end of the nineteenth century, the discrepancy between the Romantic concepts and the world in which the artist lived had grown too great to be bridged by any illusory magic. For the poet who could no longer endure the world around him, the most obvious recourse was withdrawal into a "hushed cult of beauty," into an almost religious preoccupation with art for its own sake. Such a withdrawal we find in the Pre-Raphaelites and *fin-de-siècle* poets in England and the symbolists in France. It was the logical end product of the process that began with Shelley and Keats. But, where the English poets cultivated excesses of the style and sentiments they had inherited and were driven into esthetic exhaustion, the symbolists concentrated upon revitalizing language and structure by almost literally tearing apart the traditional syntax and forcing words into new and dissonant relationships. Ironically, one of the major reasons why the symbolists achieved what the

[304]

English could not is that they had been emancipated from the compulsive desire of the English poets to affirm the vision of a man-oriented, ordered universe and the guilty need to justify art as an instrument of moral uplift and prophetic illumination. The revolutions and social upheavals in France in the nineteenth century, so much more violent than in England, had disillusioned the French artists with Rousseauistic concepts of man, nature, and society. They were the disenchanted, for whom heaven had been revealed as a mirage and the earthly paradise as a wasteland. Their sense of a chaotic and disorganized world was reflected in their compulsive desire to derange the senses, to dislocate language, to make the private world of the self utterly independent and self-sufficient, the microcosm from which to draw all the materials for their art and gaze in ironic contemplation on the shattered world without. They were free to explore the complex resources of language for symbol and ambiguity and to define the limits of poetry in terms of a highly professional and personal craft. Their way out of the Romantic impasse was to make withdrawal itself a virtue by creating their own private cosmic syntax.

When symbolist attitudes and techniques were carried into English poetry by Eliot and Pound, the difference between their poetry and that of Swinburne or even of the early Yeats appeared so enormous that artists and critics alike leaped to the conclusion that a complete break with the Romantic tradition had been effected. Certainly Eliot and Pound, disillusioned like the symbolists with Rousseauistic concepts and tending to equate them with Romanticism, saw themselves as leaders in a revolt against the nineteenth century. In their early essays and in polemics like T. E. Hulme's "Romanticism and Classicism" they issued their manifestos and set up their battle lines. But now, after half a century has passed, the revolt seems not nearly so sharp or significant as it did then. Insofar as a successful revolution took place, it was a formal revolution, and even as such it can be seen not as originating from outside the Romantic tradition but as taking place within it. John Bayley in his book *The Romantic Survival* makes the same point in regard to Eliot, Pound, and Hulme in England, and Valéry in France, that has been made here in regard to the symbolists:

The Classical Revival—to give it for the moment a text book title—which took place at the beginning of the present century . . . arose directly out of the Romantic absorption in the nature of the creative process. Classicism is always associated with form, with careful craftsmanship, and with an interest in techniques for their own sake, and paradoxically it was precisely these things to which Romantic solipsism and self-consciousness began to tend.[4]

Indeed, the term "classicism" is so obviously inappropriate for the kind of daring technical and linguistic experimentation with which modern poetry has been concerned that it has been abandoned even by those like Eliot who first used it.

In attitudes and themes, Eliot and Pound are quite clearly in the main line of descent from the Romantics. Now that we can see in particular the full pattern of Eliot's poetry, we are aware of the extent to which his preoccupations are those prescribed by the Romantics: the search for personal security and salvation, the exploration of the self, the revulsion against modern society, the futility of social action. What obscures the relationship is that he begins with none of the optimistic faith in the goodness of man and the perfectibility of society with which the Romantics began; he begins in disillusionment with a society that pays lip service to the Romantic ideals at the same time that it wantonly disregards and perverts them. Yet his disillusionment differs only in degree from that to which, in one way or another, the Romantics came in the end. His retreat into religious and political conservatism, into traditional patterns of belief, is very like that of the older Wordsworth, but it is the more egregiously Romantic precisely because it comes a hundred years later.

With Eliot this survey of the aftermath of Romanticism can appropriately end. There is neither time nor space to trace the relationship between Romanticism and the poetry of the last quarter century. But this much can safely be said. Between Eliot's generation and the present has occurred no violent break or striking innovation. Modern poetry moves steadily in the echoing footsteps of its predecessors. It is more intensely concerned with craft than any previous poetry has been, and with craft reduced to its essence—the ambiguities of word and symbol. And similarily it is more intensely concerned with itself as subject than any previous poetry has been. This concern is finally inseparable from the obsessive self-consciousness of the artist. He uses his craft as means by which to probe, analyze, and reveal his deepest self. To an increasing degree the poem has become the medium through which the ventriloquist poet attempts to release the unconscious, to give it voice and form apart from his conscious self. Insofar as this is the function of modern poetry, it carries to its inevitable end the movement from public to private poetry that began in the eighteenth century.

NOTES

I: INTRODUCTION

1. Arthur Lovejoy, *The Great Chain of Being* (Cambridge, Mass.: Harvard University Press, 1936). See in particular chaps. ix and x.

2. Earl Wasserman, *The Subtler Language* (Baltimore, Md.: Johns Hopkins Press, 1959), pp. 10–11.

3. For all the complex and conflicting elements in the evolution of Romantic religious attitudes, see H. N. Fairchild, *Religious Trends in English Poetry* (5 vols.; New York: Columbia University Press, 1939–62), especially I, 535 ff. (chap. xii), and II, 365 ff. (chap. xi).

4. Ernest Tuveson, *The Imagination as a Means of Grace* (Berkeley and Los Angeles: University of California Press, 1960), p. 97.

5. Samuel Taylor Coleridge, *Biographia Literaria,* edited by J. Shawcross (2 vols.; London: Oxford University Press, 1907), I, 105.

6. See Coleridge's *The Eolian Harp,* lines 26–33 and 44–48, and *Dejection: An Ode,* lines 56–58. For the importance of the harp in Romantic critical theory, see M. H. Abrams, *The Mirror and the Lamp* (New York: Oxford University Press, 1953), pp. 51–52, 61.

7. Cf. William Blake, *Jerusalem,* chap. i (*Poetry and Prose of William Blake,* edited by Geoffrey Keynes [London: Nonesuch Press, 1927], pp. 435–36):

> I rest not from my great task!
> To open the Eternal Worlds, to open the immortal Eyes
> Of Man inwards into the Worlds of Thought, into Eternity
> Ever expanding in the Bosom of God, the Human Imagination.

8. Clarence Thorpe, Carlos Baker, and Bennett Weaver (eds.), *The Major English Romantic Poets: A Symposium in Reappraisal* (Carbondale: Southern Illinois University Press, 1957), p. xv.

Notes to Chapter 2: Wordsworth

9. During the last half century William Blake has been elevated to a position of equality with the poets with whom I am concerned, and by some modern critics he would be considered the greatest of them all. Certainly in his own right he deserves as full attention as the others. But I have omitted him because ultimately I am concerned with the development of a literary tradition and the formulation of critical attitudes, and Blake had almost no influence on literary or critical tradition. I have concentrated upon the poets who have been traditionally grouped together, and whose work has been the basis of most of the generalizations about English Romanticism.

2: WORDSWORTH

1. William Wordsworth, *Poetical Works of William Wordsworth,* edited by Ernest de Selincourt and Helen Darbishire (5 vols.; Oxford: Clarendon Press, 1940–49), V, 2; hereafter referred to as *PW.* All references to Wordsworth's poetry with the exception of *The Prelude* are from this edition. References to *The Prelude* are from *The Prelude,* edited by E. de Selincourt; 2nd ed., revised by Helen Darbishire (Oxford: Clarendon Press, 1959).

2. G. M. Harper, *William Wordsworth* (London: John Murray, 1929), p. 515.

3. *PW,* V, 372.

4. See William Empson, "Sense in *The Prelude,*" in *The Structure of Complex Words* (New York: New Directions, 1952), pp. 289–305, for an analysis of Wordsworth's use of the word "sense."

5. All quotations are from the 1805 version unless otherwise noted.

6. F. R. Leavis, *Revaluations* (New York: George W. Stewart, 1947), pp. 159–60.

7. *PW,* V, 313–39 (Appendix A).

8. See *This Lime Tree Bower,* lines 37–43; *Fears in Solitude,* lines 183–91.

9. The conflict in Wordsworth's poetry between nature and man has been emphasized in quite different ways from my own in two recent studies: David Perkins, *The Quest for Permanence* (Cambridge, Mass.: Harvard University Press, 1959), and David Ferry, *The Limits of Mortality: An Essay on Wordsworth's Major Poems* (Middletown, Conn.: Wesleyan University Press, 1959).

10. *PW,* I, 270–83. See especially lines 416 ff. (pp. 279–80), which present the earliest version of the "spots of time" passage on his father's death.

11. For dating, see *Prelude,* p. xxviii.

12. For dating, see *Prelude,* pp. xxix, xxxii, 444, 448.

13. The most valuable discussion of the extent of Hartley's influence in relation to that of other eighteenth-century philosophers upon Wordsworth is by J. W. Beach in *The Concept of Nature in Nineteenth Century English*

Notes to Chapter 2: Wordsworth

Poetry (New York: Macmillan Co., 1936), chaps. iv and v. For an excellent survey of the debate over the philosophical influences upon *The Prelude,* see J. V. Logan, *Wordsworthian Criticism* (Columbus: Ohio State University Press, 1947), chap. vi.

14. It is interesting that this is the passage singled out for adverse criticism in the *Biographia Literaria.* "Home at Grasmere" was written before Coleridge came to the lake country in 1800, and so the ideas of rustic life advanced are pretty much Wordsworth's own, or at least they have been developed more or less free of Coleridge's hypnotic influence. It is likely that they therefore went further than Coleridge would willingly have gone, even in 1800. See in *The Notebooks of Samuel Taylor Coleridge,* edited by Kathleen Coburn (2 vols.; New York: Pantheon Books, 1957–61), Miss Coburn's notes for entries 764, 787, 815, and 818 in Vol. I.

15. F. W. Bateson, *Wordsworth: A Reinterpretation* (London: Longmans, Green and Co., 1954), pp. 151 ff.

16. For dating of *The Leech Gatherer,* see *PW,* II, 510–11. For details of the return home from the Clarksons' in April, 1802, see *Early Letters of William and Dorothy Wordsworth,* edited by Ernest de Selincourt (Oxford: Clarendon Press, 1935), pp. 287–91; hereafter referred to as *Early Letters.* See also Mary Moorman, *William Wordsworth: 1770–1803* (Oxford: Clarendon Press, 1957), pp. 556–57.

17. That the poem was of unusual importance to Wordsworth is indicated by his remarkable defense of an early draft in a letter of June 14, 1802, to Sara Hutchinson, who had apparently criticized the poem adversely. See *Early Letters,* pp. 305–7.

18. For dating of the poem, see *PW,* IV, 464–66. The ode was finished probably before September, 1804. The "timely utterance" may have been the "Rainbow" poem, written on March 26, 1802, the day before he began the ode.

19. Compare Shelley's use of the phrase "too deep for tears" in the conclusion of *Alastor* to indicate the extent of the loss resulting from the death of the poet.

20. To Beaumont, March 12, 1805 (*Early Letters,* p. 460).

21. Wordsworth first saw Peele Castle in the summer of 1794 when he visited his cousin Mrs. Barker at Rampside. This was just after his first long reunion with Dorothy. See Bateson, *Wordsworth: A Reinterpretation,* p. 117, and Mary Moorman, *William Wordsworth: 1770–1803,* pp. 245–50.

22. For dating of Book III, see *The Prelude,* pp. xlviii–l.

23. A fascinating example of the way in which Wordsworth adapted lines written long before to later needs, and vivid evidence, in the shift from one context to another, of his shift in attitude, can be found by comparing lines 80 ff. in Book III with lines 270–300 in the draft of *The Ruined*

Cottage finished in the spring of 1798. The growth of the Pedlar has been described in language that anticipates that of Books I and II of *The Prelude*, with the same emphasis upon the interaction of nature and mind (the first version of *The Prelude*, II.416–34, is applied to the Pedlar). As he trudges along he repeats the songs of Burns:

> . . . though he was untaught,
> In the dead lore of schools undisciplined,
> Why should he grieve? he was a chosen son
> To him was given an ear which deeply felt
> The voice of Nature in the obscure wind
> The sounding mountain and the running stream.
> To every natural form, rock, fruit and flower
> Even the loose stones that cover the highway
> He gave a moral life, he saw them feel
> Or linked them to some feeling. In all shapes
> He found a secret and mysterious soul,
> A fragrance and a spirit of strange meaning.
> Though poor in outward shew he was most rich,
> He had a world about him, 'twas his own
> He made it, for it only lived to him
> And to the God who looked into his mind.
>   [*PW*, V, 388]

To watch the casual transfer of "chosen son" from Pedlar to Poet is disconcerting. The whole shift in attitude is symbolized in this gesture. For applied to the Pedlar "chosen son" means, in the familiar Romantic idiom, natural genius; but applied by Wordsworth to himself in the context of Cambridge it takes on sophistication, as the formal poetic "boast" of his God-appointed singularity and superiority to other men—and nature. Furthermore, the references that indicate an independent power and life in nature have been removed in the transfer, and the passages added that throw the weight of the scales toward the perceiving mind and its community with "highest truth."

24. These lines (1–65) were composed as early as the beginning of 1804. See *The Prelude*, p. 619.

25. Coleridge's references to Associationism after 1800 show that he saw it as a philosophy of "death." See his letter of May 30, 1815, to Wordsworth expressing his disappointment with *The Excursion*. He had hoped, he says, that Wordsworth would have demonstrated "the necessity of a general revolution in the modes of developing and disciplining the human mind by the substitution of Life and Intelligence . . . for the philosophy of mechanism, which in everything that is most worthy of the human Intellect, strikes *Death* . . ." (*Collected Letters of Samuel Taylor Coleridge*, edited by E. L. Griggs [4 vols.; Oxford: Clarendon Press, 1956–59], IV, 575; hereafter referred to as *Collected Letters*). See also *Biographia Literaria*, edited by J. Shawcross (2 vols.; Oxford: Clarendon Press, 1907), I, 98.

Notes to Chapter 2: Wordsworth

26. *Biographia Literaria,* II, 109.

27. Charles Moorman, "Wordsworth's *Prelude:* I, 1–269," *Modern Language Notes,* LXXII (1957), 416–20, argues that in the opening lines Wordsworth anticipates the conclusion of the poem, but the lines simply will not bear him out. Mrs. Moorman (*William Wordsworth: 1770–1803,* p. 419) believes that the lines were first written down in autumn, 1803, when Wordsworth was trying to get started again on the poem. See also *The Prelude,* p. xlviii.

28. A recent article by Edwin Morgan, "A Prelude to *The Prelude,*" *Essays in Criticism,* V (1955), 341–53, argues the case for Wordsworth's deliberate consistency in purpose and method.

29. *The White Doe of Rylstone* is the most extreme expression of the doctrine of suffering. As G. M. Harper says (*William Wordsworth,* pp. 474–75), the poem "teaches that active life is vanity that passeth away, though the soul, through suffering and submission to nature, may yet win communion with what endures for ever. . . . Regarded in connection with the general trend of Wordsworth's thinking at the time he wrote it, it is a confession of human failure so sweeping that the Western mind refuses to join in it."

30. See J. L. and Barbara Hammond, *The Village Laborer* (London: Longmans, Green and Co., 1911), especially chap. vi, for a detailed account of the conditions of the poor and the bitter controversies that raged at this time in regard to methods of alleviation.

31. For dating, see *The Prelude,* pp. xxv, xlvi.

32. See *PW,* V, 379 ff., for the 1798 draft of *The Ruined Cottage.*

33. *PW,* V, 400. De Selincourt's comment. The three passages follow on pp. 400–4.

34. Coleridge quoted these lines in a letter of April, 1798, to George Coleridge (*Collected Letters,* I, 397–98), and in lines 11–28 of *Fears in Solitude* he develops a similar argument.

35. O. J. Campbell in "Sentimental Morality in Wordsworth's Narrative Poetry," in *University of Wisconsin Studies in Language and Literature,* No. 11 (Madison: University of Wisconsin Press, 1920), points out that Wordsworth here and in other poems like *The Old Cumberland Beggar* is following in his argument the sentimental tradition of the eighteenth century in which "a central place [was] given to compassion for undeserved human suffering."

36. See *PW,* V, 387, for the first version of these lines inserted at the very beginning of the Wanderer's narrative.

37. G. W. Meyer in *Wordsworth's Formative Years* (Ann Arbor: University of Michigan Press, 1943) defends Wordsworth by arguing that he quite deliberately turned from poems of social protest because he believed

that they only irritated the reader and sharpened his aversions, and that he began to write "carefully insulated tales of undeserved and unnecessary suffering bravely borne to cultivate in his readers those particular virtues which were certain to produce in the end, a harmonious society founded on universal love" (p. 237). "The readers of *The Ruined Cottage* he hoped to leave in a lush condition of benevolent tranquillity" (p. 225). "In other words, the whole truth about nature and society was not congenial to the educational and reformatory purpose to which Wordsworth chose to dedicate his verse" (p. 249). This is a curiously damning way of justifying Wordsworth's practice.

38. Cf. *The Excursion*, I.368–70, where "within" is changed significantly to "without."

39. *PW,* V, 375. See also Judson Lyon, *The Excursion: A Study* (New Haven, Conn.: Yale University Press, 1950), pp. 44–45.

40. Two recent critics have assumed that Wordsworth was presenting a personal experience to be interpreted like those in *The Prelude.* Professor Abbie Potts, assuming that the original version of the vision is to be found in MS x, which contains passages later to become part of Book VII of *The Prelude,* believes that the Solitary was first conceived of in the spirit of Bunyan's Pilgrim on the Delectable Mountains coming out of the Valley of the Shadow of Death and looking toward the Celestial City (*Wordsworth's Prelude* [Ithaca, N.Y.: Cornell University Press, 1953], pp. 11, 238). But the textual note in *PW,* V, 415, indicates that the vision passage was not part of MS x. Furthermore, both the story of the old man and the vision are based upon an experience related to Wordsworth in November, 1805. See *PW,* V, 417–18.

John Jones sees the Solitary's experience as Wordsworth's own vision of paradise "in an exact Christian and literary sense. . . . We must believe that Wordsworth was in the spirit when he beheld this vision" (*The Egotistical Sublime* [London: Chatto and Windus, 1954], pp. 170–72). But both Potts and Jones overlook the fact that, whatever the circumstances under which he first wrote the passage, Wordsworth has quite deliberately given it to one who wants to but cannot believe in such a vision.

41. For dates of composition of Book III, see *PW,* V, 418–19. The first draft was probably written in 1806.

42. *Early Letters,* p. 460.

43. See notes, *PW,* V, 418–19, 421.

44. The last two lines are an echo of lines 1174–75 of *The Borderers* (*PW,* I, 198), in which Oswald describes his state of mind upon learning that the captain he has marooned is innocent.

45. H. N. Fairchild, *Religious Trends in English Poetry* (5 vols.; New York: Columbia University Press, 1939–62), III, 218.

Notes to Chapter 3: Coleridge

46. See *PW*, V, 367–68, for other comments and letters between 1815 and 1845 on the unfinished *Recluse*.

3: COLERIDGE

1. Thomas Carlyle, *The Life of John Stirling,* in *Collected Works* (Centenary ed.; 31 vols.; New York: Charles Scribner's Sons, 1897–1901), XI, 52–62.

2. *Collected Letters of Samuel Taylor Coleridge,* edited by E. L. Griggs (4 vols.; Oxford: Clarendon Press, 1956–59), I, 259–60; hereafter referred to as *CL.*

3. *The Notebooks of Samuel Taylor Coleridge,* edited by Kathleen Coburn (2 vols.; New York: Pantheon Books, 1957–61), Vol. I, entries 161, 165, 174; hereafter referred to as *Notebooks.*

4. *Ibid.,* entry 1153. In her note on the entry, Miss Coburn suggests that the poem is *The Picture.* But in *The Picture* the lover is endeavoring to emancipate himself from "Passion's dreams" or quite simply his love for the girl who traps him at the end. Coleridge's entry suggests a much more elaborate and philosophical poem than this.

5. A. C. Swinburne, *Essays and Studies* in *Complete Works,* edited by Edmund Gosse and Thomas Wise (20 vols.; London: William Heinemann, 1926), XV, 145.

6. John Livingston Lowes, *The Road to Xanadu* (Boston: Houghton, Mifflin Co., 1927), p. 412.

7. Elisabeth Schneider, *Coleridge, Opium and Kubla Khan* (Chicago: University of Chicago Press, 1953), pp. 22 ff.

8. Samuel Taylor Coleridge, *The Complete Poetical Works,* edited by E. H. Coleridge (2 vols.; London: Oxford University Press, 1912), I, 296; hereafter referred to as *PW.* All quotations from Coleridge's poetry are from this edition. For the Crewe MS, see Schneider, *Coleridge, Opium and Kubla Khan,* p. 24. Coleridge's notebooks show how alert and aware his conscious mind remained during his reveries. His dreams were usually "waking dreams."

9. Schneider, *Coleridge, Opium and Kubla Khan,* p. 10.

10. *Ibid.,* p. 241.

11. See letter to Southey, July 17, 1797 (*CL,* I, 335).

12. Lowes, *The Road to Xanadu,* pp. 368–69.

13. Richard Harter Fogle, "The Romantic Unity of 'Kubla Khan,'" *College English,* XXII (1960), 115.

14. Schneider, *Coleridge, Opium and Kubla Khan,* pp. 248 ff.

15. *CL,* I, 349–50. The date of the poem is a subject of much debate. Griggs argues for the fall of 1797, mainly on the basis of the letter to Thelwall. Miss Schneider (*Coleridge, Opium and Kubla Khan,* pp. 153–236)

argues for October, 1799, or summer, 1800. The exact date of the poem is not vitally important to the present discussion, but the abrupt shift from Kubla Khan to the vision of the Abyssinian Maid would suggest that the closing lines were composed separately and probably at a later date than the body of the poem—after he had given up trying to complete it. So perhaps the composition of the poem stretches across the years 1797–1800.

16. Schneider (*Coleridge, Opium and Kubla Khan,* pp. 245–46) points out the parallels between this portrait and the ancient conventional descriptions of the god-intoxicated poet, as given for example in Plato's *Ion.*

17. The dome and caves become the fabrics of art, suggesting the range of art from dome to cave, from sun to ice, the extremes that meet. J. V. Baker (*The Sacred River* [Baton Rouge: Louisiana State University Press, 1957], p. 181) sees the dome as the "heaven of art" equivalent to Keats' urn, Eliot's Chinese jar, Yeats' holy city of Byzantium. And the caves of ice, as Wilson Knight says in *The Starlit Dome* (London: Oxford University Press, 1941), p. 94, "hint cool cavernous depths in the unconscious mind."

18. Sigmund Freud, *A General Introduction to Psychoanalysis,* translated by Joan Riviere (New York: Permabooks, 1953), pp. 384–85.

19. Coleridge was aware of and not too disturbed by these faults. To Thelwall, December 17, 1796 (*CL,* I, 278), he admits that in many of his poems "there is a garishness & swell of diction" which he hopes his future poems may be clear of. In defending Bowles from the charge of Della Cruscanism he says, "As to my own poetry, I do confess that it frequently both in thought & language deviates from 'nature & simplicity.'"

20. Stephen Potter, *Coleridge and S. T. C.* (London: Jonathan Cape, 1935), pp. 11–21.

21. See autobiographical letters to Poole (*CL,* I, 348, 388).

22. God's Image is presumably his soul. See *Notebooks,* Vol. I, entry 272.g and note.

23. Cf. letter to Joseph Cottle, April, 1797 (*CL,* I, 320), in which he describes how he would go about writing an epic.

24. Cf. in the letter to Thelwall, December 17, 1796 (*ibid.,* p. 279): "My philosophical opinions are blended with, or deduced from my feelings: & this, I think, peculiarizes my style of Writing."

25. See below, pp. 132 ff.

26. *The Portable Coleridge,* edited by I. A. Richards (New York: Viking Press, 1950), pp. 21, 27, 35.

27. See Marginalia to *Polemical Discourses,* "Liberty," sec. 2, in *Coleridge on the Seventeenth Century,* edited by Roberta F. Brinkley (Durham, N.C.: Duke University Press, 1955), p. 796.

28. What he says of Shakespeare was undoubtedly his own ideal. Shakespeare kept *"at all times the high road of life.* With him there were no

innocent adulteries; he never rendered that amiable which religion and reason taught us to detest; he never clothed vice in the garb of virtue, like Beaumont and Fletcher, the Kotzebues of his day . . ." (*Coleridge's Shakespearean Criticism*, edited by Thomas M. Raysor [2 vols.; Cambridge, Mass.: Harvard University Press, 1930], II, 266).

29. There were of course specific personal miseries that aggravated the agony of composition: opium addiction and the frustration of his love for Sara Hutchinson. See below, pp. 123 and 132.

30. Compare Byron's description of Lara, below, pp. 273–74. Byron had encouraged Coleridge to revise his play, which was produced as *Remorse* at Drury Lane in January, 1813.

31. Douglas Angus in "The Theme of Love and Guilt in Coleridge's Three Major Poems," *Journal of English and Germanic Philology*, LIX (October, 1960), 658, sees the rivalry of Osorio with Albert, rightly, I think, as reflecting Coleridge's old rivalry with Francis. He goes on, more doubtfully, to see Ferdinand as a father figure. He finds at the core of Coleridge's sense of guilt an Oedipal complex—an unconscious hatred of his father and incestuous desire for his mother—and he interprets the symbolic action of the major poems in terms of this complex.

32. On the occasion of Coleridge's first visit to Racedown, June 5, 1797, Dorothy writes: "after tea he repeated to us two acts and a half of his tragedy *Osorio*. The next morning William read his tragedy *The Borderers* . . ." (*Early Letters of William and Dorothy Wordsworth*, edited by Ernest de Selincourt [Oxford: Clarendon Press, 1935], p. 169). It is in the second half of *Osorio* that the similarities between Oswald and Osorio are most marked. Coleridge was wildly enthusiastic about *The Borderers*. He called it "absolutely wonderful" and compared Wordsworth with Schiller and Shakespeare (*CL*, I, 325).

33. Compare *Childe Harold*, Canto IV, stanza 135, where Byron says grandly to his wife that his "curse shall be forgiveness."

34. Ernest de Selincourt, *Wordsworthian and Other Studies* (Oxford: Clarendon Press, 1947), p. 30.

35. *Ibid.*, p. 31.

36. In the 1818 edition of *The Friend*. See *The Poetical Works of Samuel Taylor Coleridge*, edited by James Dykes Campbell (London: Macmillan Co., 1893), p. 591.

37. Lawrence Hanson, *The Life of S. T. Coleridge: The Early Years* (London: George Allen and Unwin, 1938), p. 493.

38. See *The Table Talk and Omniana of Samuel Taylor Coleridge* (London: Oxford University Press, 1917), p. 106.

39. To Wordsworth, January, 1801 (*The Complete Works and Letters of Charles Lamb* [New York: Modern Library, 1935], p. 689).

40. The question of whether or not the deaths of the men are ethically justified has provoked much solemn debate. The most recent and elaborate justification is by Robert Penn Warren in his essay "A Poem of Pure Imagination" (in *The Rime of the Ancient Mariner* [New York: Reynal and Hitchcock, 1946], pp. 85–86). Warren argues that the men have "duplicated the Mariner's own crime of pride" and "have violated the sacramental conception of the universe, by making man's convenience the measure of an act, by isolating him from Nature and the 'One Life.'" But this seems to me a specious and largely irrelevant argument, which ignores the vast difference between the Mariner's act and the petty human frailties of the men; the fact that the Mariner lives and the men die; and the implications of the dice game discussed below.

41. *Ibid.,* p. 106.

42. Kenneth Burke, *The Philosophy of Literary Form* (Baton Rouge: Louisiana State University Press, 1941), pp. 71–73.

43. H. N. Fairchild, *Religious Trends in English Poetry* (5 vols.; New York: Columbia University Press, 1939–62), III, 292–93.

44. *Ibid.,* p. 294.

45. This is the error into which Warren has fallen in his influential interpretation. He proceeds on the assumption that the poem presents a "sacramental view of the universe" thoroughly consistent with Coleridge's philosophical view of the "One Life" as found in the famous lines in *The Eolian Harp* and later prose writings. He is led, therefore, into forcing the universe of the poem to fit into a pattern of fundamentally benevolent order and law by which the Mariner is brought to the point "where he discovers the joy of human communion in God, and utters the moral, 'He prayeth best who loveth best, etc.' We arrive at the notion of a universal charity . . . the sense of the 'One Life' in which all creation participates" ("A Poem of Pure Imagination," p. 78). For an extended discussion of Warren's interpretation see my article, "The Nightmare World of *The Ancient Mariner,*" *Studies in Romanticism,* I (Summer, 1962), 241–54.

46. See, for example, Burke, *The Philosophy of Literary Form,* pp. 71 ff.; Knight, *The Starlit Dome,* pp. 84–89; David Beres, "A Dream, a Vision, and a Poem: A Psycho-analytic Study of the Origins of *The Rime of the Ancient Mariner,*" *International Journal of Psycho-analysis,* XXXII (1951), Part II.

47. See, in particular, *Notebooks,* Vol. I, entry 1726 (December 13, 1803).

48. See *ibid.,* entry 979 (September, 1801), in which Coleridge refers openly to Sara's frigidity: "Sara is uncommonly *cold* in her feelings of animal Love."

49. See letters to Poole on March 16, 1801 (*CL,* II, 706), and January 15,

1804 (*ibid.*, p. 1035), for examples of the frenzied manner in which periodically he claimed to have refuted the doctrine of necessity.

50. *Aids to Reflection* (Bohn's Library [London: George Bell and Sons, 1890]), p. 192.

51. Quoted by E. H. Coleridge in his edition of *Christabel* (London: H. Frowde, 1907), p. 52.

52. The relationship between opium and dreams has been discussed by Miss Elisabeth Schneider, who points out that sexual desire is deadened by the taking of opium but is "reawakened under withdrawal with increased intensity, often during sleep" (*Coleridge, Opium and Kubla Khan,* p. 63). The dreams described in the notebooks and in *The Pains of Sleep* express sexual attitudes whose origins are undoubtedly independent of opium. But the dreams occurred apparently during periods in which Coleridge was trying to abandon opium. His use of sexual imagery for the description of opium indicates that the two evils were inextricably entangled in his mind. By the time Coleridge began *Christabel* in 1798 he was already taking opium with some regularity, so that the particular pattern of the relationship between Christabel and Geraldine may reflect the blurred interaction of opium and sexual desire. The primary imagery for Geraldine is sexual, but her effect is narcotic. As the focal detail linking the sexual and narcotic imagery, Geraldine's touch drugs and paralyzes Christabel and at the same time provokes fearful dreams.

53. Notebook 30. Quoted by Kathleen Coburn in "Coleridge and Wordsworth and 'the Supernatural,'" *University of Toronto Quarterly,* XXV (1956), 127.

54. See Lionel Trilling's essay "Freud and Literature" in *The Liberal Imagination* (New York: Viking Press, 1950), pp. 54–57.

55. *Christabel* (E. H. Coleridge ed.), p. 32.

56. See, for example, Dorothy Wordsworth's letter to Catherine Clarkson of April 12, 1810, after Sara Hutchinson had left for Wales. Dorothy says that she is glad Sara is gone because Coleridge "harassed and agitated her mind continually, and we saw that he was doing her health perpetual injury" (*The Letters of William and Dorothy Wordsworth: The Middle Years,* edited by Ernest de Selincourt [2 vols.; Oxford: Clarendon Press, 1937], I, 365–67). Obviously Coleridge tormented himself as much as his friends by his recurrent fears and suspicions. In 1807 he was persuaded that the Wordsworths were censoring Sara's letters to him and cruelly infusing into her mind the notion "that [his] attachment to her had been the cause of all [his] unhappiness." And in numerous notebook entries he tortured himself with the fear that Sara admired Wordsworth more than him. See George Whalley, *Coleridge and Sara Hutchinson, and the Asra Poems* (Toronto: University of Toronto Press, 1955), pp. 64 ff.

Notes to Chapter 4: Keats

57. *The Ode to Tranquillity* and the *Hymn* were sent in the same letter. See *CL,* II, 995–98.

4: KEATS

1. *The Letters of John Keats,* edited by Hyder E. Rollins (2 vols.; Cambridge, Mass.: Harvard University Press, 1958), II, 167; hereafter referred to as *Letters.* All quotations from the letters are from this edition, unless otherwise noted.

2. Hyder E. Rollins (ed.), *The Keats Circle: Letters and Papers* (2 vols.; Cambridge, Mass.: Harvard University Press, 1948), II, 72; hereafter referred to as *KC.*

3. All quotations from the poetry are from *The Poetical Works of John Keats,* edited by H. W. Garrod (Oxford: Clarendon Press, 1939).

4. Kenneth Muir, "The Meaning of *Hyperion,*" *Essays in Criticism,* II (1952), 61, 75.

5. See below, pp. 167 ff.

6. Charles Cowden Clarke, Biographical Note, reprinted in *KC,* II, 149.

7. *Blackwood's Edinburgh Magazine,* IV (August, 1818), 519–24, reprinted in *Complete Poems and Selected Letters of John Keats,* edited by H. L. Briggs (New York: Modern Library, 1951), pp. 478–85.

8. Quoted in *The Letters of John Keats,* edited by Maurice Buxton Forman (2nd ed.; London: Oxford University Press, 1935), p. 25.

9. See Dorothy Hewlitt, *A Life of John Keats* (2nd ed.; London: Hurst and Blackett, 1949), chap. iii, pp. 35 ff., for a description of conditions in the hospitals.

10. *Ibid.,* p. 42.

11. *KC,* II, 56.

12. To George and Tom Keats, December 27, 1817. Earlier in the letter he had written: "The excellence of every Art is its intensity, capable of making all disagreeables evaporate, from their being in close relationship with Beauty and Truth. Examine 'King Lear' and you will find this exemplified throughout." As the context here and in the letter to Bailey of November 22 makes clear, the word "truth" carries quite positive connotations for Keats. On the highest level, it connotes the morally good and beneficent; on a more personal level, it connotes the "essence" of sensuous enjoyment, the fullest realization of health and happiness (immortality will consist of "what we called happiness on Earth repeated in a finer tone"). The implications of the speculations in both letters are that the beautiful is ultimately the good, and so preoccupation with beauty can be safely indulged. Contrariwise, the evil and disagreeable could not be truth.

13. The attitude Keats struck in the letter grew to a considerable extent

out of a desire to convince himself and his friends that he was indifferent to criticism. He wanted also to reassure Woodhouse, who was inclined to take his every word literally. At a party at Hessey's he had burst into a "rhodomontade" to Woodhouse that "there was now nothing original to be written in poetry; that its riches were already exhausted, & all its beauties forestalled—& that [he] should consequently write no more." Immediately thereafter, Woodhouse had seen the attack in the *Quarterly Review* and had written an anxious letter to bolster up Keats' confidence (*Letters*, I, 378 ff.). The letter of October 18 was Keats' reply.

14. Muir, "The Meaning of *Hyperion*," p. 63. Another typical comment is John Middleton Murry's: Philosophy meant for Keats "one thing and one thing alone—a comprehension of the meaning of life. That is to say, it meant precisely the kind of speculations of which his letter is composed; and the conclusions he reached through them are what he meant by Truth. So that when he said that Poetry was not so fine a thing as Philosophy, he was saying simply that one kind of poetry is not as fine as another kind of poetry: and that one kind of poet is not so fine as another kind of poet" (*Keats and Shakespeare* [London: Oxford University Press, 1925], p. 121). But to say this is willfully to substitute what Murry wants Keats to say for what he does say.

15. Keats had long felt for Hazlitt an admiration that bordered on idolatry. On April 27, 1818, he wrote Reynolds that he intended to prepare himself through study "to ask Hazlitt in about a years time the best metaphysical road I can take" (*Letters*, I, 274). For Hazlitt's influence on Keats' theories, particularly his conception of Negative Capability, see Claude Finney, *The Evolution of Keats's Poetry* (2 vols.; Cambridge, Mass.: Harvard University Press, 1936), II, 478–79. See also Clarence Thorpe, "Keats and Hazlitt," *PMLA*, LXXII (1947), 487–502.

16. Further evidence that Keats had Hazlitt's *Letter* in mind in developing his speculations is the fact that the concluding section of Hazlitt's *Letter* is devoted to a summary of his arguments in *An Essay on the Principles of Human Action* against "the metaphysical doctrine of the innate and necessary selfishness of the human mind" and in favor of the doctrine that, "as a voluntary agent, I am necessarily . . . a disinterested one. I could not love myself, if I were not so formed as to be capable of loving others." The object of his essay is "to leave free play to the social affections, and to the cultivation of the more disinterested and generous principles of our nature" (*Collected Works of William Hazlitt*, edited by A. R. Waller and Arnold Glover [13 vols.; London: J. M. Dent and Co., 1902–6], I, 403–11). Keats owned a copy of Hazlitt's *Principles of Human Action*. Obviously, though he accepted Hazlitt's conception of disinterestedness,

he had come to question Hazlitt's conviction that as a voluntary agent man was necessarily disinterested.

17. The theme of the poem recalls the letter to Woodhouse in which Keats "speaks of his solitary indifference to applause" and of the yearning he has for beauty that would inspire him to write—even if his night's labors were burnt each morning.

18. I. A. Richards, *Mencius on the Mind* (London: K. Paul, Trench, Trubner and Co., 1932), p. 116. For a useful summary of the many recent interpretations of the ode, see Harvey T. Lyon, *Keats' Well-read Urn* (New York: Henry Holt, 1958).

19. I. A. Richards, *Science and Poetry* (New York: W. W. Norton and Co., 1926), pp. 70–72.

20. T. S. Eliot, *Selected Essays* (New York: Harcourt, Brace and Co., 1950), p. 231.

21. He had also gone further than Hazlitt, who had said that "poetry delights in power *as well as* in truth, in good, in right" (my italics). Hazlitt's attitude might be summed up in the aphorism: "Truth is beauty; and beauty is sometimes truth." Keats probably found in such statements by Hazlitt as "Truth with beauty suggests the feeling of immortality" the stimulus for his own aphorism at the end of the ode. For examples of the coupling of truth and beauty in Hazlitt's essays, see the section on "Keats and Hazlitt" in James Caldwell, *John Keats' Fancy* (Ithaca, N.Y.: Cornell University Press, 1945), pp. 172–86.

22. See Kenneth Burke, "Symbolic Action in a Poem by Keats," in *A Grammar of Motives* (New York: Prentice-Hall, 1945), pp. 456 ff. The poignant and, in effect, involuntary address to the desolate little town in the last lines of the fourth stanza reveals how precariously and at what cost the final affirmation has been achieved, and how inadequate as symbol the urn ultimately is to the demands placed upon it. For an excellent discussion of the unresolved tensions in the poem see David Perkins, *The Quest for Permanence* (Cambridge, Mass.: Harvard University Press, 1959), pp. 233–42.

23. Hazlitt, *Collected Works*, V, 9. The kind of generalization Keats was making was common among artists of the time, and the rainbow was a favorite symbol. Nearly two years before, at Haydon's "immortal dinner-party," Lamb and Keats agreed that Newton "had destroyed all the poetry of the rainbow by reducing it to the prismatic colours . . . we all drank Newton's health, and confusion to mathematics" (B. R. Haydon, *Autobiography* [World's Classics series (London: Oxford University Press, 1927)], p. 360).

24. See M. H. Abrams, *The Mirror and the Lamp* (New York: Oxford University Press, 1953), pp. 303–12, for an excellent discussion of these

lines in relation to the historical background and the attitudes of other Romantic artists.

25. C. D. Thorpe's influential interpretation that Keats intended both Apollonius and Lamia to represent falsities seems to me to make Keats too coolly judicious and fails to take into account the turbulent tone of the inserted lines as well as the concluding action of the poem. See Thorpe's *The Mind of John Keats* (New York: Oxford University Press, 1926), pp. 102–3, 119–20; and *Complete Poems and Selected Letters of Keats,* edited by Thorpe (New York: Odyssey Press, 1935), pp. xliii–xliv.

26. On August 24 he wrote Reynolds: "I feel it in my power to become a popular writer—I feel it in my strength to refuse the poisonous suffrage of a public—My own being which I know to be becomes of more consequence to me than the crowds of Shadows in the Shape of Man and women that inhabit a kingdom. The Soul is a world of itself and has enough to do in its own home" (*Letters*, II, 146).

27. Two letters written at the time that he was recasting *Hyperion* reaffirm his statement in the journal letter on the relation of poet to philosopher. To Bailey, August 14, he writes, "I am convinced more and more every day that (excepting the human friend Philosopher) a fine writer is the most genuine Being in the World" (*ibid.,* p. 139). And in the letter to Reynolds of August 25 he says, "I am convinced more and more day by day that fine writing is next to fine doing the top thing in the world" (*ibid.,* p. 146). As in the journal letter where philosophy is equated with "the pure desire of the benefit of others," here philosophy and fine doing are equated. Apollonius is, in one sense, the philosopher in whom "the pure desire of the benefit of others" has been pushed to the extremity that Keats foresaw in the journal letter, in which it injures instead of benefits. (To Lycius, Apollonius says,

> ". . . from every ill
> Of life have I preserv'd thee to this day,
> And shall I see thee made a serpent's prey?")

28. See Garrod, *The Poetical Works of John Keats,* p. 512. Middleton Murry's argument (in *Keats and Shakespeare,* pp. 178–80) for rejecting these lines in an interpretation of the poem seems to me sophistical; and De Selincourt's rebuttal (in *The Poems of John Keats* [5th ed.; London: Methuen and Co., 1926], pp. 583–84), completely convincing. Most recent critics consider the lines necessary to the argument.

29. De Selincourt, *The Poems of John Keats,* p. 582.

30. The conclusions to which I have been led stand in opposition to the optimistic interpretations of *The Fall of Hyperion* by recent critics. Muir, for example, says ("The Meaning of *Hyperion*," p. 75): "In the meeting with Moneta imagination and reality had been reconciled. . . . To *Autumn*

represented the first fruits, and the last fruits, of Keats' new understanding." But to say this is to take the wish for the deed: to confuse the insistence upon the necessity for reconciliation with the reconciliation. It is to ignore the confusion and near-hysteria of the passage, to overlook the fact that Moneta neither explains nor shows how the reconciliation is to be made. As for *To Autumn,* it is certainly not the kind of poem Keats or Moneta had in mind; the understanding it represents is nothing new, but rather an understanding that Keats had had almost from the beginning, given at last almost perfect expression. Insofar as it represents the aftereffect of the experience in *The Fall of Hyperion,* it reflects the abandonment of struggle, the languid relaxation of energy, and, in the final stanza, the quiet resignation to death. As Professor Kingsley Widmer has pointed out to me, the poem illustrates, in all its poignant implications, Shakespeare's "Ripeness is all."

In an elaborate and confusing examination of "The Disputed Lines in *The Fall of Hyperion,*" *Essays in Criticism,* VII (1957), 28–41, Brian Wicker sees Keats as working his way through an unconsciously Christian sacramental process in the journey from Garden to Altar in which "the redemption of mankind is accomplished." In the expression of transcended suffering in the deathless countenance of Moneta, the poet sees "reflected his own transfiguration. He has become, like Shakespeare, a 'miserable and mighty poet of the human heart.'" It seems to me that Wicker, even more than Muir, is arbitrarily imposing his own wishful thinking upon the poem.

31. For the probable satire on literary figures in *The Cap and Bells,* see the essay by Robert Gittings in *The Mask of Keats* (London: William Heinemann, 1956).

32. See letters of October 13 and 19 (*Letters,* II, 223–24).

33. This statement would hold true, I think, for the effect of the reviews and the lack of widespread recognition also. That he brooded over the reviews and the contempt or indifference of the "public" is evident, but his brooding had hitherto acted as a stimulant to almost feverish activity rather than as a depressant. The reaction to the reviews seems probably one of many factors hastening the development of tuberculosis. But in itself this reaction was certainly a cause neither of his silence nor of death. One can see, however, how his morbid brooding over failure during the "posthumous year" of 1820 would lead Brown and other friends to believe that he had been "destroyed by hirelings under the imposing name of reviewers." See H. L. Briggs, "Keats's Conscious and Unconscious Reactions to Criticisms of *Endymion,*" *PMLA,* LX (1945), 1106–29.

34. See also letter of June, 1820, to Brown: "I do not begin composition yet, being willing, in case of a relapse, to have nothing to reproach myself with" (*Letters,* II, 299).

Notes to Chapter 5: Shelley

5: SHELLEY

1. T. S. Eliot, "A Talk on Dante," *Kenyon Review*, XIV (Spring, 1952), 183–84. F. R. Leavis, *Revaluations* (New York: George Stewart, 1947), p. 231.

2. Ernest Dowden, *Life of Percy Bysshe Shelley* (2 vols.; London: Kegan Paul, 1886), II, 507.

3. Newman I. White, *Shelley* (2 vols.; New York: Alfred A. Knopf, 1940), II, 372.

4. Peter Butter, *Shelley's Idols of the Cave* (Edinburgh: Edinburgh University Press, 1954), p. 30, suggests plausibly on the basis of line 256, "The star that ruled his doom was far too fair," that Plato's sin was his reputed love for the Greek youth, Aster.

5. Several critics have interpreted this scene as "a symbolic representation of Rousseau's birth" because of the evident implications of mountain and cavern and the similarity of language to Wordsworth's *Intimations* ode. See Carlos Baker, *Shelley's Major Poetry* (Princeton, N.J.: Princeton University Press, 1948), pp. 265–66, and Kenneth Allott, "Bloom on 'The Triumph of Life,'" *Essays in Criticism*, X (April, 1960), 222–28. Perhaps so, but a number of details argue against so narrow an interpretation. Rousseau emphasizes the dream nature of the episode. The valley is the valley of "perpetual dream." There is nothing to indicate present or potential imperfection in it. Rousseau cannot remember whether life had been heaven or hell before. He tells the poet that in this valley he could forget all ills, as the king would cease to mourn his lost crown and a mother her dead baby. These images imply that it is as a mature human being that one enters the valley. Furthermore, if this dream is symbolic of birth into this world from a more perfect world, then one would expect the Shape to be fading from the beginning, rather than the active agent who stamps out the knowledge of pre-existence. To make her the one who blots out the memory of the ideal turns her into a delicately sinister figure. Actually, all the imagery of the valley is "Platonic" and suggests that the episode can most meaningfully be interpreted as a symbolic transportation of Rousseau into the ideal world of which he—and Shelley—had always dreamed.

Baker sees the Shape as entirely beneficent and interprets the cup detail thus: "The usual explanation is that as a result of drinking from the cup, Rousseau's spiritual senses were overcome by the cold new vision. Actually, however, he is not said to drink, but only to touch his lips to the cup. Had he drunk the bright Nepenthe, he could have quenched his youthful thirst for knowledge of the mysteries. But at the crucial moment his courage failed, his brain became as sand, his thirst remained unquenched, and the bright cold vision of worldly life burst in" (p. 267). But this is to read into the account, it seems to me, an explanation that is carefully avoided. The interesting thing about the passage is its *deliberate* ambiguity. It presents a series of details: Rousseau rises; he bends at her command; he touches the cup with faint lips; and suddenly his brain becomes as sand, and the vision bursts upon his sight. The description is as enigmatic as Coleridge's Mariner's account of shooting the Albatross. It raises questions to which no definite answers can be given. But the very order of details indicates a cause and effect relationship between the touching of the cup and the coming of the vision.

The most recent commentator on the poem, Harold Bloom in *Shelley's Mythmaking* (New Haven, Conn.: Yale University Press, 1959), pp. 220–75, goes to the opposite extreme from Baker. He sees the valley as symbolic of the natural world, in which the ideal vision fades into the light of common day as in Wordsworth's *Intimations* ode. The Shape is a parody of the ideal, the goddess of nature like Blake's Vala, "a type of Rahab, the New Testament Great Whore embodied in the Natural World which is a snare for the visionary." Once Rousseau "has given in to the supposed beauty and good of nature, forgetting . . . his early imaginative powers which transcended nature and which alone could have given his eyes vision that the icy glare of life would not obscure, then life substitutes its glare for the illusory light of the natural sun" (pp. 270–71). But, though undoubtedly the Shape plays an ironic role, there is no more evidence in the poem for reducing her to parody than for insisting upon divorcing her totally from the pageant.

6. *The Complete Works of Percy Bysshe Shelley*, edited by Roger Ingpen and Walter Peck (The Julian Edition; 10 vols.; London: Ernest Benn, 1926–30), VII, 133; hereafter referred to as *Works*. For his characterization of Rousseau, Shelley undoubtedly drew upon the *Reveries of a Solitary*. "The creed of a Savoyard Priest" in *Emile*, where among other themes the famous comparison of Socrates and Christ occurs, must also have been in his mind. Shelley's statement in the *Essay on Christianity* is interesting in this connection: "Rousseau has vindicated this opinion [the equality of mankind] with all the eloquence of sincere and earnest faith, and is perhaps the philosopher among the moderns who in the structure of his feelings and understanding resembles most nearly the mysterious sage of Judaea" (*Works*, VI, 247). Yeats in his *Ideas of Good and Evil* (London: A. H. Bullen, 1914), p. 90, calls Rousseau "the typical poet of *The Triumph of Life*."

7. Between the initial presentation of Rousseau and the presentation at the end exists a curious contradiction or at least shift in conception. The Rousseau who introduces himself and identifies the characters in the triumph indicates that he is there because of a specific flaw in himself: a

lack of "purer nutriment." But the story he tells indicates that he is an unwitting victim or passive pawn. Perhaps this discrepancy would have been explained as Rousseau answered the poet's questions; and perhaps it is an example of the kind of inconsistency—resulting from haste in composition and impatience with logical sequence—typical of Shelley's other poems.

8. *Selected Poetry and Prose of P. B. Shelley,* edited by Kenneth N. Cameron (New York: Rinehart and Co., 1951), p. 527.

9. Leavis, *Revaluations,* p. 215.

10. T. S. Eliot, *The Use of Poetry and the Use of Criticism* (London: Faber and Faber, 1933), pp. 89 ff.

11. *Ibid.,* p. 99.

12. *The Poems of Percy Bysshe Shelley,* edited by C. D. Locock (2 vols.; London: Methuen and Co., 1911), II, 453; *The Complete Poetical Works of Percy Bysshe Shelley,* edited by George E. Woodberry (Boston: Houghton Mifflin Co., 1901), p. 630; White, *Shelley,* II, 256; Baker, *Shelley's Major Poetry,* p. 237. It is refreshing to note that the two most recent commentators on the poem, Milton Wilson in *Shelley's Later Poetry* (New York: Columbia University Press, 1959), and Harold Bloom in *Shelley's Mythmaking,* take for granted the physical elements in the ideal union.

13. *Epipsychidion,* edited by Robert Potts (facsimile reprint; London: Published for the Shelley Society by Reeves and Turner, 1887), Introduction, p. xxix.

14. In his Advertisement prefixed to the poem, Shelley says, "The present Poem, like the *Vita Nuova* of Dante, is sufficiently intelligible to a certain class of readers without a matter-of-fact history of the circumstances to which it relates . . ." (*Works,* II, 355).

15. The essay was written in the summer of 1818. Page references are to *Shelley's Prose,* edited by David Lee Clark (Albuquerque: University of New Mexico Press, 1954), since only the first half of the essay is in *Works.*

16. The section was first privately printed by Ingpen. It can be found in James Notopoulos, *The Platonism of Shelley* (Durham, N.C.: Duke University Press, 1949), pp. 375–413, as well as in Clark, *Shelley's Prose.*

17. The canceled sentences are given in Notopoulos, *The Platonism of Shelley,* pp. 533–34.

18. In the concluding lines of the fragment *Fiordispina* (1820), the old nurse says to Fiordispina on her wedding night:

> And say, sweet lamb, would you not learn the sweet
> And subtle mystery by which spirits meet?
> Who knows whether the loving game is played,
> When once of mortal [vesture] disarrayed,
> The naked soul goes wandering here and there
> Through the wide deserts of Elysian air?

19. For the ultimate variation on this process, see the conclusion of *The Witch of Atlas* (stanza 76), where timid lovers, under the spell of dreams induced by the Witch,

> Would rise out of their nest, and take sweet joy,
>   To the fulfilment of their inmost thought;
> And when next day the maiden and the boy
>   Met one another, both, like sinners caught,
> Blushed at the thing which each believed was done
> Only in fancy—till the tenth moon shone. . . .

20. This is the notebook version. See *Works,* III, 299, 351; and Walter Peck, *Shelley: Life and Works* (2 vols.; Boston: Houghton Mifflin Co., 1927), II, 162.

21. This is the notebook version. For MS readings and discussion of where the fragment belongs, see *Works,* III, 350; Peck, *Shelley: Life and Works,* II, 161; and White, *Shelley,* II, 562, 587.

22. In a canceled passage following the song (II.v.71 ff.), Panthea tells Asia that Prometheus was speaking through her: "I mixed my own weak nature with his love" (*Works,* II, 267).

23. Compare the description of Cosimo in *Fiordispina:*

> He faints, dissolved into a sea of love;
> But thou art as a planet sphered above;
> But thou art Love itself—ruling the motion
> Of his subjected spirit.

24. Leavis, *Revaluations,* p. 211.

25. These observations are borne out by *The Cenci,* which Shelley was writing in the interim between composition of the third and fourth acts of *Prometheus.* The world of *The Cenci* is one of almost completely unrelieved evil and gloom. The theme in part determines this, but the particular handling of details and the dominant tone are Shelley's own. One need only think of the difference between his handling of the Renaissance world and Browning's or even Byron's to realize how completely lacking are the positive qualities of that world, including its exuberant enjoyment of life. We are reminded of the visions of the Furies in *Prometheus.* Most importantly, the characters are singularly unattractive and never really emerge as human beings. There is nothing, either, to suggest that they are redeemable or perfectible, and ironically nowhere is this more depressingly true than in the character of Beatrice. Shelley's intent in regard to Beatrice is baffling. Most critics try to see her actions in the fifth act, particularly her ruthless betrayal of Marzio, as the effect of the tragic flaw, the hardening of soul that results from the decision to murder her father (see Baker, *Shelley's Major Poetry,* pp. 147–50). Even if this were the intent, she is no tragic character. There is no sign of self-awareness, of a sense of guilt or remorse, such as even Lady Macbeth reveals—only an absolute conviction of rightness

that borders on madness. The disturbing thing is that not only is she presented with complete sympathy, but she is also given speeches that echo Shelley's attitudes in other poems. It is quite likely that he took for granted that her sense of innocence and her attitudes toward the others in the play were justified, if not her behavior.

26. Ernest Bernbaum, *Guide through the Romantic Movement* (2nd ed.; New York: Ronald Press, 1949), p. 255.

27. Joseph Warren Beach, *The Concept of Nature in Nineteenth Century English Poetry* (New York: Macmillan Co., 1936), p. 259.

28. Yeats, *Ideas of Good and Evil*, p. 72.

29. For the first incident see Edward Trelawny, *Recollections of the Last Days of Shelley and Byron,* edited by Edward Dowden (London: Oxford University Press, 1923), chap. vii, pp. 39–40. The second incident is related in his revision, *Records of Shelley, Byron and the Author* (London: B. M. Pickering, 1878), and is probably, therefore, less reliable.

30. Thomas Medwin, *Life of Percy Bysshe Shelley,* edited by H. B. Forman (London: Oxford University Press, 1913), p. 237.

31. Also in Trelawny, *Recollections,* chap. x, p. 67.

32. See H. N. Fairchild in *Religious Trends in English Poetry* (5 vols.; New York: Columbia University Press, 1939–62), III, 300: "What he had always wanted was a life on this side of the grave in which the apparent would be redeemed by the ideal while the ideal took on the warmth and color of the apparent."

33. Shelley's recognition of the potential danger of his way of life and thought is perhaps indicated by his question to Peacock (*Works,* X, 343) about the possibility of being "employed politically at the court of a native prince" in India (the momentary mental picture of Shelley in India is one of the most bizarre and tantalizing "imaginary" events in the history of Romanticism), and by his remarks in a letter to Hogg on October 22, 1821, in which the association of his future plans with *Adonais* is interesting: "I have some thoughts, if I could get a respectable appointment, of going to India, or anywhere where I might be compelled to active exertion, and at the same time enter into an entirely new sphere of action. But this I daresay is a mere dream. I shall probably have no opportunity of making it a reality but finish as I have begun. Have you seen a poem I wrote on the death of Keats. . . . It is perhaps the least imperfect of my pieces" (*New Shelley Letters,* edited by W. S. Scott [New Haven, Conn.: Yale University Press, 1949], p. 133).

34. Beach, *The Concept of Nature in Nineteenth Century English Poetry,* p. 591.

35. For the confused question of Shelley's attitudes toward immortality, see Ellsworth Barnard, *Shelley's Religion* (Minneapolis: University of

Minnesota Press, 1937), chap. v; B. P. Kurtz, *The Pursuit of Death* (New York: Oxford University Press, 1933), pp. 122–35, 266–94; Beach's note, *The Concept of Nature in Nineteenth Century English Poetry,* pp. 590–91; Fairchild, *Religious Trends in English Poetry,* III, 361–65; C. E. Pulos, *The Deep Truth: A Study of Shelley's Scepticism* (Lincoln: University of Nebraska Press, 1954), p. 86 and *passim.* I agree with Pulos and other recent commentators in their insistence on Shelley's persistent skepticism and his indebtedness to Hume. The views Shelley expressed in *On Life* (*Works,* VI, 193–97) and in *On a Future State* (*ibid.,* pp. 205–9) he held more or less consistently to the end of his life.

36. Shelley to the end of his life had a particular regard for *Adonais.* He obviously felt that in it he had succeeded in "the province of the poet." On June 5, 1821, he wrote Gisborne, "It is a highly wrought *piece of art,* perhaps better in point of composition than anything I have written" (Shelley's italics; *Works,* X, 270). And on September 25 he wrote Ollier, his publisher, "The 'Adonais' in spite of its mysticism, is the least imperfect of my compositions" (*ibid.,* p. 328).

37. Mary Shelley's note to *The Revolt of Islam.*

38. Albert Guerard, "Prometheus and the Aeolian Lyre," *Yale Review,* XXXIII (March, 1944), 492.

39. Leavis, *Revaluations,* p. 208.

40. *The Letters of John Keats,* edited by Hyder Rollins (2 vols.; Cambridge, Mass.: Harvard University Press, 1958), II, 323.

41. Medwin, *Life of Percy Bysshe Shelley,* p. 266. See also Mary Shelley's letter to Leigh Hunt, December 29, 1820, in *Letters of Mary Shelley,* edited by Frederick L. Jones (2 vols.; Norman: University of Oklahoma Press, 1944), I, 122–23.

42. Edmund Blunden, *Shelley* (New York: Viking Press, 1947), p. 285.

43. Leavis, *Revaluations,* pp. 209 ff. See above, pp. 193 f.

44. D. G. James, *The Romantic Comedy* (London: Oxford University Press, 1948), p. 66.

45. Trelawny, *Recollections,* chap. viii, pp. 47–50.

46. See *Works,* IV, 111–15, 197–201, 205–6.

47. For the first drafts of *Epipsychidion,* see *ibid.,* II, 377–82.

48. Thomas Love Peacock, *Memoirs of Percy Bysshe Shelley,* in *Collected Works,* edited by H. F. B. Brett-Smith and C. E. Jones (10 vols.; London: Constable and Co., 1928–34), VIII, 131.

6: BYRON

1. Edward Trelawny, *Recollections of the Last Days of Shelley and Byron,* edited by Edward Dowden (London: Oxford University Press,

1923), chap. xxii, p. 158. The fragment was first published by E. H. Coleridge in *The Poetical Works of Lord Byron* (7 vols.; London: John Murray, 1898–1904), VI; hereafter referred to as *PW*.

2. Elizabeth Boyd, *Byron's Don Juan* (New Brunswick, N.J.: Rutgers University Press, 1945), p. 70.

3. Countess of Blessington, *A Journal of Conversations with Lord Byron* (Boston: Cottrell, 1859), pp. 301–2.

4. Thomas Medwin, *Conversations of Lord Byron at Pisa* (London: Henry Colburn, 1824), pp. 37, 47–48.

5. To Woodhouse, October 27, 1818 (*The Letters of John Keats*, edited by Hyder E. Rollins [2 vols.; Cambridge, Mass.: Harvard University Press, 1958], I, 387).

6. See Ernest J. Lovell, Jr., *Byron: The Record of a Quest* (Austin: University of Texas Press, 1949), pp. 185–228, for full discussion.

7. See G. Wilson Knight, *Lord Byron: Christian Virtues* (London: Routledge and Kegan Paul, 1952), particularly pp. 163 ff.

8. *Letters and Journals of Lord Byron,* edited by R. E. Prothero (6 vols.; London: John Murray, 1898–1901), V, 457; hereafter referred to as *LJ*.

9. Lovell, *Byron: The Record of a Quest,* p. 180.

10. See H. N. Fairchild, *Religious Trends in English Poetry* (5 vols.; New York: Columbia University Press, 1939–62), III, 394 ff., for an effort to distinguish between Calvinism as a genuinely formative influence and as an after-the-fact explanation seized upon by Byron.

11. See Lucifer's last statement to Cain at the end of Act II, scene ii, lines 452 ff.

12. I. A. Richards, *Practical Criticism* (London: Routledge and Kegan Paul, 1929), pp. 290–91.

13. March 5, 1855 (quoted in *LJ*, VI, 262).

14. Fairchild, *Religious Trends in English Poetry,* III, 391.

15. Southey to Henry Taylor, March 3, 1830, quoted in Earl of Lovelace, *Astarte* (new ed.; London: Christophers, 1921), p. 17.

16. G. Wilson Knight, *Lord Byron's Marriage* (New York: Macmillan Co., 1957), pp. 220 ff. For the most judicious and balanced discussion of the relationship with Augusta and all the factors leading to the separation, see Leslie Marchand, *Byron* (3 vols.; New York: Alfred A. Knopf, 1957), chaps. xii–xv. Much hitherto unpublished material from the Lovelace papers has been made available by Doris Langley Moore in *The Late Lord Byron* (Philadelphia: J. B. Lippincott Co., 1961).

17. See also p. 373, "I wish I could leave off eating altogether."

18. Medwin, *Conversations of Lord Byron at Pisa,* p. 42.

19. See in the letter to Hodgson of September 13, 1811 (*LJ*, II, 35), the

remark: "You degrade the Creator, in the first place, by making Him a begetter of children."

20. See letter to Murray, January 2, 1817: "As for poesy, mine is the dream of my sleeping Passions; when they are awake, I cannot speak their language, only in their Somnambulism, and just now they are not dormant" (*ibid.*, IV, 43).

21. He goes on to say that poets are so near madness that "I cannot help thinking rhyme is so far useful in anticipating and preventing the disorder. I prefer the talents of action—of war, or the senate, or even of science,— to all the speculations of those mere dreamers of another existence (I don't mean religiously but fancifully) and spectators of this apathy."

22. See also letter to Moore for November 24, 1813 (*LJ*, II, 345). The asterisks refer possibly to Lady Frances Webster, but more probably to Augusta.

23. Lovell, *Byron: The Record of a Quest*, p. 35.

24. Thomas B. Macaulay, *Critical and Historical Essays Contributed to the Edinburgh Review* (2 vols.; London: Longmans, Green and Co., 1870), I, 149 (review of Moore's *Life of Byron*, June, 1831). Marchand (*Byron*, II, 598, 602, and *passim*) has pointed out that Byron greatly exaggerated the obloquy heaped upon him. But the reaction, partly political, in the journals and the personal cuts he received were real enough. He probably read into the public attitude his own feelings of self-condemnation and humiliation. The important point in respect to his poetry is that his agony is real and acute.

25. "Existentialism Is a Humanism" in *Existentialism from Dostoevsky to Sartre*, edited by Walter Kaufmann (New York: Meridian Books, 1957), p. 295.

26. See Byron's footnote to *Don Juan*, XVI.97–98, where he attributes the characteristic to Lady Adeline, and Moore's comment on it in relation to Byron (*PW*, VI, 600–1). See also the chapter, "Lord Byron's Mobility," in Countess Guiccioli, *My Recollections of Lord Byron* (2 vols.; Philadelphia: J. B. Lippincott and Co., 1869), II, 147 ff.

27. See also I.212–16, where Lucifer tells Cain that men may still achieve the joy and power of knowledge:

> By being
> Yourselves, in your resistance. Nothing can
> Quench the mind, if the mind will be itself
> And centre of surrounding things—'tis made
> To sway.

28. Blake makes an interesting comment on *Cain*. Though he would certainly not have sympathized with Byron's skepticism, he was completely

sympathetic with his attack on the "God of this World." In the *Ghost of Abel,* etched in 1822 and addressed to "Lord Byron in the Wilderness," he presents the ghost of Abel demanding revenge in his turn from Jehovah, who is here the symbol of gentleness and forgiveness, the equivalent of Jesus in *Jerusalem.* Jehovah refuses, and Abel sinks into the grave from which arises Satan (not Byron's Lucifer but Blake's "God of this World") to cry that he is the God of men, and that Jehovah himself will be sacrificed to Satan on Calvary. The point of interest here is Blake's perception that in the obsequious Abel is the spirit of revenge, and that it is from such as he that the "God of men" arises or gains his power.

29. See Teresa Guiccioli's delightfully malicious comment on Lady Blessington's *Conversations:* "She has also tried to suggest that Lord Byron conceived a great liking for her. Nothing could be more untrue. She did all she could to seduce his mind (at least) but Lord Byron was aware of the trick and said so to me, adding, 'I am studying her character for Don Juan's Adeline' " (quoted in Iris Origo, *The Last Attachment* [New York: Charles Scribner's sons, 1949], p. 342).

30. Medwin, *Conversations of Lord Byron at Pisa,* p. 210.

31. Origo, *The Last Attachment,* p. 17. The quoted phrase is from Lady Blessington's *Idler in Italy.*

32. See Sartre, "Existentialism Is a Humanism," pp. 307–8.

33. Origo, *The Last Attachment,* p. 18.

34. Trelawny, *Recollections,* chap. xix, p. 137.

35. Blessington, *Conversations,* p. 151.

36. William Parry, *Last Days of Lord Byron,* quoted in Ernest Lovell, Jr. (ed.), *His Very Self and Voice* (New York: Macmillan Co., 1954), p. 577.

37. Blessington, *Conversations,* p. 302.

38. *Ibid.,* pp. 365–66.

39. Pietro Gamba, *A Narrative of Lord Byron's Last Journey to Greece,* quoted in *His Very Self and Voice,* p. 593.

40. Harold Nicolson, *Byron: The Last Journey* (London: Constable and Co., 1924), p. ix.

7: AFTERMATH

1. F. R. Leavis, *New Bearings in English Poetry* (London: Chatto and Windus, 1932), p. 15.

2. Matthew Arnold, *Essays in Criticism: First Series* (London: Macmillan and Co., 1895), p. 177.

3. Leavis, *New Bearings in English Poetry,* p. 18.

4. John Bayley, *The Romantic Survival* (London: Constable and Co., 1957). A number of recent studies have been concerned with exploring the

line of descent from Romantic to modern poetry. See, for example, Frank Kermode, *Romantic Image* (New York: Macmillan Co., 1957); Robert Langbaum, *The Poetry of Experience* (New York: Random House, 1957); and Richard Foster, *The New Romantics: A Reappraisal of the New Criticism* (Bloomington: Indiana University Press, 1962).

SELECTED BIBLIOGRAPHY

❧❧❧❧❧❧❧❧❧❧❧❧❧❧❧❧❧❧❧❧❧❧❧❧❧❧❧❧❧❧❧❧

THE following list is made up of books and articles cited in the notes, and a few other books frequently consulted. But my indebtedness extends far beyond these works and is finally incalculable. The bibliography of critical and scholarly writings on Romanticism and the individual Romantic poets is immense, and if I were to attempt to list all the works that I have read and drawn upon I would not know where to draw the line. For fuller bibliographies, therefore, the reader is referred to Ernest Bernbaum, *Guide through the Romantic Movement* (2nd ed.; New York: Ronald Press, 1949); *The English Romantic Poets: A Review of Research,* edited by Thomas M. Raysor (2nd ed. rev.; New York: Modern Language Association, 1956); *The Cambridge Bibliography of English Literature,* Vols. II and III, edited by F. W. Bateson (Cambridge, Eng.: Cambridge University Press, 1941), and Vol. V, Supplement, edited by George Watson (1957); and the annual bibliographies in *Publications of the Modern Language Association, Philological Quarterly,* and *The Keats-Shelley Journal.*

Abrams, M. H. *The Mirror and the Lamp: Romantic Theory and the Critical Tradition.* New York: Oxford University Press, 1953.

Allott, Kenneth. "Bloom on 'The Triumph of Life,' " *Essays in Criticism,* X (April, 1960), 222–28.

Angus, Douglas. "The Theme of Love and Guilt in Coleridge's Three Major Poems," *Journal of English and Germanic Philology,* LIX (1960), 655–68.

Arnold, Matthew. *Essays in Criticism: First Series.* London: Macmillan and Co., 1895.

Selected Bibliography

Baker, Carlos. *Shelley's Major Poetry*. Princeton, N.J.: Princeton University Press, 1948.

Baker, James V. *The Sacred River: Coleridge's Theory of the Imagination*. Baton Rouge: Louisiana State University Press, 1957.

Barnard, Ellsworth. *Shelley's Religion*. Minneapolis: University of Minnesota Press, 1937.

Bate, W. J. *From Classic to Romantic: Premises of Taste in Eighteenth-Century England*. Cambridge, Mass.: Harvard University Press, 1946.

————. *The Stylistic Development of Keats*. New York: Modern Language Association of America, 1945.

Bateson, F. W. *Wordsworth: A Reinterpretation*. London: Longmans, Green and Co., 1954.

Bayley, John. *The Romantic Survival*. London: Constable and Co., 1957.

Beach, J. W. *The Concept of Nature in Nineteenth Century English Poetry*. New York: Macmillan Co., 1936.

Beer, J. B. *Coleridge the Visionary*. London: Chatto and Windus, 1959.

Beres, David. "A Dream, a Vision and a Poem: A Psycho-analytic Study of the Origins of *The Rime of the Ancient Mariner*," *International Journal of Psycho-analysis*, XXII (1951), Part I.

Bernbaum, Ernest. *Guide through the Romantic Movement*. 2nd ed. New York: Ronald Press, 1949.

Blackstone, Bernard. *The Consecrated Urn: An Interpretation of Keats in Terms of Growth and Form*. London: Longmans, Green and Co., 1959.

Blake, William. *Poetry and Prose*, edited by Geoffrey Keynes. London: Nonesuch Press, 1927.

Blessington, Countess of. *A Journal of Conversations with Lord Byron*. Boston: Cottrell, 1859.

Bloom, Harold. *Shelley's Mythmaking*. New Haven, Conn.: Yale University Press, 1959.

Blunden, Edmund. *Shelley*. New York: Viking Press, 1947.

Boyd, Elizabeth. *Byron's Don Juan*. New Brunswick, N.J.: Rutgers University Press, 1945.

Briggs, H. L. "Keats' Conscious and Unconscious Reactions to Criticisms of *Endymion*," *PMLA*, LX (1945), 1106–29.

Brooks, Cleanth. *The Well Wrought Urn*. New York: Harcourt, Brace and Co., 1947.

Burke, Kenneth. *A Grammar of Motives*. New York: Prentice-Hall, 1945.

————. *The Philosophy of Literary Form*. Baton Rouge: Louisiana State University Press, 1941.

Bush, Douglas. *Mythology and the Romantic Tradition in English Poetry*. Cambridge, Mass.: Harvard University Press, 1937.

[334]

Selected Bibliography

Butter, Peter. *Shelley's Idols of the Cave.* Edinburgh: Edinburgh University Press, 1954.

Byron, George Gordon, Lord. *Byron, a Self-Portrait: Letters and Diaries,* edited by Peter Quennell. 2 vols. London: John Murray, 1950.

———. *Don Juan: A Variorum Edition,* by Truman Guy Steffan and Willis W. Pratt. 4 vols. Austin: University of Texas Press, 1957.

———. *Letters and Journals,* edited by R. E. Prothero. 6 vols. London: John Murray, 1898–1901.

———. *Lord Byron's Correspondence,* edited by John Murray. 2 vols. London: John Murray, 1922.

———. *Poetical Works,* edited by E. H. Coleridge. 7 vols. London: John Murray, 1898–1904.

Caldwell, James. *John Keats' Fancy.* Ithaca, N.Y.: Cornell University Press, 1945.

Cameron, Kenneth N. *The Young Shelley.* London: Victor Gollancz, 1951.

Campbell, O. J. "Sentimental Morality in Wordsworth's Narrative Poetry," *University of Wisconsin Studies in Language and Literature,* No. 11. Madison: University of Wisconsin Press, 1920.

Carlyle, Thomas. *Collected Works.* Centenary edition. 31 vols. New York: Charles Scribner's Sons, 1897–1901.

Chambers, E. K. *S. T. Coleridge.* London: Oxford University Press, 1938.

Coburn, Kathleen. "Coleridge and Wordsworth and 'the Supernatural,'" *University of Toronto Quarterly,* XXV (1956), 121–30.

Coleridge, S. T. *Aids to Reflection.* (Bohn's Library.) London: George Bell and Sons, 1890.

———. *Biographia Literaria,* edited by J. Shawcross. 2 vols. Oxford: Clarendon Press, 1907.

———. *Christabel,* edited by E. H. Coleridge. London: H. Frowde, 1907.

———. *Coleridge on the Seventeenth Century,* edited by R. F. Brinkley. Durham, N.C.: Duke University Press, 1955.

———. *Collected Letters* (1785–1819), edited by E. L. Griggs. 4 vols. Oxford: Clarendon Press, 1956–59.

———. *The Complete Poetical Works,* edited by E. H. Coleridge. 2 vols. London: Oxford University Press, 1912.

———. *The Inquiring Spirit,* edited by Kathleen Coburn. London: Routledge and Kegan Paul, 1951.

———. *The Notebooks* (1794–1808), edited by Kathleen Coburn. 2 vols. New York: Pantheon Books, 1957–61.

———. *The Poetical Works,* edited by James Dykes Campbell. London: Macmillan and Co., 1893.

———. *The Portable Coleridge,* edited by I. A. Richards. New York: Viking Press, 1950.

[335]

Selected Bibliography

——. *Shakespearian Criticism,* edited by T. M. Raysor. 2 vols. Cambridge, Mass.: Harvard University Press, 1930.

——. *The Table Talk and Omniana.* London: Oxford University Press, 1917.

Dowden, Ernest. *The Life of Percy Bysshe Shelley.* 2 vols. London: Kegan Paul, 1886.

Dunklin, Gilbert T. (ed.). *Wordsworth: Centenary Studies.* Princeton, N.J.: Princeton University Press, 1951.

Eliot, T. S. *Selected Essays.* New York: Harcourt, Brace and Co., 1950.

——. "A Talk on Dante," *Kenyon Review,* XIV (Spring, 1952), 178–88.

——. *The Use of Poetry and the Use of Criticism.* London: Faber and Faber, 1933.

Elwin, Malcolm. *Lord Byron's Wife.* London: Macdonald and Co., 1962.

Empson, William. *The Structure of Complex Words.* New York: New Directions, 1952.

Fairchild, H. N. *Religious Trends in English Poetry.* 5 vols. New York: Columbia University Press, 1939–62.

——. *The Romantic Quest.* New York: Columbia University Press, 1931.

Ferry, David. *The Limits of Mortality: An Essay on Wordsworth's Major Poems.* Middletown, Conn.: Wesleyan University Press, 1959.

Finney, Claude. *The Evolution of Keats's Poetry.* 2 vols. Cambridge, Mass.: Harvard University Press, 1936.

Foakes, R. A. *The Romantic Assertion.* New Haven, Conn.: Yale University Press, 1958.

Fogle, Richard Harter. *The Imagery of Keats and Shelley: A Comparative Study.* Chapel Hill: University of North Carolina Press, 1949.

——. "The Romantic Unity of 'Kubla Khan.'" *College English,* XXII (1960), 112–16.

Ford, Newell F. *The Prefigurative Imagination of John Keats.* Stanford, Calif.: Stanford University Press, 1951.

Foster, Richard. *The New Romantics: A Reappraisal of the New Criticism.* Bloomington: Indiana University Press, 1962.

Freud, Sigmund. *A General Introduction to Psychoanalysis,* translated by Joan Riviere. New York: Permabooks, 1953.

Gittings, Robert. *John Keats: The Living Year.* London: William Heinemann, 1954.

——. *The Mask of Keats.* London: William Heinemann, 1956.

Guerard, Albert. "Prometheus and the Aeolian Lyre," *Yale Review,* XXXIII (March, 1944), 482–97.

Guiccioli, Countess. *My Recollections of Lord Byron,* translated by Hubert E. H. Jerningham. 2 vols. Philadelphia: J. B. Lippincott and Co., 1869.

Selected Bibliography

Hammond, J. L., and Barbara. *The Village Laborer.* London: Longmans, Green and Co., 1911.

Hanson, Lawrence. *The Life of S. T. Coleridge: The Early Years.* London: George Allen and Unwin, 1938.

Harper, G. M. *William Wordsworth: His Life, Works, and Influence.* London: John Murray, 1929.

Havens, R. D. *The Mind of a Poet: A Study of Wordsworth's Thought with Particular Reference to the Prelude.* Baltimore, Md.: Johns Hopkins Press, 1941.

Haydon, B. R. *Autobiography.* (World's Classics Series.) London: Oxford University Press, 1927.

————. *The Diary* (1808–24), edited by W. B. Pope. 2 vols. Cambridge, Mass.: Harvard University Press, 1960.

Hazlitt, William. *Collected Works,* edited by A. R. Waller and Arnold Glover. 13 vols. London: J. M. Dent and Co., 1902–6.

Henley, Elton F., and David H. Stam (comps.). *Wordsworthian Criticism, 1945–1959: An Annotated Bibliography.* New York: New York Public Library, 1960.

Hewlitt, Dorothy. *A Life of John Keats.* 2nd ed. London: Hurst and Blackett, 1949.

House, Humphrey. *Coleridge: The Clark Lectures, 1951–52.* London: Rupert Hart-Davis, 1953.

Jones, John. *The Egotistical Sublime: A History of Wordsworth's Imagination.* London: Chatto and Windus, 1954.

Kaufmann, Walter (ed.). *Existentialism from Dostoevsky to Sartre.* New York: Meridian Books, 1957.

Keats, John. *Complete Poems and Selected Letters,* edited by H. L. Briggs. New York: Modern Library, 1951.

————. *Complete Poems and Selected Letters,* edited by C. D. Thorpe. New York: Odyssey Press, 1935.

————. *The Letters,* edited by Maurice Buxton Forman. 2nd ed. London: Oxford University Press, 1935.

————. *The Letters,* edited by Hyder E. Rollins. 2 vols. Cambridge, Mass.: Harvard University Press, 1958.

————. *The Poems,* edited by Ernest de Selincourt. 5th ed. London: Methuen and Co., 1926.

————. *The Poetical Works,* edited by H. W. Garrod. Oxford: Clarendon Press, 1939.

————. *Selected Poems and Letters,* edited by Douglas Bush. Boston: Houghton Mifflin Co., 1959.

Kermode, Frank. *Romantic Image.* New York: Macmillan Co., 1957.

Selected Bibliography

Knight, G. Wilson. *Lord Byron: Christian Virtues.* London: Routledge and Kegan Paul, 1952.

——. *Lord Byron's Marriage: The Evidence of Asterisks.* New York: Macmillan Co., 1957.

——. *The Starlit Dome.* London: Oxford University Press, 1941.

Kurtz, B. P. *The Pursuit of Death.* New York: Oxford University Press, 1933.

Lamb, Charles. *The Complete Works and Letters.* New York: Modern Library, 1935.

Langbaum, Robert. *The Poetry of Experience.* New York: Random House, 1957.

Leavis, F. R. *New Bearings in English Poetry.* London: Chatto and Windus, 1932.

——. *Revaluations.* New York: George Stewart, 1947.

Logan, J. V. *Wordsworthian Criticism: A Guide and Bibliography.* Columbus: Ohio State University Press, 1947.

Lovejoy, Arthur. *The Great Chain of Being.* Cambridge, Mass.: Harvard University Press, 1936.

Lovelace, Earl of. *Astarte.* A new edition, with additional letters, edited by Mary, Countess of Lovelace. London: Christophers, 1921.

Lovell, Ernest J., Jr. *Byron: The Record of a Quest.* Austin: University of Texas Press, 1949.

—— (ed.). *His Very Self and Voice.* New York: Macmillan Co., 1954.

Lowes, John Livingston. *The Road to Xanadu.* Boston: Houghton Mifflin Co., 1927.

Lyon, Harvey T. *Keats' Well-Read Urn.* New York: Henry Holt, 1958.

Lyon, Judson. *The Excursion: A Study.* (Yale Studies in English, No. 114.) New Haven, Conn.: Yale University Press, 1950.

Macaulay, Thomas B. *Critical and Historical Essays Contributed to the Edinburgh Review.* 2 vols. London: Longmans, Green and Co., 1870.

MacGillivray, J. R. *Keats: A Bibliography and Reference Guide.* Toronto: University of Toronto Press, 1949.

Marchand, Leslie A. *Byron: A Biography.* 3 vols. New York: Alfred A. Knopf, 1957.

Medwin, Thomas. *Conversations of Lord Byron at Pisa.* London: printed for Henry Colburn, 1824.

——. *Life of Percy Bysshe Shelley,* edited by H. B. Forman. London: Oxford University Press, 1913.

Meyer, G. W. *Wordsworth's Formative Years.* (University of Michigan Publications in Language and Literature, No. 20.) Ann Arbor: University of Michigan Press, 1943.

Selected Bibliography

Moore, Doris Langley. *The Late Lord Byron*. Philadelphia: J. B. Lippincott Co., 1961.

Moorman, Charles. "Wordsworth's *Prelude:* I, 1–269," *Modern Language Notes,* LXXII (1957), 416–20.

Moorman, Mary. *William Wordsworth: 1770–1803*. Oxford: Clarendon Press, 1957.

Morgan, Edwin. "A Prelude to *The Prelude,*" *Essays in Criticism,* V (1955), 341–53.

Muir, Kenneth. "The Meaning of *Hyperion,*" *Essays in Criticism,* II (1952), 54–75.

Murry, John Middleton. *Keats and Shakespeare*. London: Oxford University Press, 1925.

———. *Keats*. Rev. ed. New York: Noonday Press, 1955.

Nethercott, A. H. *The Road to Tryermaine*. Chicago: University of Chicago Press, 1939.

Nicolson, Harold. *Byron: The Last Journey*. London: Constable and Co., 1924.

Notopoulos, James. *The Platonism of Shelley*. Durham, N.C.: Duke University Press, 1949.

Origo, Iris. *The Last Attachment: The Story of Byron and Teresa Guiccioli*. New York: Charles Scribner's Sons, 1949.

Peacock, Thomas Love. *Collected Works,* edited by H. F. B. Brett-Smith and C. E. Jones. 10 vols. London: Constable and Co., 1928–34.

Peck, Walter. *Shelley: Life and Works*. 2 vols. Boston: Houghton Mifflin Co., 1927.

Perkins, David. *The Quest for Permanence*. Cambridge, Mass.: Harvard University Press, 1959.

Pettet, E. C. *On the Poetry of Keats*. Cambridge, Eng.: Cambridge University Press, 1957.

Potter, Stephen. *Coleridge and S. T. C.* London: Jonathan Cape, 1935.

Potts, Abbie F. *Wordsworth's Prelude: A Study of Its Literary Form*. Ithaca, N.Y.: Cornell University Press, 1953.

Pulos, C. E. *The Deep Truth: A Study of Shelley's Scepticism*. Lincoln: University of Nebraska Press, 1954.

Quennell, Peter. *Byron: The Years of Fame*. New York: Viking Press, 1935.

———. *Byron in Italy*. New York: Viking Press, 1941.

Raysor, Thomas M., *et al. The English Romantic Poets: A Review of Research*. 2nd ed. rev. New York: Modern Language Association, 1956.

Read, Herbert E. *The True Voice of Feeling*. New York: Pantheon, 1953.

Richards, I. A. *Coleridge on the Imagination*. London: Routledge and Kegan Paul, 1934.

Selected Bibliography

——. *Mencius on the Mind*. London: K. Paul, Trench, Trubner and Co., 1932.

——. *Practical Criticism*. London: Routledge and Kegan Paul, 1929.

——. *Science and Poetry*. New York: W. W. Norton and Co., 1926.

Rogers, Neville. *Shelley at Work: A Critical Enquiry*. Oxford: Clarendon Press, 1956.

Rollins, Hyder E. (ed.). *The Keats Circle: Letters and Papers*. 2 vols. Cambridge, Mass.: Harvard University Press, 1948.

Rutherford, Andrew. *Byron, a Critical Study*. Palo Alto, Calif.: Stanford University Press, 1961.

Schneider, Elisabeth. *Coleridge, Opium and Kubla Khan*. Chicago: University of Chicago Press, 1953.

Shelley, Mary. *Letters*, edited by Frederick L. Jones. 2 vols. Norman: University of Oklahoma Press, 1944.

Shelley, Percy Bysshe. *Complete Works*, edited by Roger Ingpen and Walter Peck. The Julian Edition. 10 vols. London: Ernest Benn, 1926–30.

——. *The Complete Poetical Works*, edited by George E. Woodberry. Boston: Houghton Mifflin Co., 1901.

——. *Epipsychidion*, edited by Robert Potts. London: published for the Shelley Society by Reeves and Turner, 1887.

——. *New Shelley Letters*, edited by W. S. Scott. New Haven, Conn.: Yale University Press, 1949.

——. *The Poems*, edited by C. D. Locock. 2 vols. London: Methuen and Co., 1911.

——. *Prometheus Unbound: A Variorum Edition*, edited by Lawrence J. Zillman. Seattle: University of Washington Press, 1959.

——. *Selected Poetry and Prose*, edited by Kenneth N. Cameron. New York: Rinehart and Co., 1951.

——. *Shelley's Prose, or, The Trumpet of a Prophecy*, edited by David Lee Clark. Albuquerque: University of New Mexico Press, 1954.

Slote, Bernice. *Keats and the Dramatic Principle*. Lincoln: University of Nebraska Press, 1958.

Stallknecht, N. P. *Strange Seas of Thought*. Durham, N.C.: Duke University Press, 1945.

Suther, Marshall. *The Dark Night of Samuel Taylor Coleridge*. New York: Columbia University Press, 1960.

Swinburne, A. C. *Complete Works*, edited by Edmund Gosse and Thomas Wise. 20 vols. London: William Heinemann, 1926.

Thorpe, Clarence. "Keats and Hazlitt," *PMLA*, LXXII (1947), 487–502.

——. *The Mind of John Keats*. New York: Oxford University Press, 1926.

——, Carlos Baker, and Bennett Weaver (eds.). *The Major English*

Selected Bibliography

Romantic Poets: A Symposium in Reappraisal. Carbondale: Southern Illinois University Press, 1958.

Trelawny, Edward. *Recollections of the Last Days of Shelley and Byron,* edited by Edward Dowden. London: Oxford University Press, 1923.

———. *Records of Shelley, Byron and the Author.* London: B. M. Pickering, 1878.

Trilling, Lionel. *The Liberal Imagination.* New York: Viking Press, 1950.

Trueblood, Paul. *The Flowering of Byron's Genius: Studies in Byron's Don Juan.* Stanford University, Calif.: Stanford University Press, 1945.

Tuveson, Ernest. *The Imagination as a Means of Grace.* Berkeley and Los Angeles: University of California Press, 1960.

Warren, Robert Penn. "A Poem of Pure Imagination: An Experiment in Reading," in *The Rime of the Ancient Mariner.* New York: Reynal and Hitchcock, 1946.

Wasserman, Earl. *The Finer Tone: Keats' Major Poems.* Baltimore, Md.: Johns Hopkins Press, 1953.

———. *The Subtler Language.* Baltimore, Md.: Johns Hopkins Press, 1959.

Whalley, George. *Coleridge and Sara Hutchinson, and the Asra Poems.* Toronto: University of Toronto Press, 1955.

White, Newman I. *Shelley.* 2 vols. New York: Alfred A. Knopf, 1940.

Wicker, Brian. "The Disputed Lines in *The Fall of Hyperion," Essays in Criticism,* VII (1957), 28–41.

Willey, Basil. *The Eighteenth Century Background.* London: Chatto and Windus, 1940.

Wilson, Milton. *Shelley's Later Poetry.* New York: Columbia University Press, 1959.

Wordsworth, William. *Poetical Works,* edited by Ernest de Selincourt and Helen Darbishire. 5 vols. Oxford: Clarendon Press, 1940–49.

———. *The Prelude: A Variorum Edition,* edited by Ernest de Selincourt. 2nd ed., revised by Helen Darbishire. Oxford: Clarendon Press, 1959.

———, and Dorothy Wordsworth. *The Early Letters,* edited by Ernest de Selincourt. Oxford: Clarendon Press, 1935.

———, and Dorothy Wordsworth. *The Letters: The Middle Years* (1806–20), edited by Ernest de Selincourt. 2 vols. Oxford: Clarendon Press, 1937.

Woodring, Carl. *Politics in the Poetry of Coleridge.* Madison: University of Wisconsin Press, 1961.

Yeats, William Butler. *Ideas of Good and Evil.* London: A. H. Bullen, 1914.

INDEX

🦉 🦉

[343]

Index

titudes of, 92, 95, 96, 99, 113–16; as poet seer, 93–97; his theory of epic, 94, 314; last poems of, 98, 135; and problem of evil, 99, 112, 120–23; childhood experiences of, 99–100; on will and volition, 99, 124–25; on theme of violence in poetry, 99–100; on significance of dreams, 103, 118–20, 121, 122, 123–24; relation of love and hate in his poetry, 104, 121, 125, 126, 128, 129, 130; his collaboration with Wordsworth in *Lyrical Ballads,* 104–5, 107, 108, 109, 117, 118; his treatment of wife and friends, 112, 125, 131, 317; and necessitarianism, 114, 122, 317, *see also* and association-ism; his definition of madness, 121; sexual attitudes of, 121–22, 317; and associationism, 122, 310, *see also* and necessitarianism

—*Prose*

Aids to Reflection, 123
Biographia Literaria, 50, 95, 105, 309
The Friend, 104, 134, 315
Letters: quoted, 83, 88, 91, 94, 99, 100, 101, 116, 124–25, 128, 135, 310, 314
Notebooks: quoted, 83–84, 120, 122, 123, 126, 129, 316
Shakespearean Criticism, 314–15
Table Talk, 109, 121, 126–27

—*Poetry*

The Ballad of the Dark Ladie, 91, 117
Christabel, 6, 84, 85, 91, 97, 99, 117, 118–32; and character of Geral-dine, 8, 120–21, 125–26, 130, 131, 317; compared with *Osorio,* 103–4; compared with *The Three Graves,* 106, 107, 108; compared with *The Rime of the Ancient Mariner,* 112, 117, 123, 131; its relation to Coleridge's life, 118, 123–28, 130–31; Conclusion to Part I, 118–19; its relation to opium habit, 118–19, 124–25; compared with *Pains of Sleep,* 118–19, 131; its relation to Cole-ridge's dreams, 120–21; Cole-ridge's plans for completion of, 126–28; Conclusion to Part II, 128–31; and character of Sir Leo-line, 129; compared with *Dejec-tion: An Ode,* 133

Dejection: An Ode, 98, 123, 132–33, 135, 307
The Destiny of Nations, 93
The Eolian Harp, 92, 307, 316
Fears in Solitude, 19, 93, 94, 134, 308, 311
Hymn before Sunrise in the Vale of Chamouni, 134–35, 318
Kubla Khan, 6, 7, 8, 84–91, 98, 99, 219, 317; preface to, 84–85; Crewe note on, 84–85, 313; sig-nificance of Mount Abora (Amara) in, 85, 88, 89; literary parallels to, 85–86; compared with earthly paradises, 85–86, 89; anticipations of in earlier poems, 86–87, 89, 98; analysis of, 87–90; dating of, 88, 313–14; significance of song of Abyssinian Maid in, 88–90; significance of dome and caves in, 89–90, 314; compared with *Religious Musings,* 96; com-pared with *Three Graves,* 105; compared with *Hymn before Sunrise,* 135; compared with Plato's *Ion,* 314
Lines on a Friend Who Died of a Frenzy Fever Induced by Ca-lumnious Reports, 97
Love, 91
Monody on the Death of Chatter-ton, 97, 98
Ode to the Departing Year, 93–94, 134
Ode to Tranquillity, 133–34, 318
Osorio, 88, 100–4; ending com-pared with *Remorse,* 101; preface to, 101; summarized, 101; and character of Osorio, 101–3; as anticipation of Byronic hero, 102, 315; and *The Borderers,* 103; and Coleridge's own con-flicts, 103; and *Christabel,* 103–4; and *The Rime of the Ancient Mariner,* 104, 110, 115; Freudian implications in, 315
The Pains of Sleep, 118–19, 131, 317
The Picture, 313
Quae Nocent Docent, 97
The Raven, 108–9, 115
Religious Musings, 87, 93, 94–96
Remorse, 100, 101, 315
The Rime of the Ancient Mariner, 58, 84, 85, 91, 97, 99–100, 109–18; Mariner in relation to Cole-

Index

Hutchinson, Sara, 108, 131, 135, 309, 315, 317

Imagination: religious function of, 4. *See also under* Coleridge, Samuel Taylor; Keats, John; Wordsworth, William

James, D. G., 235
Jeffrey, Miss (Keats' correspondent), 177–78
Johnson, Samuel, 85, 89
Jones, John, 312

Kafka, Franz, 123
Keats, Fanny, 179
Keats, George, 172, 318
Keats, George and Georgiana: John Keats' letters to, 139, 151–54, 178–79
KEATS, John, 6, 8–9, 39, 42, 45, 74, 135, 136–79, 190, 200, 225, 226, 227, 232, 302, 303, 304, 318–22, 327; on beauty as truth, 8, 137, 145, 147, 148, 149, 155–58, 162–63, 318, 320; on dream as revelation of truth, 8, 137, 139, 144–49, 154, 158–59, 160, 162–63, 164, 169–71, 172–73, 178; and imagination, 8, 137, 145, 147, 152, 154, 155–57, 162–63; his relation to Wordsworth, 42, 149, 150, 168; on vale of soul-making, 138, 170; and dream journey in poetry, 139, 144–47, 158–59, 160, 164–65, 171, 178; his relation to Milton, 139, 149, 170; on various functions of poetry, 139, 140–43, 150–52, 155–59, 160, 163, 164, 174, 178–79; his attitudes toward surgery, 140, 143, 144; his attitude toward Byron, 141, 142, 152, 168, 173; his reaction to critical attack, 142, 318–19; his attitude toward public, 142, 161, 320, 321, 322; his problems of poetic composition, 143, 177–79, 322; on negative capability, 147, 148, 150, 152, 319; his relation to Shakespeare, 147, 150, 152, 170, 176; on beauty as evil, 148, 151, 153; on cruelty in nature, 148, 151, 153; on mansion of many chambers, 148–49; on perfectibility, 149, 151, 153–54; his conflict between theory and practice, 150, 154, 155, 164, 170–71, 179; on poetic detachment, 150, 151, 152, 153, 156, 168, 174, 176, 253, *see also* on negative capability; on poetry and philosophy,

150–52, 162–64, 319, 321; on truth, 151–52, 155, 318, *see also* on beauty and truth, on poetry and truth; on poetry and truth, 151–53, 157–59, 163; on disinterestedness, 151–54, 155–58, 165–66, 190, 319–20; Hazlitt's influence on, 152–53, 162–63, 319, 320; on beauty as good, 153–54; on beauty as power, 153–54; skepticism of, 159, 163, 171, 176, 179; his tuberculosis, 159, 173, 179, 322; his love for Fanny Brawne, 159–61, 172, 173; on writing for profit, 161, 172–73; on poetry and science, 162–63, 320–31; his dramatic talents, 170, 174–75, 176; his proposal to write for liberal journals, 171–72; his attitude toward Shelley, 232
—*Works*
    The Cap and Bells, 172–73, 179, 322
    Earl of Leicester (proposed drama), 174–75
    Endymion, 141–42, 147, 158, 160, 161, 169, 171, 176, 177
    Epistle to My Brother George, 140–41, 143
    Epistle to Reynolds, 147, 148, 151
    The Eve of St. Agnes, 142, 174
    The Eve of St. Mark, 173, 174
    The Fall of Hyperion, 6, 9, 136–40, 142, 143, 145, 164–71, 172, 173, 175, 178, 179, 180, 321–22; Moneta's dialogue with dreamer in, 9, 142, 166–71, 172, 174, 175, 178; Moneta compared with Mnemosyne, 136–38; and differences from *Hyperion,* 136–38, 170–71; reasons for abandoning, 139, 170–71; dreamer versus poet in, 140, 167–69, 170, 321, 322; and journey in dream, 164–65; "induction" of, 164–70; *see also Hyperion*
    Hyperion, 6, 8–9, 136–37, 142, 149, 150; and character of Apollo, 8, 136–38, 149, 153–54, 165; and Keats' identification with Apollo, 8, 137–38; and Mnemosyne, 8, 136–38, 149, 154, 165; and character of Hyperion, 137, 138, 153, 154, 171; theme of progress in, 149, 153–55, 170–71; reasons for abandoning, 149, 154; *see also The Fall of Hyperion*
    I Stood Tiptoe, 141
    King Stephen, 175–76

Index

Index

Index